A BEHAVIORAL THEORY
OF THE FIRM

PRENTICE-HALL INTERNATIONAL SERIES IN MANAGEMENT

PRENTICE-HALL BEHAVIORAL SCIENCES IN BUSINESS SERIES

Herbert A. Simon, Editor

PRENTICE-HALL INTERNATIONAL, INC., UNITED KINGDOM AND EIRE

PRENTICE-HALL OF CANADA, LTD., CANADA

C. BERTELSMANN VERLAG, GERMANY AND AUSTRIA

DE BUSSY, HOLLAND AND FLEMISH-SPEAKING PART OF BELGIUM

DUNOD, FRANCE AND FRENCH-SPEAKING PART OF BELGIUM

HERRERO HERMANOS, SUCS., SPAIN AND SPANISH-SPEAKING COUNTRIES OF LATIN AMERICA

MARUZEN, FAR EAST

A BEHAVIORAL THEORY
OF THE FIRM

Richard M. Cyert

Dean, Graduate School of
Industrial Administration
Carnegie Institute of Technology

James G. March

Professor, Graduate School
of Industrial Administration
Carnegie Institute of Technology

With contributions by:

G. P. E. Clarkson
K. J. Cohen
W. R. Dill
E. A. Feigenbaum
E. Grunberg
C. G. Moore
P. O. Soelberg
W. H. Starbuck
O. E. Williamson

PRENTICE-HALL, INC.
Englewood Cliffs, New Jersey   1963

ACKNOWLEDGMENTS

Our research on a behavioral theory of the firm began with a casual conversation over a pair of bag lunches. Although in subsequent years the work has been semiformalized into a "project," the research has been conducted by a fluid, informal circle of individuals, each interested at different times to different degrees in different aspects of the effort to develop a theory of business decision making. As a result, the work summarized in this volume is a collaborative endeavor in more than the usual sense. Some of our colleagues have made major contributions to specific parts of the work; others, without being intensively involved at any one point, have offered suggestions and other help at many times. To all of these, our thanks.

We have tried to indicate a number of major specific contributions by reference on the title page and by appropriate footnote references in the text. In particular, O. E. Williamson and G. P. E. Clarkson have prepared chapters especially for this book (Chapters 9 and 10, respectively). K. J. Cohen is a co-author of Appendix B and a major contributor to the model presented in Chapter 8. E. Grunberg is a co-author of Appendix A. C. G. Moore and P. O. Soelberg are senior collaborators on the models presented in Chapters 7 and 8, respectively. W. R. Dill, E. A. Feigenbaum, and W. H. Starbuck have individually collaborated with us on published articles from which we have drawn freely. To each of these collaborators we owe a debt for the specific contributions identified explicitly here and for their continuing stimulation, criticism, and enthusiasm.

We are grateful for three special contributions: To W. W. Cooper for his original and stimulating ideas on the relevance of business practice to the theory of the firm. To F. Modigliani for his friendly criticism and helpful clarification of the relation between our work and more conventional economic theory. To H. A. Simon for his insights into the process of decision making in complex organizations, for his administrative support, and for his careful and constructive comments on the manuscript. Among many others who have contributed ideas and comment, we should like to acknowledge particularly C. P. Bonini, P. Cagan, J. Feldman, G. H. Haines, Jr., H. L. Johnson, J. Marschak, W. H. McWhinney, A. H. Meltzer, R. R. Nelson, and A. Whinston.

Parts of the book are based on articles previously published in professional journals or other books. We wish to thank John Wiley & Sons, the McGraw-Hill Book Company, *Administrative Science Quarterly*, *Management Science*, *American Economic Review*, *Quarterly Journal of Economics*, *Behavioral Science*, and the University of California at Los Angeles for their permission to borrow freely from our earlier publications.

Mrs. Ethel Blank, Miss Judith Brunclik, and Mrs. Rosemary Domyslawski both typed the manuscript and supervised us during its preparation. We are glad to acknowledge both services, the typing with pleasure — the supervision with reluctance. We are also glad to acknowledge the usually tolerant help of M. Nathenson in reproducing the preliminary versions of the book.

Through a series of generous grants to us as individuals and to the Graduate School of Industrial Administration, the Ford Foundation has supported the research reported here. We want to thank the Foundation for that support, and particularly for the opportunities for basic research provided by the terms of their awards.

Finally, we owe a twofold debt to G. L. Bach. First, we are grateful for the uniquely exciting research climate in the Graduate School of Industrial Administration over the past decade. Second, Lee Bach's decision to resign as dean of the school provides us with a legitimate opportunity to acknowledge his primary responsibility for that climate by dedicating this book to him.

R. M. Cyert
J. G. March

CONTENTS

A BEHAVIORAL THEORY
OF THE FIRM

1

INTRODUCTION

This book is about the business firm and the way it makes economic decisions. We propose to make detailed observations of the procedures by which firms make decisions and to use these observations as a basis for a theory of decision making within business organizations. Our articles of faith are simple. We believe that, in order to understand contemporary economic decision making, we need to supplement the study of market factors with an examination of the internal operation of the firm — to study the effects of organizational structure and conventional practice on the development of goals, the formation of expectations, and the execution of choices.

The rationale for such a belief is also simple. The modern "representative firm" is a large, complex organization. Its major functions are performed by different divisions more or less coordinated by a set of control procedures. It ordinarily produces many products, buys and sells in many different markets. Within the firm, information is generated and processed, decisions are made, results are evaluated, and procedures are changed. The external environment of the firm consists, in part, of other firms with comparable characteristics. If the market completely determined the firm's economic behavior, these internal attributes would be little more than irrelevant artifacts. But the market is neither so pervasive nor so straightforward. The modern firm has some control over the market; it has discretion within the market; it sees the market through an organizational filter.

The elaboration of these articles of faith into a theory of the firm involved four major research commitments. They are commitments that evolved during the course of the research, but they constitute a general retrospective characterization of our research strategy:

1. *Focus on a small number of key economic decisions made by the firm.* In the first instance, these were price and output decisions; subsequently they included internal allocation and market strategy decisions.

2. *Develop process-oriented models of the firm.* That is, we viewed decisions of the firm as the result of a well-defined sequence of behaviors in that firm; we wished to study the decisions by studying the process.

3. *Link models of the firm as closely as possible to empirical observations* of both the decision output and the process structure of actual business organizations. The models were to be both explicitly based on observations of firms and subject to empirical test against the actual behavior of identifiable firms.

4. *Develop a theory with generality beyond the specific firms studied.* We wanted a set of summary concepts and relations that could be used to understand the behavior of a variety of organizations in a variety of decision situations.

Each of these commitments was critical to the research; each in some way characterizes the theory that resulted.

The focus on a specific set of economic decisions (i.e., price and output) was intended to constrain the tendency of theories of decision making to become excessively general. Quite simply, we wanted models that could predict actual decisions (if provided with necessary data), not simply models that could predict some qualitative properties of those decisions. Obviously, we wanted both kinds of predictions if we could manage them, but by restricting our focus we hoped to strengthen the specificity of the models.

The emphasis on studying actual decision processes implies a description of the firm's decision in terms of a specific series of steps used to reach that decision. The process is specified by drawing a flow diagram and executing a computer program that simulates the process in some detail. We wanted to study the actual making of decisions and reproduce the behavior as fully as possible within the confines of theoretical manageability.

The insistence on empirical content follows naturally from the emphasis on identifying the actual process of decision. It is hard to imagine constructing a process model without detailed observation of the ways in which business organizations make decisions. Thus, the empirical commitment has forced us to reconsider the traditional truculence of the firm with respect to outside investigation. We were constrained to secure research access to a number of firms under conditions that protected the competitive position of the firm without interfering with the disclosure needs of a research study.

Finally, the commitment to theoretical generality was intended to complement the insistence on specificity in models with a similar insistence on generality of concepts and broad structure. We did not want the theory to be limited to descriptive models of specific firms making specific decisions. We required a set of explanatory concepts that would serve as a framework for analysis and further research.

The results of our efforts to develop an empirically relevant, process-oriented, general theory of economic decision making by a business firm are summarized in this book. We hope they suggest both the utility and some of the problems of theoretical research on decision making in the firm. More generally, we hope they support the case for the legitimacy and importance of the business firm as a unit for detailed empirical study and theoretical analysis. More specifically, we hope that the rudiments of a behavioral theory of the firm presented in the following chapters will prove relevant both to economic theory and to the theory of complex organizations.

2

ANTECEDENTS OF THE BEHAVIORAL THEORY OF THE FIRM[1]

In a modern market society, economic decisions on price, output, product lines, product mix, resource allocation, and other standard economic variables are made not by individual entrepreneurs but by a complex of private and public institutions. Many of these decisions are made within the large, multifunctional, and complicated organizations called firms. These are simple facts. They may not be facts with which economic theory should concern itself, but the disparity between the process by which business decisions appear to be made by complex organizations in the real world and the way in which they are explained by economic theory has provided material for several decades of debate.[2] In this chapter, we propose

[1]This chapter is based in part on a paper given in December, 1959, at the annual meeting of the Econometric Society and a paper published in *Contributions to Scientific Research in Management* (UCLA).

[2]There are a large number of articles that might be cited in this connection. Perhaps the articles stimulated by the so-called "marginalist" controversy are representative. See R. A. Lester, "Shortcomings of Marginal Analysis for Wage-Employment Problems," *American Economic Review*, **36** (1946), 63–82; "Marginalism and Labor Markets," *American Economic Review*, **37** (1947), 135–148; F. Machlup, "Marginal Analysis and Empirical Research," *American*

to discuss the theory of the firm, the debates over it, and the relevance of existing theories of organizations to a revised theory of the firm. With such a discussion, we hope to articulate both our view of the limitations of existing theories and our motives for developing the behavioral theory of the firm outlined in this volume.

2.1 The Theory of the Firm

Any brief presentation of a body of theory is likely to suffer from the distortion dictated by condensation. This problem is severe when the theory has been a focus for controversy and the writers making the condensation are parties to the controversy. We are in such a position in describing the theory of the firm. Nevertheless, without completely concealing our prejudices, we describe in this section the current consensus on the theory of the firm, the challenges to that theory, and the rejoinders of the defenders of orthodoxy.

2.1.1 Current consensus on the theory of the firm

It will become clear below that there is disagreement about the theory of the firm in three respects. There is disagreement about (1) what the theory is, (2) the extent to which the theory is defective, and (3) appropriate methods for improving the theory.

The first of these disagreements makes it difficult to describe any current consensus on the theory of the firm. We are sympathetic with the view that, in fact, there is no consensus. At the same time, a case can be made for moderate agreement. We believe a fair number of economists would agree, except for questions of detail, on the general characterization of the theory of the firm given in this section.[3]

Assuming that the firm is operating within a perfectly competitive market, the generally received theory asserts that the objective of the firm is to maximize net revenue in the face of given prices and a technologically determined production function. Net revenue (profits, or expected profits) is the difference between receipts and the sum of fixed and variable costs. The production function is a relation between factors of production and their corresponding outputs determined by physical conditions within the

---

Economic Review, **36** (1946), 519–554; "Rejoinder to an Antimarginalist," *American Economic Review*, **37** (1947), 148–154; R. A. Gordon, "Short-Period Price Determination," *American Economic Review*, **38** (1948), 265–288.

[3]See R. G. D. Allen, *Mathematical Economics* (London: St. Martins, 1957), 608–617; R. Dorfman, *Application of Linear Programming to the Theory of the Firm* (Berkeley: U. of Cal., 1951), 5–10; J. M. Henderson and R. E. Quandt, *Microeconomic Theory* (New York: McGraw-Hill, 1958), 42–75; P. Samuelson, *Foundations of Economic Analysis* (Cambridge: Harvard University Press, 1947), 57–89.

firm. Maximization of profit is accomplished by determining the optimal mix of outputs (products) and inputs (factors), i.e., the equilibrium position.

Existing theory of the firm treats two main areas — the conditions for maximum net revenue, and the analysis of shifts in equilibrium positions. The usual method for obtaining a solution is first to derive the conditions for minimum cost at any fixed output and subsequently to determine the optimal level of output. This analysis, however, is usually limited to the single-product firm. A somewhat more general treatment is gained from the Hicks-Allen analysis of the multiproduct firm.

Using the methods of differential calculus, the Lagrangean multiplier, and the theory of quadratic forms, the propositions listed below are generally derived. The first two are given by a direct consideration of the sufficient conditions for an equilibrium.

1. n equations may be derived and solved for the optimal quantities of the firm's n commodities (both inputs and outputs).

2. At equilibrium, the marginal rate of substitution between two products, or between two factors, is equal to the ratio of their prices.

If we turn to variations near the equilibrium, the necessary conditions yield further relations.

3. The marginal physical productivity of a factor with respect to a product (the rate of change of the amount of the factor used with respect to the product's output) is equal to their price ratio.

4. The quantity of a good produced is selected so that its marginal cost (with respect to this product) is equal to its (given) price.

The sufficient conditions for equilibrium insure a maximum (rather than a minimum) of net revenue. From them the remainder of the theory is derived.

5. A price increase for a product raises its supply; a price increase for a factor reduces its demand.

6. "Cross" price effects are symmetric. That is, the rate of change of a first commodity with respect to the price of a second commodity is equal to the rate of change of the second with respect to the price of the first.

7. A price increase of a good tends to affect the other commodities by decreasing the outputs of products and increasing the inputs of factors.

Thus product-factor substitution is seen to dominate generally. However, within this framework complementarity with respect to a group of products *or* factors (a single price increase raising all their supplies *or* reducing all their demands, respectively) may operate.

In our judgment, the above description (see the appendix to this chapter for a mathematical description) is the closest thing to a consensus on the content of the theory of the firm. The theory has been extended to cover either imperfect factor markets, imperfect product markets, or both.[4] Although agreement on such extensions is somewhat less complete than for the perfectly competitive case, we can still describe them as "standard." These elaborations, while extending the theory to new market situations, retain the basic framework and decision-making process postulated for the firm in perfect competition.

Both the theory of monopolistic competition and attempts at oligopoly theory are such elaborations. In the theory of monopolistic competition, it is assumed that the firm no longer has a demand curve of infinite elasticity because its product is not a perfect substitute for the products of other firms in the industry. For example, Chamberlin's analysis is worked out essentially with three curves — a demand curve for the firm assuming the quality of the products of competitors and the prices of competitors' products given, a demand curve for the firm assuming that competitors' prices are always identical with the firm's price, and an average cost curve for the firm.[5] Predictions are derived from the model by assuming profit maximization by the firm and by assuming that each firm expects competitors not to follow its behavior (because competitors are so numerous, none is significantly affected by the behavior of a single firm). Within this framework Chamberlin handles three decision variables — price, product quality, and selling expense. From the standpoint of the theory of the firm, the theory of monopolistic competition adds two dimensions (selling expense and product quality) to the kinds of decisions the firm makes but leaves the decision process essentially unchanged from the traditional model.[6]

Similarly, efforts to develop a theory of oligopoly have generally retained the classical assumptions about firm behavior.[7] The theories focus on the interdependence among firms in oligopolistic markets, and this focus is characterized by an emphasis on such concepts as conjectural variations. A major difficulty in developing the theory is the assignment of proper values to conjectural variation terms.[8] Once meaning is given to the con-

---

[4] In recent years linear programing has been applied to the analysis of the firm. Linear programing can be viewed as an alternative optimizing technique to that of the differential calculus employed in the marginal analysis of the firm. From the standpoint of the present discussion, this innovation does not alter the basic nature of the theory.

[5] E. H. Chamberlin, *The Theory of Monopolistic Competition*, 5th ed. (Cambridge: Harvard University Press, 1946), 90.

[6] For another point of view see Chamberlin's "Full Cost and Monopolistic Competition," *Economic Journal*, **62** (1952), 318–325.

[7] G. J. Stigler, *The Theory of Price* (New York: Macmillan, 1946), 269.

[8] A. L. Bowley, *Mathematical Groundwork of Economics* (Oxford: Clarendon Press, 1924).

jectural variation terms, the postulated decision process remains essentially the same as in the conventional model.[9]

Both the theory of monopolistic competition and oligopoly theory have taken the basic theory of the firm as given and changed the market assumptions.[10] Dissatisfaction with this limited revision has led to a re-examination of the basic theory of the firm itself. In the debate over the theory of the firm, we can identify two major difficulties perceived by economists who view the basic theory as deficient. First, the motivational and cognitive assumptions of the theory appear unrealistic. Profit maximization, it is commonly alleged, is either only one among many goals of business firms or not a goal at all. As we shall see, this general criticism and its rejoinders have periodically filled the pages of economic journals with a host of subtleties both economic and philosophic. On the cognitive side, both the classical assumption of certainty and its modern equivalent — knowledge of the probability distribution of future events — have been challenged.

Second, the "firm" of the theory of the firm has few of the characteristics we have come to identify with actual business firms. It has no complex organization, no problems of control, no standard operating procedures, no budget, no controller, no aspiring "middle management." To some economists it has seemed implausible that a theory of an organization can ignore the fact that it is one.

In the next two sections, we discuss each of these criticisms and some of the forms each has taken, especially some of the proposals for revision. The objective is not to provide an exhaustive list of the large number of variations on the two themes but to suggest the nature of the criticisms and the problems the criticisms create in turn, for it is striking that the revisions have failed to secure widespread acceptance.

2.1.2 Challenges to the motivational and cognitive assumptions of the theory

The assumptions of rationality in the theory of the firm can be reduced to two propositions: (1) firms seek to maximize profits; (2) firms operate with perfect knowledge. Of course, a number of attempts have been made to adapt these assumptions to make them somewhat more sophisticated.

[9]It is as a solution to such problems that game theory seems plausible. However, the strategic decision rules of game theory thus far have offered more in formulation than they have been able to deliver in detailed economic models. Even the recent efforts in this direction by Shubik, although they develop economic game theory substantially, still leave a significant gap between the phenomena with which the theory would like to deal and the present power of n-person game theory. M. Shubik, *Strategy and Market Structure* (New York: Wiley, 1959). It is true, however, that the decision process is not identical with the conventional one when game theory is used. See A. Henderson, "The Theory of Duopoly," *Quarterly Journal of Economics*, **68** (1954), 565–584.

[10]J. Robinson, *Economics of Imperfect Competition* (London: Macmillan, 1942).

Thus, we can assume that firms maximize the discounted value of future profits, and that firms have perfect knowledge only up to a probability distribution of all possible future states of the world. We are not concerned at this point with such adaptations, for we wish first to consider a set of more frontal assaults on the assumptions.

Proposed substitutes for profit maximization. There have been two basic challenges to the profit maximization assumption. First, is profit the only objective of business firms? Second, does maximization describe what the business firms do about the profits? As we shall see, some current critics link these two queries, but they need not be linked.

If not profit, what? Perhaps the simplest attack on profits as a motive is also the most destructive. We can argue that entrepreneurs, like anyone else, have a host of personal motives.[11] Profit is one, perhaps, but they are also interested in sex, food, and saving souls. It is rather difficult to deny the proposition, but if we accept it as critical, it is not easy to see how to devise a theory of the firm in anything approximating its present form (or even with its present goals). We can adopt the strategy of introducing subjective utility, but this cannot help us until the utile becomes a better-behaved measure. In a related fashion, we can argue (as Papandreou does) that organizational objectives grow out of interaction among the various participants in the organization.[12] This interaction produces a "general preference function." Whether we agree with Papandreou that this leaves us in no more vague a position than profit maximization, we must concede his point that little can be done with a general preference function unless it can be measured in some nontautological fashion (see Chapter 9).

An alternative to a utility-like preference function is substituting a different *summum bonum* for profits. For example, Rothschild has suggested that the primary motive of the entrepreneur is long-run survival.[13] In this view, decisions aim to maximize the security level of the organization (i.e., the probability that the organization will survive over the indefinite future). Another such suggestion is Baumol's, that firms seek to maximize sales subject to a profit constraint.[14]

The second attack on the assumption of profit maximization does not deny the importance of profits but questions the assumption of maximiza-

[11]G. Katona, *Psychological Analysis of Economic Behavior* (New York: McGraw-Hill, 1951).

[12]A. Papandreou, "Some Basic Problems in the Theory of the Firm," in *A Survey of Contemporary Economics*, ed. B. F. Haley (Homewood, Ill.: Richard D. Irwin, 1952), vol. 2, 183–219.

[13]K. W. Rothschild, "Price Theory and Oligopoly," *Economic Journal*, **42** (1947), 297–320.

[14]W. J. Baumol, *Business Behavior, Value and Growth* (New York: Macmillan, 1959), 45–53.

tion. Gordon, Simon, and Margolis have all argued that profit maximizing should be replaced with a goal of making satisfactory profits.[15] Satisfactory profits represent a level of aspiration that the firm uses to evaluate alternative policies. The aspiration level may change over time, but in the short run it defines a utility function with essentially only two values — good enough and not good enough.

This critique of maximizing is linked with other proposals for revision in at least two ways. First, representing goals by a two-valued utility function avoids many of the problems involved in reducing the various dimensions of a multitude of goals to a single scale. Each goal enters as a simple constraint. All of the goals taken together define a space of acceptable solutions. Second, combining the acceptable level goal with a search theory (as found in Simon) suggests some possible solutions not only to the difficulties about motives, but also to objections about the cognitive side of the rationality assumptions.

Proposed substitutes for perfect knowledge. As we have already noted, it is awkward to assume perfect knowledge in the theory of the firm, and introducing expected value calculations in the case of risk solves only some of the problems. In particular, Simon and others have argued that information is not given to the firm but must be obtained, that alternatives are searched for and discovered sequentially, and that the order in which the environment is searched determines to a substantial extent the decisions that will be made.[16] In this way, the theory of choice and the theory of search become closely interwined and take on prime importance in a general theory of decision making.

A more conventional attempt to deal with the same problem is reflected in recent contributions to a normative theory of search.[17] In this theory, search activity is one of the competitors for internal resources, and expenditures for search are made up to the point where the marginal cost of search equals the marginal expected return from it. These elaborations of the theory are clearly more traditional than Simon's suggestions, but they do not seem to meet the burden of the complaint.

2.1.3 Challenges to the conventional concept of the firm

If we take seriously the concept of a firm as something distinct from an individual entrepreneur, there is no consensus on a theory of the firm.

[15]Gordon, *op. cit.;* J. Margolis, "The Analysis of the Firm: Rationalism, Conventionalism, and Behaviorism," *Journal of Business,* **31** (1958), 187–199; H. A. Simon, "A Behavioral Model of Rational Choice," *Quarterly Journal of Economics,* **69** (1952), 99–118.

[16]J. G. March and H. A. Simon, *Organizations* (New York: Wiley, 1958).

[17]A. Charnes and W. W. Cooper, "The Theory of Search: Optimum Distribution of Search Effort," *Management Science,* **5** (1958), 450–458.

As we have seen, the theory in all its standard forms ignores the fact that decisions are made in large-scale organizations. There is only one conspicuous exception to this statement. Marshall, as others before him, was impressed by the apparent increasing returns to scale.[18] He undertook to explain the historical reduction in production costs by introducing the concepts of internal and external economies, and it is this germ of an idea about the effect of organizational size on organizational performance, by the way of "internal economies," that became important to several decades of theory development.[19] This development, however, ignored other organizational aspects of the firm.

In recent years there has been speculation about the effects of other organizational factors. We will not try to describe all the suggestions for revision that have come from observing, or reflecting on, the behavior of actual business organizations. However, a sample of them will suggest the nature of the difficulties perceived in the theory and the kinds of revisions suggested.

First, the failure to view the firm as an organization has been criticized.[20] Papandreou has made perhaps the most detailed argument for expanding the framework of the firm.[21] He views the firm as a cooperative system. The executive tasks are accomplished by a "peak coordinator." The firm has certain goals, and it is the peak coordinator's job to achieve these by allocating resources rationally. This involves three actions: (1) substantive planning — constructing the firm's budget; (2) procedural planning — constructing a system of communication and authority; (3) executing both plans.

Within such a model of the firm, Papandreou sees certain areas of psychology playing a helpful role. The goals of the firm are strongly influenced by both internal and external forces. The internal influences come from such entities as stockholders, unions, government, and so forth. The preference function discussed above is a "resultant of the influences which are exerted upon the firm. The peak coordinator's job is to maximize the preference function." The greatest difficulty with the analysis is that it does not relate the model specifically to decision making. Hence, it provides a general analysis of the firm from the standpoint of organization theory without specifying precisely how the model can be used in economics.

[18]A. Marshall, *Principles of Economics*, 8th ed. (London: Macmillan, 1936), 278–290. See also G. J. Stigler, *Production and Distribution Theories* (New York: Macmillan, 1941), 76–83.

[19]P. Sraffa, "The Laws of Return Under Competitive Conditions," *Economic Journal*, **36** (1926), 535–550.

[20]W. W. Cooper, "Revisions to the Theory of the Firm," *American Economic Review*, **39** (1949), 1204–1222; G. F. Thirlby, "Notes on the Maximization Process in Company Administration," *Economica*, **17** (1950), 266–282.

[21]A. Papandreou, *op. cit.*

Second, the way in which the theory portrays the process of decision making in business firms has been criticized. It is alleged that firms, in fact, do not equate marginal cost and marginal revenue in deciding on either output or price; rather they follow one or another of a series of rules of thumb.

Consider on the price side, for example, the full cost (or mark-up) method of pricing.[22] Under this method, average variable cost is taken as a base and this cost is marked up to obtain the selling price. The mark-up presumably covers overhead costs and some profit. There are problems with this decision rule. There are unsettled questions as to how the size of the mark-up and the quantity of output are determined. However, the skepticism that greeted the original study of Hall and Hitch in 1939 seems to have been unwarranted. We now have evidence suggesting strongly that mark-up pricing is common in both England and the United States.

Consider similarly, on the output side, Eiteman's suggestion for using inventory turnover as a surrogate for demand estimation.[23] Inventory turnover then determines output. (As we have noted, the indeterminacy of output under mark-up pricing is bothersome.) Output is increased at the given price until inventories increase at abnormal rates. Output is then adjusted until inventories are stable. Price is determined on a mark-up basis for the costs at that output which represents "the minimum reasonable use of the plant available." No doubt, in actual practice the role of inventory change in determining output is more complicated than this. However, if one drops the assumption that the firm knows with certainty its demand curve, or even a few points on it, it is clear that the firm must use feedback from the environment in fixing its price and output. Inventory change is one way of obtaining such feedback (normative inventory models largely build on this). Although there are other feedback devices, many firms do use information on inventory turnover in making the output decision.

Consider similarly the apparent sharp difference between the economic concept of costs on the one hand and the accounting concept of costs on the other. Cooper has outlined tentatively how standard costs and common control systems in business firms might be introduced into a meaningful theory of the firm.[24] It seems quite unlikely that firms use very frequently anything approaching the conventional marginal calculation of costs.

Consider finally some broader observations on the process of organiza-

[22]R. L. Hall and C. J. Hitch, "Price Theory and Business Behavior," in *Oxford Studies in the Price Mechanism*, ed. T. Wilson and P. W. S. Andrews (Oxford: Oxford University Press, 1951), 107–138.

[23]W. J. Eiteman, *Price Determination*, Bureau of Business Research Report No. 16 (Ann Arbor, Mich., 1949).

[24]W. W. Cooper, "A Proposal for Extending the Theory of the Firm," *Quarterly Journal of Economics*, **65** (1951), 87–109.

tional decision making. As we observed earlier, Gordon[25] suggested the substitution of "satisfactory profits" for "profit maximization" as the goal of the firm. Even more important was his suggestion that standard business procedures influence the content of the decisions. For example, virtually every study of business decision making reveals the use of what Gordon called "shortcuts." These shortcuts, or guides to policy, take the form of dicta: "Thou shalt not allow thy share of the market to go below 10 per cent." "Honor thy dealers above all." "Thou shalt not unionize." Since the relation between these dicta and profit maximization is vague and the imperative "Optimize!" is less operational than the shortcuts, it is reasonable to expect that the so-called shortcuts will in fact dominate the decisions, at least in the short run.

Gordon extended his general process-oriented comments further. He argued that (1) the theory should reflect the way in which costs are actually used in a firm (e.g., selling expense); (2) the treatment of uncertainty in the theory is considerably at variance with the way in which firms react to uncertainty; (3) there is a critical discrepancy between theoretical time and real time; (4) the executive in the firm deals with only a subset of the decision variables specified in the theory — treating the others as essentially outside his control.

The details of Gordon's argument (and of similar more recent proposals) indicate that substantial differences have been found between the decision-making process of firms and the decision-making process of the theory of the firm.[26] They reflect a rather understandable discontent with what at least appears to be a very substantial disparity between theory and reality.

2.1.4 In defense of orthodoxy

The suggestions for revision have not gone unchallenged by the defenders of the classical theory. In fact, one writer or another has questioned the methodological relevance, the factual premises, or the theoretical utility of virtually all of the proposed revisions.

The methodological argument asserts simply that it is irrelevant whether the assumptions are valid. The only crucial test of a theory is its predictive power. The foremost proponent of this view is Friedman.[27] Friedman hits sharply at the view that the realism of assumptions is important. He maintains that concern over descriptive accuracy has led to a misunderstanding of economic theory. The function of economic

[25]R. A. Gordon, *op. cit.*

[26]R. M. Cyert, H. A. Simon, and D. B. Trow, "Observation of a Business Decision," *The Journal of Business*, **29** (1956), 237–248.

[27]M. Friedman, "The Methodology of Positive Economics," in *Essays in Positive Economics* (Chicago: University of Chicago Press, 1953), 3–46.

theory is to build propositions with which the world can be analyzed and not to reproduce the world. The most crucial part of the Friedman argument, however, is also the most difficult to demonstrate. He argues that the current theory meets the predictive test, though the "evidence is extremely hard to document; it is scattered in numerous memorandums, articles, and monographs concerned primarily with specific concrete problems rather than with submitting the hypothesis to test." (See Appendix A.)

A second defense, not altogether consistent with the first, attempts to demonstrate the reality of some of the controversial assumptions underlying conventional theory. This approach has followed two lines. In one the theory has been interpreted to show that the assumptions are reasonable. Machlup's well-known paper represents the most elaborate defense of this type.[28] The important step he takes is to argue that cost and revenue are subjective.

> "It should hardly be necessary to mention that all the relevant magnitudes involved — cost, revenue, profit — are subjective — that is, perceived or fancied by the men whose decisions or actions are to be explained (the business men) — rather than 'objective'. . . . Marginal analysis of the firm should not be understood to imply anything but subjective estimates, guesses and hunches."

Although this approach runs the danger of turning the theory into a tautology, it is, of course, an answer to those who criticize the cognitive assumptions of the theory.

The second line attempts to demonstrate empirically that the assumptions are valid. For example, Earley argues that modern accounting techniques such as direct costing (as well as the techniques of operations research) enable businessmen to behave as postulated in the theory of the firm. By use of an elaborate questionnaire he has gathered some data from which he infers that they generally do so.[29]

The third general method of defending conventional theory might be called "evolutionary analysis."[30] The argument concedes that firms do not (or at least may not) consciously pursue the marginal calculations specified in the theory, that firms may have many different goals, and that therefore there may not be a one-to-one relation between the decision process in the firm and the analytic tools used by economists to "describe" that process. However, since in the long run firms will survive only if they (by whatever

[28]F. Machlup, "Marginal Analysis and Empirical Research," *American Economic Reveiw*, **36** (1946), 519–554.

[29]J. S. Earley, "Marginal Policies of 'Excellently Managed' Companies," *American Economic Review*, **46** (1956), 44–70.

[30]A. Alchian, "Uncertainty, Evolution and Economic Theory," *Journal of Political Economy*, **58** (1950), 211–221.

process) make the decisions dictated by economic theory, the theory will predict the behavior of viable firms. Since only the fittest survive, we need only a theory of the fit.

The fourth defense of conventional theory depends on a proposition in the technology of theory construction. It is argued that the proposed changes in the theory cannot be dealt with analytically.[31] Even though it might be desirable to substitute other assumptions for those currently found in economic theory, there is too large a gap between the proposals and the mathematical tools available for developing a theory. With the introduction of the high-speed electronic computer, this defense has been somewhat muted — or at least deflected to an examination of the problems of constructing and testing computer models. (See Appendix B.)

2.1.5 Some observations on the debate

The debates summarized in the previous sections seem to have remarkable powers of reincarnation.[32] They neither die nor fade away with much permanence. Instead, with each publication of new empirical evidence or a new theoretical treatise, the argument is resumed. We will leave the more esoteric features of this remarkable immortality to students of the sociology of knowledge and the metaphysics of wisdom. On a more mundane level, it seems to us that much of the controversy is based on a misunderstanding of the questions the conventional theory of the firm was designed to answer. The theory of the firm, which is primarily a theory of markets, purports to explain at a general level the way resources are allocated by a price system. To the extent to which the model does this successfully, its gross assumptions will be justified. However, there are a number of important and interesting questions relating specifically to firm behavior that the theory cannot answer and was never developed to answer, especially with regard to the internal allocation of resources and the process of setting prices and outputs.

Thus, many of the attacks on the theory of the firm are not so much proper critiques of existing theory as they are suggestions for the development of a theory appropriate to this different set of questions. Ultimately, a new theory of firm decision-making behavior might be used as a basis for a theory of markets, but at least in the short run we should distinguish

---

[31]A. Papandreou and J. Wheeler, *Competition and Its Regulation* (Englewood Cliffs, N.J.: Prentice-Hall, 1954), 73–74.

[32]T. C. Koopmans, *Three Essays on the State of Economic Science* (New York: McGraw-Hill, 1957), 137–142; E. T. Penrose, "Biological Analogies in the Theory of the Firm," *American Economic Review*, **42** (1952), 804–819; E. Rotwein, "On 'The Methodology of Positive Economics'," *Quarterly Journal of Economics*, **73** (1959), 554–575.

between a theory of microbehavior, on the one hand, and the microassumptions appropriate to a theory of aggregate economic behavior on the other. In the present volume we will argue that we have developed the rudiments of a reasonable theory of firm decision making. Our arguments for the utility of the theory in developing a theory of markets are, at least at the moment, more modest.

Thus, for present purposes, three characteristics of the conventional theory of the firm need emphasis:

1. It deals with a particular set of decisions (e.g., price, production) that are viewed as functions of a few "catch-all" variables (e.g., demand, costs).

2. The theory uses aggregation as a tactic; it attempts to specify total market supply and demand curves.

3. There is no attention to, or interest in, the actual process by which individual firms reach decisions.

Despite the record of controversy over the theory, these attributes are more conspicuous than bad. However, they will (in conjunction with a similar characterization of organization theory below) suggest some reasons why little success has been realized in the efforts to merge economic and organization theories of the firm.

2.2 Organization Theory

Although there have been a number of recent efforts to bring some rough order to the field,[33] the study of organizations is even more diffuse than the study of the economic activities of the firm; as a result, it is harder to characterize briefly. To avoid some of the difficulties, we limit our attention to one aspect of organization theory — its possible relevance to a revised theory of the firm. In a sense, what many of the critics of the theory of the firm propose is an integration of organization theory and the theory of the firm. On occasion, such a proposal has been made explicit, and some efforts to achieve an integration have been made.[34] We can consider whether such a proposal is reasonable.

Like the theory of the firm, organization theory means different things to different people. Only those meanings of the term that emphasize the empirical study of behavior in organizations are relevant to our present purpose. If we thus limit the focus, there are (as we view it) three major

[33]J. G. March and H. A. Simon, *op. cit.;* M. Haire, ed., *Modern Organization Theory* (New York: Wiley, 1959); A. Etzioni, *Complex Organizations* (New York: Holt, Rinehart and Winston, 1961).

[34]H. Leibenstein, *Economic Theory and Organizational Analysis* (New York: Harper, 1960).

branches of organization theory. The first of these, which can best be described as "sociological," lists as its founding fathers Weber, Durkheim, Pareto, and Michels and centers on phenomena of bureaucracy. The second is "social psychological" and has been built primarily on an experimental base with an emphasis on an "efficiency" criterion. The third is "administrative" in the sense that it focuses on the problems of the executive in dealing with an organization and is centered on classic administrative axioms.

The early sociological theories of organization (e.g., Weber, Durkheim) emphasized the phenomena of division of labor and specialization as broad social trends and the importance of large-scale organizations in utilizing specialized competences. Weber, for example, placed considerable emphasis on the rationality of bureaucratic organization. Such theorists tended to compare the depersonalized professionalization of bureaucracies with a (probably overdrawn) view of earlier personal and unspecialized systems of social organization. To a certain extent the early theorists and, to a much greater extent, modern sociological students of organizations emphasized what Merton has labeled the "unanticipated consequences of purposive social action." Thus, the major variables tend to be such things as subgoal differentiation and conflict, individual personality changes, and organizational life-cycle.[35]

Social psychological approaches to organizational phenomena have tended to be less grandiose in scope. In general, they have taken a relatively obvious criterion of efficiency (e.g., productivity, speed) in a relatively simple task and examined experimentally the effect of some small set of independent variables on the efficiency of the organization. In this tradition have been the studies of communication nets, simulated radar warning stations, and small problem-solving groups. Somewhat less experimental have been the studies of morale and productivity, which also emphasize explicitly a criterion of efficiency.[36]

The final branch of organization theory dates in a sense from the earliest political and social philosophers. Speculation about centralization and decentralization and the problems of coordination can be found in pre-Christian writings. In this case, however, modern administrative theorists generally reject the earlier formulations with considerable vigor. In particular, Barnard and Simon have argued against the excessively formalistic and nonoperational analyses of early administrative theory.

Much of the recent work in this branch of organization theory takes the decision-making process as its specific focus of concern. The theory

[35]P. Blau, *Dynamics of Bureaucracy* (Chicago: University of Chicago Press, 1955); A. W. Gouldner, *Patterns of Industrial Bureaucracy* (Glencoe, Ill.: Free Press, 1954).
[36]C. Argyris, *Understanding Organizational Behavior* (Homewood, Ill.: Dorsey, 1960); R. Likert, *New Patterns of Management* (New York: McGraw-Hill, 1961).

tends to subdivide, then, into two main parts, each concerned with a certain class of decisions of significance to organizations. The first subdivision views the organization as a clearing house through which transfer payments are arranged among participants (e.g., workers, investors, customers). The theory describes the "decision to belong," and specifies the conditions of organizational survival in terms of the methods of motivating organizational participants.[37]

The second subdivision aims at the development of theory explaining how decisions are made in organizations, with special emphasis upon the processes of executive influence and the impact of organizational position on individual goals and perceptions.[38]

Without attempting to describe the various forms that theoretical arguments have assumed within organization theory, we think this brief sketch of the focus of attention is enough to illustrate three major points:

1. The theory focuses on a set of problems that are different from those of the economic theory of the firm. Its problems are not specifically economic; virtually nothing is said about how output levels are set, advertising expenditures determined, and so forth.

2. Although it places considerable emphasis on the study of "process" — the study of what goes on in an organization — only the third branch of the theory focuses primarily upon organizational decision-making processes.

3. Unlike the theory of the firm, there is no consideration of "aggregation." Indeed, there is nothing to aggregate.

Thus, existing organization theory provides only a very partial basis for a new theory of the firm. The sociological and social psychological approaches have emphasized questions that are only marginally relevant to either the objectives of conventional theories of the firm or the objective of predicting individual firm behavior. The decision-making approach has developed a substantial theory of decision-making processes in an organizational context, but has not applied the theory to the specific environmental conditions in which the business firm operates nor applied the

---

[37]H. A. Simon, *Administrative Behavior* (New York: Macmillan, 1947); C. I. Barnard, *Functions of the Executive* (Cambridge: Harvard University Press, 1938); H. A. Simon, D. W. Smithburg, and V. A. Thompson, *Public Administration* (New York: Knopf, 1950). This subdivision of organization theory has many points of contact with the social psychological — largely with the motivational aspects of decisions.

[38]C. I. Barnard, *op. cit.;* H. A. Simon, *op. cit.* This subdivision has derived its basic framework from cognitive psychology [H. A. Simon, *Models of Man* (New York: Wiley, 1957), introduction to pt. IV; J. G. March and H. A. Simon, *op. cit.*, chaps. 6 and 7] but historically has derived its problems primarily from economics — the theory of the firm (Barnard), and public expenditure theory [C. E. Ridley and H. A. Simon, *Measuring Municipal Activities* (Chicago: International City Managers' Association, 1938)].

theory in detail to the particular decision variables that characterize the firm's operation.

2.3 Research Questions in a Revised Theory of Firm Decision Making

Given these characteristics of organization theory — or much of it — and the theory of the firm — or much of it, it is clear that much more is needed than a simple integration of the two. *Our conception of the task we face is that of constructing a theory that takes (1) the firm as its basic unit, (2) the prediction of firm behavior with respect to such decisions as price, output, and resource allocation as its objective, and (3) an explicit emphasis on the actual process of organizational decision making as its basic research commitment.* The remainder of this book is directed toward that task. The task involves two main problems: determining the major attributes of decision making by business firms and identifying a theoretical language appropriate to a revised theory. We defer a discussion of the language problem until we attempt to describe explicit models of organizational decision making (Chapters 5, 7, 8, and 10). Assuming that we can solve the language problem, the substantive problem becomes pressing. If we can afford the luxury of greater complexity in the theory, to what questions do we require answers?

Much of this book is aimed at answering this last question. At the outset, however, we can anticipate the direction of the research. We start with a simple conception that an organizational decision is the execution of a choice made in terms of objectives from among a set of alternatives on the basis of available information. This leads to an examination of how organizational objectives are formed, how strategies are evolved, and how decisions are reached within those strategies.

Organizational objectives of a business firm. Once we drop the concept of a single, universal, organizational goal (e.g., profit maximization) and look instead at the process for defining objectives in organizations, we need some propositions about the development of goals. What is the effect of departmental structure on the goals actually pursued in an organization? It is commonly alleged that one of the most frequent phenomena in an organization is the differentiation of subunit goals and the identification of individuals with the goals of the subunits, independently of the contribution of that goal to the organization as a whole. What difference does this make for a business firm and its decisions on such matters as resource allocation?

What effect do planning and plans have on organizational objectives? Plans are a conspicuous part of organizational functioning, yet their impact on organizational goals is little understood. We would especially emphasize the study of the role of the budget in determining goals. Thus, we would argue that more information is necessary about how budgets are determined.

How do objectives change? If we allow goals to develop within the organization, we must also allow them to change over time. To what extent can we deduce propositions about shifts in organizational objectives from the theories and research on individual aspiration levels?

What characterizes the objectives that are defined in an organization? Assuming that profit maximization is sometimes replaced by the use of profit surrogates, acceptable-level criteria, or other goals, can we predict under what conditions a given objective will be used? Even more awkward, how do we deal with (i.e., what are the consequences of) conflict of interest within organizations?

Decision strategies. We are assuming that the decisions of the firm are not always uniquely determined by its external environment — for example, the market. Where the firm has discretion, we think it forms what we have called *decision strategies* or *rules*. Many important aspects of those strategies turn on the distinction made by the firm between decision variables and parameters. What is taken as given and what is treated as subject to manipulation by the firm? Here, a number of organizational characteristics seem to us to be important. Are some things treated as variable only at specified points in time? What difference does such time spacing of decisions make? To what extent are one department's decision variables another department's parameters and what difference does it make?

Decision making within strategies. Once organizational objectives and decision strategies are determined, the organization can be viewed as an information-processing and decision-rendering system. We need more reliable information on where and how organizations secure information, how that information is communicated through the organization, how authoritative decisions are reached, and finally, how such decisions are implemented in the organization.

To what extent does the market serve as a source of information about consumers, competitors, and so forth? What alternative sources of data exist and are used? What determines which sources of information will be used by an organization? Specifically, what predictable informational biases can be identified? If it is true that typically only a very small portion of the total available information is ever recorded by the organization, the processes by which the initial screening takes place has extraordinary importance in determining the final decision.

What happens to information as it is processed through the organization? What predictable screening biases are there in an organization? What is the effect of conflict of interest on communication? What difference does time pressure make?

What characterizes authoritative decision makers under different conditions? How do their prior experience and reference group identifications affect their decisions? How are executive expectations determined? What differences are there between individual and group decision making? How do hierarchical groups make decisions? If gradual commitment distinguishes decision making in business firms, in what respect does this affect the content of the decisions?

What is the relation between decisions made by the responsible executives and the final "decision" implemented by the organization? How do variations in the control systems (e.g., accounting systems) affect the implementation of decisions? What is the function and consequence of "organizational slack"? In what systematic ways are decisions elaborated or changed by the organization?

In general, there are many questions about the behavior of business firms but only a few answers. Existing theory is not equipped to answer most of the questions we have raised. Where an answer can be derived by brute force, it tends to be ambiguous or conspicuously inadequate. In order to develop an alternative theory, we need more satisfactory theories of organizational *goals*, organizational *expectations*, organizational *choice*, and organizational *control*. In our view, these are the four major subtheories of a behavioral theory of the firm. A theory of organizational goals would consider how goals arise in an organization, how they change over time, and how the organization attends to them. A theory of organizational expectations would treat how and when an organization searches for information or new alternatives and how information is processed through the organization. A theory of organizational choice would characterize the process by which the alternatives available to the organization are ordered and a selection made among them. A theory of organizational control would specify the differences between executive choice in an organization and the decisions actually implemented.

2.4 Summary

We have suggested that there are serious problems in using the theory of the firm and organization theory to predict and explain the behavior of business firms with respect to such economic decisions as price, output, capital investment, and internal resource allocation. In the remaining chapters we attack these problems in three ways:

1. We indicate partial answers to some of the questions posed in the previous section. Thus, in Chapter 3 we consider organizational goals; in Chapter 4, organizational expectations; in Chapter 5, organizational choice and (to a limited extent) organizational control.

2. We present some explicit models of organizational decision making. In Chapters 7 and 10 models of specific organizations are described. In

Chapters 8 and 9 we indicate two general models of price and output determination.

3. In Chapter 11 we suggest some implications of the revised theory for future work, on both the micro and the macro levels.

Appendix. Mathematical Theory of the Firm[39]

The derivation of the seven propositions of Chapter 2 is shown in this appendix.

1. The production function for a multiproduct firm is given by

$$f(x_1, x_2, \ldots, x_n) = 0$$

where x_r $(r = 1, \ldots, n)$ is the output of the rth commodity. If $x_r > 0$, the commodity is a product, and if $x_r < 0$, it is a factor. Assume p products and $n - p$ factors.

Within a perfectly competitive market, the commodity prices p_r $(r = 1, \ldots, n)$ are given to the firm. It must then choose the optimal mix to maximize net revenue:

$$R = \sum_r p_r x_r - A$$

subject to

$$f(x_1, \ldots, x_n) = 0$$

where A is fixed cost.

The equilibrium position is determined using the Lagrangean multiplier λ by maximizing the new function

$$Z = R - \lambda f$$

for the n variables, x_r $(r = 1, \ldots, n)$.

The necessary conditions give

$$\frac{\partial Z}{\partial x_r} = p_r - \lambda f_r = 0$$

where $f_r = \partial f / \partial x_r$, i.e.,

$$\left. \begin{array}{l} p_r = \lambda f_r \\ f(x_1, \ldots, x_n) = 0 \end{array} \right\} \quad (r = 1, \ldots, n) \tag{1}$$

and

as $(n + 1)$ equations to determine the quantities of the n commodities and λ.

---

[39]We are indebted to M. A. H. Dempster for this way of summarizing the literature.

2. From Eq. (1), the marginal rate of substitution between the rth and the sth product, or the rth and the sth factor, becomes

$$\frac{f_r}{f_s} = \frac{p_r}{p_s} \quad \text{or} \quad \begin{array}{l} (r, s = 1, \ldots, p) \\ (r, s = p + 1, \ldots, n) \end{array}$$

3. The marginal physical productivity, with respect to the rth product, of the sth factor,

$$M_{r,s} = \frac{\partial(-x_s)}{\partial x_r} = \frac{f_r}{f_s} = \frac{p_r}{p_s} \quad \begin{array}{l} (r = 1, \ldots, p) \\ (s = p + 1, \ldots, n) \end{array}$$

where $\partial(-x_s)/\partial x_r$ is the rate of change of the amount of the factor used $(x_s < 0)$ with respect to the product.

4. Total costs are given by

$$C = \sum_s p_s(-x_s) + A \qquad (s = p + 1, \ldots, n)$$

such that the marginal cost of the rth good produced,

$$\frac{\partial C}{\partial x_r} = \sum_s p_s \frac{\partial(-x_s)}{\partial x_r} = \sum_s p_s M_{r,s} = \sum_s p_s \frac{p_r}{p_s} = p_r$$

5. The sufficient conditions for a maximum of net revenue, R, are

$$d^2Z = -\lambda \, d^2f < 0$$

This is equivalent to

$$d^2f = \sum_r \sum_s f_{rs} \, dx_r \, dx_s > 0$$

(i.e., d^2f is positive definite) subject to

$$df = \sum_r f_r \, dx_r$$

From the theory of quadratic forms the sufficient conditions may be written in the following manner:

$$\begin{vmatrix} 0 & f_1 & f_2 \\ f_1 & f_{11} & f_{12} \\ f_2 & f_{12} & f_{22} \end{vmatrix} < 0; \quad \ldots; \quad F = \begin{vmatrix} 0 & f_1 & f_2 & \ldots & f_n \\ f_1 & f_{11} & f_{12} & \ldots & f_{1n} \\ f_2 & f_{12} & f_{22} & \ldots & f_{2n} \\ \ldots & \ldots & \ldots & f_{rs} & \ldots \\ f_n & f_{1n} & f_{2n} & \ldots & f_{nn} \end{vmatrix} < 0$$

where

$$f_r = \frac{\partial f}{\partial x_r}, \qquad f_{rs} = \frac{\partial^2 F}{\partial x_r \, \partial x_s}$$

These can be interpreted as stability conditions for arbitrary finite variations x_r, x_s. Note that F and all its principal minors are symmetric. Alternatively,

$$\sum_r \sum_s \frac{F_{rs}}{F} y_r y_s > 0 \qquad (2)$$

where the y's are any finite variations (not all zero) from the equilibrium position of the quantities of products or factors. F_{rs} is the cofactor of f_{rs} in F.

The effect of a variation in any one price, p_r, is determined by differentiating (1) to yield $(n + 1)$ equations in $(n + 1)$ variables,

$$\left(\frac{1}{\lambda}\frac{\partial \lambda}{\partial p_r}\right) \qquad \text{and} \qquad \frac{\partial x_s}{\partial p_r} \qquad (s = 1,\ldots, n)$$

Thus,

$$\sum_s f_s \frac{\partial x_s}{\partial p_r} = 0$$

$$f_i\left(\frac{1}{\lambda}\frac{\partial \lambda}{\partial p_r}\right) + \sum_s f_{is} \frac{\partial x_s}{\partial p_r} = 0 \qquad (i = 1, \ldots, r - 1, r + 1, \ldots, n)$$

$$f_r\left(\frac{1}{\lambda}\frac{\partial \lambda}{\partial p_r}\right) + \sum_s f_{rs} \frac{\partial x_s}{\partial p_r} = \frac{1}{\lambda}$$

This linear system is solved by Cramer's rule to yield

$$\frac{\partial x_s}{\partial p_r} = \frac{F_{rs}}{\lambda F} \qquad (r, s = 1, \ldots, n) \qquad (3)$$

Substituting in (2) (since λ positive),

$$\sum_r \sum_s \frac{\partial x_s}{\partial p_r} y_r y_s > 0$$

For all y's zero except y_r,

$$\frac{\partial x_r}{\partial p_r} > 0 \qquad (r = 1, \ldots, n)$$

If $x_r > 0$, $\partial x_r/\partial p_r > 0$, and if $x_s < 0$, $\partial(-x_s)/\partial p_r < 0$.

6. Since F is symmetric, $F_{rs} = F_{sr}$ and (from (3))

$$\frac{\partial x_s}{\partial p_r} = \frac{\partial x_r}{\partial p_s}$$

7. The effects of a change in the price of the rth commodity, p_r, are determined by the expansion rule for determinants operating on F, and (1):

$$0 = \sum_s f_s F_{rs} = F \sum_s p_s \left(\frac{F_{rs}}{\lambda F} \right) = F \sum_s p_s \frac{\partial x_s}{\partial p_r}$$

Now, $F < 0$; hence

$$\sum_s p_s \frac{\partial x_s}{\partial p_r} = 0 \qquad (r, s = 1, \ldots, n)$$

and

$$\sum_s^* p_s \frac{\partial x_s}{\partial p_r} = p_r \left(-\frac{\partial x_r}{\partial p_r} \right) < 0 \qquad (4)$$

where $\sum_s^*$ sums over all $s \neq r$.

Note that the negative values of the $(\partial x / \partial p_r)$'s on the left-hand side of (4) outweigh the positive.

3

ORGANIZATIONAL GOALS[1]

3.1 The Problem of Collective Goals

If we wish to develop a theory that predicts and explains business decision-making behavior, we face a problem that can be paraphrased in terms of the following:

1. People (i.e., individuals) have goals; collectivities of people do not.
2. To define a theory of organizational decision making, we seem to need something analogous — at the organization level — to individual goals at the individual level.

For the moment, let us accept this paraphrase (not everyone does). The theorist's problem is then to identify some concept of organization goals that is consistent with the apparent denial of their existence. Since (rightly or wrongly) individual goals are perceived as lodged in the individual human mind, the problem is to specify organizational goals without postulating an "organizational mind." In order to solve the problem we must (1) specify what an organization is in terms of the individual-organization dichotomy, (2) agree on the nature of the theoretical

[1]This chapter is based extensively on R. M. Cyert and J. G. March, "A Behavioral Theory of Organizational Objectives," *Modern Organization Theory*, ed. M. Haire (New York: Wiley, 1959).

problems created by such a conception for the notion of organizational goals, and (3) identify a plausible solution to the theoretical problems. We will argue that there is substantial agreement on the first two requirements, but that the classic procedures for meeting the third requirement are deficient.

3.1.1 Conception of an organization

Let us view the organization as a coalition. It is a coalition of individuals, some of them organized into subcoalitions. In a business organization the coalition members include managers, workers, stockholders, suppliers, customers, lawyers, tax collectors, regulatory agencies, etc. In the governmental organization the members include administrators, workers, appointive officials, elective officials, legislators, judges, clientele, interest group leaders, etc. In the voluntary charitable organization there are paid functionaries, volunteers, donors, donees, etc.

Drawing the boundaries of an organizational coalition once and for all is impossible. Instead, we simplify the conception by focusing on the participants in a particular "region" — either temporal or functional. That is, over a specified (relatively brief) period of time we can identify the major coalition members; or, for a particular decision we can identify the major coalition members. More generally, for a certain class of decisions over a relatively long period of time we can specify the major classes of coalition members. As a result, we will be able to develop models of organizational decision making (for the short run) that pay only limited attention to the process by which the coalition is changed; but any such simplification involves some clear risks when we generalize to long-run dynamics.

This conception of an organization fits a number of recent formulations: the inducements-contributions schema, game theory, and the theory of teams. Each of these theories assumes a coalition of participants; each (with the exception of the inducements-contributions schema) assumes that by some procedure the coalition arrives at a statement of organization goals. However, the idea of an organization goal and the conception of an organization as a coalition are implicitly contradictory. Basic to the idea of a coalition is the expectation that the individual participants in the organization may have substantially different preference orderings (i.e., individual goals). That is to say, any theory of organizational goals must deal successfully with the obvious potential for internal goal conflict inherent in a coalition of diverse individuals and groups.

3.1.2 Classic devices for defining organization goals

There are two classic economic solutions to the problem of organization goals. The first, or entrepreneurial, solution is to describe an organization

as consisting of an entrepreneur (either the top of the managerial hierarchy
or some external control group such as stockholders) and a staff. The goals
of the organization are then defined to be the goals of the entrepreneur.
Conformity to these goals is purchased by payments (wages, interest, love)
made by the entrepreneur to the staff and by a system of internal control
that informs the staff of the entrepreneurial demands. This solution to the
problem is characteristic of the economic theory of the firm, some political
theories of public bureaucracies, and most theories of management.

The second solution to the problem is to identify a common or con-
sensual goal. This is a goal that is shared by the various participants in the
organization. It may be a priori sharing, as in many theories of political
institutions in which the goal of "public interest" or "social welfare" is
introduced. It may be a posteriori sharing, as in some theories of small-
group goal formation through discussion. In either case, conflict is eliminated through consensus.

Neither solution is entirely happy. Both attempt to define a joint
preference ordering for the coalition. In our view, such attempts are mis-
directed. Actual organizational goals cannot normally be described in
terms of a joint preference ordering. Studies of organizational objectives
suggest that agreement on objectives is usually agreement on highly
ambiguous goals.[2] Such agreement is undoubtedly important to choice
within the organization, but it is far from the clear preference ordering
usually assumed. The studies suggest further that behind this agreement
on rather vague objectives there is considerable disagreement and uncertainty about subgoals, that organizations appear to be pursuing different
goals at the same time.[3] Finally, the studies suggest that most organization
objectives take the form of an aspiration level rather than an imperative
to "maximize" or "minimize," and that the aspiration level changes in
response to experience.[4]

Unless we choose to ignore such observations, we need to reconsider our
conceptions of objectives. Since the existence of unresolved conflict is a
conspicuous feature of organizations, it is exceedingly difficult to construct
a useful positive theory of organizational decision making if we insist on
internal goal consistency. As a result, recent theories of organization
objectives describe goals as the result of a continuous bargaining-learning
process. Such a process will not necessarily produce consistent goals.

[2]D. B. Truman, The Governmental Process (New York: Knopf, 1951); A. D. H.
Kaplan, J. B. Dirlam, and R. F. Lanzillotti, Pricing in Big Business (Washington, D.C.:
Brookings Institution, 1958).

[3]Kaplan, et al., op. cit.; P. Selznick, TVA and the Grass Roots (Berkeley: University
of California Press, 1949).

[4]P. M. Blau, The Dynamics of Bureaucracy (Chicago: University of Chicago Press,
1955); R. M. Alt, "The Internal Organization of the Firm and Price Formation: An
Illustrative Case," Quarterly Journal of Economics, 63 (1949), 92–110.

3.2 The Goal Formation Process

In the theory to be outlined here, we consider three major ways in which the objectives of a coalition are determined. These are:

1. the bargaining process by which the composition and general terms of the coalition are fixed;

2. the internal organizational process of control by which objectives are stabilized and elaborated;

3. the process of adjustment to experience by which coalition agreements are altered in response to environmental changes.

3.2.1 Formation of coalition objectives through bargaining

A basic problem in developing a theory of coalition formation is that of handling side payments. It seems certain that the side payments by which organizational coalitions are formed do not satisfy the requirements of unrestricted transferability of utility. Side payments are made in many forms: money, personal treatment, authority, organization policy, and so forth. A winning coalition does not have a fixed booty that it then divides among its members. Quite to the contrary, the total value of side payments available for division among coalition members is a function of the composition of the coalition, and the total utility of the actual side payments depends on the distribution made within the coalition. There is no conservation of utility. For example, if we can imagine a situation in which any dyad is a viable coalition (e.g., a partnership to exploit the proposition that two can live more cheaply in coalition than separately), we would predict a greater total utility for those dyads in which needs were complementary than for those in which they were competitive.

Such a situation makes game theory as it currently exists virtually irrelevant for a treatment of organizational side payments,[5] but the problem is in part even deeper than that. The second requirement of theories such as game theory, theory of teams, and inducements-contributions theory is that after the side payments are made, a joint preference ordering is defined. All conflict is settled by the side-payment bargaining. The employment-contract form of these theories, for example, assumes that the entrepreneur has an objective. He then purchases whatever services he needs to achieve the objective. In return for such payments employees contract to perform whatever is required of them — at least within the range of permissible requirements. For a price, the employee adopts the "organization" goal.

One feature of such a conception is that it describes a coalition asym-

[5] D. Luce and H. Raiffa, *Games and Decisions* (New York: Wiley, 1957), chaps. 7 and 10.

metrically. To what extent is it arbitrary, in conventional accounting procedures, that we call wage payments "costs" and dividend payments "profit" rather than the other way around? Why is it that in our quasi-genetic moments we are inclined to say that in the beginning there was a manager and he recruited workers and capital? For the development of our own theory we make two major arguments. First, the emphasis on the asymmetry has seriously confused the understanding of organizational goals. The confusion arises because ultimately it makes only slightly more sense to say that the goal of a business organization is to maximize profit than to say that its goal is to maximize the salary of Sam Smith, Assistant to the Janitor.

Second, despite this, there are important reasons for viewing some coalition members as quite different from others. For example, it is clear that employees and management make somewhat different demands on the organization. In their bargaining, side payments appear traditionally to have performed the classical function of specifying a joint preference ordering. In addition, some coalition members (e.g., many stockholders) devote substantially less time to the particular coalition under consideration than do others. It is this characteristic that has been used to draw organizational boundaries between "external" and "internal" members of the coalition. Thus, there are important classes of coalition members who are passive most of the time. A condition of such passivity is that the payment demands they make be of such a character that most of the time they can be met rather easily.

Although we thereby reduce substantially the size and complexity of the coalition relevant for most goal setting, we are still left with something more complicated than an individual entrepreneur. It is primarily through bargaining within this active group that what we call *organizational objectives* arise. Side payments, far from being the incidental distribution of a fixed, transferable booty, represent the central process of goal specification. That is, a significant number of these payments are in the form of policy commitments.

The distinction between demands for monetary side payments and demands for policy commitments seems to underlie management-oriented treatments of organizations. It is clear that in many organizations this distinction has important ideological connotations. Indeed, the breakdown of the distinction in our generation has been quite consistently violent. Political party machines in this country have changed drastically the ratio of direct monetary side payments (e.g., patronage, charity) to policy commitments (e.g., economic legislation). Labor unions are conspicuously entering into what has been viewed traditionally as the management prerogatives of policy making and demanding payments in that area. Military officers have given up the substance — if not entirely the pretense

— of being simply hired agents of the regime. The phenomenon is especially obvious in public[6] and voluntary[7] organizations, but all organizations use policy side payments. The marginal cost to other coalition members is typically quite small.

This trend toward policy side payments is especially noticeable in contemporary organizations, but the important point is that we have never come close to maintenance of a sharp distinction in the kinds of payments made and demanded. Policy commitments have (one is tempted to say *always*) been an important part of the method by which coalitions are formed. In fact, an organization that does not use such devices can exist in only a rather special environment.

To illustrate coalition formation under conditions where the problem is not scarce resources for side payments but varying complementarities of policy demands, imagine a nine-man committee appointed to commission a painting for the village hall. The nine members make individually the following demands:

A: The painting must be an abstract monotone.
B: The painting must be an impressionistic oil.
C: The painting must be small and oval in shape.
D: The painting must be small and in oil.
E: The painting must be square in shape and multicolored.
F: The painting must be an impressionistic square.
G: The painting must be a monotone and in oil.
H: The painting must be multicolored and impressionistic.
I: The painting must be small and oval.

In this case each potential coalition member makes two simple demands. Assuming that five members are all that are required to make the decision, there are three feasible coalitions: A, D, C, G, and I can form a coalition and commission a small, oval, monotone, oil abstract; B, C, D, H, and I can form a coalition and commission a small, oval, multicolored, impressionistic oil; B, D, E, F, and H can form a coalition and commission a small, square, multicolored, impressionistic oil.

Committeeman D, it will be noted, is in the admirable position of being included in every possible coalition. The reason is clear; his demands are completely consistent with the demands of everyone else.

Obviously, at some level of generality the distinction between money and policy payments disappears because any side payment can be viewed

[6]R. A. Dahl and C. E. Lindblom, *Politics, Economics, and Welfare* (New York: Harper, 1953); H. A. Simon, D. W. Smithburg, and V. A. Thompson, *Public Administration* (New York: Knopf, 1950).

[7]D. L. Sills, *The Volunteers* (Glencoe, Ill.: Free Press, 1957); S. L. Messinger, "Organizational Transformation: A Case Study of a Declining Social Movement," *American Sociological Review*, **20** (1955), 3–10.

as a policy constraint. When we agree to pay someone \$35,000 a year, we are constrained to the set of policy decisions that will allow such a payment. Any allocation of scarce resources (such as money) limits the alternatives for the organization. However, the scarcity of resources is not the only kind of problem. Some policy demands are strictly inconsistent with other demands. Others are completely complementary. To be sure, the problems of policy consistency are in principle amenable to explicit optimizing behavior, but they add to the computational difficulties facing the coalition members and make it even more obvious why the bargaining leading to side payment and policy agreements is only slightly related to the bargaining anticipated in a theory of omniscient rationality.

In the process of bargaining over side payments, many of the organizational objectives are defined or clarified. Because of the form the bargaining takes, the objectives tend to have several important attributes:

1. They are imperfectly rationalized. The extent to which the new demands will be tested for consistency with existing policy will depend on the skill of the leaders involved, the sequence of demands leading to the new bargaining, the aggressiveness of various parts of the organization, and the scarcity of resources. This testing is normally far from complete.

2. Some objectives are stated in the form of aspiration-level constraints. This occurs when demands that are consistent with the coalition are thus stated; for example: "We must allocate ten per cent of our total budget to research."

3. Some objectives are stated in a nonoperational form. In our formulation such objectives arise when potential coalition members have demands that are nonoperational or demands that can be made nonoperational. The prevalence of objectives in this form can be partly explained by the fact that nonoperational objectives are consistent with virtually any set of objectives.

3.2.2 Stabilization and elaboration of objectives

The bargaining process goes on more or less continuously, turning out a long series of commitments — but a description of goal formation in such terms alone is not adequate. Organizational objectives are, first of all, much more stable than would be suggested by such a model, and second, such a model does not handle satisfactorily the elaboration and clarification of goals through day-to-day bargaining.

Human beings have limited capacities and limited time to devote to any particular aspect of the organizational system; such limitations constrain the bargaining process. Let us return to our conception of a coalition having monetary and policy side payments. These side-payment agreements are incomplete. They do not anticipate effectively all possible future situations, and they do not identify all considerations that might be viewed as important by the coalition members at some future time. Nevertheless, the coalition members are motivated to operate under the agreements and to develop some mutual control-systems for enforcing them.

One such mutual control-system in many organizations is the budget. A budget is an explicit elaboration of previous commitments. Although it is usually viewed as an asymmetric control-device (i.e., a means for superiors to control subordinates), it is clear that it represents a form of mutual control — just as there are usually severe costs to the department in exceeding the budget, so also are there severe costs to other members of the coalition if the budget is not paid in full. As a result, budgets in every organization tend to be self-confirming (see Chapter 5).

A second major, mutual control-system is the allocation of functions. Division of labor and specialization are commonly treated in management textbooks simply as techniques of rational organization. If, however, we consider the allocation of functions in much the way we would normally view the allocation of resources during budgeting, a somewhat different picture emerges. When we define the limits of discretion, we constrain the individual or subgroup from acting outside those limits; but at the same time, we constrain any other members of the coalition from prohibiting action within those limits. Like the allocation of resources in a budget, the allocation of discretion in an organization chart is largely self-confirming.

The secondary bargaining involved in such mutual control-systems serves to elaborate and revise the coalition agreements made on entry.[8] In the early life of an organization, or after some exceptionally drastic organizational upheaval, this elaboration occurs in a context where relatively deliberate action must be taken on everything from pricing policy to paper clip policy. Reports from individuals who have lived through such early stages emphasize the lack of structure that typifies settings for day-to-day decisions.[9]

In most organizations most of the time, however, the elaboration of objectives occurs within much tighter constraints. Much of the structure is taken as given. This is true primarily because organizations have memories in the form of precedents, and individuals in the coalition are strongly motivated to accept the precedents as binding. Whether precedents are formalized in the shape of an official standard operating procedure or are less formally stored, they remove from conscious consideration many agreements, decisions, and commitments that might well be subject to renegotiation in an organization without a memory (see Chapter 5). Past

---

[8]J. D. Thompson and W. J. McEwen, "Organizational Goals and Environment: Goal-setting as an Interactive Process," *American Sociological Review*, **23** (1958), 23–31.

[9]H. A. Simon, "The Birth of an Organization: The Economic Cooperation Administration," *Public Administration Review*, **13** (1953), 227–236.

bargains become precedents for present situations; a budget becomes a precedent for future budgets; an allocation of functions becomes a precedent for future allocations. Through all the well-known mechanisms, the coalition agreements of today are institutionalized into semipermanent arrangements. A number of administrative aphorisms come to mind: an unfilled position disappears; see an empty office and fill it up; there is nothing temporary under the sun. As a result of organizational precedents, objectives exhibit much greater stability than would typify a pure bargaining situation. The "accidents" of organizational genealogy tend to be perpetuated.

3.2.3 Changes in objectives through experience

Although considerably stabilized by internal processes, the demands made on the coalition by individual members do change with experience. Both the nature of the demands and their quantitative level vary over time.

Since many of the requirements specified by individual participants are in the form of attainable goals rather than general maximizing constraints, objectives are subject to the usual phenomena associated with aspiration levels. As an approximation to the aspiration-level model, we can take the following set of propositions:

1. In the steady state, aspiration level exceeds achievement by a small amount.

2. Where achievement increases at an increasing rate, aspiration level will exhibit short-run lags behind achievement.

3. Where achievement decreases, aspiration level will be above achievement.

These propositions derive from a set of assumptions requiring that current aspiration be an optimistic extrapolation of past achievement and past aspiration. Although such assumptions are sometimes inappropriate, the model seems to be consistent with a wide range of human goal-setting behavior.[10] Two kinds of achievement are, of course, important. The first is the achievement of the participant himself. The second is the achievement of others in his reference group.[11]

Because of these phenomena, our theory of organizational objectives must allow for drift in the demands of members of the organization. No one doubts that aspirations with respect to monetary compensation vary substantially as a function of payments received — so do aspirations regarding advertising budget, quality of product, volume of sales, product

[10]K. Lewin, T. Dembo, L. Festinger, and P. Sears, "Level of Aspiration," in *Personality and the Behavior Disorders*, ed. J. M. Hunt (New York: Ronald, 1944), vol. 1.

[11]L. Festinger, "A Theory of Social Comparison Processes," *Human Relations*, 7 (1954), 117–140.

mix, and capital investment. Obviously, until we know a great deal more than we now do about the parameters of the relation between achievement and aspiration, we can make only relatively weak predictions. However, some of these predictions are quite useful, especially in conjunction with search theory (see Chapter 4).

The nature of the demands also changes with experience in another way. We do not conceive that individual members of the coalition will have a simple listing of demands, with only the quantitative values changing over time. Instead we imagine each member as having a rather disorganized file case full of demands. At any point in time, the member attends to only a rather small subset of his demands, the number and variety depending again on the extent of his involvement in the organization and on the demands of the other commitments on his attention.

Since not all demands receive attention at the same time, one important part of the theory of organizational objectives is to predict when particular units in the organization will attend to particular goals. Consider the safety goal in a large corporation. For the safety engineers this is an important goal most of the time. Other parts of the organization rarely even consider it. If, however, the organization has some drastic experience (e.g., a multiple fatality), attention to a safety goal is much more widespread and safety action quite probable (see Chapter 4).

Whatever the experience, it shifts the attention focus. In some cases (as in the safety example), adverse experience suggests a problem area to be attacked. In others, solutions to problems stimulate attention to a particular goal. An organization with an active personnel-research department will devote substantial attention to personnel goals, not because it is necessarily an especially pressing problem but because the subunit keeps generating solutions that remind other members of the organization of a particular set of objectives they profess.

The notion of attention focus suggests one reason why organizations are successful in surviving with a large set of unrationalized goals. They rarely see the conflicting objectives simultaneously. For example, consider the case of a common pair of organizational demands within business organizations, the demands for: (1) specific tailoring of product specifications and delivery times to individual customer needs — primarily from the sales department and customers; (2) product standardization and delivery times consistent with production smoothing — primarily from the production department and cost analysts. In large part, these demands are logically inconsistent; one is satisfied at the expense of the other. They cannot both be completely satisfied simultaneously. However, since the probability is low that both of these demands will be made simultaneously, the organization can remain viable by attending to the demands sequentially.

The sequential attention to goals is a simple mechanism. A consequence of the mechanism is that organizations ignore many conditions that outside observers see as direct contradictions. They are contradictions only if we imagine a well-established, joint preference ordering or omniscient bargaining. Neither condition exists in an organization. If we assume that attention to goals is limited, we can explain the absence of any strong pressure to resolve apparent internal inconsistencies. This is not to argue that all conflicts involving objectives can be resolved in this way, but it is one important mechanism that deserves much more intensive study.

3.2.4 Organizational slack

In terms of the present framework, an organizational coalition is viable if the payments made to the various coalition members are adequate to keep them in the organization. If resources exist to meet all demands and those resources are distributed so as to meet demands, the coalition is a feasible one. Since demands adjust to actual payments and alternatives external to the organization, there is a long-run tendency for payments and demands to be equal. In this sense, what we have called *coalition demands* are analogous to the factor prices of a more conventional view of the firm.

There is a critical difference, however. In the present theory we focus on the short-run relation between payments and demands and on the imperfections in factor markets. The imperfections, in fact, dominate the behavior. The imperfections are dominant for three primary reasons:

1. As we have already noted, payments and demands are in the form of a variety of money payments, perquisites, policies, personal treatments, and private commitments. As a result, information on actual factor "prices" is hard to obtain, easily misinterpreted, and often unreliable.

2. Information about the "market" is not obtained automatically; it must be sought. Typically, the participants in the organization do not seek information until stimulated to do so by some indication of failure.

3. Adaptations in demands are slow — even in the face of strong pressure.

Because of these frictions in the mutual adjustment of payments and demands, there is ordinarily a disparity between the resources available to the organization and the payments required to maintain the coalition. This difference between total resources and total necessary payments is what we have called *organizational slack*. Slack consists in payments to members of the coalition in excess of what is required to maintain the organization. Many interesting phenomena within the firm occur because slack is typically not zero.

In conventional economic theory slack is zero (at least at equilibrium). In treatments of managerial economics, attention is ordinarily focused on only one part of slack — payments to owners — and it is assumed that other slack is maintained at zero. Neither view is an especially accurate portrayal of an actual firm. Many forms of slack typically exist: stockholders are paid dividends in excess of those required to keep stockholders (or banks) within the organization; prices are set lower than necessary to maintain adequate income from buyers; wages in excess of those required to maintain labor are paid; executives are provided with services and personal luxuries in excess of those required to keep them; subunits are permitted to grow without real concern for the relation between additional payments and additional revenue; public services are provided in excess of those required.

From time to time virtually every participant in any organization obtains slack payments. However, some participants ordinarily obtain a greater share of the slack than do other participants. In general, we would expect that members of the coalition who are full-time, in a position to perceive potential slack early, or have some flexibility in unilateral allocation of resources will tend to accumulate more slack than will other members. Although we have not attempted to pursue in detail the implications of such differential distribution of slack within the organization, the general model presented in Chapter 8 distinguishes between two kinds of organizational slack (essentially slack in the marketing-sales functions on the one hand and slack in the production function on the other) that are related by their mutual dependence on external conditions but are partially independent.

In most cases we have used the organizational slack concept not to explain differential payments but as a hypothetical construct for explaining over-all organizational phenomena. In particular, it seems to be useful in dealing with the adjustment of firms to gross shifts in the external environment. For example, consider what happens when the rate of improvement in the environment is great enough so that it outruns the upward adjustment of aspirations. In a general way, this seems to be the situation that faces business firms during strong boom periods. When the environment outruns aspiration-level adjustment, the organization secures, or at least has the potential of securing, resources in excess of its demands. Some of these resources are simply not obtained — although they are available. Others are used to meet the revised demands of those members of the coalition whose demands adjust most rapidly — usually those most deeply involved in the organization. The excess resources would not be subject to general bargaining because they do not involve allocation in the face of scarcity.

When the environment becomes less favorable, organizational slack represents a cushion. Resource scarcity brings on renewed bargaining and tends to cut heavily into the excess payments introduced during plush times. It does not necessarily mean that precisely those demands that grew abnormally during better days are pruned abnormally during poorer ones, but in general we would expect this to be approximately the case. More important, the cushion provided by organizational slack permits firms to survive in the face of adversity. Under the pressure of a failure (or impending failure) to meet some set of demands on the coalition, the organization discovers some previously unrecognized opportunities for increasing the total resources available. For example, M. W. Reder reports that after losses of about fifty million dollars for the first three quarters of 1946, the Ford Motor Company "announced that it had found methods of reducing operating costs (on a given volume of output) by about twenty million dollars per year."[12]

Organizational slack absorbs a substantial share of the potential variability in the firm's environment. As a result, it plays both a stabilizing and adaptive role. We have already noted that the demands of participants adjust to achievement. Aspiration-level adjustment, however, tends to be a relatively slow process — especially downward adjustment. If the only adaptive devices available to the organization were adjustments in aspirations of the members of the coalition, the system would be quite unstable in the face of an environment of even moderate fluctuation. Slack operates to stabilize the system in two ways: (1) by absorbing excess resources, it retards upward adjustment of aspirations during relatively good times; (2) by providing a pool of emergency resources, it permits aspirations to be maintained (and achieved) during relatively bad times.

This is not to argue that slack is deliberately created for such a stabilizing purpose; in fact, it is not. Slack arises from the bargaining and decision process we have described, without conscious intent on the part of the coalition members to provide stability to the organization. In a sense, the process is reinforced because it "works" and it "works" partly because it generates slack, but we have seen no significant evidence for the conscious rationalization of slack in business firms. From the point of view of a behavioral theory of the firm, however, the critical question is whether predictions based on the concept can be verified. For example, we would predict that the costs of firms that are successful in the market place will, *ceteris paribus*, tend to rise. Such predictions are susceptible to more or less direct test.[13] They also are tested by testing more complicated models of which they form a part (see Chapter 5).

[12]M. W. Reder, "A Reconsideration of Marginal Productivity Theory," *Journal of Political Economy*, **55** (1947), 450–458.

[13]R. M. Cyert and J. G. March, "Organizational Factors in the Theory of Oligopoly," *Quarterly Journal of Economics*, **70** (1956), 44–46.

3.2.5 Constructing a predictive theory

Before the general considerations outlined above can be transformed into a useful predictive theory, a considerable amount of precision must be added. The introduction of precision depends, in turn, on the future success of research into the process of coalition formation. Nevertheless, some steps can be taken now to develop the theory. In particular, we can specify a general framework for a theory and indicate its needs for further development.

We assume a set of coalition members, actual or potential. Whether these members are individuals or groups of individuals is unimportant. Some of the possible subsets drawn from this set are viable coalitions. That is, we will identify a class of combinations of members such that any of these combinations meet the minimal standards imposed by the external environment of the organization. Patently, therefore, the composition of the viable set of coalitions will depend on environmental conditions.

For each of the potential coalition members we require a set of demands. Each such individual set is partitioned into an active part currently attended to and an inactive part currently ignored. Each demand can be characterized by two factors: (1) its marginal resource requirements, given the demands of all possible other combinations of demands from potential coalition members; (2) its marginal consistency with all possible combinations of demands from potential coalition members.

For each potential coalition member we also require a set of problems, partitioned similarly into an active and an inactive part.

This provides us with the framework of the theory. In addition, we need five basic mechanisms:

1. A mechanism that changes the quantitative value of the demands over time. In our formulation, this becomes a version of the basic aspiration-level and mutual control theory outlined earlier.

2. An attention-focus mechanism that transfers demands among the three possible states: active set, inactive set, not-considered set. We have said that some organizational participants will attend to more demands than other participants and that for all participants some demands will be considered at one time and others at other times, but we know rather little about the actual mechanisms that control this attention factor.

3. A similar attention-focus mechanism for problems. As we have noted, there is a major interaction between what problems and what demands are attended to, but research is also badly needed in this area.

4. A demand-evaluation procedure that is consistent with the limited capacities of human beings. Such a procedure must specify how demands are checked for consistency and for their resource demands. Presumably

such a mechanism will depend heavily on a rule that much of the problem be taken as given and only incremental changes considered.

5. A mechanism for choosing among the potentially viable coalitions. In our judgment, this mechanism will probably look much like the recent suggestions of game theorists that only small changes be evaluated at a time.[14]

Given these five mechanisms and some way of expressing environmental resources, we can describe a process for the determination of objectives in an organization that will exhibit the important attributes of organizational goal determination. At the moment, we can approximate some of the required functions. For example, it has been possible to introduce into several models substantial parts of the first four mechanisms (see Chapters 5, 7, 8, and 9).

3.3 Business Goals and Price and Output Decisions

Suppose we wish to use the general considerations noted above to construct a model of organizational decision making by a business firm determining price, output, and general sales strategy. As we have already noted, we are not yet in a good position to develop a theory that focuses intensively on the formation of objectives through bargaining and coalition formation (rather than on the revision of such objectives and selective attention to them). As a result, when we look at price and output determination in business firms, we do three things:

1. We assume a small set of operational goals. In making such an assumption we suggest that the demands of many parts of the coalition are not operative for this class of decisions most of the time or are substantially satisfied when the set of goals assumed is satisfied.

2. We assume that this set of goals is fixed in the sense that no other classes of goals will arise within the coalition. Such an assumption does not exclude changes in the levels of the goals nor in the attention directed at specific goals within the set.

3. We attempt to determine by empirical investigation what specific goals ordinarily enter into the price and output decisions. In general, we have observed that we can represent organizational goals reasonably well by using about five different goals. In any organization, other considerations sometimes arise. For example, governmental demands occasionally become of prime importance. In a few organizations other considerations are as important as those we have identified. For example, in some organizations considerations of prestige or tradition are major goal factors. However, for most price, output, and general sales strategy decisions in

[14]D. Luce and H. Raiffa, *op. cit.*

most organizations, we think we can limit our primary attention to five goals.

We list the five goals here in an arbitrary order without attempting to establish any necessary order of importance; most of the time no order of importance is required. All goals must be satisfied. However, it should be clear in the models we will present in later chapters that there is an implicit order in the models reflected in the way in which search activity takes place and in the speed and circumstances of goal-level change. These latent priorities appear to vary from organization to organization in a way that is not clear. It seems most probable that their variation should be explained in terms of differences in the bargaining position of the several participants in the coalition either current or historical, but at present we treat the implicit priorities simply as organizational parameters.

3.3.1 Production goal

We assume that an organization has a complex of goals surrounding the production operation. These can be summarized in terms of a production goal. Such a goal has two major components. The first is a smoothing goal: we do not want production to vary more than a certain amount from one time period to another. The second is a level-of-production goal: we want to equal or exceed a certain production level. These two components can be summarized in terms of a production range: we want production to fall within a range of possible production.

The production goal represents in large part the demands of those coalition members connected with production. It reflects pressures toward such things as stable employment, ease of scheduling, development of acceptable cost performance, and growth. Thus, the goal is most frequently evoked in the production part of the organization and is most relevant to decisions (e.g., output) made in that part.

3.3.2 Inventory goal

We assume certain aspirations with respect to finished-goods inventory levels. As in the case of the production goal, the inventory goal summarizes a number of pressures, most conspicuously the demands of some participants to avoid runouts in inventory and to provide a complete, convenient source of inventoried materials. We summarize these demands in terms of either an absolute level of inventory goal or an inventory range (in which case we also attend to demands to avoid excessive inventory costs).

The inventory goal reflects the demands of those coalition members connected with inventory. Primarily, thus, it builds on the pressures of the inventory department itself, salesmen, and customers. Since the inventory serves essentially as a buffer between production and sales, the goal is evoked most frequently and is most relevant to decisions in the output and sales areas.

3.3.3 Sales goal

We assume that most participants in business firms believe the firm must sell produced goods in order to survive. Thus, various members of the coalition make demands that the organization meet some general criteria of sales effectiveness. The sales goal and the market share goal (below) summarize these demands. In addition, the sales department itself (and the personnel in it) link subunit goals with sales. The sales goal is simply an aspiration with respect to the level of sales. It may be in terms of dollars, units, or both.

The sales goal represents primarily the demands of those members of the coalition closely connected with sales and secondarily those members of the coalition who view sales as necessary for the stability of the organization. The goal is most frequently evoked and is most relevant to decisions with respect to sales strategy.

3.3.4 Market share goal

The market share goal is an alternative to the sales goal insofar as the concern is for a measure of sales effectiveness. Either or both may be used, depending on the past experience of the firm and the traditions of the industry. In addition, the market share goal is linked to the demands of those parts of the organization that are primarily interested in comparative success (e.g., top management, especially top sales management) and to the demands for growth.

Like the sales goal, the market share goal is most frequently evoked and most relevant to sales strategy decisions.

3.3.5 Profit goal

We assume that the business firm has a profit goal. This goal is linked to standard accounting procedures for determining profit and loss. It summarizes the demands for two things: (1) demands for accumulating resources in order to distribute them in the form of capital investments, dividends to stockholders, payments to creditors, or increased budgets to subunits; (2) demands on the part of top management for favorable performance measures. In general, we assume that the profit goal is in terms of an aspiration level with respect to the dollar amount of profit. In principle, of course, this goal might also take the form of profit share or return on investment.

The profit goal reflects the pressure of those parts of the coalition that share in the distribution of profits and in the distribution of credit for profitability. Thus, in general, this pressure comes from top-level managers throughout the firm, from stockholders, creditors, and from those parts of the organization seeking capital investment. The goal is usually most closely linked to pricing and resource allocation decisions.

Although such a specification of goals deviates substantially from the conventional theory of the firm, it will not necessarily satisfy anyone who would like to reflect all of the goals that might conceivably be of relevance to price, output, and sales strategy decisions. Without insisting on the necessary efficacy of five goals, we think a strong case can be made for expanding the set of goals beyond that represented by the conventional theory, and even beyond the elaboration suggested by Baumol.[15] We also think that expanding the list of assumed goals much beyond the present list rapidly meets a point of diminishing returns. In the models presented in later chapters we restrict attention to this list of goals; in some cases a subset of goals seems satisfactory.

3.4 Summary

We have argued that the goals of a business firm are a series of more or less independent constraints imposed on the organization through a process of bargaining among potential coalition members and elaborated over time in response to short-run pressures. Goals arise in such a form because the firm is, in fact, a coalition of participants with disparate demands, changing foci of attention, and limited ability to attend to all organizational problems simultaneously.

In the long run, studies of the goals of a business firm must reflect the adaptation of goals to changes in the coalition structure. Except for some dramatic shifts, however, such changes are quite gradual, and it is possible to construct reasonable, short-run models in which a few specific types of goals are taken as given (subject to aspiration-level changes). With respect to the contemporary firm — and price, output, and sales strategy decisions — we have argued that we can identify five major goals: production, inventory, sales, market share, and profit. These goals, or a subset of them, are postulated in the models presented in later chapters (see Chapters 5, 7, 8, 9, and 10).

Finally, we have argued that, because of the form of the goals and the way in which they are established, conflict is never fully resolved within an organization. Rather, the decentralization of decision making (and goal attention), the sequential attention to goals, and the adjustment in organizational slack permit the business firm to make decisions with inconsistent goals under many (and perhaps most) conditions.

[15]W. J. Baumol, *Business Behavior, Value and Growth* (New York: Macmillan, 1959).

4

ORGANIZATIONAL

EXPECTATIONS[1]

Just as a theory of the firm requires certain assumptions about organizational goals, it also requires certain assumptions about expectations. Since the theory is predicated on the essential purposiveness of the firm, it assumes some attempt on the part of the organization to react to its environment through observation and interpretation. In this chapter we consider the formation and handling of information in a business firm and the ways in which information about the environment enters into the decisions made by a firm.

4.1 Expectations in Theories of Business Decision Making

Theories of business decision making generally assume that estimates of cost and return *in some form* are made by the firm and that decision behavior depends heavily on such estimates. For example, the standard theory of price treats investment and internal resource allocation as

[1]This chapter is based on two previously published papers, R. M. Cyert, W. R. Dill, and J. G. March, "The Role of Expectations in Business Decision Making," *Administrative Science Quarterly*, **3** (1958), 307–340; R. M. Cyert, J. G. March, and W. H. Starbuck, "Two Experiments on Bias and Conflict in Organizational Estimation," *Management Science*, **8** (1961), 254–264.

problems in maximization. The firm invests in each available alternative to the extent that the marginal return from each alternative will equal the opportunity costs. Except insofar as sunk costs are involved, the firm makes no fundamental distinction between internal and external investment; that is, all marginal returns are equal to the best alternative return available. Under these conditions, "efficiency" — the ratio of obtained to potential return — is equal to one.

What conception of organizational decision making is implicit in such theories? They assume that the organization scans all alternatives continuously and just as continuously adjusts its portfolio of investments to changes in the pattern of alternatives available. They assume that firms have accurate information on the costs to be incurred and returns to be received from alternatives and that decisions are made on the basis of this information. These assumptions have been attacked by both economists and organization theorists.

Attempts to revise the standard theories have been designed primarily to modify the assumptions through the introduction of probability distributions and the substitution of expected profit (or utility) for the profit (or utility) originally specified. The "modern entrepreneur" is probabilistically omniscient. He knows the probability distribution of outcomes from all alternatives. He can, therefore, compute the expected value of any particular alternative and equate expected marginal return with expected marginal cost.

At the same time, the assumption of infinite search has been replaced by a theory of search that recognizes certain costs to search and thus makes the allocation of resources for securing information one of the investment decisions to be made. The modern entrepreneur does not scan all alternatives nor does he have all information about all alternatives. He invests in information only so long as the expected marginal return from the information gained exceeds the expected marginal cost.

There is general consensus that these theories, specifically their economic versions, have been valuable in both normative and empirical analyses of aggregate behavior. Since this has been the major traditional interest of economic analysis, macroeconomists have found no pressing reasons for re-examining the assumptions of the standard theories.

On the other hand, economists and others interested in the behavior of the individual firm have not been entirely satisfied with the classic assumptions. As normative theory, the theories have been challenged for accepting too easily Bernoullian expected utility. Alternative formulations, arising primarily from game theory considerations, are preferred by a vocal, but apparently minority, group. The normative uses of the theories, however, are tangential to our main interest here. We are more concerned with the challenges to these theories as explanations of business behavior.

Because we wish to consider some empirical studies of business decision making, we will elaborate upon these challenges.

There have been four major objections to the more or less "pure" theory of expectations insofar as it has been applied to the behavior of individual firms.

1. The theories assume continuous competition among all alternatives for all resources. As Coase has pointed out, the perfectly competitive market for internal resources is a major implicit assumption of the standard theory of the firm.[2] Such a description of organizational behavior is distinctly different from that implicit in many treatments of other organizations. For example, some public administration models seem to emphasize local adaptation to specific problems; they stress problem solving much more than planning.

2. The theories make search activity (and thus information) simply one of the several claimants for resources to be evaluated in terms of calculable costs and expected returns.[3] Simon and others have questioned this treatment of search behavior.[4] They have placed considerable emphasis on dissatisfaction as a stimulant to search, on the "conspicuousness" of alternatives as a factor in their consideration, on the external effects on the generation of information, and on the sequential characteristics of alternative evaluation.

3. The theories require substantial computational activity on the part of the organization. Shackle and others have argued that the theory grossly exaggerates both the computational ability and, more important, the usual computational precision of human beings.[5] There have been a number of suggestions for constraining the amount of information that must be digested. For example, the heart of Shackle's theory (still completely untested) lies in the ϕ-functions by which the attention value of a particular outcome is determined.

4. The theory treats expectations as exogenous variables; they are given, not explained. But such an eminently logical extension of certainty theory to the treatment of uncertainty ignores a number of important (or potentially important) phenomena. On the one hand, it sidesteps a major aspect of uncertain situations, the interaction of expectation and desire. On the other hand, it ignores the ways in which information is obtained and processed through the organization. For example, pricing

---

[2]R. H. Coase, "The Nature of the Firm," *Economica*, **4** (1937), 368–405.

[3]A. Charnes and W. W. Cooper, "The Theory of Search: Optimum Distribution of Search Effort," *Management Science*, **5** (1958), 44–50.

[4]H. A. Simon, "A Behavioral Model of Rational Choice," *Quarterly Journal of Economics*, **69** (1955), 99–118.

[5]G. L. S. Shackle, *Expectations in Economics* (Cambridge: Cambridge University Press, 1949).

decisions are assumed to be based on expectations concerning future sales, costs, and competitors' behavior. The firm is organized to provide information on which such expectations can be based, and it seems at least plausible that some features of the communication system in the firm will affect the kinds of information made available.

To examine the ways in which information about the external environment is obtained and processed by an organization, we consider two sets of recent observations on organizational expectations. First, case studies of four major decisions in three business firms and, second, two experimental studies of organizational communication are discussed. From an analysis of these studies we arrive at some tentative reformulations of the role of expectations in business decision making.

4.2 Four Case Studies in the Use of Expectations

The three firms observed are all well-established, successful organizations: a large, heavy manufacturing concern, a medium-sized construction firm, and a medium-large manufacturing and retailing concern. Each of the firms gave the research group full access to files and to the activities of the organization. The decisions and the studies were made during 1953–1956. Three basic techniques of observation were used: (1) detailed analysis of memoranda, letters, and other written file material, (2) intensive interviews with participants in the decisions, and (3) direct observation of the decision process. The first two techniques were used in every case. All pertinent documents (all those relating in any way to the decision being studied) in the companies' files were examined. All participating members of the organization were interviewed at least once; key members were interviewed repeatedly. In two cases (the second and fourth below), an observer from the research team was present virtually full-time in the organization during the time the decision was being made. He was attached directly to a staff member in the organization and attended staff meetings. In the fourth case, the observer was permitted, in addition, to tape record important meetings.

The data on the decisions are, therefore, as complete as the limits of memory (both organizational and personal), interview technique, and observer ability permitted. Since those limits can be surprisingly restrictive, some questions of detail could not be answered. Nevertheless, the case studies described below are based on substantial information, direct and indirect. For purposes of presentation they have been condensed considerably, and emphasis has been placed on one aspect of the situation — the role of expectations. We are well aware of the dangers in such an abstraction, and we scarcely hope that four case studies, however detailed, will allay the skepticism of critical readers. The justification lies in our belief that the key propositions we want to make are conspicuous in the data and in our hope that the data will provide a start for empirical research in an area of extensive *ad hoc* theory.

4.2.1 Decision 1: a problem in accelerated renovation of old equipment

The first decision problem we shall analyze arose in a branch plant of a heavy manufacturing corporation employing several thousand workers and divided into semiautonomous operating divisions — seven major and several smaller divisions. Auxiliary service departments (such as safety) reported to the plant manager and his assistants, but most such departments had liaison personnel assigned to the operating division.

An important goal of management was to achieve a better safety record than other plants in the corporation and in the industry. Particular stress was placed on eliminating fatal accidents and on achieving annual reductions in the frequency of lost-time injuries. Making the plant as safe a place to work as possible was more than a plant goal; it was a personal objective of most members of top management in the firm.

All the large divisions and most of the small ones made extensive use of overhead cranes, and the movement of most cranes was governed by an old type of controller. Most cranemen and supervisors preferred magnetic controllers, a newer type that had been installed on many cranes in the plant. Because magnetic controllers operated on low-voltage control circuits, there was less danger of severe shock or of "flash" — visible arcing of current across contact points — than with the old type, which operated on full-line voltage. Magnetic controllers also allowed operators to direct crane movements more precisely — there was less danger of "drift" or unanticipated movements. Since they used less cab space than some older controllers, they offered the craneman better visibility and more work space. They were also supposedly cooler and less fatiguing to operate, as well as easier to maintain.

The actual safety benefits that would accrue from the replacement of old-type controllers with magnetic controllers were hard to estimate. Burns, shocks, and eye injuries resulted from "flash" in the older controller circuits, but they were infrequent and were not often disabling. Injuries caused by movements of cranes were more frequently attributable to human error by cranemen or ground crews than to mechanical failure of the controllers or to drift.

Changeovers to magnetic controllers were being made only as the older controllers wore out, until a fatal accident in the plant triggered recommendations for an accelerated replacement program. A worker was killed when the unexpected movement of a crane load pinned him against a wall. Investigation by top management and by the safety department led to recommendations for a general review of the problems of crane safety.

The plant manager appointed a special committee to recommend steps that could be taken to improve a craneman's view of his working areas and to give him better control over crane movements. The committee consisted of the director of safety, the superintendents of two operating divisions, and a man from the plant engineering department.

At the initial investigation of the accident, the craneman had been asked the type of controller with which the crane was equipped, but no links had been suggested between type of controller and the accident. Blame was assigned to the victim for standing in an unsafe position, to the craneman for moving a lift when his view was obscured, and to management for improper stacking of materials on the floor.

The special crane-safety committee did not mention magnetic controllers in its first report of recommendations for the division where the accident had occured. Not until their seventh meeting several weeks after the accident, while investigating conditions in a second division, did the committee discuss a suggestion for accelerated changeover of magnetic controllers. The change would "save space in the crane cab" and provide better control levers, but the committee feared initially that "the cost would be excessive."

Apparently the committee changed its evaluation of the costs of the change, although minutes of the meetings do not report any further discussion. In its final report to the plant manager, the committee recommended as one of several changes that the controllers then in use "be replaced by magnetic controllers as quickly as feasible." The plant manager circulated the entire list of recommendations without change to the division superintendents and asked that they all be adopted and implemented promptly.

After the order for implementation, specific questions of cost were raised and searches for information were initiated. Most division superintendents individually made quick estimates of the minimum cash outlays required for purchase and installation of the new controllers and checked with the plant manager to see if these expenditures would be approved. Their estimates ranged from $27,000 to $50,000 per division and were described by the safety director as "an absolute minimum" since they did not cover all expected costs of installation.

To supplement the divisional estimates and to fit the accelerated replacement program into operating budgets, the plant manager asked the chief engineer to make a plant-wide survey of requirements and installation costs. Four months after the accident the chief engineer asked the special crane-safety committee to draw up detailed plans for the replacement program and suggested that the program be included in the following year's budget. He wrote, "It may be an expenditure between $150,000 and $200,000."

Seven months later, in another memorandum to division superintendents, the chief engineer was still asking for an itemized list of cranes that required the new controllers and of the number of replacements each such crane would need. At this time he described the program as a five-year job with budgeted expenditures of $100,000 a year.

The chief engineer was not the only one to explore the costs and benefits of the program. In the meantime one of the division superintendents had announced the program to a plant-wide conference of management personnel. He said that the installation of magnetic controllers would "virtually eliminate" injuries to cranemen from flashes and burns. Several other division superintendents prepared a memorandum summarizing their objections to the old-type controllers. The chief industrial engineer reported to management that, for the new magnetic controllers, "any increased costs in operation will be negligible." He mentioned the old-type controllers as a "cause" of the fatality that had initiated the program.[6]

Early in the second year of the program the plant manager asked the superintendent of maintenance to coordinate the replacement program over the next several years. By the ninetieth week after the accident, the superintendent of maintenance had developed a revised plan for replacements. The estimated number of replacements had been decreased from 344 to 250, the estimated total cost increased from $500,000 to $600,000, and the estimated time for completion of the program increased from five to six or seven years. He reported costs in terms of the program's encroachment on men and facilities needed for other projects to which the maintenance division was committed. This was the first time in the written memoranda on the program that an estimate of available manpower to install the controllers was cited as a limit to the completion of the program.

Initially, then, the program for accelerated replacement of controllers had been judged expensive but feasible. The original recommendation for the program had been promulgated along with a number of other suggestions for increasing crane safety that could be implemented less expensively in the short run.

The first eighteen months after the program was approved by the plant manager were used to explore the scope of the decision and to plan for its implementation. Specific estimates of cost quadrupled in that time (rising from $150,000 to over $600,000), and the estimated time for completion changed from about two years to seven or more. Apparently the firm's commitment to an accelerated replacement program was made before the cost of new installations and the impact of the project on other commitments for maintenance and expansion were fully known. The development of cost information is summarized in Table 4.1.

[6]If this had been the case, it definitely was not brought out in the detailed records of the inquiries following the accident.

Table 4.1. The sources and uses of cost information in crane control decision

Time since fatality (wks)	Evaluation expressed in available correspondence	Source of evaluation	Context of evaluation
6–11	New controls would save space in cabs and offer better control levers; cost of plant-wide program might be "excessive"	Crane-safety committee	Series of meetings to find ways to increase the safety of crane operations
11	Accelerated, plant-wide installation of new controls is feasible	Plant manager	Directive to division superintendents to carry out such a program
13–19	"Absolute minimum" costs for purchase and basic installation would be $27,000–$50,000 per division	Division superintendents	Individual requests to plant manager for approval of expenditures
20	Program will take at least a year and may mean expenditure of $150,000–$200,000	Chief engineer	Guide to plant manager for fitting program into next budget
22	New controls will virtually eliminate injuries to cranemen from flashes and burns	Division superintendent	Speech at annual management safety conference on his division's progress
49	Program will take five years and will involve budgeted expenditures of $100,000 a year	Chief engineer	A request to division superintendents for more precise information on their requirements
52	Increased costs of operation with new controls will be negligible	Chief industrial engineer	Memorandum to the plant manager and division superintendents
55	New controls will be safer, easier to use, and cheaper to maintain	Group of division superintendents	Memorandum to inform others in management
95	Program will take 6–7 years, will require 250 installations, and cost $650,000; rate of progress is limited by other maintenance commitments	Maintenance division superintendent	Report of plans to the chief engineer
106–112	Lack of funds prevents further work on program	Two division superintendents	Report to director of safety on progress of program

In the end the commitment proved vulnerable — not to revised estimates of cost but to short-run declines in available resources. At the end of two years two divisions stopped work on the program because a decline in operations had reduced their funds. One year later almost all divisions had reverted, for similar reasons, to the policy they were following before the accident; they were installing magnetic controllers only as the older control systems wore out.

Three major features of this decision process are especially interesting from the point of view of the place of expectations in a theory of business decision making:

1. It is clear that search behavior by the firm was apparently initiated by an exogenous event, was severely constrained, and was distinguished by "local" rather than "general" scanning procedures.

2. The noncomparability of cost expectations and expected returns led to estimates that were vague or easily changed and made the decision exceptionally susceptible to the factors of attention focus and available organizational slack.

3. The firm considered resources as fixed and imposed feasibility, rather than optimality, tests on the proposed expenditure.

The search behavior is difficult to interpret. The apparent sequence is quite simple: accident, concern for safety, and focus (among other foci) on magnetic controllers. As a view of top management, such a sequence seems to be reasonably accurate. Underlying this sequence, however, are a number of factors that make too simple a theory of organizational search unwarranted. Most conspicuous is the fact that the connection between the stimulus (fatal accident) and the organizational reaction (new controllers) is remote. There is no evidence that the fatal accident depended on the type of controller used on the crane. At the same time, there is little doubt that the accident had made members of management give greater priority to any device that would improve crane safety and that the possibility of new controllers was well known to parts of the organization. Thus, organization search for safety alternatives at the level of top management can be viewed at lower levels as the promotion of favored projects under the impetus of a crisis. The alternative of magnetic controllers was discovered not so much because the organization at this time searched everywhere for solutions to a problem but because some parts of the organization were already (for whatever reason) predisposed toward the project and (1) thought of it as relevant and (2) were able to present it as relevant to the perceived problem in safety.

The decentralized characteristics of information gathering in this case are particularly striking in the pursuit of cost information. Cost information was not readily available, especially to the men who were charged with investigating crane safety. Each knew something about the costs of a single installation since some of these had already been made, but none of the four had the information needed for even a rough approximation of the over-all costs of an accelerated replacement program. Furthermore, as later searches showed, many people and much time would have been needed to gather such information. Even after the decision to make the plant-wide installations, when detailed cost and return data were sought, every new group brought in costs and advantages that other groups had not considered (see Table 4.1).

One of the reasons why detailed information on costs seems to play such an insignificant role in all but the final stages of the process is that at no time did the organization make a conscious calculation of costs and return in comparable figures. This feature of the decision is conspicuous in Table 4.1. Information about costs was not necessary to persuade members of management to order the installation of the controllers. All members of management apparently favored the new controls, and they were supported by noncompany technical literature. They had been putting the new controllers in as the old systems wore out. Statements made by the division superintendents indicated that they were placing strong positive emphasis on the safety advantages of the new controls. These gains were usually expressed in absolute rather than relative terms. None of the safety advantages and few of the operating advantages were ever formally expressed in dollar terms. There was consensus that the program would be beneficial and evidence that the benefits — whatever their size — would apply in several departments: safety, maintenance, and operating divisions.

Under these conditions it is not surprising that the early cost estimates were too optimistic (at least if we can assume later ones were more accurate). It is also not surprising to discover that variations in cost expectations had little impact on the basic decision until the focus on safety became less intense and free funds became scarce.

Measurable expectations entered in the decision only in the feasibility test. Do we have money for the controls? Initially, agreement by various groups in management that the step was a good one and an estimate that costs — although unknown — would not be unreasonable were apparently sufficient to carry the decision. For costs to be reasonable under the usual theory of investment, they must be better (relative to the gain) than other available alternatives. This was not, however, how the issue was formulated here. Rather, the question of "reasonableness" hinged on whether the expenditure could be made without appreciably affecting existing organizational arrangements adversely (e.g., profits, dividends, wages, output).

As long as estimated costs were modest and output high, the costs were reasonable. As the costs grew and business activity declined, accelerated installation of the magnetic controllers became less "reasonable." This was obviously not because they became suboptimal whereas they had previously been optimal but simply because the supply of uncommitted resources (one form of organizational slack — see Chapter 3) had been substantially reduced. The later stages of the decision were dominated by the necessity for making specific provisions for the program in the plant budgets and for preparing tentative time schedules for installation. When, at this stage, there was not enough money for all of the approved projects, some comparisons of the relative merits were made. At that time the hierarchy of preferred projects seemed to reflect such considerations as the tangibility of their expected return, the importance of their major supporters, and the conspicuousness of the problem for which they were designed. It is, of course, possible that such a process also generates the optimum set of investments. We will note only that the explicit decisions made by two divisions to abandon the program corresponded in time with declines in their level of operations. When it became apparent that cash would not be available to meet more than the bare minimum of repair and maintenance commitments, the two divisions stopped work on the accelerated program completely and returned to preaccident policies.

4.2.2 Decision 2: a problem of new working quarters for a department with a doubtful future

The second decision was an attempt in a medium-sized construction firm to find new working and storage quarters for its home specialties department, which held a unique and somewhat insecure position in the firm. Its customers were not often shared by other departments. Like other departments of the firm but unlike most of its competitors, it used union labor; therefore, its labor costs were too high to enable it to bid successfully on many projects. Its labor costs and changes in style and technology in the construction industry were causing the department's market to shrink, though it had shared with other departments in the growth from new construction activity during and after the Korean War. Top management expected its sales to decline, and its members outside the Home Specialties Department had negative feelings toward the department for two reasons:

1. The head of the department was a senior man in the firm and his earnings under a profit-sharing contract were higher than the earnings of almost all other department heads.

2. Other departments were also expanding, and some of these were anxious to take over space being used by Home Specialties.

The problem of making a decision about the long-run importance of Home Specialties operations and of providing plant facilities to accommodate expanded operations had been current for at least two years.

Management had long been aware of the need for some kind of action. However, there was no consensus on the critical problem nor on a satisfactory alternative. The president, who believed centralized operations were most efficient, initially viewed the problem as one of finding a way to expand facilities at (or in the immediate vicinity of) the current site. The head of the Home Specialties Department wanted to move the department to a new location, where it would not be in conflict with the operations of other units. Some members of general management thought that the department should be dropped from the firm in order to release working capital for units that had a brighter future. The president and the branch manager had talked of maintaining the department but limiting it to a size that fitted the existing site, reducing the share of profits going to departmental personnel, and forcing the head of the department to take a cut in earnings. Some years earlier, a few men had almost managed to force the department manager out of the firm.

The president's show of interest when a local plot of land became available, coupled with continuing pressure from departmental management to investigate possible new sites, resulted in a decision to concentrate on the search for a new site. Study of the feasibility of moving the department may have seemed timely, too, because of the president's independent decision to renegotiate profit-sharing contracts with departmental management. Since the department manager and his assistant wanted to move, a decision to support their search for a new location might have been regarded as an inducement to them to accept a cut in earnings. In addition, the move might make it easier to follow the cut in earnings with a later decision to curtail departmental operations or to ease the department out of the firm.

Requirements for the new site were set forth in a conference attended by the branch manager, the department head for Home Specialties, his assistant, and a specialist in estimating building alteration costs. The pressures on current facilities, at least, were not expected to increase greatly over the next year or two; in fact, the space requirements of Home Specialties were expected to decline. The Home Specialties facilities were probably not grossly unsuited to their operations; in defining the requirements for a new site, the head men in the department were merely trying, on most measures, to find something that would be equivalent to what they already had. The assistant head of the Home Specialties Department initiated most suggestions for site requirements; he worked from a memorandum he had prepared earlier. The final set of requirements was drafted by the branch manager after the meeting. The key specifications are set forth in Table 4.2.[7]

[7]Other specifications were discussed initially, but they did not figure explicitly in the later evaluations of actual sites.

Table 4.2. Selected site characteristics: aspirations vs. actions

Features of sites	Existing facilities	Proposed requirements			Characteristics of 3 best sites		
		Requested by dept.	Agreed on in meeting	Listed by branch mgr.	2	14	10
Total space, sq ft	25,000	25,000+	24,000	26,000	24,000+	18,500	15,500
Yard storage space	8850	8850	8850	9000	Available	Not available	Available separately
Heating facilities	..	..	Work area to 60°	Work area to 60°	..	Will cost $150/yr	Will cost $183/yr
Location (minutes from main office)	0	..	10	10	9	More than 10	About 10
Dock-height unloading space	..	Desired	Desired	Desired	Has	Has	Does not have
R.R. siding	..	Not mentioned	Worth $500 extra rent	Worth $500 extra rent	No	No	1-1/2 blocks from R.R.
Annual rent	$6–7000	..	$10,000	$10,000	Bid of $10,000 submitted	Bid of $12,025 submitted	Bid of $17,000 submitted

The conference was notable for the absence of real debate about or explicit consideration of the relative importance of different kinds of requirements. The discussion was oriented towards ensuring that the new site would offer the same facilities as the old one at no greater cash outlay for rent, rather than toward determining what would be a "most efficient" site for the Home Specialties Department. The most intensive discussion with respect to several requirements centered on reaching an agreement as to what facilities the department had in its current location. The question of the flexibility of various requirements was hardly raised, although it was unreasonable to expect to find a site that corresponded to all of the committee's specifications.

An intensive search for sites that lasted for four months followed the conference. The evaluation of each site about which information was received was a three-phase process. First, the branch manager or another member of the central management group looked at the initial information that was available from advertisements, phone calls, or cursory visits to the site to decide whether the site was worth further inspection. As Table 4.3

Table 4.3. The consideration and disposition of possible sites

Site No.	Period of consideration	Disposition of site
1	June 14	Rejected: Inadequate access
2	June 20–Sept. 13	Bid upon: Bid of $10,000+ not accepted
3	June 23–July 12	Rejected: Considered in detail but too large and too liable to flood damage
4	July 6	Rejected: Too small, too far away
5	July 12	Rejected: Would have to be purchased
6	July 12	Rejected: Too far away
7	July 12	Rejected: Too far away
8	July 17	Rejected: Too large
9	Aug. 9	Rejected: Unsatisfactory layout
10	Aug. 18–Oct. 24	Rejected: Bid prepared but not submitted: considered too expensive by president
11	Aug. 24	Rejected: Reason unknown
12	Aug. 24	Rejected: Reason unknown
13	Aug. 30	Rejected: Too small (13,000 sq ft)
14	Aug. 30–Sept. 25	Bid upon: Bid not accepted by owner, who preferred commercial use of property
15	Sept. 7	Rejected: Too far away
16	Sept. 7	Rejected: Too far away
17	Sept. 12	Rejected: Would have to be purchased
18	Sept. 12	Rejected: Would have to be purchased
19	Sept. 12	Rejected: Too far away, wrong size
20	Sept. 17	Rejected: Reason unknown
21	Sept. 18	Rejected: Reason unknown
22	Sept. 21	Rejected: Reason unknown

indicates, at least 18 sites were rejected at this stage because they failed to meet one of a small set of requirements. The most important considerations at this stage were (1) whether the site could be rented (the company did not want to purchase), (2) whether the site was located near the company's existing facilities (something within 10 minutes' driving distance was preferred), and (3) whether the site was approximately the right size (sites with 15,000 to 25,000 sq ft were preferred). One or more of these three factors underlay the rejection of 11 of the 18 sites in this early phase. (Of the remaining seven, one was rejected because of problems of access, one because of an unsatisfactory layout, and five for unknown reasons.)

The second phase consisted of a more detailed evaluation of the site's potentialities. Four sites were given detailed consideration. Members of the home specialties department staff estimated the expenditures required to make the necessary heating, lighting, and ventilating installations. One of the four sites was rejected after detailed inspection because the branch manager found it liable to frequent flood damage and because the company would have had to buy other leases on the property.

There were, then, three sites that management thought worth preparing bids on. Looking at the major criteria of space, price, and nearness to existing facilities, we note in Table 4.3 that management relaxed its requirements as time went on. Site 2, the first one for which a bid was prepared, had an area about the same as the specifications required, but sites 10 and 14 were both smaller. Site 10 was at and site 14 was beyond the distance limits set by management. Management expected to acquire site 2 with a bid of $10,000–$15,000 for 24,000 sq ft of space; the bid on site 14 was $12,000 for 18,500 sq ft. On site 10, the third one for which a bid was prepared, management considered offering $17,000 for 15,500 sq ft of space (excluding yard space, which had to be obtained separately).

The bids on sites 2 and 14 were turned down by the agents for the properties, but the bid on site 10 was never submitted. The president refused to approve the bid because he thought it offered too much money for too little space. The search for a new site for the home specialties department apparently ended with the president's refusal to approve a bid for site 10.

Why were other sites not considered? Among the reasons for ending the search, the following were perhaps most important:

1. The branch manager and the others who had been most active in the search felt that they had explored most of the available possibilities. They had even resorted to driving around the neighborhood looking for "for rent" signs.

2. The earnings contracts of the departmental managers had been renegotiated — most of them successfully. Use of the search for a new location as an inducement to counteract the negative effects of renegotiation

was no longer of any importance, and, with renegotiation completed, one point of friction between Home Specialties and other departments had been eliminated.

3. Contrary to expectations, Home Specialties had continued to maintain a fairly high level of operations over the summer, while its most direct competitor for work space had suffered a decline in business.

The decision-making process in this case has some significant similarities to that connected with the purchase of automatic controllers. As before, search activity represented a response to some specific events rather than a form of continued planning. Second, detailed expectation data entered into the decision relatively late, after a conditional commitment to secure space had been made. Finally, most of the tests were primarily feasibility tests rather than checks on optimality.

From the present point of view, perhaps the most interesting aspect of this study is the fact that the organization focused on the problem of outside space for the department. Although the decision was contingent (and was in fact never executed because bids were rejected), it represented a commitment to a course of action; yet the commitment was made not because it was shown to have the best return (in terms of organization goals) of a number of alternatives. Quite the contrary, the decision to find new quarters was made because a number of important parts of the organization, for apparently different reasons, viewed such a step as desirable. Had there been agreement, for example, between the Home Specialties Department and other departments about the probable long-run consequences of this step, one or the other of those groups would probably have opposed the move. Since this was an important aspect of the decision situation, some of the more important expectations were not discussed in open meetings. The role of ambiguity of expectations in securing agreement where there is a conflict of interests has previously been noted with respect to political and labor-management decision making.[8] There is some suggestion here that it is also important for the formation of business policy.

Once the decision to secure additional space had been made, data on alternatives were organized around a set of more or less independent criteria. These criteria are interesting in two respects:

1. They represent for the most part a simple statement of current facilities. The adequacy of some aspects of these facilities was discussed, but the general question of what would constitute an ideal site was not raised.

2. With one or two exceptions (e.g., an attempt to place a rental value on the existence of a railroad siding), the specifications represented a check

[8]David B. Truman, *The Governmental Process* (New York: Knopf, 1951).

list. Sites that were unsatisfactory on one or more of the major criteria were rejected immediately. Only among the more or less "satisfactory" alternatives was there an attempt at comparison with a different dimension; and even at that point this comparison was somewhat halting and not always easily understood. Some of the sites rejected at an early stage might have been considered more thoroughly later, after management's aspirations declined.

In one conspicuous feature the site purchase decision was different from the decision to purchase new automatic controllers. The search for alternative sites was much more exhaustive than the search for alternatives in the first case; the organization had no ready-made site alternative. Although it is conceivable that the organization did not discover all the alternatives that were within 10 minutes of the central office, it seems unlikely that they missed any that would have been suitable. To be sure, the use of the 10-minute criterion as a device for defining the range within which one would search made that criterion into an absolute one, in the sense in which the others (e.g., the size requirement) were not. However, the difference between the number of alternatives considered in this instance and in the crane case is substantial. Similarly, the specific cost estimates reflected in proposed bids for sites and the decisions on whether to make the bids, seem, in this case, to be more attempts to determine the intrinsic worth of the property to the organization and less a function of available resources than they were in the previous case.

4.2.3 Decision 3: selection of a consulting firm

The third decision is part of a larger decision regarding the installation of an electronic data-processing system. It relates specifically to the selection of a consulting firm. The company, a medium-large manufacturing concern, had made some preliminary investigation of the problem and decided that a consultant was necessary. At the beginning of the process of deciding which firm should be chosen, there was no clear program as to how many firms would be evaluated. A list of possible consultants was prepared, but a series of chance circumstances led to a meeting with Alpha, a relatively new consulting firm specializing in the design of electronic data-processing systems.

On February 21 consultants from Alpha and people from the company discussed the problem of improving business methods. By March 23 Alpha had submitted a step-by-step program that would survey and analyze the company's operations and data-processing procedures. Alpha stated that the objective of this program would be (1) the estimation of savings that could be realized through the use of electronic equipment and (2) the specification of the price class and characteristics of equipment required. The fee expected for this work was stated as $180 per man-day (i.e., $3600 per month assuming one man works a 20-day month). The initial consulting task was to be limited to 100 man-days, and consequently the fee was limited to $18,000. Traveling expenses of some $4000 would also be charged.

The report was well received by company officials, who generally agreed that Alpha would be retained until the question of investigating other alternatives was raised. As will be obvious, this was a crucial point in the process, but it is not clear what prompted the suggestion for additional search effort. The suggestion was rather quickly accepted, and a list of about a dozen potential consultants, which had been prepared earlier by a staff member, was presented. The controller decided that only one more firm, Beta, should be asked to submit a proposal. Beta was more widely known, older, and larger than Alpha, although it did not specialize in electronic data-processing feasibility studies.

Following analysis of the problem, Beta submitted a contract proposal covering an investigation of the company's problems. The stated objectives were two: (1) to reduce the costs of the accounting and clerical operation and (2) to improve the quality of information available for accounting and control. Beta stated in the contract proposal that employing electronic data-handling equipment was to be considered as a possible means of attaining these objectives. This contract outlined service charges that would not exceed $5000 a month. The initial study was to be completed and a report submitted three to four months after active work began.

After Beta had submitted a report, it became necessary to choose between the two firms. At the request of the controller a staff member wrote a memorandum that listed the criteria on which the decision should be based and also evaluated the two firms on each of the criteria. The results of this memorandum are summarized in Table 4.4.

The staff member who wrote the memorandum believed that as far as quality of personnel, cost of services, and estimated time were concerned, the two firms were equal or could be made equal by negotiation. Regarding the other criteria — commitment made, availability and scope, and geographic situation — he felt Beta had an advantage. He was supported in this opinion by an academician who had previously served as a consultant to the company. Analysis of the memorandum seems to show, however, that the only advantage that can objectively be given to Beta is its geographic situation. Even here, aside from availability, it is difficult to see any advantage; the only possibility would be higher traveling expenses for Alpha, but presumably this would mean a reduction in some part of the fee. Again it should have been possible to negotiate on availability and scope, assuming that geographic proximity is divorced from availability. It is quite obvious that the commitment could have been negotiated

Table 4.4. Comparison of consulting firms

Criteria	Alpha	Beta
Quality of personnel	Depth in quality of computer personnel	More experienced in business problems
Cost of services	$180 per man-day ($3600 per month); $18,000 max. charge plus traveling expenses	$5000 per month max. plus traveling expenses
Commitment made	Committed themselves *primarily* to study of feasibility of application of E.D.P. equipment	Will give consideration to both *methods* and *possibility* of using E.D.P. equipment, in order noted
Estimated time	100 man-days maximum; possibility of doing work in 15 weeks	Longer time allowed because of greater commitment (actual time stated in contract was 3–4 months)
Availability and scope	No quantitative evaluation mentioned	
Geographic situation	Main office approx. 2500 miles from company's office	Main office approx. 500 miles from company's office

because Alpha, as a new organization in the field, was open to suggestion with respect to the kind of commitments it should make.

On the cost side (ignoring possible negotiation) there was some ambiguity. The approximate monthly charges were $1400 less for Alpha than for Beta. The total charge for Beta to the company varied according to the length of time it would take. The estimated length of time for Beta was three to four months, which would mean a price between $15,000 and $20,000. Alpha, on the other hand, had a maximum price of $18,000. Exact price comparisons under the circumstances were difficult to make. Since Alpha gave a maximum total price whereas Beta used only a maximum monthly charge and no upper limit on the time, what advantage there was in the cost situation was probably in Alpha's favor. However, the costs were close enough and the circumstances blurred enough so that relative cost was difficult to evaluate.

This fact was recognized by the staff members involved, who proposed that the decision be made on collateral grounds (e.g., geographic proximity, possible future uses). As noted above, the grounds specified seemed to favor Beta, and this preference of the staff was apparent almost from the moment that the decision to expand the search to Beta was made. That is, the staff members most closely involved seemed to view Alpha as a reasonable solution until the suggestion for further search was made. There is some suggestion that they interpreted the instruction to expand their search to include Beta and only Beta as a preference for Beta by their supervisors. The controller and assistant controller, on the other hand, felt that the final decision was based on the independent recommendations of their staff members and did not acknowledge the possibility that such an outcome was implicit in the decision not to accept Alpha until further investigation. The firm decided to hire Beta.

How did expectations with respect to cost and return enter the decision to hire Beta? First, the methods of search resulted in casual consideration of about a dozen possible firms, intensive consideration of two. Second, a comparison of the two firms finally considered was difficult. Expected costs and expected return were measured in a number of dimensions (e.g., fee, quality of personnel, convenience) that were not readily reduced to a single index. Third, given the difficulties of evaluation, there appears to have been substantial interaction between expectations and desires and between desires and perceptions of others' desires.

As in the case of the search for a new site for the Home Specialties Department, there was some attempt here to be reasonably inclusive in searching for potential firms. Presumably, if that original scanning had uncovered a firm that was conspicuously more appropriate than all others, that fact would have been noted. Since there were no conspicuous alternatives, it is not surprising to discover that not many were evaluated in detail and that the factors affecting the choice of firms to consider in large part determined which firm would be selected. Alpha was considered because it was exceptionally visible to a key staff member when the organization needed a detailed proposal. Beta was conspicuous to the controller because it was well known in the business community and had apparently been considered as a potential consultant on other occasions.

In evaluating the proposal by Alpha and later in comparing it with the one made by Beta, the people involved in the decision seemed to have done two things: (1) They asked whether the charges were within the range of what it was reasonable for the organization to pay for the services offered. There does not appear to have been any significant problem on this score. (2) They asked which of the two proposals offered the better return on investment. As the description of the two firms indicates, this was by no means an easy job. The simple comparison of the two consulting firms in Table 4.4 has some interesting features. Perhaps most conspicuous is the fact that the conclusion to be drawn from the comparison is not at all clear. Reasonable men could quite easily disagree as to its implications. It was not that part of the return was in the form of intangibles; all of the factors explicitly considered were reasonably tangible. The problem was that they were not reducible to a single dimension (or at least were not reduced to one) and that neither firm was better on all dimensions.

The ambiguity in expectations that arose from the difficulty of making objective rankings of Alpha and Beta resulted in a decision process that seemed to be dominated in large part by nonexpectational factors. The final staff memorandum on the decision clearly recommended Beta. This recommendation was accepted by the controller. As he put it, "I asked the boys to set down the pros and cons. The decision was Beta. It was entirely their decision."

The staff members involved, on the other hand, seemed to have felt that the decision to search further rather than hire Alpha immediately reflected some bias in favor of Beta on the part of top management, and this was probably reinforced by the fact that the controller specified that Beta and only Beta would be asked to make a proposal. Since the differences between the two firms were not particularly striking, it is not surprising that these plausible assumptions about the attitudes of others were consistent with subsequent perceptions of the alternatives and the final recommendation.

4.2.4 Decision 4: choosing a data-processing system

In November, six months after the original contract had been signed, Beta submitted a report which outlined some alternative proposals designed to improve the company's accounting and merchandising procedures. Essentially three alternatives were discussed in the report: (1) a centralized electronic data-processing center employing an IBM 705 or a Remington-Rand Univac, (2) an improvement on the current procedures requiring the addition of some Electrodata equipment, and (3) an improvement on the current procedures requiring the use of punched-card electronic equipment instead of Electrodata equipment. These alternatives were differentiated on the basis of projected savings and improved management control. In each, savings were to accrue from the elimination of personnel. Management control was to be increased by additional reports, which would be more complete and more readily available.

The report shows a breakdown of the savings and reports provided under each system. A comparison of the savings for the three alternatives is shown in Table 4.5. The three alternatives have several significant differences. (1) The decentralized system with punched-card equipment has a larger projected direct savings than either of the other alternatives ($7515 savings for this system as opposed to $5000 savings, and $1455 additional cost for the other systems). (2) Only when the less direct savings of $7500 per month are added to the centralized system does this system become more attractive in price than the punched-card program. (3) The centralized system gives management six reports not provided by the other alternatives. On the other hand, the two decentralized alternatives give management four reports that are not provided by the centralized

Table 4.5. Comparison of savings of alternative proposals (per month)

Factors Considered	Centralized with IBM-705 or Univac	Decentralized	
		With punched cards	With Electrodata
Direct Savings			
Personnel reduction	$33,000*	$8570	$8390
Equipment added	*26,500*	*1055*	*9845*
Space needed	*1500*		
Net savings	$ 5000	$7515	*$1455*
Less direct Savings			
(a) Reduction in cost of compiling physical inventory	1500		
(b) Elimination of stock record personnel (20)	6000		
	$ 7500		
	$12,500	$7515	*$1455*

Note: Figures representing costs rather than savings are italicized.

system. The centralized system has some additional advantage in that some of its reports are prepared daily. The other two systems require more time in the preparation of reports. Over all, there is a net advantage of two reports with the centralized system.

The savings of $7500 a month for the centralized system noted in Table 4.5 are estimates for the time when the inventory is put on the machine. Since the estimates were rough and the time for converting the inventory was indefinite, no specific discounting factors were used. The consultants originally drafted a report that showed equal savings for a system using a computer and a system that was basically a revision of the company's current practices with the addition of electronic equipment. When it was pointed out to the consultants that a recommendation was expected from them, the additional savings from converting inventory were added and the centralized system was recommended.

The implication of the foregoing should not be that cost and savings estimates were unimportant. During the six months of the consultants' investigations, cost estimates played a prominent role in the analysis. For example, time and motion studies were made to derive time estimates, and the resulting estimates were closely scrutinized. Some time estimates were revised as many as three times. In the meeting of the management committee where the formal decision was made, the questions pertained primarily to costs. There was concern for the break-even point of the investment and the pay-back period.

Despite their explicit importance, however, costs entered into the decision in a way somewhat different from that anticipated by traditional theory. As in the previous cases, the first question apparently asked was whether the computer installation or the other new installations studied would be economically *feasible*. The original report of the consultants as well as the analysis by management indicated that two of the three systems studied were feasible and preferable to the existing system. Given this basic conclusion, the use of cost data and the attitude toward that data became much more flexible than they probably would have been otherwise. Since two of the systems were defensible as replacements for the existing system, the choice between them seems to have depended less on an objective effort to assign meaningful values to intangible or uncertain advantages than on important individual preferences. Thus the controller was interested in a system that produced more information faster and with better control. He, and others, felt that the computer might become an important general managerial tool. Although they obviously felt the necessity of justifying the installation on comparative cost-savings grounds, their attitude toward the hypothetical savings of $7500 was undoubtedly generous. Their attitude would have been different had they not been favorably inclined toward a computer nor persuaded that straightforward, tangible benefits made the centralized system an "acceptable" solution.

In addition, the relation between the consulting firm and the organization points up some interesting features of the role of expectations. In this case, the organization relied on an outside source for information, but some of the behavior of the ambiguous situation in the third case also occurred here. The consultants made a detailed, careful, and responsible analysis of the proposed installations. Nevertheless, when asked to make a specific recommendation, they were able to change the summary figures on cost savings from a set that indicated indifference between two major alternatives to a set that indicated the clear superiority of the computer. The point is not that the consultants falsified their data. They clearly would have refused to do this, and the organization would not have countenanced it. However, they had to make a judgment as to which uncertain costs and savings should be counted, and this judgment was almost certainly affected, as had been the earlier judgments of staff members within the organization, by their perception of management's attitudes and predilections.

In each of these case studies we have seen the interaction among the problem situation, the data collected, and the expectations formed. In addition, in at least three of the cases, information gathering is clearly decentralized. Special subunits gather information and provide it to other parts of the organization. Thus, before attempting to examine the implications of these studies, we need to consider the special features of information transmission within a decision system in which conflict is only partially resolved.

4.3 Communications in Theories of Business Decision Making

An organization not only seeks information through search behavior, it also processes information. In most theories of business decision making, communication effects are ignored. *Prima facie* this exclusion seems implausible. If, for example, pricing decisions are assumed to be based on expectations concerning future sales, costs, and competitors' behavior, it is hard to see how we can ignore the process through which such information is communicated in the organization.

The classic solution has two characteristics: It eliminates any time delays implicit in a communication structure by essentially ignoring the time dimension, and it eliminates any bias by assuming homogeneity of goals. It is possible that the time-delay problem may reasonably be assumed away in many circumstances, but unless our analysis of organizational goals is incorrect, we cannot dispose of bias problems by assuming goal homogeneity. Where different parts of the organization have responsibility for different pieces of information relevant to a decision, we would expect some bias in information transmitted due to perceptual differences among the subunits and some attempts to manipulate information as a device for manipulating the decision.

Basically, we need information on two points: we need (1) to examine the effect of differing goals on the estimations prepared by individual members of the organization, and (2) to consider the net organizational effect of an information system operating under partial conflict of interest.

4.4 Two Experiments on Organizational Communication

In order to explore the effect of conflict (as reflected in presumed payoffs) on communicated information, we undertook two experiments on organizational communication. The first looks at individual bias, the second at organizational bias.

4.4.1 An experiment on communication bias

We wish to test the proposition that individuals can and do modify their subjective estimates of reality to accommodate their expectations about the kind of payoffs associated with various possible errors. In the experiment, subjects were asked to determine a summary statistic for an array of numbers. Since the experiment involved the switching of labels, it is of some importance to investigate the "theory" of descriptive statistics to determine the importance, if any, of the substantive origin of the numbers in the array to be summarized.

Essentially, a descriptive statistic is a procedure for transforming any arbitrary array of numbers into a coded number (or set of numbers) that in some sense "represents" the original array. The procedure is independent of the labels attached to the numbers in the original array. The arithmetic mean of the array {10, 8, 5, 1} is 6, and this result does not depend on whether we are talking about apples, revolutions per minute, or shoe size. According to the theory, the choice of a descriptive statistic (for example, a choice between an arithmetic mean and a median as a measure of central tendency) should be made on the basis of the characteristics of the distribution.

The implicit model underlying much of the treatment of descriptive statistics can be characterized as follows: For any array of numbers there exists a set of summary numbers (smaller in size than the original array) appropriate to that array. This set of summary numbers depends on the values of the numbers within the array and not on the labels attached to those numbers. Given an array of numbers and a set of instructions we can determine a statistic, and that statistic is uniquely defined, at least for any particular practitioner at any particular point of time.

Suppose, however, that the statistic is imbedded as an estimate in a decision-making system. In particular, suppose that the summary set of numbers represents information processed through an organization as a basis for a decision. We wish to investigate whether a summary estimate is uniquely determined for a given practitioner, a given array, and a given set of instructions. We do this by introducing variations in the labels attached to specific numbers in an array and comparing the summary statistic chosen by relatively sophisticated subjects.

In accordance with the model described above, it is hypothesized that cost analysts will tend to overestimate costs and that sales analysts will tend to underestimate sales. The rationale for the hypothesis relates to the presumption of a biased payoff schedule within the organization. The experiment described here does not test the rationale but only the treatment of the estimation problem.

Subjects. Subjects were 32 first-year graduate students in a program leading to a master's degree in industrial administration. Almost all held undergraduate degrees in engineering or science; all were men; all had had some introduction to techniques of statistical description and estimation.

Experimental material. The basic experimental form was a paper-and-pencil test requiring each subject to make ten estimates on the basis of the estimates of others. There were two versions of the test, the first of which (the *cost* version) was introduced by the following preamble:

> Assume you are the chief cost analyst of a manufacturing concern considering the production of a new product. You have been asked to submit *a single figure* as your estimate of unit cost for the product if 750,000 are produced. You have two assistants (A and B) in each of whom you have equal confidence and who make preliminary estimates for you. For each of the cases below, indicate what estimate of cost you would submit.

The second version (the *sales* version) was introduced by the following preamble:

> Assume you are the chief market analyst of a manufacturing concern considering the production of a new product. You have been asked to submit *a single figure* as your estimate of sales of the product if the price is set at $1.50. You have two assistants (A and B) in each of whom you have equal confidence and who make preliminary estimates for you. For each of the cases below, indicate what estimate of sales you would submit.

Each preamble was followed by a list of ten pairs of numbers representing the 10 pairs of estimates by two subordinates. These numbers and their pairings were identical in the two cases except that in the cost version they were presented as unit costs in cents and in the sales version they were presented as sales in 1000's. The numbers ranged from 108 to 907. The pairs were arranged such that there were two pairs in which the difference was approximately 100, two pairs in which the difference was approximately 200, two pairs in which the difference was approximately 400, and two pairs in which the difference was approximately 500. For those eight pairs, one pair in each of the four difference levels was toward the high end of the over-all number range and one pair was toward the low end of the over-all range. The other two pairs did not fit the same pattern. One involved a difference of approximately 800; the other was simply a repeat of an earlier pair. The ten pairs in the order they were presented to the subjects are indicated below:

	A's estimate	B's estimate
1	594	194
2	901	396
3	113	609
4	894	796
5	311	108
6	451	848
7	901	396
8	641	836
9	162	257
10	111	907

Experimental procedure. The subjects were divided into two groups of 16 subjects each. One group was given the cost version, the other the sales version. The two groups met in separate classes and completed the versions at approximately the same time without opportunity for communication. Ten weeks later the same groups were again given the forms. This time the versions were reversed. The group receiving the cost version first received the sales version ten weeks later. The group receiving the sales version first received the cost version ten weeks later. In all cases subjects were assured that the questions did not have a "correct" answer, that they should use their own best judgment, and that the test was not being used as an evaluative device.

Analysis. To analyze the data we define a number representing the weight attached to the larger of the two given numbers in the pair presented to the subject. We specify $E = \alpha U + (1 - \alpha)L$, where E is the estimate made by the subject, U is the higher number in the pair, and L is the lower number in the pair. For each of the ten pairs for each subject, the value of α was computed as well as a mean α for the 10 pairs. The mean value of α represents the average weight attached to the higher of the two numbers in the given pair. Thus, a subject with $\alpha = 1$ always chose the higher estimate; a subject with $\alpha = 0.50$ on the average took the mean; a subject with $\alpha = 0$ always chose the lower estimate. Since we have two estimates of α for each subject, we compare the α used in the cost version with the α used in the sales version. We treat the group that received the cost version first separately from the group that received the sales version first.

Results. The mean results for each group are indicated in Table 4.6.

Table 4.6. Mean value of α by group

	Sales estimates	Cost estimates
Sales version first	0.499	0.606
Cost version first	0.346	0.738
Total mean value	0.423	0.672

There is some suggestion in the data that the order of presentation might have affected the results. Therefore, before merging the two groups a test was run. Specifically, we tested the hypothesis that the two samples, sales version first and cost version first, came from the same population. The technique used was the Wald-Wolfowitz run test and the hypothesis was not rejected at the 5 per cent level of significance. The hypothesis that the total means are equal was then tested and the hypothesis was rejected.

A stronger test is one that utilizes the individual values. Specifically, we asked whether the value of α for a given subject was greater for the sales version, equal in the two versions, or greater in the cost version. The results for the 32 subjects are indicated in Table 4.7.

Table 4.7. Comparison of individual values

	Greater in sales version	Equal	Greater in cost version
Sales version first	2	3	11
Cost version first	3	1	12

The results for both the sales version first and the cost version first are significant at the 0.05 level by the sign test.

In the most simplified terms, we can make the following generalizations from this study (and another to be discussed below): Individuals will treat estimates, information, and communication generally as active parts of their environment. They will tend to consider the decision for which the information is relevant, the probable outcomes of various possible biases in information, and the payoff to them of various possible decision results. They adjust the information they transmit in accordance with their perceptions of the decision situation.

Such considerations led us in one early paper to develop some assumptions about the effect of communication structure (as well as some other attributes of the organization) on decision making. These assumptions formed the basis for a Cournot duopoly model in which the two firms had different communication structures and thus different biases. The result was a solution substantially different from that obtained in the conventional Cournot model.[9]

Subsequently, however, we have concluded that this approach was not fruitful. In the light of more recent research, it has two deficiencies as an approach to the study of organizational decision making.

1. An approach that emphasizes expectations in the classic sense is inconsistent with our observations about how business organizations obtain and use information (see above). If, as we believe, organizations often substitute feedback mechanisms for anticipation data, models imputing bias in communication are more appropriately linked to the processing of feedback data than to anticipatory data.

2. We cannot reasonably introduce the concept of communication bias without introducing its obvious corollary — "interpretive adjustment." Those parts of the organization receiving data include human beings accustomed to the facts of communicative life. In short, they ordinarily use counterbiases to adjust for such biases as they anticipate in the data they receive.

The second deficiency represents an especially complex difficulty. Once we take the simple biases suggested by the study of the effect of labels on estimation and combine them in an organization, we compound the situation enough to make no simple model obviously appropriate. In order to study the organizational phenomena, we constructed a three-person experimental organization operating under a partial conflict of interest.

4.4.2 An experiment on organizational estimation under partial conflict of interest

The decision-making system in the experiment had four critical organizational characteristics:

1. *Subunit interdependence.* Major decisions are not made by individuals or groups at the lowest level of the organization. Rather, the major

[9]R. M. Cyert and J. G. March, "Organizational Structure and Pricing Behavior in an Oligopolistic Market," *American Economic Review*, **45** (1955), 129–139.

decision-making units base their actions on estimates formulated at other points in the organization and transmitted to them in the form of communications. The estimates so received cannot be verified directly by the decision-making unit.

2. *Subunit specialization.* The estimates used in decision making come from more or less independent subunits of the organization. Each such subunit specializes in a particular function and usually processes a particular type of information.

3. *Subunit discretion.* Organizational constraints on the subunits that formulate and process estimates do not completely determine subunit behavior. The subunits have appreciable discretion in making, filtering, and relaying estimates.

4. *Subunit conflict.* The freedom available to a subunit in satisfying organizational constraints is devoted to the satisfaction of subunit goals. Each subunit develops its own goals and procedures reflecting the particular interests of its members. Such subunit goals will be consistent with the organizational requirements, but within those limits they will take the direction most compatible with individual and group objectives.

Subjects. Subjects were 108 male students. They included both undergraduate and graduate students but were predominately undergraduate. Most of the subjects were either engineering or science majors. They were divided into 36 three-man groups.

Experimental situation: apparatus. Each member of a group sat in a booth designed to prevent him from seeing other members. Each subject was prevented from speaking to other members except when desired by the experimenter and then only over the communication system. This system provided each subject and the experimenter with a headset, microphone, and a display board that indicated what communication was currently feasible over the system. This system was controlled automatically by a mechanical timer which stepped the system through the various communication links required according to a predetermined schedule. When a particular subject was not currently able to use the communication system, a noise signal was transmitted over his line. This served both as a mask for room noise and as an auditory supplement to the visual display board signal.

Experimental situation: task. The task of the group was to estimate the area of a series of 30 rectangles. On each of the 30 trials, one member of the group (the length estimator) saw projected on the wall in front of him a line segment. The line segments varied in length from 2.27 to 4.92 in. There were 15 different lengths. The 15 were ordered randomly for presentation in the first 15 trials. The same lengths were presented in the last 15 trials (in a different random order). This line segment was designated as the length of the rectangle. It was not seen by the other two members of the group. A second member of the group (the width estimator) saw a different line segment projected on the wall in his booth. This line segment was designated as the width of the rectangle and was not seen by the other members of the group. The line segments were the same as for the length estimator and were presented in the same way but in a different random order. The third group member (the area estimator) received from the length estimator a number representing his estimate of the length. The area estimator received from the width estimator a number representing his estimate of the width. Neither the width estimator nor the length estimator heard the estimate of the other. The area estimator then communicated to the experimenter an estimate of the area of the rectangle. This estimate was compared with the correct area and the magnitude of the error was reported by the experimenter to all three group members. Aside from the communications indicated here, no communication among the members of the group was permitted.

Experimental situation: rewards. Each subject was given a card in his booth showing the basis on which he would be rewarded for the group's performance during the experiment. The reward was in the form of cash-convertible points. The actual money involved was small (subjects normally "earned" about $1 in an experiment lasting about 40 minutes), but was adequate to obtain subjects. The major motivational factor was probably not the modest cash rewards but the point score. The experiment was presented as an experimental test for managerial potential, and most subjects reported after the experiment that they thought it measured some dimensions of managerial ability. There were three different payoff cards used in the experiment, as shown in Table 4.8.

Table 4.8. Payoff cards

Card	Magnitude and direction of error on the area estimate	Score
	More than 15% high	0
	5% high to 15% high	2
A	5% high to 5% low	5
	5% low to 15% low	2
	More than 15% low	0
	More than 15% high	0
	5% high to 15% high	0
B	5% high to 5% low	5
	5% low to 15% low	4
	More than 15% low	0
	More than 15% high	0
	5% high to 15% high	4
C	5% high to 5% low	5
	5% low to 15% low	0
	More than 15% low	0

Each card indicated the highest payoff for estimates within 5 per cent of the true area. However, they differed in the extent to which they valued errors. Card A is symmetric around the true area. Card B suggests a preference for errors on the low side. Card C suggests a preference for errors on the high side. Subjects knew only their own payoff card.

Experimental treatment. There were six different experimental treatments; in each treatment six groups were run. They were defined in terms of the assignment of payoff cards to the various members of the group. We will represent each treatment by three letters. The first letter is the payoff card given the length estimator; the second letter is the payoff card given the width estimator; the third letter is the payoff card given the area estimator.

> *AAA treatment.* Each member of the group has the same payoff and it is symmetric.
> *BBB treatment.* Each member of the group has the same payoff but it is not symmetric around the true area.
> *BCA treatment.* The two line estimators have opposing biases and the area estimator has a symmetric payoff.
> *ACB treatment.* All three payoffs are used. One of the line estimators has the symmetric payoff; the other two subjects have opposing biases.
> *CCB treatment.* There are only biased payoffs. The two line estimators have the same bias and are opposed to the area estimator.
> *BCB treatment.* There are only biased payoffs. One of the line estimators and the area estimator have the same bias. They are opposed by the other line estimator.

These six treatments represent six of the ten basic types of conflict possible in the experiment. That is, we feel that the following equivalences are reasonable:

> BBB is equivalent to CCC.
> ACB is equivalent to ABC, BAC, and CAB.
> BCA is equivalent to CBA.
> CCB is equivalent to BBC.
> BCB is equivalent to CBB, BCC, and CBC.

Unrepresented in the experiment are the following types: ABA (equivalent to ACA, BAA, and CAA), AAB (equivalent to AAC), ABB (equivalent to BAB, ACC, CAC), and BBA (equivalent to CCA).

Analysis. In the analysis we are primarily interested in the performance of the groups operating under the different conflict treatments. However, first we need to discuss the evidence bearing on the effectiveness of the experimental conditions in inducing consciously biasing behavior by subjects. Three pieces of evidence are available, none fully satisfactory. First, we compare the regression of estimates on actual line lengths for the three kinds of payoff cards used for line estimators. Second, we compare the values of δ in the equation $A = \delta LW$ (where A is the area estimate, L is the length estimate, and W is the width estimate) for the two kinds of payoff cards (A and B) used for area estimators. Third, we compare the frequency of overt strategy comments indicating a conscious manipulation of estimates by individuals having biased payoff cards (B and C) as compared with persons having unbiased payoffs (A). The basic problem with all techniques is that the various individuals were involved in different kinds of groups such that it is impossible to make firm inferences as to the effect of the payoff cards on individual behavior independent of all group effects. These effects include both the pattern of payoffs to other participants and the local adaptation to area error.

To measure the performance of groups, we compute the mean absolute error and the mean algebraic error in estimating the area of the rectangle. Specifically, we consider the mean absolute and algebraic errors in estimating the area for each treatment for each of six five-trial periods.

Results. The regressions of estimated line segment length (E) on actual length (L) for subjects having the various payoff cards have the following equations:

$$A \text{ (no bias)}: \quad E = 3.28 + 1.05(L - 3.60)$$
$$B \text{ (low bias)}: \quad E = 3.51 + 1.20(L - 3.60)$$
$$C \text{ (high bias)}: \quad E = 3.65 + 1.19(L - 3.60)$$

The difference between the means is significant and in the predicted direction for the AC and the BC comparisons. The AB difference is significant but not in the predicted direction. The differences between the slopes of A and B and A and C are significant. The difference between the slopes of B and C is not significant. All tests were made at the 5 per cent level of significance.

The values of the "fudge factor," δ, for the several area estimators are indicated below for each treatment:

Card	Treatment	δ
A	AAA	1.0268
	BCA	1.0015
B	ACB	0.977
	BCB	0.968
	BBB	1.138
	CCB	0.974

Subjects' responses to a question eliciting comments on individual strategies were divided into those that showed some conscious biasing of subjective estimates and those that did not. Forty-four of the 78 subjects with biased payoffs expressed overtly such strategies. Nine of the 30 subjects with unbiased payoffs did so.

We conclude that the payoff cards did have the desired effect of introducing individual behavior directed toward biasing the organization
estimate. The data in general support such a proposition.

The basic results with respect to the performance of the various groups
are indicated in Fig. 4.1. We plot the mean absolute performance over

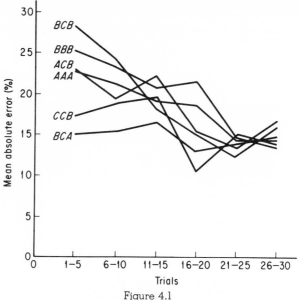

Figure 4.1

each of the six five-trial periods for each treatment. Two things are
conspicuous: (1) No treatment has any very clear advantage from the
point of view of such performance. (2) There is an apparent convergence
in performance over time.

Table 4.9. Mean algebraic error performance results

Treatments	Trials					
	1–5	6–10	11–15	16–20	21–25	26–30
CCB	−6.26	−5.07	−6.70	−0.90	+0.43	+1.79
AAA	−1.67	−8.88	−5.96	+2.34	−8.73	−5.29
ACB	−0.14	−2.90	−4.10	−6.72	−5.53	−3.00
BCA	−1.56	−1.50	−1.03	−7.07	−2.59	+1.17
BCB	+6.13	+6.07	−4.31	−6.10	−5.43	−5.30
BBB	−9.97	−6.07	−10.10	−13.53	−2.48	−5.87

The results (Table 4.9) with respect to algebraic error show no such
consistency except for the treatment (BBB) involving bias without

conflict. As might be expected, that treatment shows rather consistently the greatest negative error. The other five treatments are apparently indistinguishable (by Kendall's test for concordance). There is a suggestion in the data for the final trials that net group bias may affect performance, but that result cannot be clearly distinguished from more transitory variations.

We conclude that there are no persistent differences among the performances of the groups that are a function of the extent or type of conflict imposed on them within this experiment.

The anomaly that variations in behavior at the micro level can exist actively without being reflected at a macro level is a common enough phenomenon. It does not elicit surprise after the fact. In the present situation we can understand how such a result might have been produced. In particular, it seems clear that in an organization of individuals having about the same intelligence, adaptation to the falsification of data occurs fast enough to maintain a more or less stable organizational performance. For the bulk of our subjects in both experiments, the idea that estimates communicated from other individuals should be taken at face value (or that their own estimates would be so taken) was not really viewed as reasonable. For every bias, there was a bias discount.

If such a result can be shown to be a general one, however, it has substantial implications for a theory of organizational decision making. We, as well as others, have argued that internal informational bias has to be dealt with explicitly in a theory of the firm. These results cast doubt on such an argument in extreme form. They indicate that such phenomena, important as they may be to the understanding of the internal operation of the organization, have a severely constrained significance to a theory of organizational choice.

The generality of such a result and such an implication, of course, needs to be explored further. However, our own experience in attempting to develop models of organizational price and output determination without explicit attention to internal information bias is consistent with the conclusion based on the experiment. Both because of the tendency toward counterbiasing and because of the relative unimportance of anticipatory data, we have been able to ignore such apparently important factors as communication effects on organizational expectations — at least in the development of the relatively frequent type of decision involved in determining price and output.

4.5 Implications for a Theory of Organizational Expectations

We can now examine in more general terms the kind of expectations model that is suggested by the studies reported above and by our present under-

standing of human organization problem solving. As before, we consider
the organization to be a coalition having a series of more or less independent
goals imperfectly rationalized in terms of more general goals. From time
to time this coalition (or parts of it) makes decisions that involve organizational resources of one sort or another. These decisions depend on certain
information and expectations formed within the organization.

From the point of view of such a coalition, the classic theory of expectations is somewhat awkward. In fact, we would expect that an organization
that attempted to obtain the information required in such a theory would
ordinarily incur heavy costs in internal conflict. An organizational coalition
does not require either consistency or completeness in information; in fact,
as we have already seen in our case studies, consistency or completeness
would, at times, create problems in finding feasible solutions.

At the same time, we do not expect to find — and do not find — anything like a constant level of search. Rather, there are search procedures
called into play on various cues such that for any given situation there is a
standard search response. In the extreme case, we may want to say simply
that either there is search or there is not; there is search when existing
decisions are perceived as inadequate. More elaborately, we will want to
allow several equivalence classes representing different intensities and types
of search. For example, we will want to specify a hierarchy of search
activities. If one fails, we proceed to the next.

More generally, the analysis of these studies suggests some problems
with both the neoclassical conception of organizational use of expectations
and some recent suggestions for revision. On balance, however, it suggests
that many of the criticisms of the conventional theory of decision making
are warranted, at least in part.

Resource allocation within the firm reflects only gross comparisons of
marginal advantages of alternatives. All the decisions studied in actual
organizations were made within budgetary constraints and to that extent
reflected any marginal calculations that entered into the formation of a
general budget. When the rising estimates of costs for the crane controllers
(Decision 1) and the decline of business created an internal problem of
scarce resources, there were some attempts to compare the advantages of
the safety devices with alternative investments. These attempts, however,
focused on such considerations as prior commitment rather than marginal
return.

In the other cases, there were distinct conceptions of "appropriate"
costs or net return. Undoubtedly these were related in a relatively un-
systematic way to the comparable statistics (e.g., "payoff period") on the
other acceptable alternatives. If we ignore for the moment the problem of
bias in estimates, the studies indicate that rules of thumb for evaluating
alternatives provide some constraints on resource allocation even though

the allocation is substantially decentralized and there is no conscious comparison of specific alternative investments. Thus, a theory that predicts grotesquely large deviations from a return on investment norm is probably not accurate.

On the other hand, it seems clear that the constraints do not guarantee very close adjustment, especially where business conditions permit organizational slack. Any alternative that satisfies the constraints and secures suitably powerful support within the organization is likely to be adopted. This means that decision making is likely to reflect a response to local problems of apparent pressing need as much as it will reflect continuing planning on the part of the organization.

In a rough sense we can say that the first two case decisions considered here arose primarily as responses to "crisis" situations, the last two as the results of planning. In the computer decisions the organization had been alerted to the potential utility of electronic data-processing and had actually instituted procedures for continuing attention to possible applications. In the other cases the organization was stimulated to search for solutions to conspicuously unsatisfactory conditions. In every case, once an alternative was evoked, it was accepted if it satisfied the general cost and return constraints and enjoyed the support of key people in management. This support in turn came about through a rather complex mixture of personal, suborganizational, and general organizational goals. In Decision 2, the support came for mutually contradictory reasons from two or three different parts of the organization. In Decision 1 the support from top management came for reasons that were not directly relevant to the events that had triggered the search. In Decision 4 the support from top management came in considerable part from collateral expectations about the action.

Search activity is not viewed as simply another use of internal resources. In general these studies suggest that there are several stages to motivated search activity on the part of an organization. If a problem area is recognized, there is ordinarily a search for possible alternatives. At this stage only rough expectational data are used to screen obviously inappropriate actions. In each case considered this early scanning generated only a few suitable possibilities, which were then considered in greater detail. In most cases a rather firm commitment to an action was taken before the search for information proceeded very far, but the search became more and more intensive as the decision approached implementation. This was especially obvious in the case of the crane controls.

One major reason why this seems to be true is that organizational "search" consists in large part of evoking from various parts of the organization considerations that are important to the individual subunits; the relevance of such considerations, and the impetus to insist on them, are not manifest until the implications of the decision are made specific through implementation. An obvious corollary of such a conception of the search process is the proposition that search will be much more intensive where organizational slack is small than where it is large. Where there are enough excess resources in the organization, the interdependence of allocation decisions is uncertain; search consequently becomes relatively routine.

At the same time a conspicuous factor in these cases is frequently ignored in search theory. Whether in its classical form or in the level of aspiration form, the theory of search is basically a prospecting theory. It assumes that the objects of search are passive elements distributed in some fashion throughout the environment. Alternatives and information about them are obtained as a result of deliberate activities directed toward that end. Not all information comes to an organization in this way, however. Many of the events in these studies suggest a mating theory of search. Not only are organizations looking for alternatives; alternatives are also looking for organizations. In the computer decisions the intensity of search activity by the organization would scarcely have generated as much information as it did if the manufacturers of electronic data-processing equipment and the consulting firms had not been pursuing as well as being pursued. In Decision 1, too, many efforts had presumably been made by producers of magnetic controllers to sell management on a change. In fact, the timing of the major spurts of activity on those decisions was as much a function of the pressure from such outside groups as it was from internal factors.

Computations of anticipated consequences used by the organizations seem to be quite simple. Although there is no particularly strong evidence for Shackle's specific concept of what computations are made, at most only a half-dozen criteria were used explicitly in making the decisions. There appear to be two main reasons for the simplicity. First, in one form or another the major initial question asked about a proposed action was not how it compared with other alternatives but whether it was feasible. In the decisions discussed here there were two varieties of feasibility. The first was a budgetary constraint: Is money available for the project? The second was an improvement criterion: Is the project clearly better than existing procedures? In one form or another these questions were extremely important in all of the decisions discussed here. In some cases they were rather hard to answer, but they were almost always considerably easier than the question required by the classical theory of expectations: Does the expected net return on this investment equal or exceed the expected return on all alternative investments?

The second apparent reason for simplicity in establishing decision criteria was the awkwardness of developing a single dimension on which all relevant considerations could be measured. In each of the decisions described above, costs in dollars were factors; so were dollar savings. But so, too, were such considerations as speed and accuracy of work, safety of personnel, distance from railroad transportation, quality of performance, and reputation of company. Unless one is prepared to make explicit the dollar value of such diverse factors — and none of these firms did do so to any great extent — they must be treated substantially as independent constraints. Detailed expectations on these dimensions seemed substantially irrelevant to efforts to estimate costs because the organization had no way of using such information.

Expectations are by no means independent of such things as hopes, wishes, and the internal bargaining needs of subunits in the organization. Information about the consequences of specific courses of action in a business organization is frequently hard to obtain and of uncertain reliability. As a result, both conscious and unconscious bias in expectations is introduced. In each of the cases studied there is some suggestion of unconscious or semiconscious adjustment of perceptions to hopes. The initial estimates of cost for the crane controllers appear to have been fairly optimistic. The expectations about the consequences of moving the home specialties department seem to have been substantially a function of subunit goals. The evaluation of consulting firms seems to have shifted before detailed expectations were formed; subsequently, the expectations supported the evaluation. Expectations about net return from alternative data-processing systems apparently were influenced by some feelings of *a priori* preferences.

In addition, there is some evidence of more conscious manipulation of expectations. The classic statement came from a staff member involved in one of the decisions. He told a group of men outside of the company, "In the final analysis, if anybody brings up an item of cost that we haven't thought of, we can balance it by making another source of savings tangible."

It would be a mistake to picture the biases introduced in either of these fashions as exceptionally great. In almost every case there are some feasonably severe reality constraints on bias. But where the decision involves choice between two reasonably equal alternatives, small biases will be critical. Consequently, research on selective perception and recall is of substantial importance to an empirical theory of business decision making.

Communication in a complex organization includes considerable biasing, but also considerable bias correction. The communication system is not passive, nor is it viewed as passive. Information on critical variables in the system is seen as an important element in the decision process. In both of the experiments on communication, organization members modified their communicated judgments in the light of their picture of the decision consequences of various information.

Despite the bias in communication introduced in this manner, however, the system does not become hopelessly confused. Most biases are recognized by other parts of the organization. Whether the recognition is a logical inference drawn from the goals in the organization or an experienced inference drawn from past cases, long-run biases are detected. Once detected, the bias is vitiated by a correction factor. In addition, organizations seem to protect themselves from the worst effects of bias by focusing on easily verified data in lieu of uncertain estimates and by using easily checked feedback information instead of more remote anticipations.

5

ORGANIZATIONAL CHOICE[1]

The theories outlined in earlier chapters have emphasized several important characteristics of the decision-making process that are dealt with awkwardly in the neoclassical theory of the firm. First, organizational decisions depend on information, estimates, and expectations that ordinarily differ appreciably from reality. These organizational perceptions are influenced by some characteristics of the organization and its procedures. The procedures provide concrete estimates — if not necessarily accurate ones. Second, organizations consider only a limited number of decision alternatives. The set of alternatives considered depends on some features of organizational structure and on the locus of search responsibility in the organization. This dependence seems to be especially conspicuous in such planning processes as budgeting and price-output determination. Finally, organizations vary with respect to the amount of resources they devote to organizational goals on the one hand and suborganizational and individual goals on the other. In particular, conflict and partial conflict of

[1]This paper is based in part on our paper published as "Business Operating Procedures," in *Industrial Psychology*, ed. B. von Haller Gilmer (New York: McGraw-Hill, 1961), pp. 67–87; in part on our paper, "Organizational Factors in the Theory of Oligopoly," *Quarterly Journal of Economics*, **70** (1956), 44–64; and in part on an article we wrote with E. A. Feigenbaum, "Models in a Behavioral Theory of the Firm," *Behavioral Science*, **4** (1959), 81–95.

interests is a feature of most organizations, and under some conditions organizations develop substantial internal slack susceptible to reduction under external pressure.

In this chapter we suggest first how such considerations lead to a partial model of organizational choice and second how an examination of the actual decision procedures used in business firms leads to a more complete model. For, as we shall see when we consider organizational standard operating procedures, organizational choice is heavily conditioned by the rules within which it occurs. These rules, in turn, reflect organizational learning processes by which the firm adapts to its environment.

5.1 A Partial Model of Organizational Choice

The objective in this section is to show how the general attributes of decision making indicated in Chapters 3 and 4 can be introduced into a choice model. Because the elaboration is an obvious simplification of some important features of choice procedures in a complex organization, we call it a *partial model*. It summarizes in a relatively simple way some implications of our concepts of organizational goals and organizational expectations.

5.1.1 The decision process

We have specified a decision process that involves nine distinct steps:

1. *Forecast competitors' behavior.* The assumption that firms anticipate something about the reactions of their rivals is a part of virtually any theory of oligopoly. The approach in this model is to reflect some propositions about the ways in which organizations gain, analyze, and communicate information about competitors.

2. *Forecast demand.* The model includes assumptions about the process by which the demand curve is estimated in the firm. In this manner, we introduce organizational biases in estimation and allow for differences among firms in the way in which they adjust their current estimates on the basis of experience.

3. *Estimate costs.* The model does not assume that the firm has achieved the optimum combination of resources and the lowest cost per unit of output for any given plant size. Factors are introduced that affect the firm's costs, estimated as well as achieved.

4. *Specify objectives.* As we noted in earlier chapters, organizational "objectives" may enter at two distinct points and perform two quite distinct functions. First, in this step they consist in goals the organization wishes to achieve and which it uses to determine whether it has at least one viable plan [see step (5)]. Although we actually restrict ourselves to one

objective (profit), there is no requirement that there be only one objective or that the objectives be comeasurable since they enter as separate constraints all of which "must" be satisfied. Second, the objectives may be used as decision criteria [see step (9)]. As will become clear below, the fact that objectives serve this twin function rather than the single (decision-rule) function commonly assigned to them is of major importance to the theory.

The order of steps 1, 2, 3, and 4 is irrelevant in the present formulation. We assume that a firm performs such computations more or less simultaneously and that all are substantially completed before any further action is taken. Since the subsequent steps are all contingent, the order in which they are performed may have considerable effect on the decisions reached. This is especially true with respect to the order of steps 6, 7, and 8. Thus, one of the structural characteristics of a specific model is the order of the steps.

5. *Evaluate plan.* On the basis of the estimates of steps 1, 2, and 3, alternatives are examined to see whether there is at least one alternative that satisfies the objectives defined by step 4. If there is, we transfer immediately to step 9 and a decision. If there is not, however, we go on to step 6. This evaluation represents a key step in the planning process that is ignored in a model that uses objectives solely as the decision rule. Certain organizational phenomena (e.g., organizational slack) increase in importance because of the contingent consequences of this step.

6. *Re-examine costs.* We specify that the failure to find a viable plan initially results in the re-examination of estimates. Although we list the re-examination of costs first here, the order is dependent on some features of the organization and will vary from firm to firm. An important feature of organizations is the extent to which a firm is able to "discover" under the pressure of unsatisfactory preliminary plans "cost savings" that could not be found otherwise. In fact, we believe it is only under such pressure that firms begin to approach an optimum combination of resources. With the revised estimate of costs, step 5 occurs again. If an acceptable plan is possible with the new estimates, the decision rule is applied; otherwise, step 7.

7. *Re-examine demand.* As in the case of cost, demand is reviewed to see whether a somewhat more favorable demand picture cannot be obtained. This might reflect simple optimism or a consideration of new methods for influencing demand (e.g., an additional advertising effort). In either case, we expect organizations to revise demand estimates under some conditions and different organizations to revise them in different ways. Evaluation 5 occurs again with the revised estimates.

8. *Re-examine objectives.* Where plans are unfavorable, we expect a tendency to revise objectives downward. The rate and extent of change we

can attempt to predict. As before, evaluation 5 is made with the revised objective.

9. *Select alternative.* The organization requires a mechanism (a) for generating alternatives to consider and (b) for choosing among those generated. The method by which alternatives are generated is of considerable importance since it affects the order in which they are evaluated. Typically, the procedures involved place a high premium on alternatives that are "similar" to alternatives chosen in the recent past by the firm or by other firms of which it is aware. If alternatives are generated strictly sequentially, the choice phase is quite simple: choose the first alternative that satisfies the objectives. If more than one alternative is generated at a time, a more complicated choice process is required. For example, at this point maximization rules may be applied to select from among the evoked alternatives. In addition, this step defines a decision rule for the situation in which there are no acceptable alternatives (even after the re-examination of each of the estimates).

5.1.2 A specific duopoly model

The framework outlined in the preceding section can be viewed as an executive program for organizational decisions. That is, the model specifies that any large-scale oligopolistic business organization pursues the steps indicated. A change in decision must (within the model) be explained by some change in one of the processes. Such a conception of the model seems to suggest computer simulation as a way of exploring the implications of the theory. Unfortunately, when we attempt to develop models exhibiting the process characteristics discussed above, it becomes clear that our knowledge of how actual firms do, in fact, estimate demand, cost, and so forth is discouragingly small. Moreover, what knowledge we have (or think we have) tends to be qualitative in nature in situations where it would be desirable to be quantitative.

For these reasons, the models of firms with which we will deal here should be viewed as tentative (as well as partial) approximations. They contain substantial elements of arbitrariness and unrealistic characterizations. For example, we believe that the models presented in this chapter exaggerate the computational precision of organizational decision making. We have not attempted to introduce all of the revisions we consider likely primarily because we wish to show how some major revisions produce results which reasonably approximate observed phenomena.

The model is developed for a duopoly situation. The product is homogeneous, and therefore only one price exists in the market. The major decision that each of the two firms makes is an output decision. In making this decision each firm must estimate the market price for varying outputs.

When the output is sold, however, the actual selling price will be determined by the market. No discrepancy between output and sales is assumed, and thus no inventory problem exists in the model.

We assume the duopoly to be composed of an ex-monopolist and a firm developed by former members of the established firm. We shall call the latter the "splinter" and the former the "ex-monopolist" or, for brevity, the "monopolist." Such a specific case is taken so that some rough assumptions can be made about appropriate functions for the various processes in the model. The assumptions are gross, but hopefully not wholly unreasonable. To demonstrate that the model as a whole has some reasonable empirical base, we will compare certain outcomes of the model with data from the can industry in the United States, where approximately the same initial conditions hold.

We can describe the specific model at several levels of detail. In Table 5.1, the skeleton of the model is indicated — the "flow diagrams" of the

Table 5.1. Process model for output decision of firm

1. *Forecast:* Competitor's reactions	Compute conjectural variation term for period t as a function of actual reactions observed in the past
2. *Forecast:* Demand	Keep slope of perceived demand curve constant but pass it through the last realized point in the market
3. *Estimate:* Average unit costs	Cost curve for this period is the same as for last period. If profit goal has been achieved two successive times, average unit costs increase
4. *Specify objectives:* Profit goal	Specify profit goal as a function of the actual profits achieved over past periods
5. *Evaluate:* Examine alternatives	Evaluate alternatives within the estimate space. If an alternative which meets goal is available, go to (9). If not, go to (6)
6. *Re-examine:* Cost estimate	Search yields a cost reduction. Go to (5). If decision can be made after evaluation there, go to (9). If not, go to (7)
7. *Re-examine* Demand estimate	Estimate of demand increased after search. Go to (5). If decision can be made after evaluation, go to (9). If not, go to (8)
8. *Re-examine:* Profit goal	Reduce profit goal to a level consistent with best alternative in the estimate space as modified after (6) and (7)
9. *Decide:* Set output	Selection of alternative in original estimate space to meet original goal, in modified estimate space to meet original goal, or in modified estimate space to meet lowered goal

decision-making process. This will permit a quick comparison of the two firms. In the remainder of this section we will attempt to provide somewhat greater detail (and rationale) for the specific decision and estimating rules used.

The decision-making process postulated by the theory begins with a forecast phase (in which competitor's reaction, demand, and costs are estimated) and a goal specification phase (in which a profit goal is established). An evaluation phase follows, in which an effort is made to find the "best" alternative, given the forecasts. If this "best" alternative is inconsistent with the profit goal, a re-examination phase ensues, in which an effort is made to revise cost and demand estimates. If re-examination fails to yield a new best alternative consistent with the profit goal, the immediate profit goal is abandoned in favor of "doing the best possible under the circumstances." The specific details of the models follow this framework.

Forecasting competitor's behavior. Since we deal with a duopoly, one of the significant variables in the decision on the quantity of output to produce for each firm becomes an estimate of the rival firm's output. For example, assume the monopolist in period t is considering a change in output from period $(t - 1)$ and makes an estimate of the change the splinter will make. At the end of period t the monopolist can look back and determine the amount of change the splinter made in relation to his own change. The ratio of changes can be expressed as follows:

$$V_{m,t} = \frac{Q_{s,t} - Q_{s,t-1}}{Q_{m,t} - Q_{m,t-1}}$$

where $V_{m,t}$ = the change in the splinter's output during period t as a proportion of the monopolist's output change during period t,

$Q_{s,t} - Q_{s,t-1}$ = the actual change in the splinter's output during period t,

$Q_{m,t} - Q_{m,t-1}$ = the actual change in the monopolist's output during period t.

In the same way we have for the splinter the following:

$$V_{s,t} = \frac{Q_{m,t} - Q_{m,t-1}}{Q_{s,t} - Q_{s,t-1}} = \frac{1}{V_{m,t}}$$

We assume that the *monopolist* first makes an estimate of the fractional change in the splinter's output in relation to his own change, that is, an estimate of $V_{m,t}$. We have assumed that the monopolist will make this estimate on the basis of the splinter's behavior over the past three time periods. More specifically, we have assumed that the monopolist's estimate is based on a weighted average, as follows:

$$V'_{m,t} = V_{m,t-1} + \tfrac{1}{7}[4(V_{m,t-1} - V_{m,t-2}) + 2(V_{m,t-2} - V_{m,t-3})$$
$$+ (V_{m,t-3} - V_{m,t-4})]$$

where $V'_{m,t}$ = the monopolist's estimate of the change in the splinter's output during period t as a proportion of the monopolist's output change during period t, that is, an estimate of $V_{m,t}$.

Note that $(V'_{m,t}) \cdot (Q_{m,t} - Q_{m,t-1})$ is the monopolist's estimate of the splinter's change in output, $Q_{s,t} - Q_{s,t-1}$.

We would expect the *splinter* firm to be more responsive to recent shifts in its competitor's behavior and less attentive to ancient history than the monopolist, both because it is more inclined to consider the monopolist a key part of its environment and because it will generally have less computational capacity as an organization to process and update the information necessary to deal with more complicated rules. Our assumption is that the splinter will simply use the information from the last two periods. Thus,

$$V'_{s,t} = V_{s,t-1} + (V_{s,t-1} - V_{s,t-2})$$

In the same manner as above, $(V'_{s,t}) \cdot (Q_{s,t} - Q_{s,t-1})$ is the splinter's estimate of the monopolist's change in output, $Q_{m,t} - Q_{m,t-1}$.

Forecasting demand. We assume that the actual market demand curve is linear. That is, we assume the market price to be a linear function of the total output offered by the two firms together. We also assume that the firms forecast a linear market demand curve (not necessarily the same as the actual demand curve). There has been considerable discussion in the economics literature of an alleged discrepancy between the "imagined" demand curve and the actual demand curve, and it is this concept that is incorporated in the model. The values of the parameters of the imagined demand curve are based on rough inferences from the nature of the firms involved.

We assume that, because of its past history of dominance and monopoly, the *ex-monopolist* will be overly pessimistic with respect to the quantity that it can sell at lower prices, i.e., we assume the initially perceived demand curve will have a somewhat steeper slope than will the actual market demand curve. On the assumption that information about actual demand is used to improve its estimate, we assume that the monopolist changes its demand estimate on the basis of experience in the market. The firm assumes that its estimate of the slope of the demand curve is correct and it repositions its previous estimate to pass through the observed demand point.

We posit that the *splinter* firm will initially be more optimistic with respect to the quantity that it can sell at low prices than the ex-monopolist. Secondly, we assume that initially the splinter firm perceives demand as increasing over time. Thus, until demand shows a downward turn, the splinter firm estimates its demand to be 5 per cent greater than that found by repositioning its perceived demand through the last point observed in the marketplace.

Estimating costs. We do not assume that the firm has achieved optimum costs. We assume, rather, that the firm has a simplified estimate of its average cost curve, that is, the curve expressing cost as a function of output. It is horizontal over most of the range of possible outputs; at high and low outputs (relative to capacity) costs are perceived to be somewhat higher.

Further, we make the assumption that these cost estimates are "self-confirming," i.e., the estimated costs will, in fact, become the actual per-unit cost. The concept of organizational slack as it affects costs is introduced at this point. Average unit cost for the present period is estimated to be the same as the last period, but if the profit goal of the firm has been achieved for two consecutive time periods, then costs are estimated to be 5 per cent higher than "last time." The specific values for costs are arbitrary.

The *monopolist's* initial average unit cost is assumed to be $800 per unit in the range of outputs from 10 to 90 per cent of capacity. Below 10 per cent and above 90 per cent the initial average unit cost is assumed to be $900.

It is assumed that the *splinter* will have somewhat lower initial costs. This is because its plant and equipment will tend to be newer and its production methods more modern. Specifically, initial average costs are $760 in the range of outputs from 10 to 90 per cent of capacity. Below 10 per cent and above 90 per cent costs are assumed to average $870 per unit produced.

Specifying objectives. The multiplicity of organizational objectives is a fact with which we deal in later models. For the present, however, we limit ourselves to a single objective defined in terms of profit. In this model the function of the profit objective is to restrict or encourage search as well as to determine the decision. If, given the estimates of rival's output, demand, and cost, there exists a production level that will provide a profit that is satisfactory, we assume the firm will produce at that level. If there is more than one satisfactory alternative, the firm will adopt that quantity level that maximizes profit.

We assume that the *monopolist*, because of its size, substantial computational ability, and established procedures for dealing with a stable rather than a highly unstable environment, will tend to maintain a relatively stable profit objective. We assume that the objective will be the moving average of the realized profit over the last ten time periods. Initially, of course, the monopolist will seek to maintain the profit level achieved during its monopoly.

The *splinter* firm will presumably be (for reasons indicated earlier) inclined to consider a somewhat shorter period of past experience. We assume that the profit objective of the splinter will be the average of experienced profit over the past five time periods and that the initial profit objective will be linked to the experience of the monopolist and the relative capacities of the two. Thus, we specify that the initial profit objectives of the two firms will be proportional to their initial capacities.

Re-examination of costs. We assume that when the original forecasts define a satisfactory plan, there will be no further examination of them. If, however, such a plan is not obtained, we assume an effort to achieve a satisfactory plan in the first instance by reviewing estimates and finally by revising objectives. We assume that cost estimates are reviewed before demand estimates and that the latter are only re-examined if a satisfactory plan cannot be developed by the revision of the former. The re-evaluation of costs is a search for methods of accomplishing objectives at lower cost than appeared possible under less pressure. We believe this ability to revise estimates when forced to do so is characteristic of organizational decision making. It is, of course, closely related to the organizational slack concept previously introduced. In general, we have argued that an organization can ordinarily find possible cost reductions if forced to do so and that the amount of the reductions will be a function of the amount of slack in the organization.

It is assumed that the re-examination of costs under the pressure of trying to meet objectives enables each of the organizations to move in the direction of the "real" minimum cost point. For purposes of this model it is assumed that both firms reduce costs 10 per cent of the difference between their estimated average unit costs and the "real" minimum.

Re-examination of demand. The re-evaluation of demand serves the same function as the re-evaluation of costs. In the present model it occurs only if the re-evaluation of costs is not adequate to define an acceptable plan. It consists of revising upward the expectations of market demand. The reasoning is that some new alternative is selected that the firm believes will increase its demand. The new approach may be changed advertising procedure, a scheme to work salesmen harder, or some other alternative that leads the firm to an increase in optimism. In any event, it is felt the more experienced firm will take a slightly less sanguine view of what is possible. As in the case of estimating demand, we assume that all firms persist in seeing a linear demand curve and that no changes are made in the perceived slope of that curve. In the case of the *ex-monopolist*, it is assumed that as a result of the re-examination of demand estimates, the firm revises its estimates of demand upward by 10 per cent. In the case of the *splinter*, the assumption is that the upward revision of demand is 15 per cent.

Re-examination of objectives. Because our decision rule is one that maximizes among the available alternatives and our rule for specifying objectives depends only on outcomes, the re-evaluation of objectives does not, in fact, enter into our present models in a way that influences behavior. The procedure can be interpreted as adjusting aspirations to the "best possible under the circumstances." If our decision rule were different or if we made (as we do in later chapters) objectives at one time period a function of both outcomes and previous objectives, the re-evaluation of objectives would become important to the decision process.

Decision. We have specified that the organization will follow traditional economic rules for maximization with respect to its perception of costs, demand, and competitor's behavior. The specific alternatives selected, of course, depend on the point at which this step is invoked (i.e., how many re-evaluation steps are used before an acceptable plan is identified). The output decision is constrained in two ways:

Table 5.2. Initial and structural conditions for models exhibited in Table 5.3

Initial market demand (unknown to firms)	$p = 2000 - q$
Ex-monopolist's initial perception of demand schedule	$p = 2200 - 3q$
Splinter's initial perception of demand schedule	$p = 1800 - q$

Ex-monopolist's average unit cost

$$\begin{cases} 0.1q_{\max,m} < q_m < 0.9q_{\max,m} & \cdots \cdots \$800 \\ q_m > 0.9q_{\max,m}, \quad q_m < 0.1q_{\max,m} & \cdots \cdots \$900 \end{cases}$$

Splinter average unit cost

$$\begin{cases} 0.1q_{\max,s} < q_s < 0.9q_{\max,s} & \cdots \cdots \$760 \\ q_s > 0.9q_{\max,s}, \quad q_s < 0.1q_{\max,s} & \cdots \cdots \$870 \end{cases}$$

"Real" minimum average unit cost	$700
Ex-monopolist's capacity	400
Splinter's capacity	50
Market quantity	233
Market price	$1500
Ex-monopolist's profit goal	$163,100
Splinter's profit goal	$20,387
Conjectural variations ($V'_{m,t}$ and $V'_{s,t}$)	All 0 initially
Splinter's overoptimism of demand in forecast phase	5%
Splinter's raise of demand forecast upon re-examination	15%
Ex-monopolist's raise of demand forecast upon re-examination	10%
Cost reduction achieved in M's and S's search for lower costs (% of costs above "real" min. av. unit cost)	10%
Cost rise attributable to increase in "internal slack"	5%
Shift of actual demand schedule to right each time period	8%
Constraint on changing output from that of the last period	$\pm 25\%$
Per cent of capacity at which firm must be producing before it may expand (subject to other conditions)	90%
Change in capacity, upon expansion	20%

1. A firm cannot produce, in any time period, beyond its present capacity. Both models allow for change in plant capacity over time. The process by which capacity changes is the same for both firms. If profit goals have been met for two successive periods and production is above 90 per cent of capacity, then capacity increases 20 per cent.

2. A firm cannot change its output from one time period to the next more than ±25 per cent. The rationale behind the latter assumption is that neither large cutbacks nor large advances in production are possible in the very short run, since there are large organization problems connected with either.

The various initial conditions specified above are summarized in Table 5.2, along with the other initial conditions required to program the models.

5.1.3 Results of the duopoly model

We have now described a decision-making model of a large ex-monopolist and a splinter competitor. In order to present some detail of the behavior that is generated by the interacting models, we have reproduced in Table 5.3 the values of the critical variables on each of the major decision

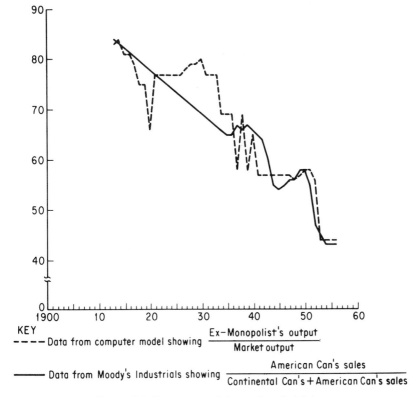

KEY

---- Data from computer model showing $\dfrac{\text{Ex-Monopolist's output}}{\text{Market output}}$

——— Data from Moody's Industrials showing $\dfrac{\text{American Can's sales}}{\text{Continental Can's + American Can's sales}}$

Figure 5.1 Comparison of share of market data.

Table 5.3. Values of selected variables at two-period intervals

	I	III	V	VII	IX	XI	XIII	XV	XVII	XIX	XXI	XXIII
Market												
Price	1420	1710	2196	2763	3283	3927	4430	4942	5425	3722	2785	2573
Output	290	311	262	205	209	195	303	466	713	914	855	534
Ex-monopolist												
Aspiration level	163,100	165,671	169,631	176,800	173,221	178,385	203,693	246,746	319,561	348,006	247,455	182,580
Conjectural variations	0	0	0.74	−22.4	1.09	0.74	0.26	0.35	0.28	0.30	−0.38	0.05
Costs (A.U.C.)	826	813	881	944	1041	1106	1219	1344	1482	1634	1801	1986
Output	240	251	206	153	161	150	233	363	566	703	658	369
No. of re-exam. steps	2	0	0	3	0	0	0	0	0	0	0	0
Splinter												
Aspiration level	20,387	27,107	31,448	39,763	46,218	39,684	54,245	79,090	113,595	121,973	86,083	60,742
Conjectural variations	0	0	9.2	−1.78	−6.58	8.72	3.39	3.96	4.76	3.91	6.3	−17.1
Costs	760	798	865	954	1023	1057	1166	1285	1417	1562	1623	1790
Output	50	60	56	52	48	45	70	103	147	211	197	165
No. of re-exam. steps	0	0	0	3	3	0	0	0	0	0	0	3
Profit ratio												
Splinter's profit ÷ ex-monopolist's profit	0.19	0.21	0.26	0.34	0.30	0.30	0.30	0.28	0.26	0.30	0.34	0.68
Share of market												
Ex-monopolist's output ÷ total output	0.83	0.81	0.79	0.75	0.77	0.77	0.77	0.78	0.79	0.77	0.77	0.69

Table 5.3. (cont.)

	XXV	XXVII	XXIX	XXXI	XXXIII	XXXV	XXXVII	XXXIX	XLI	XLIII	XLV
Market											
Price	2229	1719	2286	2970	3355	3742	4099	4546	5463	6730	7294
Output	360	335	250	140	218	340	529	735	777	727	1126
Ex-monopolist											
Aspiration level	157,664	148,648	154,010	158,120	159,060	179,859	203,892	239,045	280,940	260,501	340,745
Conjectural variations	0.64	−1.07	28.4	−1.40	0.85	0.95	0.96	0.65	3.77	1.91	1.35
Costs (A.U.C.)	2085	1710	1609	1436	1363	1502	1656	1826	2013	2071	2283
Output	207	193	143	80	125	195	303	432	342	320	500
No. of re-exam. steps	1	3	0	3	0	0	0	0	0	0	0
Splinter											
Aspiration level	37,977	19,272	28,402	37,123	38,627	53,005	77,001	109,136	164,566	266,512	396,911
Conjectural variations	2.21	−0.32	2.43	50.7	1.32	1.31	1.32	2.3	−0.8	3.16	0.79
Costs	1853	1821	1608	1669	1840	2029	2237	2466	2719	2771	3055
Output	153	142	107	60	93	145	226	303	435	407	626
No. of re-exam. steps	0	1	0	0	0	0	0	0	0	0	0
Profit ratio											
Splinter's profit ÷ ex-monopolist's profit	0.98	0.74	0.75	0.64	0.49	0.49	0.49	0.47	0.90	0.97	0.95
Share of market											
Ex-monopolist's output ÷ total output	0.57	0.58	0.57	0.57	0.57	0.57	0.57	0.59	0.44	0.44	0.44

and output factors.[2] By following this chart over time, we can determine
the time path of such variables as cost, conjectural variation, and output
for both of the firms.

In addition, we have compared the share of market and profit-ratio
results with actual data generated from the competition between American

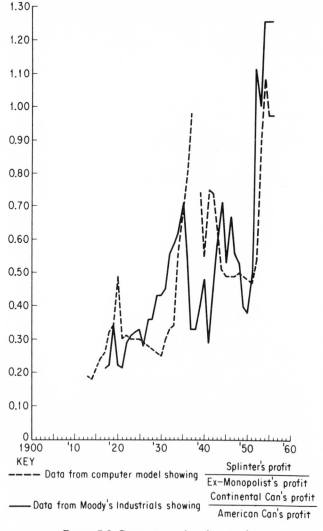

Figure 5.2 Comparison of profit-ratio data.

[2]Market demand was varied in the following way: (1) The slope of the demand curve
was held constant. (2) At each time period the intercept I_t was set equal to aI_{t-1}.
The value of a was 1.08 for periods 1–16, 0.90 for periods 17–20, 1 for periods 21–26, and
1.08 for periods 27–43.

Can Company and its splinter competitor, Continental Can Company, over the period from 1913 to 1956. These comparisons are indicated in Figs. 5.1 and 5.2.[3] In general, we feel that the fit of the behavioral model to the data is surprisingly good, although we do not regard this fit as validating the approach.[4]

It should be noted that the results in period XLV do not necessarily represent an equilibrium position. By allowing the firms to continue to make decisions, changes in output as well as changes in share of market would result. One of the reasons for the expected change is that the demand curve is shifting upward. Another more interesting reason is that no changes have been made within the organizations. In particular, the splinter firm is a mature firm by period XLV, but in the model it behaves as a new, young firm.

An examination of Table 5.3 indicates that the re-examination phase of the decision-making process was not used frequently by either firm. This characteristic is the result of a demand function that is increasing over most of the periods. Whether this also stems from an inadequacy in the model's description of organizational goal setting or is a characteristic of the real world of business decision making is a question that can be answered only by empirical research.

5.1.4 Deficiencies

The results of the model indicate that it is feasible to construct a choice model based on the general concepts outlined in Chapters 3 and 4. The theory we have used differs from conventional theory in six important respects:

1. The models are built on a description of the decision process. That is, they specify organizations that evaluate competitors, costs, and demand in the light of their own objectives and (if necessary) re-examine each of these to arrive at a decision.

2. The models depend on a theory of search as well as a theory of choice.

---

[3]One of the parameters in the model is the length of time involved in a single cycle. In comparing the output of the model with the American-Continental data, this parameter was set at 12 months.

[4]It should be clear that the validity of the approach presented in this chapter is not conclusively demonstrated by the goodness of fit to the can industry data. We have demonstrated that under the appropriate assumptions, models of firm decision processes can be specified that yield predictions approximating some observed results. However, the situation is one in which there are ample degrees of freedom in the specification of parameters to enable a number of time series to be approximated. Although in this case we have reduced the number of free parameters substantially by specifying most of them *a priori*, the problems of identification faced by any complex model are faced by this one and will have to be solved. The general methodology for testing models that take the form of computer programs remains to be developed (see Appendix B).

They specify under what conditions search will be intensified (e.g., when a satisfactory alternative is not available). They also specify the direction in which search is undertaken. In general, we predict that a firm will look first for new alternatives or new information in the area it views as most under its control. Thus, in the present models we have made the specific prediction that cost estimates will be re-examined first, demand estimates second, and organizational objectives third.

3. The models describe organizations in which the profit objective changes over time as a result of experience. The goal is not taken as given initially and fixed thereafter. It changes as the organization observes its success (or lack of it) in the market. In these models the profit objective at a given time is an average of achieved profit over a number of past periods. The number of past periods considered by the firm varies from firm to firm.

4. Similarly, the models describe organizations that adjust forecasts on the basis of experience. Adaptation in expectations occurs as a result of observations of actual competitors' behavior, actual market demand, and actual costs. Each of the organizations we have used readjusts its perceptions on the basis of such experience.

5. The models introduce organizational biases in making estimates. For a variety of reasons we expect some organizations to be more conservative with respect to cost estimates than other organizations, some organizations to be more optimistic with respect to demand, and some organizations to be more attentive to and perceptive of changes in competitors' plans.

6. The models all introduce features of "organizational slack." That is, we expect that over a period of time during which an organization is achieving its goals, a certain amount of the resources of the organization are funneled into the satisfaction of individual and subgroup objectives. This slack then becomes a reservoir of potential economies when satisfactory plans are more difficult to develop.

Despite the substantial differences between the duopoly model and more classical models in this area, a number of important features of organizational decision making as we have observed it are omitted from the model. In particular, we would identify the following major ways in which the model is deficient as a description of the choice process in a modern firm:

1. Price is not a decision variable. In order to simplify the model, we have made a single decision variable (output) rather than a series of decision variables — including price.

2. Only one goal is considered. A more complete model would include more than a single goal.

3. Little explicit attention is given to standard operating procedures and the avoidance of uncertainty through substituting feedback data for expectational data.

4. The organizations learn from their environment in only a limited sense. Decisions are contingent on feedback but decision rules are not.

These deficiencies suggest that the duopoly model, despite its apparent success, is not a general model. Thus, we need to consider in somewhat more detail the actual procedures used by business firms to make economic decisions. We will argue that business firms adapt over time by learning a number of simple decision rules and procedures and that a behavioral theory of the firm should deal both with that adaptive process and with the procedural implications of long-run adaptation.

5.2 The Firm as an Adaptive Institution

In Chapter 2 (and subsequently) we suggested that the classic theory of an omniscient firm is inappropriate for a theory of the firm directed toward answering questions about microbehavior. Without denying the substantial abilities of organizations as problem-solving and decision-making institutions, we have suggested that a business firm is constrained by the uncertainty of its environment, the problems of maintaining a viable coalition, and the limitations on its capacity as a system for assembling, storing, and utilizing information. As a result, the theory outlined in this volume characterizes the firm as an *adaptively rational* system rather than an *omnisciently rational* system.[5]

In general, we assume that an adaptive system has the following properties:

1. There exist a number of states of the system. At any point in time, the system in some sense "prefers" some of these states to others.

2. There exists an external source of disturbance or shock to the system. These shocks cannot be controlled.

3. There exist a number of decision variables internal to the system. These variables are manipulated according to some decision rules.

4. Each combination of external shocks and decision variables in the system changes the state of the system. Thus, given an existing state, an external shock, and a decision, the next state is determined.

5. Any decision rule that leads to a preferred state at one point is more likely to be used in the future than it was in the past; any decision rule that leads to a nonpreferred state at one point is less likely to be used in the future than it was in the past.

[5]The distinction between "adaptive" and "rational" decision systems has been made by H. A. Simon. See H. A. Simon, *Models of Man* (New York: Wiley, 1957), and *Administrative Behavior*, rev. ed. (New York: Macmillan, 1956). We prefer the term "adaptively rational" to reflect some sentiments about the rationality of learning.

We argue on the basis of the above criteria that a business organization is an adaptive institution. In short, the firm learns from its experience.

With such a view of the firm, we can deal effectively with a number of classic problems in the analysis of firm decision making. However, it is important to recognize one feature of the adaptation before proceeding to a more detailed discussion of the mechanisms and procedures used by firms to make decisions. In the language and formulation of Chapter 3, an organization is a coalition of diverse subgroups; it is also a complex system in which different decisions are made at different places in the organization. Such a system adapts in a rather special way. In particular, note that we have described an adaptive system as in some sense preferring some states of the system to other states. In what sense does an organization have "preferences"? We have already indicated our perception of the sense in which organizations have goals (and therefore preferences). If we are correct in our formulation, organizational adaptation will depend, in part, on such considerations as what goals are currently evoked and what part of the system is involved in making the decision. Such phenomena can be subsumed under the rubric of adaptation without doing violence to the concept, but they suggest a somewhat more complicated form of adaptation than is commonly associated with the term in dealing with individual human systems. This will become clear when we turn to the development of actual price and output models.

If we view the business firm as an adaptive institution, we may (depending on the environment of the firm) be interested either in some long-run consequences of the adaptive process or in the short-run results of that process. Proceeding from the former point of view, some attempts have been made to indicate the long-run relation between adaptive rationality in the firm and omniscient rationality.[6] Although it is possible to show that most adaptive processes tend toward "long-run rationality," we think such demonstrations are of modest relevance for a theory of firm behavior. The conditions required for the nonfortuitous achievement of strictly rational behavior are extremely implausible as descriptions of the world. In particular, so long as the environment of the firm is unstable (and unpredictably unstable), the heart of the theory must be the process of short-run adaptive reactions. The long-run properties of the processes under stable conditions are relevant primarily as indicators of logical properties (and therefore consistency with general concepts).

Thus, our primary concern here is in the relatively short-run adaptive process and its consequences. In order to examine the major attributes of short-run adaptation by firms existing in a changing world, we need to take a new look at the standard operating procedures of a business organization and the ways in which those procedures change. Standard operating pro-

---

[6] A. Alchian, "Uncertainty, Evolution and Economic Theory," *Journal of Political Economy*, **58** (1950), 211–221.

cedures are the memory of an organization. Like any other memory or learned behavior, standard operating procedures change over time at varying rates. Some rules seem to change frequently; others appear to have been substantially unchanged for as long as the organization has existed. Because many of the rules change slowly, it is possible to construct models of organizational behavior that postulate only modest changes in decision rules. One such model has been presented in this chapter; others will be presented in Chapters 7 and 8.

When we ignore adaptation with respect to decision rules, we are simply saying that relative to the time span being considered these rules are given. For example, one might want to use a basic full-cost pricing rule in a model of a particular industry for the next ten years, without necessarily assuming that full-cost pricing (much less the mark-ups used) would persist indefinitely. In general, if we investigate a firm and determine that it uses a set of decision rules, we can ordinarily assume that within the next few years these rules will be pursued and that adaptation in the short run will be restricted largely to adaptation in goals and rule-directed reaction to feedback. From this point of view, standard operating procedures should be one of the major objects for study by students of organizational decision making. The result of adaptation rather than the adaptation itself can be studied.

At the same time we may want to extend our time span and examine the adaptation itself. Some of the main features of interest in an adaptive system are the problems of learning, and some organizational learning occurs within a time span that permits analysis. Thus, we will want to consider such questions as how the decision rules, treated as fixed in shorter-run models, change in response to long-run experience. We have introduced some assumptions about such long-run shifts in the general model presented in Chapter 8; but since little or no research has been carried out on organizational learning, the assumptions are borrowed from the study of other adaptive systems and have only limited *prima facie* validity.

In the remainder of this chapter, we consider standard operating procedures as they exist in contemporary firms in the United States. We do not think a reasonable theory of the firm can ignore such procedures. We think it is possible to characterize their main features in such a way as to contribute to the development of such a theory — that is, to abstract from the specificity of any one firm's procedures. We think they confirm — both in their form and in their changes — the description of a firm as an adaptively rational system.

5.3 Standard Operating Procedures

Any organization as complex as a firm adapts to its environment at many different (but interrelated) levels. It changes its behavior in response to short-run feedback from the environment according to some fairly well-defined rules. It changes rules in response to longer-run feedback according to some more general rules, and so on. At some point in this hierarchy of rule change, we describe the rules involved as "learning" rules. By this we mean (in effect) that we will not examine the hierarchy further, although it is clear wherever we stop that we can still imagine higher-level learning rules by which the lower-level learning rules are modified.

In this section we consider the standard operating rules used by business firms. We consider these rules at two different levels of generality. First, we examine the general decision procedure that is followed. In part, this procedure is implicit in earlier chapters; in part it comes from a look at actual operating procedures in firms. Second, we examine several of the key procedures used by large organizations to implement the general procedure. Although we would assume the procedures at both levels to be susceptible to learning, the general procedures would adapt less readily and less rapidly than the more specific rules.

5.3.1 General choice procedure

We have already considered several major features of choice procedures. In particular, we should note that organizations make decisions typically by solving a series of problems. Whether we consider what we have said about organization goals or what we have said about organizational search, it is clear that the organizations described here devote rather little time to long-run planning (that has operational significance for decision making), especially when that planning is dependent on long-run estimates. They move from one crisis to another. At the same time, they rely heavily on traditional methods, general industry practice, and standard operating procedures for making decisions.

These general choice procedures can be summarized in terms of three basic principles:

1. *Avoid uncertainty.* Rather than looking for ways of dealing with uncertainty through certainty equivalents, the firm looks for procedures that minimize the need for predicting uncertain future events. One method uses short-run feedback as a trigger to action, another accepts (and enforces) standardized decision rules.

2. *Maintain the rules.* Once it has determined a feasible set of decision procedures, the organization abandons them only under duress. The problems associated with continuously redesigning a system as complex as a modern firm are large enough to make organizations cautious about change.

3. *Use simple rules.* The firms rely on individual "judgment" to provide flexibility around simple rules. One of the most common forms of a decision rule consists in a basic, simple procedure and the specification of a list of "considerations" describing the conditions under which the procedure may be modified.

We assume that these general procedures have been learned. In fact, we can specify rather easily a set of environmental conditions and internal constraints that make these general rules sensible from the point of view of long-run rationality. It is not hard to see how an adaptive system existing in an environment such as that of the modern firm might reasonably develop a set of general rules along these lines. Moreover, we would assume that these general procedures condition changes in learning at the level of more specific decision rules. Thus, if an organization has been avoiding uncertainty about competitors' behavior by overt collusion and has had some adverse experience with the Justice Department and public opinion, we would expect it to seek some new modes of uncertainty avoidance rather than immediately abandon the general strategy.

Because of this distinction between learning at the level of general procedures and learning at the level of specific procedures, we would expect that only a long-run model would need to consider adaptation with respect to general choice procedures. A short-run model need consider no significant adaptation. Assuming that most models would probably fall somewhere between these extremes, we would expect a typical model to introduce learning with respect to some specific procedures but to treat many specific procedures (as well as all general procedures) as given.

5.3.2 Specific standard operating procedure

In general the specific procedures most likely to be treated as fixed are those incorporated in the explicit standard operating procedures of the firm. These procedures change slowly. They give stability to the organization and direction to activities that are constantly recurring. In addition to providing needed stability, the standard operating procedures influence (and in many cases dictate) the decisions made in the organization. We consider here four major types of procedures.[7]

1. *Task performance rules.* How does the part get fabricated? How are the books kept? How are the products priced? In terms of quantity of words, probably most of any given recorded standard operating procedure consists in specifications of methods for accomplishing whatever task is assigned to an individual member or subgroup of the organization.

2. *Continuing records and reports.* Every business organization maintains a set of more or less permanent records about certain aspects of its operation. Naturally, these records tend to be related to those elements of business operations that have seemed most important to the effective operation of the firm.

[7]For a more detailed discussion of some specific procedures, see W. A. Newman and C. E. Summer, Jr., *The Process of Management* (Englewood Cliffs, N.J.: Prentice-Hall, 1961), 399–411.

3. *Information-handling rules.* In any large-scale business organization, transmitting information in the form of directions, estimates, and results represents a major activity. In order to provide reasonable certainty that relevant information will be available at the proper place at the proper time, a communication system is specified in the regular operating code of the organization.

4. *Plans.* Plans for organizational behavior represent one of the major outputs of high levels in the organization as well as a significant output at other levels. Such plans take the general form of an intended allocation of resources among the alternative activities available to the firm or its subunits. They range from short-run budgets of operating expenses to long-run plans for capital expenditures.

Task performance rules. Consider a new employee in an organization who is given the simple instruction, "Set price so as to maximize profit." If such an employee lasted long enough in the organization — and the organization lasted long enough — some ways for handling the pricing problem that were reasonably satisfactory would eventually be developed. But presumably prior employees have dealt with the same problem and developed some procedures. The organization's rules permit the transfer of past learning.

There is another reason for rules, however. The organization requires solutions that are consistent with a large number of other solutions to other tasks being performed in the organization. So long as there exists a number of different "solutions" to the pricing problem and each requires a different set of coordinative mechanisms with other parts of the organization and other adjustments in the behavior throughout the organization, the problem of pricing is not adequately solved. The organization needs not only an acceptable solution (i.e., "acceptable" within the confines of the smaller unit) but also a solution that has some "uniqueness" properties. This uniqueness is needed to permit other parts of the organization to co-ordinate their activities with those of the pricing unit. Where (as is usually true) the task itself does not provide a unique solution, it is the function of the task performance rules and training to achieve the uniqueness. In this way an internally consistent, feasible schedule of activities is developed for the organization. Thus, rules not only transmit past learning; they also control (make predictable) behavior within the firm.

Task performance rules exist in considerable detail at many different levels in the organization. Highly trained engineers dealing with complex design problems may have their work as precisely described by performance rules as the individual member of the production line. More important for our purposes is the fact that in most organizations pricing, output, inventory, and sales strategy decisions are made within heavily circumscribed limits. In most of the firms we have studied, price and output decisions were almost as routinized as production line decisions. Although the procedures changed over time and the rules were frequently contingent on external feedback, price and output were fixed by recourse to a number of simple operating rules. What was apparently a complex decision problem involving considerable uncertainty was reduced to a rather simple problem with a minimum of uncertainty.

Performance rules may have several sources. For example, work procedures that stem from time study methods are generally devised for the specific job to be performed and introduced into the system by instructing and training workers. Similarly, price and output rules are learned within the organization in large part and communicated to subsequent members of the organization. Not all rules are purely internal, however. On the one hand, some rules are introduced not by training but by recruitment and selection. On the other hand, some rules are more general than the individual firm and are identified as a more pervasive code called "standard industry practice," "standard business practice," "ethical business practice," or "good business practice."

Through recruitment and selection, many employees come to a firm with established task performance rules. Their "craft" specifies how a job is to be performed (whether it is wiring a switch or scheduling production). Although some obvious examples of such pretraining can be found in the case of employees working in the standard craft areas, such a phenomenon is not limited to what are commonly called "blue collar" activities. When a business firm hires an accountant, a dietician, a doctor, or a sanitary engineer, it hires not only an individual but also a large number of standard operating procedures that have been trained into the new member of the organization by outside agencies. One of the important consequences of professionalization in general is that extraorganizational groups have the responsibility of providing task performance rules for the organization.

The rules of good business practice mentioned above have a similar effect. Enforced by management literature, management consultants, accounting firms, trade associations, and many other managerial reference groups, "good practice" — especially at management levels — tends to be shared among firms. We will not attempt to discuss in any detail the psychological reasons for the ready acceptance of such general rules. It is clear, however, that they serve the important function of providing an operational procedure for the manager to use in a situation of comparative ambiguity. Insofar as the external situation consists in other firms, it becomes predictable. Competitors' behavior can be predicted in the areas covered by standard practice. Insofar as potential failure is of concern to the decision maker, "standardization" provides a defense.

Records and reports. The continuing records and reports kept by the organization are a second major component of standard operating procedures. Just as we could describe an organization in terms of the task specifications it made, we can also describe it by the kinds of records and reports it maintains over time. In fact, an analysis of the records kept should enable us to deduce some important characteristics of the firm's decision-making system. For example, the kinds of records kept tell a good deal about the firm's perceptions of its own internal structure and the kind of world within which it exists. In most organizations record- and report-keeping serve two main purposes: control and prediction. These are, of course, the general purposes of a number of organizational subsystems.

Records, such as the financial statement or the standard cost report, have a control effect in the short run merely because they are being kept and the organization members presume that they are being kept for some purpose (or at least that their existence will induce some purpose for them). Obviously, in the long run, records that do not trigger some action within the system become simply irrelevant parts of the corporate memory. Generally, the action involved is action by a supervisor or executive administratively responsible for the department. It may also involve other individuals, however. For example, the simple publication of industry resource allocation statistics creates a reference group for the manager and generally results in modifications of behavior in the direction of homogeneity within the reference group.

A second major apparent function of records in an organization is to help the organization predict its environment. As we pointed out in Chapter 4, organizations, in fact, do not use predictions to nearly the extent suggested by classical theory. Moreover, such predictions as are used tend to be based on simple hypotheses about the relation between the past and the future. In order to make such restricted predictions, however, the firm needs both some idea of the relation between past and future events and also some records of the relevant past events.

Two important consequences stem from the organization's dependence on a particular set of records for predictive purposes:

1. The significance of records for the individual members of the organization increases substantially. To a limited extent, organizational decisions about the allocation of resources among the various subunits and individual employees depend on rough estimates of future events and information about consequences of past decisions. Thus, advertising managers feel that they should (within reason) ensure records favorable to the proposition that increases in sales revenue more than compensate for increases in advertising expenditure.

2. The records that are kept determine in large part what aspects of the environment will be observed and what alternatives of action will be considered by the firm. We have placed considerable emphasis on the process

by which organizations find alternatives to consider. Records of past behavior are one of the major sources for such a process. As a result, there is more stability of organizational decisions from one period to another than one would predict if the organization entered each situation without records of prior experience. Similarly, when the environment changes suddenly and in such a way as to make a new statistic important to decision making, the firm is likely to be relatively slow in adjusting. It will attempt to use its existing model of the world and its existing records to deal with the changed conditions. Here, as in the case of task performance rules, the standard operating procedures serve as the organization's primary memory. They permit the organization to deal more effectively with previously experienced situations than could an individual considering the situation without prior experience, but they normally retard adjustment to strikingly different situations.

Information-handling rules. As a communication system, the firm can be defined in terms of four things:

1. *The characteristics of the information taken into the firm.* Information comes to the organization from outside in a wide variety of ways and forms. Salesmen receive orders from customers and information about competitors. Executives read trade journals and formulate conclusions about general conditions in the industry. All of these bits of data comprise inputs for the firm.

2. *The rules for distributing and condensing input information.* What does the salesman do with information about competition? What does the executive do with the trade journal information?

3. *The rules for distributing and condensing internally generated information.* Different parts of the organization make decisions, issue orders, and request clarification. How are such pieces of information moved through the organization?

4. *The characteristics of the information leaving the firm.* The organization communicates with its environment through orders to suppliers, deliveries to consumers, advertising, petitions for patents, and in many other ways.

Not everyone in an organization seeks or receives all of the information needed by the firm to pursue its business. There is considerable specialization in securing information just as there is in task performance and record keeping. In large part, this specialization is defined by some operating rules linked closely to the rules for information flows that we will discuss below. Generally speaking, a firm will allocate responsibility for securing particular information to subunits having (1) regular contact with the information source or (2) special competence in securing the information. Thus, in the course of their regular contacts with customers, salesmen are ordinarily expected to provide information on market demand. A labor relations department is expected to keep management informed of impending labor demands. A purchasing department would ordinarily be responsible for providing information on the availability of supplies. All of these cases represent instances where regular contact with the relevant outside environment makes the department members obvious "experts" on the subject.

In many cases, however, the organization does not rely simply on contact as a criterion for selecting information sources. In almost all of the areas of major concern to the firm — market demand, labor supply, money market, and so forth — large firms maintain staff experts whose sole function is to secure and evaluate information. Almost any large business firm has professional market analysts, financial analysts, and economists, all providing services supplementary to the information gathered by regular operating units.

Does it make any difference who gathers the information? We show below that it is potentially important because the person who gathers the information is also the first to communicate, condense, and evaluate it. It is also important in another way. The environment of the firm generates an extremely large amount of information that might be relevant to decision making within the firm. As a result, some initial screening decisions are made at the periphery of the organization. Most of these screening decisions are trivial. The salesman learns that one of his customers is driving a new automobile, but he probably does not consider that a relevant fact for the organization. However, some screening decisions have important effects If the market analyst decides to rely on a certain informant in an outside organization, he has linked his own firm's policies to the accuracy and relevance of the informant's reports. Standardization of screening rules (e.g., by professional organizations) leads to extensive standardization in information. Similarly, all parts of the organization — from clerks dealing with visitors to vice-presidents dealing with bankers — make decisions about what questions they will direct to whom on the outside. These decisions depend on their past training and their perceptiveness of the situation. Organizational decisions, in turn, depend in part on the questions asked and the information received.

In a simple organization it would be possible to allow all information to be shared among all members of the organization and to permit this sharing in the informal manner characteristic of small groups. In a large organization with specialization of function, however, it is necessary to establish regular procedures for transmitting information, whether it be information from outside the organization or such things as decisions and instructions from within the organization. We turn now to a consideration of the rules regulating the movement of information through a firm.

There are two aspects to standard operating procedure for information flows: *routing rules* and *filtering rules*. Routing rules specify who will communicate to whom about what. The most obvious, best known, and one of the most important of such rules is the "through-channels" rule, where the organization requires that certain kinds of information be handled through channels. In such a system, the president talks only to the board of directors, his staff assistants, and vice-presidents. Vice-presidents talk only to their staff assistants, the president, and division managers. For many purposes the standard organization chart is viewed as a rule for communication. Obviously no organization can adhere strictly to such a rule without severe strains, but most business organizations observe it for a wide variety of information handling.

The reason for the extensive use of through-channels rules is clear when one considers the reasons for organizational departmentalization. Departmentalization as a basis for a business organization depends on the proposition that the activities necessary to accomplish the firm's goals can be grouped so that any given group can act more or less independently of other groups. The production division can ignore the finance division except for a rather small number of special occasions. Such atomization of the firm is complemented by a similar atomization of relevant information (e.g., it is not particularly important to the production division to know the current state of the money market in detail). The departmental organization defines reasonably well the groups within which sharing of information is needed. Since information needs and task specialization are highly correlated, it is appropriate to process information through the hierarchy defined in terms of task specialization. The rules themselves also serve to accentuate the specialization; for example, they make it relatively awkward to maintain a continuing close connection between production decisions and sales strategy decisions.

By the same token, we can predict when communication that is not through channels will become part of the operating procedures of the firm. Where it is necessary to coordinate the activities of subunits in the organization, communication through channels is frequently quite inefficient. As a result, procedures for transmitting information across channels are developed. These procedures are more likely to be the result of innovation than of conscious organizational planning at the top, but if the same problem persists over time, they develop and become as fully legitimized as the other kind.

What difference do routing rules make? Provided the information is unchanged from receipt to final destination and all information is ultimately sent everywhere, about all that can be affected by routing is the length of time required to transmit the message. What makes the routing rules important is their linkage with filtering at the various communication relay points and the fact that there are dead ends in the routes. Information is condensed and summarized as it goes through the organization and some information never reaches some points.

We have already discussed (Chapter 4) the relevance of filtering rules in the formation of organizational expectations. From the point of view of the theory, they pose a rather interesting question. On the one hand, it is clear that biases introduced in the filtering rules are real. Sales departments have consistent biases with respect to sales estimates; accounting departments filter cost data differently from other departments; the computation center provides different data on computer efficiency than other departments. On the other hand, as we have already observed, in the long run the organization learns to provide counter biases for each bias. In addition, the existence of information filtering and bias has another long-run learning effect. One of the ways in which the organization adapts to the unreliability of information is by devising procedures for making decisions without attending to apparently relevant information. Thus, the internal biases in the organization increase the pressure (from external uncertainty) to develop decision methods that do not require reliable information (other than the simplest, most easily checked information).

The dead ends in information routes similarly have short- and long-run consequences. In the short run, they result in the familiar organization problem that relevant information is frequently not available where it can be used. It is difficult for an organization to assemble all of the information that would be recognized as relevant (if known) at one point if it is buried at another point. In the long run, dead ends lead to a decision strategy that involves extensive use of essentially contingent decisions. Decisions are used as devices for learning about their hidden consequences (through outcries or other quick feedback — simulation in the raw).

Plans and planning rules. We have suggested several times that we think that long-term planning in the sense in which it is usually discussed in the theory of the firm plays a relatively minor role in decision making within the firm. However, any business firm engages in activities that come under the general rubric of planning and, in fact, are described as "planning" by the organization. These activities are usually as closely specified as other aspects of the standard operating procedures, and the fact that plans are made and features of periodicity surround them enforces a variety of interesting behaviors within the firm.

Consider, for example, the budget. Manuals on the budgeting process are commonplace in firms and many of the more interesting phenomena within the firm (especially those concerning internal resource allocation) occur within a framework defined by budget rules. The budget in a modern, large-scale corporation plays two basic roles. On the one hand, it is used as a management control device to implement policies on which executives have decided and to check achievement against established criteria. On the other hand, a budget is a device to determine feasible programs. In either case, it tends to define — in advance — a set of fixed commitments and (perhaps more important) fixed expectations. Although budgets can be flexible, they cannot help but result in the specification of a framework within which the firm will operate, evaluate its success, and alter its program. Typically, for example, one of the characteristics of a budget period in an oligopolistic firm is that it covers the period for which the firm considers prices fixed. Similarly, any budget tends to identify as given some factors that are in an absolute sense variables within the control of the organization.

More generally, we can make four observations on plans within an organization:

1. *A plan is a goal.* In classical economics the importance of planning predictions is obscured by the assumption that the predictions are always correct (and correct without benefit of an interaction between the prediction itself and firm behavior). Outside of such a utopia of perspicacity, a planning prediction functions both as a prediction of sales, costs, profit level, and so forth, and also as a goal for such factors. Under some circumstances (and within limits) an organization can induce behavior designed to confirm its prediction (goal).

2. *A plan is a schedule.* It specifies intermediate steps to a predicted outcome. Such guides take the form of both time goals and subunit goals and need not be fixed completely in advance. Frequently, however, they are fixed either absolutely or in terms of a ratio to a factor (e.g., sales) that is considered exogenously variable. In any event, the firm is forced by its plan (if for no other reason) into the specification of acceptable achievement levels for its subunits as well as for the organization as a whole, for segments of the planning period as well as for the period as a whole.

3. *A plan is a theory.* For example, the budget specifies a relationship between such factors as sales and costs on the one hand and profits on the other, and thereby permits the use of sales and cost data as guideposts to the achievement of a satisfactory level of profits. Thus, although monthly profit and loss and departmental profit and loss statements are now frequently used in firms, their use is neither so widespread nor so significant as one might anticipate. Because of the accounting difficulties involved in partial profit and loss statements (especially with respect to burden application), many operating executives appear to prefer other, plan-oriented, criteria of performance.[8]

4. *A plan is a precedent.* It defines the decisions of one year and thereby

[8]H. A. Simon, H. Guetzkow, G. Kozmetsky, and G. Tyndall, *Centralization vs. Decentralization in Organizing the Controller's Department* (New York: Controllership Foundation, 1954), 42.

establishes a *prima facie* case for continuing existing decisions. Only in quite exceptional cases do firms in fact re-examine the rationale of existing functions, for example, or alter radically the expenditures for them. This tends to be particularly true of overhead functions (e.g., advertising, research and development, clerical help).

Because of these characteristics of plans and planning, the decisions within the firm have both temporal periodicity and consistency over time that they would not necessarily have otherwise. When we say that a plan is a goal, schedule, theory, and precedent (as well as a prediction), we are suggesting that plans, like other standard operating procedures, reduce a complex world to a somewhat simpler one. Within rather large limits, the organization substitutes the plan for the world — partly by making the world conform to the plan, partly by pretending that it does. So long as achievement levels continue to be satisfactory, budgetary decisions are exceptionally dependent on decisions of previous years, with shifts tending to reflect the expansionist inclinations of subunits rather than systematic reviews by top management.[9]

5.3.3 General implications of standard operating procedures

Choice and control within an organization depend on the elaboration of standard operating procedures of the types described here. It is hard to see how a theory of the firm can ignore the effects of such procedures on decision-making behavior within the organization. The effects we have noted seem to fall into four major categories:

1. *Effects on individual goals within the organization.* The specification of a plan or other rule has a distinct effect on the desires and expectations of organizational members.

2. *Effects on individual perceptions of the state of the environment.* Different parts of the organization see different environments, and the environments they see depend on the rules for recording and processing information.

3. *Effects on the range of alternatives considered* by organization members in arriving at operating decisions. The way in which the organization searches for alternatives is substantially a function of the operating rule it has.

4. *Effects on the managerial decision rules used* in the organization. In fact, these rules frequently are specified explicitly.

The relevance of these effects for a behavioral theory of the firm is twofold. First, prediction of the price and output behavior of a specific firm

---

[9] R. M. Cyert and J. G. March, "Organizational Factors in the Theory of Oligopoly," *Quarterly Journal of Economics*, **70** (1956), 52.

will depend on a rather detailed knowledge of the standard operating procedures of that firm. Conversely, detailed knowledge of the procedures will go far toward predicting the behavior. Second, a more general model of price and output decisions by modern large-scale corporations will have to include both the dependence on standard operating procedures and the general characterization of such procedures that we have outlined here.

5.4 Summary

Having previously endowed an organization with goals, perceptions, and choice behavior somewhat different from comparable concepts in the theory of individual decision making, we have now completed the portrait with a learned set of behavior rules — the standard operating procedures. These rules are the focus for control within the firm; they are the result of a long-run adaptive process by which the firm learns; they are the short-run focus for decision making within the organization.

Considering the observations on choice in this and the preceding chapters, we can describe a skeleton of our basic theory of organizational choice and control. We assume:

1. Multiple, changing, acceptable-level goals. The criterion of choice is that the alternative selected meet all of the demands (goals) of the coalition.

2. An approximate sequential consideration of alternatives. The first satisfactory alternative evoked is accepted. Where an existing policy satisfies the goals, there is little search for alternatives. When failure occurs, search is intensified.

3. The organization seeks to avoid uncertainty by following regular procedures and a policy of reacting to feedback rather than forecasting the environment.

4. The organization uses standard operating procedures and rules of thumb to make and implement choices. In the short run these procedures dominate the decisions made.

In the chapters that follow we will attempt to show how such a conception of the choice process in a modern business organization can be used as the basis for predictive models of firm behavior.

6

A SUMMARY OF
BASIC CONCEPTS IN
THE BEHAVIORAL THEORY
OF THE FIRM

In its classic form, economic theory is simply a language designed to provide a systematic framework within which to analyze economic problems. Such a role was assigned to theory by Marshall and is clearly implicit in contemporary theory. In this view theory performs two major functions. On the one hand, it is an exhaustive set of general concepts. Any variable observed in the system can be assigned to an appropriate niche. The theory is a set of filing cabinets with each drawer bearing the title of an economic concept. Within each file drawer there is a set of folders for each economic variable relevant to the concept. Within each folder there is a further breakdown in terms of the factors affecting the variable. At the same time, the theory is a statement of critical relations among system variables. These relations may be assumptions about interdependence among variables, about the functional form of the interdependences, or about broad structural attributes of the system.

As an example in classic theory, consider the concept of market demand. The usual treatment of demand involves

(1) a description of demand in terms of a "demand curve," (2) the decomposition of the market demand curve into individual demand curves, and (3) the specification of individual demand in terms of individual preference orderings and the concept of utility. Within such a filing system we establish relations between external events and demand phenomena (e.g., a relation between demand for a particular commodity and money income) by introducing relational concepts (e.g., income elasticity).

One of the most important requirements for the usefulness of theory conceived in this general way is the requirement that all important variables in the system be conveniently represented within the concepts of the theory. The theory of the firm seems to meet this requirement reasonably well for the kinds of problems with which it has usually been faced (e.g., the perfectly competitive market). However, the theory has not been adequate to cope with oligopolistic markets. The theory outlined in this volume specifies an alternative framework and an alternative set of key relations for dealing with the modern "representative firm" — the large, multi-product firm operating under uncertainty in an imperfect market.

6.1 Goals, Expectations, and Choice

The basic framework for analysis we have proposed, like the classic one, has two major organizing devices: (1) It has a set of exhaustive variable categories; (2) it has a set of relational concepts. The exhaustive categories are implicit in the organization of this volume. We have argued that we can analyze the process of decision making in the modern firm in terms of the variables that affect organizational goals, the variables that affect organizational expectations, and the variables that affect organizational choice.

Organizational goals. Quite simply, we have identified two sets of variables affecting the goals of an organization. The first set influences the *dimensions* of the goals (what things are viewed as important). Within this set of variables, we can cite the composition of the organizational coalition, the organizational division of labor in decision making, and the definition of problems facing the organization. Thus, we have argued that organizational goals change as new participants enter or old participants leave the coalition. We have argued that the operative goals for a particular decision are the goals of the subunit making that decision. Finally, we have argued that goals are evoked by problems. The second set of variables influences the *aspiration level* on any particular goal dimension. Here we have identified essentially three variables: the organization's past goal, the organization's past performance, and the past performance of other "comparable" organizations. The aspiration level is viewed as some weighted function of these three variables.

Organizational expectations. Expectations are seen as the result of drawing inferences from available information. Thus, we consider variables that affect either the process of drawing inferences or the process by which information is made available to the organization. With respect to inference drawing, we have not attempted to reflect all of the recent efforts in the psychology of individual choice. However, we have identified some simple pattern-recognition variables (e.g., linear extrapolation) and the effect of hopes on expectations. With respect to the process by which information is made available, we have cited particularly variables affecting search activity within the firm. Affecting the intensity and success of search are the extent to which goals are achieved and the amount of organizational slack in the firm. Affecting the direction of search are the nature of the problem stimulating search and the location in the organization at which search is focused.

Organizational choice. Choice takes place in response to a problem, uses standard operating rules, and involves identifying an alternative that is acceptable from the point of view of evoked goals. Thus, the variables that affect choice are those that influence the definition of a problem within the organization, those that influence the standard decision rules, and those that affect the order of consideration of alternatives. The standard decision rules are affected primarily by the past experience of the organization and the past record of organizational slack. The order in which alternatives are considered depends on the part of the organization in which the decision is being made and past experience in considering alternatives.

In the preceding three chapters we have tried to elaborate on this simple structure in order to develop meaningful and useful theories of organizational goals, expectations, and choice. We think it is possible to subsume any variable within the theory of business decision making under one or more of these categories.

6.2 Four Major Relational Concepts

In the course of developing the three subtheories, we have developed a relatively small number of relational concepts. In many respects, they represent the heart of our theory of business decision making. The four major concepts used in the theory are (1) quasi resolution of conflict, (2) uncertainty avoidance, (3) problemistic search, and (4) organizational learning. In this section we review briefly the meaning of each of these concepts. In subsequent chapters we will use the concepts to build a number of models and to suggest implications for economic and organizational theory.

6.2.1 Quasi resolution of conflict

In keeping with virtually all theories of organizations, we assume that the coalition represented in an organization is a coalition of members having different goals. We require some procedure for resolving such conflict. The classic solution is to posit an exchange of money from some members of the coalition to other members as a way of inducing conformity to a single, consistent set of goals — the organizational objective.

We propose an alternate concept of organizational goals and an alternate set of assumptions about how conflict is resolved. Basically we have argued that most organizations most of the time exist and thrive with considerable latent conflict of goals. Except at the level of nonoperational objectives, there is no internal consensus. The procedures for "resolving" such conflict do not reduce all goals to a common dimension or even make them obviously internally consistent.

Goals as independent constraints. In our framework, organizational goals are a series of independent aspiration-level constraints imposed on the organization by the members of the organizational coalition. These constraints may include nonessential demands (i.e., demands that are already satisfied when other constraints are met), sporadic demands (i.e., demands that are made only occasionally), nonoperational demands (i.e., demands for which there are no operational measures), as well as essential, continuous, operative goals. In general, although we recognize the importance of goals that are nonessential (because they might become essential), of goals that are ordinarily sporadic (because they occasionally are enforced), and of goals that are nonoperational (because they sometimes can be made operational), we will focus on those constraints that are essential, continuous, and operative.

Specifically, in the case of price and output models of the business firm, we assume a profit goal, a sales goal, a market share goal, an inventory goal, and a production goal. In any particular firm we expect some subset of these objectives to be essential, continuous, and operative. Moreover, we expect that subset to pose problems for the organization in the form of potential conflict. Thus, we require assumptions about procedures for resolving conflict. We assume that conflict is resolved by using local rationality, acceptable-level decision rules, and sequential attention to goals.

Local rationality. We assume that an organization factors its decision problems into subproblems and assigns the subproblems to subunits in the organization. From the point of view of organizational conflict, the importance of such local rationality is in the tendency for the individual subunits to deal with a limited set of problems and a limited set of goals. At the limit, this reduces to solving one problem in terms of only one goal.

The sales department is primarily responsible for sales goals and sales strategy; the production department is primarily responsible for production goals and production procedures; the pricing department is primarily responsible for profit goals and price decisions; and so on.

Through delegation and specialization in decisions and goals, the organization reduces a situation involving a complex set of interrelated problems and conflicting goals to a number of simple problems. Whether such a system will in fact "resolve" the conflict depends, of course, on whether the decisions generated by the system are consistent with each other and with the demands of the external environment. In our theory consistency is facilitated by two characteristics of the decision process: (1) acceptable-level decision rules; (2) sequential attention to goals.

Acceptable-level decision rules. In the classic arguments for decentralization of decision making, we require strong assumptions about the effectiveness of the "invisible hand" in enforcing proper decisions on a system of local rationality. Consistency requires that local optimization by a series of independent decision centers result in over-all optimization. On the other hand, we are persuaded that organizations can and do operate with much weaker rules of consistency (i.e., we require that local decisions satisfying local demands made by a series of independent decision centers result in a joint solution that satisfies all demands). Such rules are weaker in two senses: (1) There will ordinarily be a large number of local decisions that are consistent with other local decisions under such a rule. The demand constraints do not uniquely define a solution. (2) Any such system will tend to underexploit the environment and thus leave excess resources to absorb potential inconsistencies in the local decisions.

Sequential attention to goals. Ordinarily when we talk of "consistency" of goals or decisions we refer to some way of assessing their internal logic at a point in time. As a result, in classic theories of organizations we are inclined to insist on some consistency within a cross section of goals. Such an insistence seems to us inaccurate as a characterization of organizational behavior. Organizations resolve conflict among goals, in part, by attending to different goals at different times. Just as the political organization is likely to resolve conflicting pressures to "go left" and "go right" by first doing one and then the other, the business firm is likely to resolve conflicting pressures to "smooth production" and "satisfy customers" by first doing one and then the other. The resulting time buffer between goals permits the organization to solve one problem at a time, attending to one goal at a time.

6.2.2 Uncertainty avoidance

To all appearances, at least, uncertainty is a feature of organizational decision making with which organizations must live. In the case of the business firm, there are uncertainties with respect to the behavior of the market, the deliveries of suppliers, the attitudes of shareholders, the behavior of competitors, the future actions of governmental agencies, and so on. As a result, much of modern decision theory has been concerned with the problems of decision making under risk and uncertainty. The solutions involved have been largely procedures for finding certainty equivalents (e.g., expected value) or introducing rules for living with the uncertainties (e.g., game theory).

Our studies indicate quite a different strategy on the part of organizations. Organizations avoid uncertainty: (1) They avoid the requirement that they correctly anticipate events in the distant future by using decision rules emphasizing short-run reaction to short-run feedback rather than anticipation of long-run uncertain events. They solve pressing problems rather than develop long-run strategies. (2) They avoid the requirement that they anticipate future reactions of other parts of their environment by arranging a negotiated environment. They impose plans, standard operating procedures, industry tradition, and uncertainty-absorbing contracts on that environment. In short, they achieve a reasonably manageable decision situation by avoiding planning where plans depend on predictions of uncertain future events and by emphasizing planning where the plans can be made self-confirming through some control device.

Feedback-react decision procedures. We assume that organizations make decisions by solving a series of problems; each problem is solved as it arises; the organization then waits for another problem to appear. Where decisions within the firm do not naturally fall into such a sequence, they are modified so that they will.

Consider, for example, the production-level decision. In most models of output determination, we introduce expectations with respect to future sales and relate output to such predictions. Our studies indicate, to the contrary, that organizations use only gross expectations about future sales in the output decision. They may, and frequently do, forecast sales and develop some long-run production plans on paper, but the actual production decisions are more frequently dominated by day-to-day and week-to-week feedback data from inventory, recent sales, and salesmen.

This assumption of a "fire department" organization is one of the most conspicuous features of our models. Under a rather broad class of situations, such behavior is rational for an organization having the goal structure we have postulated. Under an even broader set of situations, it is likely to be the pattern of behavior that is learned by an organization dealing with an uncertain world and quasi-resolved goals. It will be learned because by and large it will permit the organization to meet the demands of the members of the coalition.

Negotiated environment. Classical models of oligopoly ordinarily assume that firms make some predictions about the behavior of their environment, especially those parts of the environment represented by competitors, suppliers, customers, and other parts of the organization. Certainly such considerations are important to any decisions made by the firm. Our studies, however, lead us to the proposition that firms will devise and negotiate an environment so as to eliminate the uncertainty. Rather than treat the environment as exogenous and to be predicted, they seek ways to make it controllable.

In the case of competitors, one of the conspicuous means of control is through the establishment of industry-wide conventional practices. If "good business practice" is standardized (through trade associations, journals, word of mouth, external consultants, etc.), we can be reasonably confident that all competitors will follow it. We do not mean to imply that firms necessarily enter into collusive agreements in the legal sense; our impression is that ordinarily they do not, but they need not do so to achieve the same objective of stability in competitive practices.

For example, prices are frequently set on the basis of conventional practice. With time, such variables as the rate of mark-up, price lines, and standard costing procedures become customary within an industry. Some effects of such practices are indicated in Chapter 7. The net result of such activity with respect to prices (and comparable activity with regard to suppliers and customers) is that an uncertain environment is made quite highly predictable.

Such negotiation among firms is not obviously collusion for profit maximization. Rather, it is an attempt to avoid uncertainty while obtaining a return that satisfies the profit and other demands of the coalition. The lack of a profit-maximizing rationale is suggested by (1) the stability of the practices over time and (2) the occasional instances of success by firms willing to violate the conventional procedures (e.g., discount houses in retailing).

In a similar fashion, the internal planning process (e.g., the budget) provides a negotiated internal environment. A plan within the firm is a series of contracts among the subunits in the firm. As in the case of industry conventions, internal conventions are hyperstable during the contract period and tend to be relatively stable from one period to the next (e.g., in resource allocation). As a result, they permit each unit to avoid uncertainty about other units in making decisions.

6.2.3 Problemistic search

In the framework proposed in this volume, the theory of choice and the theory of search are closely intertwined. Necessarily, if we argue that organizations use acceptable-level goals and select the first alternative they see that meets those goals, we must provide a theory of organizational search to supplement the concepts of decision making. In our models we assume that search, like decision making, is problem-directed. By *problemistic search* we mean search that is stimulated by a problem (usually a rather specific one) and is directed toward finding a solution to that problem. In a general way, problemistic search can be distinguished from both random curiosity and the search for understanding. It is distinguished from the former because it has a goal, from the latter because it is interested in understanding only insofar as such understanding contributes to control. Problemistic search is engineering rather than pure science.

With respect to organizational search, we assume three things:

1. *Search is motivated.* Whether the motivation exists on the buyer or seller side of the alternative market, problemistic search is stimulated by a problem, depressed by a problem solution.

2. *Search is simple-minded.* It proceeds on the basis of a simple model of causality until driven to a more complex one.

3. *Search is biased.* The way in which the environment is viewed and the communications about the environment that are processed through the organization reflect variations in training, experience, and goals of the participants in the organization.

Motivated search. Search within the firm is problem-oriented. A problem is recognized when the organization either fails to satisfy one or more of its goals or when such a failure can be anticipated in the immediate future. So long as the problem is not solved, search will continue. The problem is solved either by discovering an alternative that satisfies the goals or by revising the goals to levels that make an available alternative acceptable. Solutions are also motivated to search for problems. Pet projects (e.g., cost savings in someone else's department, expansion in our own department) look for crises (e.g., failure to achieve the profit goal, innovation by a competitor). In the theory we assume that variations in search activity (and search productivity) reflect primarily the extent to which motivation for search exists. Thus, we assume that regular, planned search is relatively unimportant in inducing changes in existing solutions that are viewed as adequate.

Simple-minded search. We assume that rules for search are simple-minded in the sense that they reflect simple concepts of causality. Subject to learning (see below), search is based initially on two simple rules: (1) search in the neighborhood of the problem symptom and (2) search in the neighborhood of the current alternative. These two rules reflect different dimensions of the basic causal notions that a cause will be found "near" its effect and that a new solution will be found "near" an old one.

The neighborhood of symptom rule can be related to the subunits of the organization and their association with particular goals and with each other. A problem symptom will normally be failure on some goal indicator. Initial reaction, we assume, will be in the department identified with the goal. Thus, if the problem is the failure to attain the sales goal, the search begins in the sales department and with the sales program. Failing there, it might reasonably proceed to the problem of price and product quality and then to production costs.

The neighborhood of existing policy rule inhibits the movement of the organization to radically new alternatives (except under circumstances of considerable search pressure). Such an inhibition may be explained either in terms of some underlying organizational assumptions of continuity in performance functions or in terms of the problems of conceiving the adjustments required by radical shifts.

When search, using the simple causal rules, is not immediately successful, we assume two developments. First, the organization uses increasingly complex ("distant") search; second, the organization introduces a third search rule: (3) search in organizationally vulnerable areas.

The motivation to search in vulnerable areas stems from two things. On the one hand, the existence of organizational slack will tend to lead search activity in the direction of slack parts of the organization. On the other hand, certain activities in the organization are more easily attacked than others, simply because of their power position in the system. One general phenomenon is the vulnerability of those activities in the organization for which the connection with major goals is difficult to calculate concretely (e.g., research in many firms). In either case, a solution consists in either absorbing slack or renegotiating the basic coalition agreement to the disadvantage of the weaker members of the coalition.

Bias in search. We assume three different kinds of search bias: (1) bias reflecting special training or experience of various parts of the organization, (2) bias reflecting the interaction of hopes and expectations, and (3) communication biases reflecting unresolved conflict within the organization. Bias from prior experience or training is implicit in our assumptions of search learning (below), local specialization in problem solving (above), and subunit goal differentiation (above). Those parts of the organization responsible for the search activities will not necessarily see in the environment what those parts of the organization using the information would see if they executed the search themselves. The bias in adjusting expectations to hopes has the consequence of decreasing the amount of problem-solving time required to solve a problem and of stimulating the growth of organizational slack during good times and eliminating it during bad. We assume that communication bias can be substantially ignored in our models except under conditions where the internal biases in the firm are all (or substantially all) in the same direction or where biases in one direction are located in parts of the organization with an extremely favorable balance of power.

6.2.4 Organizational learning

Organizations learn: to assume that organizations go through the same processes of learning as do individual human beings seems unnecessarily naive, but organizations exhibit (as do other social institutions) adaptive behavior over time. Just as adaptations at the individual level depend upon phenomena of the human physiology, organizational adaptation uses individual members of the organization as instruments. However, we believe it is possible to deal with adaptation at the aggregate level of the organization, in the same sense and for the same reasons that it is possible to deal with the concept of organizational decision making.

We focus on adaptation with respect to three different phases of the decision process: adaptation of goals, adaptation in attention rules, and adaptation in search rules. We assume that organizations change their goals, shift their attention, and revise their procedures for search as a function of their experience.

Adaptation of goals. The goals with which we deal are in the form of aspiration levels, or — in the more general case — search equivalence classes. In simple terms, this means that on each dimension of organizational goals there are a number of critical values — critical, that is, from the point of view of shifts in search strategy. These values change over time in reaction to experience, either actual or vicarious.

We assume, therefore, that organizational goals in a particular time period are a function of (1) organizational goals of the previous time period, (2) organizational experience with respect to that goal in the previous period, and (3) experience of comparable organizations with respect to the goal dimension in the previous time period. Initially at least, we would assume a simple linear function,

$$G_t = a_1 G_{t-1} + a_2 E_{t-1} + a_3 C_{t-1}$$

where G is the organizational goal, E the experience of the organization, C a summary of the experience of comparable organizations, and where $a_1 + a_2 + a_3 = 1$. The parameters in this goal adaptation function are important attributes of the organization. a_3 reflects the organization's sensitivity to the performance of competitors or other comparable organizations. a_1 and a_2 reflect the speed at which the organization revises goals in the face of experience. In some cases, we will want to define two values for a_3 — one for when comparative experience exceeds the organization's goal and a different one for when it is below the goal. Similarly, we may want to allow the effect of the organization's experience to depend on whether it exceeds or is below the goal.

Adaptation in attention rules. Just as organizations learn what to strive for in their environment, they also learn to attend to some parts of that environment and not to others. One part of such adaptation is in learning search behavior, which we will consider in a moment. Here we wish to note two related, but different, adaptations:

1. In evaluating performance by explicit measurable criteria, organizations learn to attend to some criteria and ignore others. For example, suppose an organization subunit has responsibility for a specific organizational goal. Since this goal is ordinarily stated in relatively nonoperational terms, the subunit must develop some observable indices of performance on the goal. Among the indices objectively available to the subunit, which will be used? Observation suggests this is a typical case of learning. Subunits in the short run do not change indices significantly. However, there are long-run shifts toward indices that produce generally satisfactory results (i.e., in this case, usually show the subunit to be performing well).

2. Organizations learn to pay attention to some parts of their comparative environment and to ignore other parts. We have assumed that one of the parameters in the goal adaptation function is a parameter reflecting the sensitivity of the organization to external comparisons. This parameter is not fixed. We would expect it to change over time as such comparisons do or do not produce results (in the form of goals) that are satisfactory to the important groups in the coalition. At the same time, we have represented by C in the goal adaptation function a summary description of comparable organizations. Concealed in such an abstract form is organizational learning with respect to what is properly comparable. With which attributes of which organizations should we compare ourselves? Although in a relatively short-run model we might reasonably consider this fixed, we would expect that in the long run we would require a model in which such attention factors changed.

Adaptation in search rules. If we assume that search is problem-oriented, we must also assume that search rules change. Most simply, what we require in the models are considerations of the following type: when an organization discovers a solution to a problem by searching in a particular way, it will be more likely to search in that way in future problems of the same type; when an organization fails to find a solution by searching in a particular way, it will be less likely to search in that way in future problems of the same type. Thus, the order in which various alternative solutions to a problem are considered will change as the organization experiences success or failure with alternatives.

In a similar fashion, the code (or language) for communicating information about alternatives and their consequences adapts to experience. Any decision-making system develops codes for communicating information about the environment. Such a code partitions all possible states of the world into a relatively small number of classes of states. Learning consists in changes in the partitioning. In general, we assume the gradual development of an efficient code in terms of the decision rules currently in use. Thus, if a decision rule is designed to choose between two alternatives, the information code will tend to reduce all possible states of the world to two classes. If the decision rules change, we assume a change in the information code, but only after a time lag reflecting the rate of learning. The short-run consequences of incompatibilities between the coding rules and the decision rules form some of the more interesting long-run dynamic features of an organizational decision-making model.

6.3 The Basic Structure of the Organizational Decision-Making Process

We have described four basic concepts that seem to us fundamental to an understanding of the decision-making process in a modern, large-scale business organization. The quasi resolution of conflict, uncertainty avoidance, problemistic search, and organizational learning are central phenomena with which our models must deal. In our judgment, the natural theoretical language for describing a process involving these phenomena is the language of a computer program. It is clear that some parts of the theory are susceptible to representation and solution in other forms, but the general structure of the process can be conveniently represented as a flow chart. Such a flow chart is outlined in its most general form in Fig. 6.1. In Chapter 7 we elaborate the basic structure to illustrate the use of the framework in an empirical investigation. In Chapter 8 we elaborate the structure into a working general model.

Figure 6.1 is intended to illustrate two things. On the one hand, it shows abstractly the step-by-step decision process. For convenience, we have started the process at the point of receiving feedback from past decisions. Since the decision process is continuous, this start is arbitrary. Starting from the feedback, the figure shows the sequence of steps taken by a particular subunit in the firm with respect to a specific decision and a specific goal. Other decisions by other subunits using other goals would occur in parallel with this one. Loose connections among the subunits and decisions are secured by the environmental feedback and (when indicated) by expanded search.

At the same time, the figure shows (by the vertical columns) the relation between the basic concepts of the theory and the decision process flow chart. At a general level, each of the concepts is represented in a decision process having this structure. Obviously, when a specific decision in a specific content (e.g., Chapters 7 and 10) is considered, this abstract description of the process must be substantially elaborated with specific content.

Clearly, models based on these concepts will deviate significantly from models based on the approach of classical economics. Such differences are not surprising. We have emphasized the fact that the behavioral theory of the firm is designed to answer a set of questions different from those to

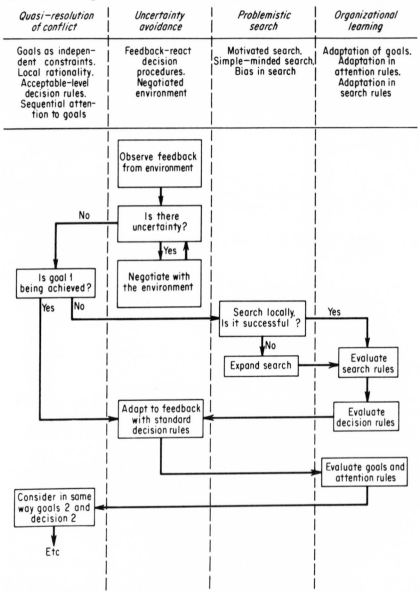

Quasi–resolution of conflict	Uncertainty avoidance	Problemistic search	Organizational learning
Goals as independent constraints. Local rationality. Acceptable–level decision rules. Sequential attention to goals	Feedback–react decision procedures. Negotiated environment	Motivated search. Simple–minded search. Bias in search	Adaptation of goals. Adaptation in attention rules. Adaptation in search rules

Figure 6.1 Organizational decision process in abstract form.

which traditional theory of the firm is directed. We think that these concepts will prove useful in dealing with organizational decision making as it is reflected in business firms. The demonstration of the utility of the concepts, however, depends on defining specific models, based on the concepts, that yield definite, testable predictions. It is to such a task that we now turn.

7

A SPECIFIC PRICE
AND OUTPUT MODEL[1]

In Chapter 6 we outlined the general form of a theory of
decision making in a complex organization. In this chapter
we propose to apply this general model to a specific
organization and a specific set of decisions. In order to
make the application, it will be necessary to elaborate
considerably the abstract model. However, we believe
that the elaboration is a special instance of the more
general theory, that it is possible to use the model as a base
for the simulation of the decision process in a specific case,
and that the predictions generated by the elaborated
model bear a close relation to actual observed behavior.

The organization chosen for intensive study is one
department in a large retail department store. The firm
involved is part of an oligopolistic market consisting (for
most purposes) of three large downtown stores. Each of
the firms involved also operates one or more suburban
stores, but the focus of this study is the downtown market
(where each store makes most of its sales). The firm is
organized into several merchandising groups, each of which

---

[1]This chapter is based on an unpublished working paper by
R. M. Cyert, J. G. March, and C. G. Moore. Mr. Moore did the
bulk of the field research and shared fully in the development of
the model.

has several departments. The firm, in total, has more than 100 major departments. We have studied, with varying degrees of intensity, the price and output decisions in about a dozen of the firm's departments. From these dozen we have chosen one for intensive investigation, and the specific model reported here is literally a model of decision making in that specific department. In our judgment, the decision processes we report for this department could be generalized with trivial changes to other departments in the same merchandising group and could be generalized with relatively modest changes to most other departments outside the immediate group. Because of the great similarity in operation among department stores, we believe the model represents many aspects of decision making in retail department stores.

We present the model at two levels of specificity. In the first section we outline the decision process in the organization in rather general terms. In the second section we elaborate some of the decision rules in order to provide specific, explicit predictions of decisions.

7.1 General View of Price and Output Determination in a Retail Department Store

As we suggested in earlier chapters, the organization makes relatively independent price and output decisions. There are loose connections between the two decision areas, but for the most part decisions are made with reference to different goals and different stimuli. Although we will want to elaborate the goals of the organization somewhat when we turn to specific decision rules, we can describe two general goals that the department pursues: (1) *a sales objective;* the department expects (and is expected by the firm) to achieve an annual sales objective; (2) *a mark-up objective;* the department attempts to realize a specified average mark-up on the goods sold. Organizational decision making occurs in response to problems (or perceived potential problems) with respect to one or the other of these goals. In this sense it is clear that the behavior of the department is problem-oriented and conforms to the general problem-solving decision model suggested earlier.

7.1.1 Sales goal

The general flow chart for decision making with respect to the sales goal is indicated in Fig. 7.1. The organization forms sales "estimates" that are consistent with its sales goal and develops a routine ordering plan for advance orders.[2] These orders are designed to avoid overcommitment,

[2]This statement may not portray the process accurately. During the period we observed it was not possible to determine the interactions between the sales estimates and the goals. They always tended to be consistent with each other but it was difficult to determine the extent to which an implicit goal of "equal or exceed last year's sales" influenced the estimates.

pending feedback on sales. As feedback on sales is provided, results are
checked against the sales objective. If the objective is being achieved,

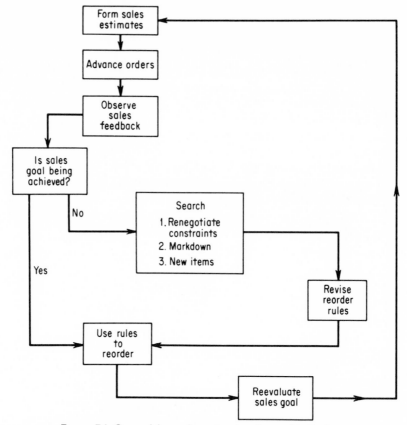

Figure 7.1 General form of reaction to sales goal indicators.

reorders are made according to standard rules. This is the usual route of
decisions, and we will elaborate it further below.

Suppose, however, that the sales goal is not being achieved. Under such
circumstances a series of steps is taken. First, the department attempts to
change its environment by negotiating revised agreements with either its
suppliers or other parts of its own firm or both. Within the firm, it seeks a
change in the promotional budget that will provide greater promotional
resources for the goods sold by the department. Outside the firm, the
department seeks price concessions from manufacturers that will permit a
reduction in retail price. If either of these attempts to relax external
constraints is successful, reorders are made according to appropriately
revised rules.

Second, the department considers a routine mark-down to stimulate sales generally and to make room for new items in the inventory. As we will indicate below, the department ordinarily has a pool of stock available for mark-downs and expects to have to reduce the mark-up in this way on some of the goods sold. It will attempt to stimulate all sales by taking some of these anticipated mark-downs. Once again, if the tactic is successful in stimulating sales, reorders are made according to slightly revised rules.

Third, the department searches for new items that can be sold at relatively low prices (but with standard mark-up). Most commonly such items are found when domestic suppliers are eliminating lines or are in financial trouble. A second major source is in foreign markets.

In general, the department continues to search for solutions to its sales problems until it finds them. If the search procedures are successful, all goes well. In the long run, however, it may find a solution in another way. The feedback on sales not only triggers action, but also leads to the re-evaluation of the sales goal. In the face of persistent failure to achieve the sales goal, the goal adjusts downward. With persistent success it adjusts upward.

7.1.2 Mark-up goal

The flow chart in Figure 7.2 outlines the departmental reaction with respect to the mark-up goal. The reactions are analogous to those shown in Fig. 7.1, but have a somewhat different impact. On the basis of the mark-up goal (and standard industry practice), price lines and planned mark-up are established. Feedback on realized mark-up is received. If it is consistent with the goal, no action is taken and standard decision rules are maintained.

If the mark-up goal is not being achieved, the department searches for ways in which it can raise mark-up. Basically, the search focuses on procedures for altering the product mix of the department by increasing the proportion of high mark-up items sold. For example, the department searches for items that are exclusive, for items that can be obtained from regular suppliers below standard cost, and for items from abroad. Where some of the same search efforts led to price reduction (and maintenance of mark-up) when stimulated by failure on the sales goal, here they lead to maintenance of price and increase in mark-up. At the same time, the organization directs its major promotional efforts toward items on which high mark-ups can be realized. In some instances, the department has a reservoir of solutions to mark-up problems (e.g., pressure selling of high mark-up items). Such solutions are generally reserved for problem solving and are not viewed as appropriate long-run solutions. Finally, as in the case of the sales goal, the mark-up goal adjusts to experience gradually.

A comparison of Figs. 7.1 and 7.2 with Fig. 6.1 will suggest the similarity between this part of the department store decision process and our basic

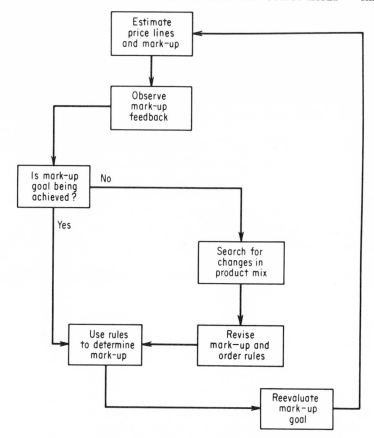

Figure 7.2 General form of reaction to mark-up goal indicators.

concepts. Those parts of the basic decision process that are not represented in the present case study (e.g., negotiation with environment to resolve uncertainty, revision of search rules) seem to us in all probability present but not easily detected in a relatively brief period of observation. Certainly our observations within the organization suggest that the motivations to avoid uncertainty through negotiation and to search where previous search was successful are present.

We think the general processes reflected in Figs. 7.1 and 7.2 correctly represent the decision process in the firm under examination. They do not, however, yield specific, precise predictions. Detailed models of the major price and output decisions need to be developed and compared with results from the organization studied. This task is undertaken in Section 7.2.

7.2 Details of Output Determination

The concept of output is not obviously relevant to a department store. In fact, if our major interest were in retail organizations, we would not describe any decisions as being output decisions. However, we are interested more generally in business firms, and we wish to identify a decision variable in the retail setting that has the same general attributes as the output decision in a production organization. A department store does not produce goods; it buys goods for resale. Consequently, orders and the process of making order decisions comprise the output determination of the firm. As the manufacturing firm adds to inventory by production, the retail firm adds to inventory by ordering.

As we have already suggested, the output decision is essentially a decision based on feedback from sales experience. No explicit calculation of the probable behavior of competitors is made, and although expectations with respect to sales are formed, every effort is made to avoid depending on any kind of long-run forecast. Output decisions are designed to satisfy two major goals. These are (1) to limit mark-downs to an acceptable level and (2) to maintain inventory at a reasonable level.

The firm divides output decisions into two classes — advance (initial) orders and reorders. Each is dependent on a different set of variables and performs a different function. Advance orders allow the firm (and its suppliers) to avoid uncertainty by providing contractual commitments. They also account for the bulk of the total orders. Reorders are only a small part of the total orders, but they provide virtually all the variance in total orders. Insofar as the output decision is viewed primarily as a decision with respect to total output, reorders are much more important than advance orders in fixing the absolute level.

7.2.1 Advance orders

Advance orders represent the base output of the department. The size of the advance order depends on two things: one is the estimated sales, the other a simple estimate of the variance in sales. In a general way, the apparent motivation with respect to advance orders is to set the commitment at such a level that the base output alone will be greater than sales only if extreme estimation errors have been made. Thus, refinements in estimation are not attempted and simple estimating procedures are used, modified somewhat by special organizational needs only remotely related to the issue of accuracy.

The estimation of sales. The store operates on a six-month planning period. The individual department estimates dollar sales expected during the next six months. At the same time, sales are estimated on a monthly basis for each product class over the six-month period. Since the accuracy of the estimate is not especially critical (at least within rather broad limits) for the total output decision, we consider the organizational setting in which the estimate is made in order to understand the decision rules. A low forecast, within limits, carries no penalties. The forecast cannot, however, be so low relative to past history that it is rejected (as being unrealistic) by top management. Limits on the high side are specified by two penalties for making a forecast that is not achieved. First, achievement of forecasts is one of the secondary criteria for judging the performance of the department. Although the department cannot significantly affect the sales goal by underestimation, it can to a limited extent soften criticism (for failure) by anticipating it. Second, an overestimate will result in overallocation of funds. If the department is unable to use the funds, it is subject to criticism. As a result, the sales estimate tends to be biased downward.

The primary data used in estimating sales are the dollar sales (at retail prices) for the corresponding period in the preceding year. Although the data are commonly adjusted slightly for "unique" events, the adjustments are not significant. The following naive rule predicts the estimates with substantial accuracy:[3]

> RULE 1. The estimate for the next six months is equal to the total of the corresponding six months of the previous year minus one-half of the sales achieved during the last month of the previous six-month period.

From the point of view of output decisions, the more critical estimates are those for the individual months. The monthly figures are used directly in determining advance orders for the individual seasons. The estimation procedure for a specific product class is as follows:

> RULE 2. *For the months of February, March, and April.* Use the weekly sales of the seven weeks before Easter of the previous year as the estimate of the seven weeks before Easter of this year. In the same way, extend the sales of last year for the weeks before and after the season to the corresponding weeks of this year.

> RULE 3. *For the months of August and September.* The same basic procedure as in Rule 2 is followed, with the date of the public schools' opening replacing the position of Easter. The opening dates of county and parochial schools also are significant. If these dates are far enough apart, the peak will be reduced, but the estimate for the two months will still represent the total sales of the corresponding two months of the previous year.

> RULE 4. *For the months of May, June, October, November, and December.* Estimated sales for this year equal last year's actual sales.

> RULE 5. *For the months of January and July.* Estimated sales for this year equal one-half of last year's actual sales rounded to the nearest $100.

This set of simple rules provides an estimate of sales that is tightly linked

---

[3]We do not mean to imply that the department consciously uses such a rule. Although the rule was inferred from a study of actual behavior, the head of the department did not describe his estimation rule in these terms.

to the experience of the immediately previous year with a slight downward adjustment (i.e., in Rule 5).

The seasonal advance order fraction. The department distinguishes four seasons — Easter, Summer, Fall, and Holiday. The seasons, in fact, do not account exhaustively for all months, but they account for most of the total sales. Estimates of sales are established on the basis of the monthly estimates. These estimates do not necessarily include all months in the season. The following estimation rules are used:

> *Easter:* Cumulate sales for the seven weeks before Easter
> *Summer:* Cumulate sales for April, May, June, and one-half of July
> *Fall:* Cumulate sales for one-half of July, August, and September
> *Holiday:* Cumulate sales for October, November, and December

These cumulations give a seasonal sales estimate for use in establishing advance orders. Once such an estimate is made, some fraction of the estimated sales is ordered.

Advance orders generally offer some concrete advantages to the department. Greater selection is possible (some goods may not be available later), and some side payments may be offered by the producer (e.g., credit terms, extra services). The department exploits these advantages by ordering a substantial fraction of its anticipated sales in advance, but an attempt is made to limit the advance order fraction to an output that would be sold even under an extreme downward shift in demand.

The size of the advance order fraction is the result of learning on the part of the organization and reflects the differences among the seasons in sales variability and the degree of seasonal specialization of the items. The greater the susceptibility of seasonal sales to exogenous variables (e.g., weather), the lower the fraction. The more specialized the merchandise sold during a season (i.e., the greater the difficulty of carrying it over to another season), the lower the fraction. At the time we observed the organization, the fraction (estimated from interviews and analysis of data) and the timing of advance orders for each of the seasons were as follows:

Seasons	% of estimated sales placed in advance orders	Time order made
Easter	50	Jan. 15–20
Summer	60	March 10–15
Fall	75	May 20–25
Holiday	65	Sept. 20–25

In general we expect this simple model to predict quite well, diverging only when the department makes *ad hoc* adjustments. Our observations lead us to believe this will not happen frequently.

7.2.2 Reorders

For all practical purposes, reorders control the total output of the department. As the word implies, a reorder is an order for merchandise made on the basis of feedback from inventory and sales. Because of lead-time problems, much of the feedback is based on early season sales information. Thus, the timing of a reorder depends on the length of time to the peak sales period as compared with the manufacturing lead-time required.

Reorder rules. Reorders are based on a re-estimate of probable sales. Data on current sales are used in a simple way to adjust "normal" sales. The reorder program specifies reorders for a given type of product class as a result of a simple algebraic adjustment.

Let T = the total period of the season

τ = the period of the season covered by the analysis

$S_{i\tau}$ = this year's sales of product class i over τ

$S'_{i\tau}$ = last year's sales of product class i over τ

$S'_{i(T-\tau)}$ = last year's sales of product class i over $T - \tau$

I_i = available stock of i at time of analysis including stock ordered

M_i = minimum amount of stock of i desired at all times

$O_{i(T-\tau)}$ = reorder estimate

Then,

$$O_{i(T-\tau)} = \left[\frac{S_{i\tau}}{S'_{i\tau}} \cdot S'_{i(T-\tau)} + M_i \right] - I_i$$

If $O_{i(T-\tau)} \leq 0$ no reorders will be made. In addition, orders already placed may be canceled, prices may be lowered, or other measures taken to reduce the presumed overstocking. Such an analysis would be made for each product class. The figure that results is tentative, subject to minor modifications in the light of anticipated special events.

7.2.3 Open-to-buy constraint

The firm constrains the enthusiasms of its departments by maintaining a number of controls on output decisions. One of the more conspicuous controls is the "open-to-buy." The open-to-buy is, in effect, the capital made available to each department for purchases. The open-to-buy for any month is calculated from the following equation:

$$B_\tau = (I^*_{\tau+1} - I_\tau) + S^*_\tau$$

where B_τ = open-to-buy for month τ

$I^*_{\tau+1}$ = expected inventory (based on seasonal plans) for beginning of month $(\tau + 1)$

I_τ = actual inventory at beginning of month τ

S^*_τ = expected sales

The department starts each month with this calculated amount (B_r) minus any advance orders that have already been charged against the month. Any surplus or deficit from the preceding month will increase or decrease the current account, as will cancellation of back orders or stock price changes.

Although the open-to-buy is a constraint in output determination, it can be violated. As long as the preceding rules are followed and the environment stays more or less stable, the open-to-buy will rarely be exceeded. From this point of view, the open-to-buy is simply a long-run control device enforcing the standard reorder procedure and altering higher levels in the organization to significant deviations from such procedure. However, the constraint is flexible. It is possible for a department to have a negative open-to-buy (up to a limit of approximately average monthly sales). Negative values for the open-to-buy are tolerated when they can be justified in terms of special reasons for optimistic sales expectations.

The open-to-buy, thus, is less a constraint than a signal — to both higher management and the department — indicating a possible need for some sort of remedial action.

7.3 Details of Price Determination

The firm recognizes three different pricing situations: *normal, sales,* and *mark-down* pricing. The first two situations occur at regularly planned times. The third is a contingent situation, produced by failure or anticipated failure with respect to organizational goals. In each pricing situation the basic procedure is the same, the application of a mark-up to a cost to determine an appropriate price (subject to some rounding to provide convenient prices).

The bulk of sales occur at prices set by either normal or sales pricing procedures. Mark-down pricing is one of the main strategies considered when search is stimulated. During the time period we observed, the demand was strong enough to permit fairly consistent achievement of the department's pricing goal — an average realized mark-up in the neighborhood of 40 per cent. As a result, we did not observe actual situations in which the pressure to reduce prices stemming from inventory feedback conflicted with the pressure to maintain or raise mark-up stemming from over-all mark-up feedback.

7.3.1 Normal pricing

Normal pricing is used when new output is accepted by the department for sale. As we have already observed, the problem of pricing is simplified considerably by the practice of price lining. In effect, the retail price is determined first and then output that can be priced (with the appropriate mark-up) at that price is obtained. Since manufacturers are aware of the standard price lines, their products are also standardized at appropriate costs.

For each product group in the firm there is a normal mark-up. Like the seasonal advance order fraction, mark-up is probably subject to long-run learning. For example, it varies in a general way from product group to product group according to the apparent risks involved, the costs of promotion or handling, the extent of competition, and the price elasticity. However, in any short run the normal mark-up is remarkably stable. The statement is frequently made in the industry that mark-ups have remained the same for the last 40 or 50 years.

Standard items. In the department under study, normal mark-up is 40 per cent. By industry practice, standard costs (wholesale prices) ordinarily end in $.75. By firm policy, standard prices (retail prices) ordinarily end in $.95. Thus, all but two of the price levels are in accord with the following rule:

> Divide each cost by 0.6 (1 − mark-up) and move the result to the nearest $.95.

The results of this rule and the effective mark-ups are shown in Table 7.1.

Table 7.1. Standard prices

Standard costs ($)	Standard price ($)	Effective mark-up (%)
3.00	5.00	40.0
3.75	5.95	37.0
4.75	7.95	40.2
5.50	8.95	38.5
6.75	10.95	38.3
7.75	12.95	40.1
8.75	14.95	41.5
10.75	17.95	40.0
11.75	19.95	41.0
13.75	22.95	40.0
14.75	25.00	41.0
18.75	29.95	37.4

Exclusive items. In some cases, the department obtains items that are not made available to competition. For such products and especially where quality is difficult to measure, the prices are set higher than the standard. The pricing rule is as follows:

> When merchandise is received on an exclusive basis, calculate the standard price from the cost, then use the next highest price on the standard schedule.

Import items. Presumably because they are frequently exclusive items, because of somewhat greater risks associated with foreign suppliers, and because of the generally lower costs of items of foreign manufacture for equal quality, the department increases the mark-up for imported items. For the product class studied the standard accepted mark-up is 50 per cent greater than normal mark-up (which gives a target mark-up of 60 per cent). This leads to the following rule for pricing imports:

> Divide the cost by 0.4 (i.e., 1 − mark-up) and move the result to the nearest standard price. If this necessitates a change of more than $.50, create a new price at the nearest appropriate ending (that is, $.95 or $.00).

7.3.2 Regular sale pricing

We can distinguish two situations in which normal pricing is not used; one is during the regular sales held by the firm a few times during the year, the other when the department concludes that a mark-down is needed to stimulate purchases or to reduce inventory levels. In this section we consider the first case. As in the case of normal pricing, sales pricing depends on a series of relatively simple rules. In almost all cases sales pricing is a direct function of either the normal price (i.e., there is a standard sales reduction in price) or the cost (i.e., there is a sales mark-up rule). Both the figures on reduction and the sales mark-up are conventional, subject perhaps to long-run learning but invariant during our observations. The general pricing rules for sales operate within a series of constraints that serve to enforce minor changes either to ensure consistency within the pricing (e.g., maintain price differentials between items, maintain price consistency across departments), or to provide attractive price endings (e.g., do not use standard price endings, if feasible use an "alliterative" price).

General constraints. The department prices for sales within a set of five policy constraints. These constraints have not changed in recent years and are viewed by the organization as basic firm policy. They are subject to review rarely.

1. If normal price falls at one of the following lines, the corresponding sale price will be used:

Normal price ($)	Sale price ($)
1.00	0.85
1.95	1.65
2.50	2.10
2.95	2.45
3.50	2.90
3.95	3.30
4.95	3.90
5.00	3.90

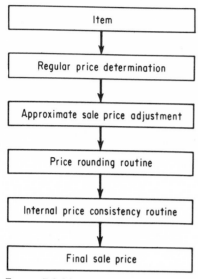

Figure 7.3 Major subroutines of sale pricing decision.

2. For all other merchandise, there must be a reduction of *at least* 15 per cent on items retailing regularly for $3.00 or less and *at least* 16⅔ per cent on higher-priced items.

3. All sales prices must end with 0 or 5.

4. No sale retails are allowed to fall on price lines normal for the product group concerned.

5. Whenever there is a choice between an ending of 0.85 and 0.90, the latter ending will prevail.

Departmental decision rules. Subject to the general policy constraints, the department is allowed a relatively free hand. Since the policy constraints do not uniquely define sales pricing, it is necessary to determine the departmental decision rules. These rules are indicated in detail in the flow charts in Figs. 7.3 and 7.4.

7.3.3 Mark-down pricing

In our earlier discussions of organizational decision making, we suggested that a general model of pricing and output determination must distinguish between the ordinary procedures (that account for most of the decisions made) and the special search procedures that are triggered by special circumstances. We have already seen how such procedures enter into the determination of output in the present case. We turn now to search and "emergency" behavior on the price side. Price is the major adaptive device open to the department in its efforts to meet its mark-up goal, maintain sales, maintain inventory control, and in general meet the demands of other parts of the organization. We have already indicated how an increase in mark-up (e.g., on imports and special items) is used by the department. We turn now to mark-downs.

The department has two decisions to make on mark-downs: when, and how much? In a general sense, the answer to the first question — the question of timing — is simple. The organization reduces price when feedback indicates an unsatisfactory sales or inventory position. The indicators include the inventory records, sales records, physical inventory, reports on competitive prices, and the open-to-buy report. Mark-downs because of product properties (e.g., defects) are of secondary importance. With respect to the amount of mark-down, the organization has a set of standard rules.

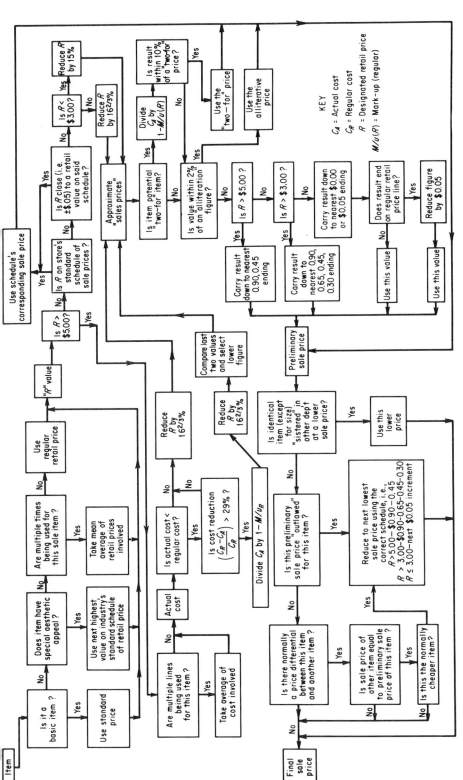

Figure 7.4 Flow chart for sale pricing decision.

These have developed over time in such a way that their rationale can only be inferred in most cases, but a general characteristic of the rules is the avoidance of pricing below cost except as a last resort.

Timing of mark-downs. Occasions for mark-downs are primarily determined by feedback on sales performance. There are three general overstock situations that account for the majority of the mark-downs:

1. *Normal remnants.* These are the odd sizes, less popular colors, and less favored styles remaining from the total assortment of an item that sold satisfactorily during the season.

2. *Overstocked merchandise.* This category includes items that have experienced a satisfactory sales rate but about which the buyer was overly optimistic in his orders. As a result, the season ends with a significant inventory that is well balanced and includes many acceptable items.

3. *Unaccepted merchandise.* This category represents merchandise that has had unsatisfactory sales. The sales personnel try to determine during the season whether the lack of acceptance is due to overpricing or to poor style, color, and so forth. The distinction is usually made by determining whether the item has been ignored. If it has, the latter causes are usually inferred. If the item gets attention but low sales, the inference is that the price is wrong.

In addition, there are a number of quantitatively less important reasons for considering mark-downs. For example, the firm will meet competition on price (if a check indicates the competitor's price is not a mistake). If a customer seeks an adjustment because of defects in the merchandise, a mark-down will be taken. If special sale merchandise is depleted during a sale, regular merchandise will be reduced in price to fill the demand. If wholesale cost is reduced during the season, price will be reduced correspondingly. If nonreturnable merchandise is substandard on arrival, it will be reduced.

Most of the merchandise that becomes excess (especially for the reasons outlined above) will be mentally transferred to an "availability pool." When a specific opportunity arises or when certain conditions develop that necessitate a mark-down, items are drawn out of this pool and marked down for the occasion involved. Store-wide clearances are scheduled by the merchandise manager on nonrecurring dates throughout the year (except during the pre-Fourth-of-July period and the after-Christmas period) to provide all departments with an opportunity to clear out their excess stocks.

However, there may be times during the year when the department cannot wait for the next scheduled clearance for reasons of limited space or limited funds. If, for example, the department is expecting a shipment of new merchandise at a time when display and storage facilities are inadequate to accommodate the new shipment, it is necessary to reduce inventory by means of mark-downs.

The department may take mark-downs when its open-to-buy is unsatisfactory. (Whenever the open-to-buy falls to the $-\$15,000$ level, it would be judged to be in unsatisfactory condition.) The department will not necessarily take mark-downs as the principal means of rectifying this state of affairs *per se* but will attempt instead to cancel merchandise on order or to charge back merchandise already received. These steps will not be taken if the department expects relief from an increased sales rate within the immediate future or if the present average mark-up is low. However, if the department has an urgent need to purchase additional merchandise and the open-to-buy at the time is in the red to the extent that the division merchandise manager will not approve any additional orders, the department will then take mark-downs for the amount necessary to permit the desired purchase to take place.

Amount of mark-down. The complete model for predicting actual mark-down prices is given in Fig. 7.5. The general rule for first mark-downs is to reduce the retail price by $\frac{1}{3}$ and carry the result down to the nearest mark-down ending (i.e., to the nearest $\$.85$). There are some exceptions. Where the ending constraint forces too great a deviation from the $\frac{1}{3}$ rule (e.g., where the regular price is $\$5.00$ or less), *ad hoc* procedures are occasionally adopted. On higher-priced items, a 40 per cent markdown is taken. On a few items manufacturers maintain price control. Occasionally, items represent a closeout of a manufacturer's line and a greater mark-down is taken.

Although the department did not seem to follow any specific explicit rule with second or greater mark-downs, the higher the first mark-down value the greater tended to be the reduction to the succeeding mark-down price. In fact, this relationship seemed to follow the top half of the parabolic curve

$$Y^2 = 5(X - 2)$$

where Y = succeeding mark-down price
  X = initial mark-down price
Accordingly, the following empirically derived rule seems to work well with second or higher mark-downs:

> Insert the value of the initial mark-down price in the parabolic formula and carry the result *down* to the nearest $\$.85$ ($\$.90$).

As a description of process, this rule is obviously deficient. However, in view of the limited number of cases involved and the inability of the department to articulate the rules, we have used this rough surrogate.

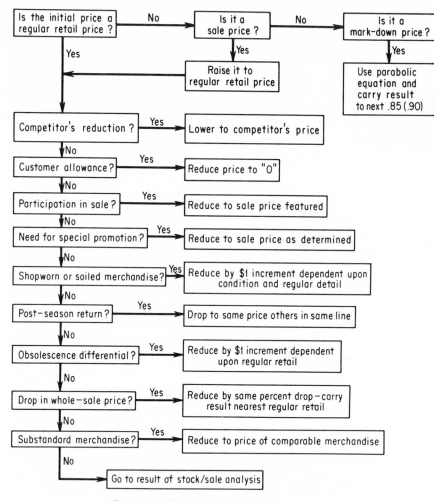

Figure 7.5 Flow chart for mark-down routine.

7.4 Tests of the Detailed Models

We have tried to develop a model that would yield testable predictions, but there are two major limits on such a goal. First, we have not been completely successful in defining a model that will make precise predictions in every decision area. Second, where we have been successful in developing a model, we are constrained by the availability of data. The value of data for the purpose of testing models has not always been controlling in data-retention decisions by the firm. Despite these limits, we have been able to develop models for the major price and output decisions and to subject all but one of the major components of those models to some empirical test.

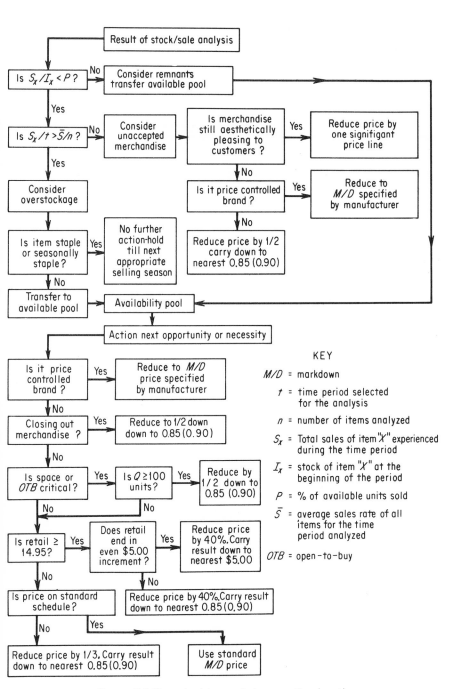

Figure 7.5 Flow chart for mark-down routine (cont.).

7.4.1 Output determination

The output determination model consists of three segments — sales estimate, advance orders, and reorders. In each of the tests described below, the data used are new and are not the data with which the model was developed.

Sales estimation. The sales estimation model is composed of the rule for estimating sales for the six-month period and the rules for the estimation of the sales of individual months. The data available were for a two-year period so that the test is far from conclusive. However, there is no reason to believe that the model would not be valid for a larger sample of data. The first part of the model, the estimation of total sales for a six-month period, predicts the total within 5 per cent in each of the four test instances. With the set of monthly rules, we can predict about 95 per cent of the monthly sales estimates within 5 per cent. There is no question that the predictive power could be increased still further by additional refinement of the rules. However, at this point it does not seem desirable to expend resources in that direction.

Advance orders. This segment of the model and the sales estimation segment are related as we have shown previously. Therefore, discrepancies between predicted and actual data are difficult to allocate precisely between the two segments although we have some clues from the above testing. Unfortunately, the firm does not keep its records of advance orders any length of time so no extensive test of the model was possible. We were able to accumulate only four instances in which the predictions of the model could be compared with the actual figures.

Season	Predicted advance orders	Actual advance orders
1	18,050	16,453
2	26,550	24,278
3	36,200	35,922
4	43,000	35,648

Reorders. This segment is one that it is most important to test. The fact is, however, that the data on reorders are not kept in a systematic fashion, and we have not been able to make any kind of test.

7.4.2 Price determination

Much more adequate data are available for the pricing models. In each case the model was tested and performed adequately.

Mark-up. In order to test the ability of the model to predict the price decisions that will be made by the buyer on new merchandise, an unrestricted random sample of 197 invoices was drawn. The cost data and classification of the item were given as inputs to the computer model. The output was in the form of a predicted price. Since the sample consisted of items that had already been priced, it was possible to make a comparison of the predicted price with the actual price.

The definition of a correct prediction was made as stringent as possible. Unless the predicted price matched the actual price to the exact penny, the prediction was classified as incorrect. The results of the test were encouraging; of the 197 predicted prices, 188 were correct and 9 were incorrect. Thus 95 per cent of the predictions were correct. An investigation of the incorrect predictions showed that with minor modifications the model could be made to handle the deviant cases. However, at this point it was felt that the predictive power was good enough so that a further expenditure of resources in this direction was not justified.

Sale pricing. In order to test the model, a random sample of 58 sales items was selected from the available records. For each item the appropriate information as determined by the model was used as an input to the computer. The output was in the form of a price that was a prediction of the price that would be set by the buyer. Again we used the criterion that to be correct the predicted price must match the actual price to the penny. Out of the 58 predictions made by the model, 56 (or 96 per cent) were correct.

Mark-downs. In testing this part of the model the basic data were taken from "mark-down slips," the primary document of this firm. Naturally such slips do not show the information that would enable us to categorize the items for use in the model. It was necessary, therefore, to use direct methods such as the interrogation of the buyer and sales personnel to get the information necessary to classify the items so that the model could be tested. All of the data used were from the previous six-month period. It would be possible on a current basis to get the information that would enable the model to make the classifications itself as part of the pricing process.

The test for a correct prediction was as before — correspondence to the penny of the predicted and the actual price. A total sample of 159 items was selected and predictions made of the mark-down price for each item. Of the 159 prices predicted, 140 were correct predictions by our criterion and 19 were wrong. This gives a record of 88 per cent correct — the poorest of the three models. Though this model does not do as well as the other two, its record is, in our view, adequate.

7.5 Summary

The tests that have been made of the model tend to support it. Clearly some of the tests are inadequate because of the paucity of the data. Also, we have not attempted to build alternative models and compare predictive ability. Undoubtedly, alternative models can be built and can be made to predict well. However, we have been interested in building a model that embodies the actual decision-making process. Our reasons for this position have been amplified elsewhere in this book. We do not believe a radically different model can be built that captures the actual decision process and predicts as well. Because our objective is to understand the actual process, we have not attempted to minimize the number of assumptions, the number of variables, or the number of inputs to the model.

The department store model is a specific application of the general model described in this book. The evidence supports the specific model and thereby presents corroborative evidence for the general model. We would not argue that the evidence is conclusive. It is not. It is, however, consistent with the model. The model lends itself to further elaboration and testing — and the world is full of firms for further empirical study.

8

A GENERAL MODEL OF

PRICE AND OUTPUT

DETERMINATION[1]

In previous chapters we have presented a verbal description of a behavioral theory of the firm as well as applications of parts of the theory to some specific problems and to some specific organizations. In this chapter, we report two things. First, we describe a general behavioral model of price and output determination in an oligopoly. The model is in the form of a computer program and includes representations of the major phenomena specified in the verbal theory. These representations are in explicit quantitative form and generate explicit price and output decisions. Second, we examine some properties of the model. A multiple regression procedure is used to identify the impact of samples of parameter values on selected output of the model. The chapter is a report on research in process rather than completed, and the analysis is preliminary to further work.

[1]The model presented in this chapter has been developed in collaboration with K. J. Cohen and P. O. Soelberg.

8.1 A General Model

In this section we describe the decision processes assumed in the model at three different levels of detail. Each description is consistent with the others; they become progressively better defined.

8.1.1 A gross description of the model

We assume an n-firm oligopolistic market. Each of the firms is similar in the sense that each makes the same decisions in generally the same way. Variations among the firms are achieved by varying parameters. Thus, in order to describe the model, we specify the internal decision process.

Decisions, goals, and departmentalization. Each of the firms makes three basic decisions each time period:

1. The price to be charged for the firm's product is determined. Price is viewed as a decision variable, not simply the direct result of market mechanisms.

2. The output to be produced during the next time period is set. Each firm decides how much of the product will be produced over a relatively brief future time period.

3. A general sales and marketing strategy is chosen. Each firm makes a decision on the amount of sales effort it will exert and the dollar expenditures it will make on sales promotion.

Associated with each of these decisions is a set of relevant goals. Each decision is related (at least in the first instance) with its own set of goals. Decisions within one decision area are made primarily with respect to the immediately relevant set of goals. The major interconnections among goals come through feedback, through expanded search where local goals cannot be achieved, and through certain checks on the feasibility of proposed action.

Thus, we have three sets of goals:

1. *A profit goal.* The profit goal is an aspiration level with respect to profits. It is connected most directly with the pricing decision.

2. *A set of inventory and production goals.* The inventory goal is in the form of minimum and maximum limits on inventory size relative to sales. The production goal is a production smoothing objective in the form of constraints on variation in output level. The inventory and production goals are related immediately to the output decision.

3. *A set of sales goals.* The firm has aspiration levels for market share and for sales. The sales goals primarily affect sales strategy. Through interconnections, they also have an important effect on price.

Because the decision process is segmented into three sets of decisions each having its own set of goals, it is convenient to think of each firm as being departmentalized into three subdivisions. These subdivisions — pricing, production, and sales — are relatively independent of each other. Each makes decisions independently, subject to cross-departmental pressures.

Feedback, adaptation, and search. Each firm makes its decisions on the basis of feedback from past results. The firms adjust goals and procedures on the basis of such feedback. Each of the firms uses search to solve problems when problems exist and avoids search when problems do not exist In fact, at the most general level the decision process in each department of each firm can be described as follows:

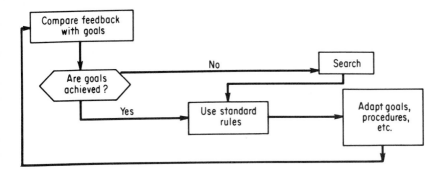

Obviously, at this level the model is an elaboration of the basic concepts presented in previous chapters.

8.1.2 A less gross description of the model

To present the model in more detail, we will describe in this section the decision process followed by each firm in each of the decision areas. In the next major section we will present the details of the actual program.

The output decision. In essence, the firm sets production in response to sales. In the steady state, production in one time period is precisely equal to sales of the preceding time period. However, such a steady state is rather infrequently attained and, when attained, is subject to shocks that make it (except under rare circumstances) transitory. More commonly, the organization seeks to establish a production level that is consistent with a set of changing inventory and production-smoothing goals. The process is indicated in Fig. 8.1.

With respect to inventory, there are two critical values:

1. *The excess limit.* This limit is a size of inventory that leads to complaints from the rest of the organization about the excessive cost of main-

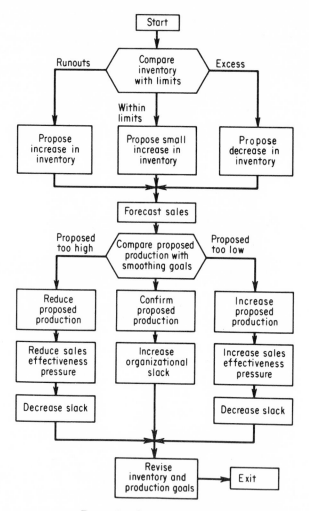

Figure 8.1 Output decision.

taining inventory. The excess limit is a lagged function of sales (becoming larger as sales increase).

2. *The runout limit.* This limit is a size of inventory that leads to complaints from the rest of the organization about the loss of sales and sales position due to stockouts. It is a lagged function of sales.

These two limits define three possible conditions. So long as the inventory lies between the limits, the proposed inventory level will show a small growth of inventory reflecting the aspirations of the inventory-production division. If the inventory exceeds the excess limit, proposed inventory will be reduced from the previous inventory level. If the inventory is below the runout limit, proposed inventory will be increased.

Proposed production is determined by proposed inventory and a sales forecast, subject to demands for production smoothing. The sales forecast is a simple lagged function of sales. Though described as a forecast, it is a simple summary of past sales data. Proposed production then becomes the forecasted sales plus the difference between proposed inventory and actual inventory. The production-smoothing goal is represented by an upper and lower production limit. If proposed production is within the limits, it is produced. If proposed production is outside the limits, production is set at the limit nearer the proposed level. Normally, the upper production limit is the maximum production in the last π periods (where π is a parameter of the model). Similarly, the lower production limit is the minimum production in the last π periods. However, if production is actually set at a limit, the limit is changed in the direction of the proposed production. Thus, so long as proposed production is within the limits, the limits tend to contract. When proposed production is outside the limits, the limits tend to expand. When a firm has a history of variable production, it is able to allow future variability. Where it has a history of smooth production, it will tolerate rather little variability.

These rules define the output decision. In addition, the inventory-production part of the model exerts some pressures on other parts of the system. First, when goals are met, organizational slack is increased. Second, when goals are not met, pressure is put on the sales division to adjust sales to inventory-production needs — that is, to smooth sales by reducing them when proposed production is too high, and by increasing them when proposed production is too low.

The price decision. Price is determined by adjusting present price in the face of feedback on goals, costs, and competitors' behavior. It is primarily responsive to a comparison between actual profits achieved and the profit goal. It is also sensitive to pressure from sales for price reduction. The process is indicated in Fig. 8.2.

The profit goal exhibits learning at two levels. First, it adapts to actual profits achieved. The goal is a lagged function of profits. Second, the parameters involved in the function change on the basis of experience. We assume two different functions for changing the goal on the basis of experience — one operates when profits achieved exceed the goal, the other when profits are less than the goal. Whenever the goal is achieved without extra search, the firm learns to attend more to recently experienced success. When the goal is achieved after initial failure triggers search activity, the firm learns to attend less to recently experienced failure. When the goal is not achieved even after extended search, the firm learns to attend more to recently experienced failure.

In setting price, the firm first checks three environmental characteristics — costs of manufacture, the effects of past price changes, and competitors' long-run price behavior. First, if exogenous costs have increased, proposed

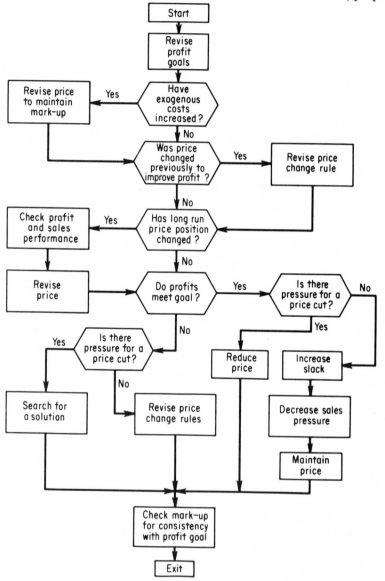

Figure 8.2 Price decision.

price is increased proportionately to the change in costs. Second, if profit performance has improved after a prior price change (either up or down) that was induced by a prior profit failure, the price change rule is altered to produce future action more in the direction of the action taken. If the prior action has been followed by a poorer performance, the rule is shifted in the other direction. Thus, "successful" price cuts will stimulate more vigorous price cuts in comparable circumstances; "unsuccessful" price cuts will stimulate less vigorous cuts and possible price raises. Similarly, successful and unsuccessful price raises lead to revision in the rule. Third, the firm also checks the long-run price behavior of competition, specifically of the lowest-priced major competitor. If competition has maintained the same relative price as the firm has, nothing is done. If competition has lowered price proportionately more than the firm, performance on market share and sales goals is checked. If market share is below goal, price is cut to restore the relative price position. If market share is above goal but sales are below, price is cut but only part of the previous relative price position is restored. If both market share and sales goals are being met, price is not changed. If competition has raised price relative to the firm, market share and profit performance are checked. If market share goals are being met, the price raise is followed. If market share goals are not being met and profit goals are being met, nothing is done. If neither goal is being met, price is raised but not as much as the competition's increase.

After these checks are made, the firm considers price from the point of view of profit and sales goals. If profit goals are being met and there is no pressure for price reduction from sales, only internal slack changes. Price is unchanged; organizational slack is increased; sales effectiveness pressure is decreased. If profit goals are not being met and there is no pressure from sales for price reduction, the firm considers its past experience in this situation and raises, cuts, or maintains price according to what has been successful in the past.

Under certain circumstances, however, there will be pressure from the sales division for price reduction. There are two kinds of pressure: the first simply indicates trouble on sales goals; the second (which we might call "emergency" pressure) indicates not only trouble but also a recent adverse change in short-run competitive price position. The feedback on price competition is faster than the feedback routinely checked above. If the firm has achieved its profit goals and the standard pressure is applied, it will cut price somewhat. If emergency pressure is applied, the firm will cut price to restore the previous relative price position. If the firm is not achieving its profit goals, the pressure from the sales division is potentially in conflict with the profit goals. Consequently, there is more resistance to price reduction. If the pressure is of the emergency variety, the firm acts to restore the price position; but it also initiates a search program for other alternatives to price cutting. If the pressure is standard, no price action is taken but the search program is triggered.

The search program consists in the following procedures. They are pursued sequentially (one each time period) until the need for search is removed. (1) Organizational slack is reduced. (2) Inventory excess limit is reduced. (3) Pressure is placed on sales for improved performance. (4) Expenditure for sales promotion is increased. (5) Expenditure for sales promotion is decreased. (6) If all of the other procedures fail, the profit goal is reduced. The order of the search changes in response to experience. If a search procedure is successful (that is, the firm does not search on the next cycle), that procedure goes to the top of the search order list. Whenever a search procedure is unsuccessful, it goes to the bottom of the list. The only exception is the profit goal reduction. Regardless of other changes, it is always the last procedure.

After this, the tentative price is checked against costs to see whether the mark-up is consistent with the profit goal. If it is not, the firm either raises price or cuts costs, depending on past experience.

The sales decision. Since the model is designed to be primarily a model of price and output determination, we have not attempted to build a detailed market strategy decision into it. However, two components of such a decision are made. One decision variable is "sales effectiveness pressure," which is an index of effectiveness in the sales strategy. It is an aggregate surrogate for decisions that influence sales efficiency. Thus, it can be viewed conveniently as the converse of organizational slack in the sales area. The second decision variable is the percentage of sales revenue used for sales promotion. Though this variable is obviously more operational than the sales effectiveness pressure, it is still an aggregate statistic. Both decision variables directly affect sales; sales promotion expenditures also are a component of costs.

There are three sales goals: (1) An aspiration level with respect to the level of sales; the organization compares its sales level with a sales goal that is a function of recent experience. (2) An aspiration level with respect to market share; the organization compares its market share with a market share goal that is also a function of recent experience. (3) A competitive price goal; the organization does not want its short-run price position relative to competitors to change adversely (i.e., to a higher relative price).

The short-run competitive price goal represents the objectives of the sales force. When relative price position changes adversely, the sales force complains and requests remedial action. Such a feedback is fast. In our model, it is received each time period. Feedback information on the sales level and the market share is somewhat slower. We assume that sales and market share are computed every λ_{SAT} and λ_{MST} periods respectively.

Figure 8.3 shows the sales decision process. The firm checks its sales goals. If the latest report on sales and market share indicates goals have been achieved, the sales department simply continues present policies with an increase in sales slack (i.e., a decrease in "sales effectiveness pressure") and an increase in general organizational slack. If the market share goal is not being met but the sales goal is, sales effectiveness pressure is increased.

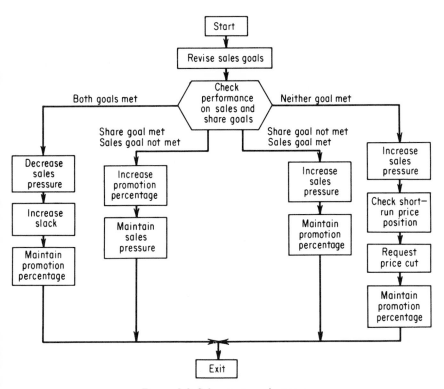

Figure 8.3 Sales strategy decision.

If the market share goal is being met but the sales goal is not, the percentage of sales revenue expended on sales promotion is increased.

If neither market share nor sales goals are achieved, sales effectiveness pressure is increased and the sales department requests remedial price action by the pricing department. If the short-run relative price position has changed adversely, it is an emergency request. If the relative price position has not changed adversely, the request is a standard one (see the pricing program for the difference in reaction to the two types of requests).

Market share and sales goals change at two levels in approximately the same way that profit goals change. Each goal is a weighted average of the previous goal and the immediate past experience. Whenever the goal is achieved, the weights attached to recently experienced success are increased and the weights attached to recently experienced failure are decreased. Whenever a goal is not achieved, the weights attached to re-

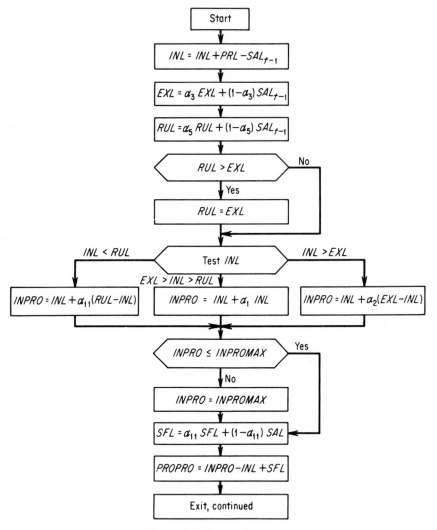

Figure 8.4 Output decision.

cently experienced failure are increased while the weights attached to recently experienced success are decreased.

8.1.3 A least gross description of the model

In this section we indicate the detailed flow charts for the model and discuss the parameters and functional forms introduced. Since such a description is necessarily rather tedious, the reader who wishes to do so may (without excess cost) omit this section.

Detail of the output decision. The detailed flow chart for the output decision is shown in Fig. 8.4. It involves first calculating proposed produc-

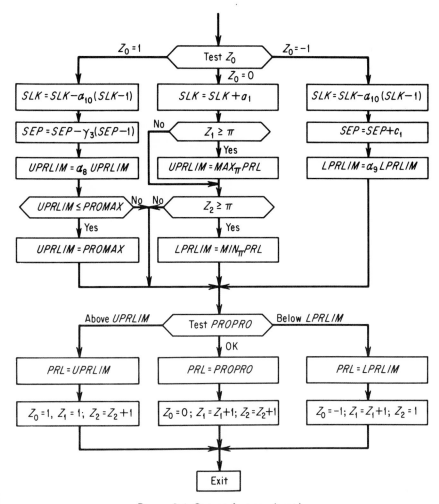

Figure 8.4 Output decision (cont.)

tion $(PROPRO)$ and then checking that proposed production against production-smoothing goals.

In order to determine proposed production, the inventory-production department determines a proposed inventory level $(INPRO)$. First, inventory level (INL) is determined by a housekeeping operation — production is added and sales subtracted from the old inventory level to obtain the new one. Second, the program determines the external constraints on the inventory, the excess limit (EXL) and the runout limit (RUL) by taking a weighted average of the old limits and sales. Thus,

$$INL \leftarrow INL + PRL - SAL$$
$$EXL \leftarrow \alpha_3 \, EXL + (1 - \alpha_3) \, SAL$$
$$RUL \leftarrow \alpha_5 \, RUL + (1 - \alpha_5) \, SAL$$

Third, the inventory level is compared with the limits. If inventory is within the limits, the proposed inventory is simply the old proposed inventory times a growth parameter (α_1). If inventory is below the runout limit, the proposed inventory increases. The increase is proportional to the differences between the inventory and the limit. Similarly, if the inventory is above the excess limit, proposed inventory represents a decrease that is proportional to the difference between the inventory and the limit. The parameters α_2 and α_4 control the magnitude of change with respect to the excess limit and the runout limit respectively.

The firm then forms a sales forecast (SFL) by taking a weighted average of the forecast in the previous period and the sales in the previous period.

$$SFL_t \leftarrow \alpha_{11}\, SFL_{t-1} + (1 - \alpha_{11})\, SAL_{t-1}$$

Given the proposed inventory level, the existing inventory level, and the forecast of sales, proposed production is simply that amount of production that will result in the proposed inventory level if the forecast of sales is accurate.

$$PROPRO_t \leftarrow INPRO_t - INL_t + SFL_t$$

To determine actual output, we compare the proposed production with the production-smoothing goals. These goals are summarized in the form of an upper production limit ($UPRLIM$) and a lower production limit ($LPRLIM$). The program first checks past performance with respect to the upper and lower production limits. If proposed production was between these limits last time, slack (SLK) is increased by a_1. If production has been below the upper limit for π or more times, the upper limit is set equal to the maximum production of the last π periods. If proposed production last time was above the upper limit, we decrease slack, decrease sales effectiveness pressure (SEP), and increase the upper production limit. (SLK and SEP are both indices whose lower bound is 1.)

$$SLK \leftarrow SLK - \alpha_{10}\,(SLK - 1)$$
$$SEP \leftarrow SEP - \gamma_3\,(SEP - 1)$$
$$UPRLIM \leftarrow \alpha_8\, UPRLIM$$

If production has not fallen below the lower limit for π periods, the lower production limit is set equal to the minimum production for π periods. If proposed production was below the lower limit last time, slack is decreased as above, sales effectiveness pressure is increased, and the lower production limit is decreased:

$$SEP \leftarrow SEP + c_1$$
$$LPRLIM \leftarrow \alpha_9\, LPRLIM$$

Having thus determined the production-smoothing goals, we set actual output at the proposed production if this lies between the upper and lower limits. If it violates one of these limits, output is set at the value of the limit.

Detail of the pricing decision. The pricing decision is indicated in Fig. 8.5. The firm bases its decisions on three considerations: (1) costs, (2) performance on profit and sales goals, and (3) competitors' pricing behavior. In a general way, price is maintained unless feedback from one of the three indicates a need for reconsideration of price.

First, every λ_{PFT} periods the firm revises its profit goal and the values of the weights in the profit goal functions. Every period the firm computes its total costs (COL) as a function of exogenous costs (EXC), slack, sales promotion percentage (SPP), and inventory costs $(INCR \cdot INL/SAL)$. It then computes a one-period profit level as a function of sales (SAL), price (PCL), and costs.

$$COL \leftarrow EXC \cdot SLK \cdot STC + INCR \frac{INL}{SAL} + SPP$$

$$PFL \leftarrow (SAL \cdot PCL) - COL$$

Profit total (PFT) is a λ period sum of profit level. There are two adjustment functions for the profit goal. If the profit goal (PFG) is achieved, the new profit goal becomes a weighted average of the goal and the profit total achieved.

$$PFG \leftarrow (1 - \beta_1) PFG + \beta_1 PFT$$

Similarly, if the goal is not achieved,

$$PFG \leftarrow (1 - \beta_2) PFG + \beta_2 PFT$$

Goal adjustment is subject to the constraint that $PFG \geq 0$. If the goal is achieved, β_1 is increased. This reflects a tendency for the firm to increase attention to its successful performance with each such performance. Similarly, if the goal is not achieved, β_1 is decreased. The firm learns (through failure) to reduce its attention to recent successes.

$$\text{If } PFT \geq PFG: \quad \beta_1 \leftarrow \beta_1 + \eta(1 - \beta_1)$$
$$\text{If } PFT < PFG: \quad \beta_1 \leftarrow \beta_1 - \eta\beta_1$$

If the goal has been achieved, the firm next checks whether that success was preceded by search activity. If it was, it observes whether the success was preceded by a reduction in the profit goal. If so, β_2 is increased, and in the future the firm pays more attention to recent failures in determining profit goal.

$$\beta_2 \leftarrow \beta_2 + \eta(1 - \beta_2)$$

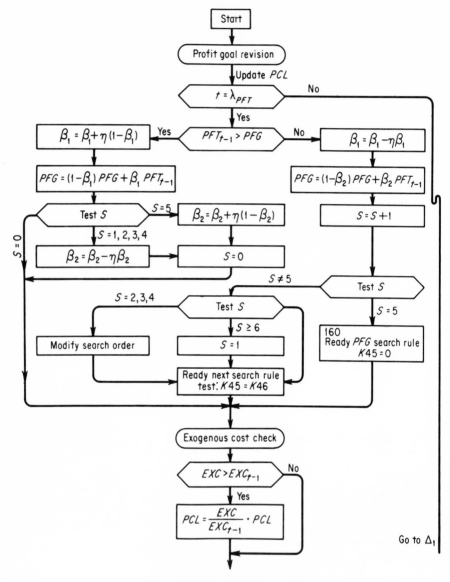

Figure 8.5 Price decision, part 1.

If search has achieved success without reducing the goal, β_2 is decreased. The firm then attends less to recent failures in determining goals.

$$\beta_2 \leftarrow \beta_2 - \eta\beta_2$$

Finally, if the profit goal has not been achieved, the firm considers whether it engaged in the search program last period. If so, it revises the search

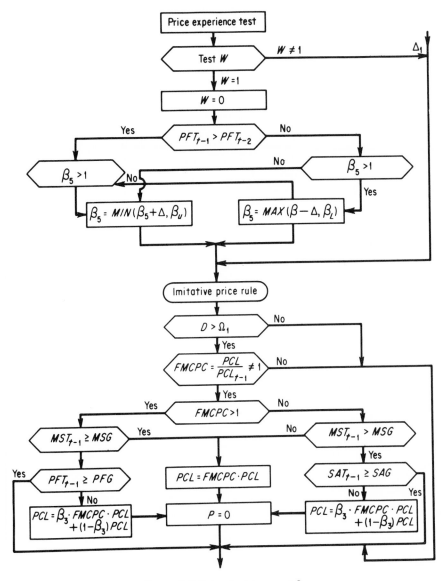

Figure 8.5 Price decision, part 2.

order by moving the unsuccessful search activity to the bottom of the list of search alternatives.

Second, every λ_{PFT} periods the firm also checks exogenous costs. If exogenous costs are up, price is increased proportionately.

$$\text{If } EXC_t > EXC_{t-1}: \quad PCL \leftarrow (EXC_t / EXC_{t-1}) \cdot PCL$$

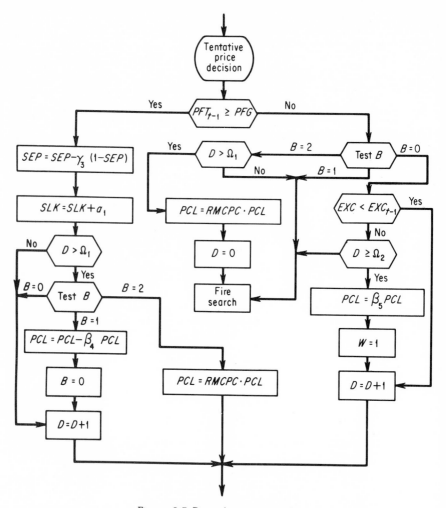

Figure 8.5 Price decision, part 3.

Third, every λ_{PFT} periods the firm checks the results of past adjustments in price designed to improve the profit position. If price has been changed last period in response to a profit failure (see below), the firm asks whether profit has gone up. If it has, β_5 (the parameter controlling the amount of movement in prices) is revised to make future price movements more pronounced in the successful direction. If profit has decreased, β_5 is revised so as to make future price movements less pronounced in the unsuccessful direction.

If profit is up and $\beta_5 > 1$: $\beta_5 \leftarrow \min\,(\beta_5 + \Delta,\, \beta_U)$

If profit is up and $\beta_5 < 1$: $\beta_5 \leftarrow \max\,(\beta_5 - \Delta,\, \beta_L)$

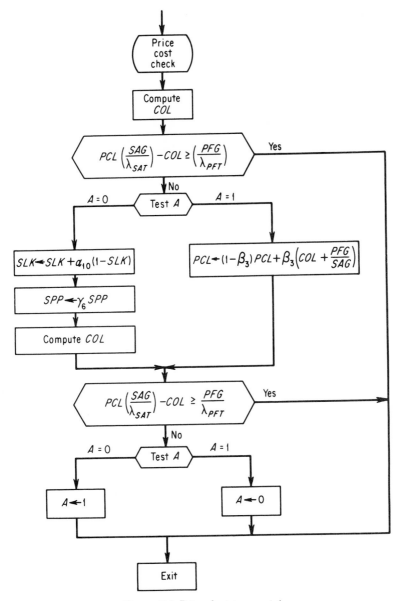

Figure 8.5 Price decision, part 4.

If profit is down and $\beta_5 > 1$: $\beta_5 \leftarrow \max(\beta_5 - \Delta, \beta_L)$

If profit is down and $\beta_5 < 1$: $\beta_5 \leftarrow \min(\beta_5 + \Delta, \beta_U)$

Fourth, whenever at least Ω_1 periods have elapsed since the last price change, the firm considers whether changes in competitors' prices over a relatively long period require some reaction. In general, a reaction is called for if the long-run relative price position has changed and certain aspiration level conditions are met. If major competitors have increased price relative to the firm's price and the firm is achieving its market share goal, the price increase will be met. That is, the firm will raise its price to restore the previous price relationship. If competition has raised price and market share goals are not being met, the firm asks whether profit goals are being achieved. If they are, no action is taken. If they are not, the firm raises price but by an amount less than proportional to competition.

$$PCL \leftarrow \beta_3 \, FMCPC \cdot PCL + (1 - \beta_3) \, PCL$$

If competition has decreased relative price, the firm again asks whether market share goals are being achieved. If they are not, the decrease is met. If market share goals are being met and sales goals are being met, no price action is taken. If market share goals are satisfied but sales goals are not, the decrease is followed in part (as above).

Fifth, each time period the firm considers its present price in the light of its profit record and pressure from the sales department. If profit exceeds the profit goal, sales effectiveness pressure is decreased and slack is increased.

$$SEP \leftarrow \gamma_3(1 - SEP)$$

$$SLK \leftarrow SLK + a_1$$

If price has been changed recently (in Ω_1 periods), no further action is taken. If price has not been changed recently, the pricing department considers whether there are any price reduction requests from the sales department. If there are no such requests, price is maintained. If there is a standard request, price is reduced.

$$PCL \leftarrow PCL - \beta_4 \, PCL$$

If there is an emergency request (and thus a recent short-run change in relative price position), price is adjusted to meet the recent major competitors' price change and restore relative price position. If profit falls below the profit goal, the department checks for price reduction requests from the sales department. If there are no such requests, if exogenous costs have not just been decreased, and if price has not been changed in the last Ω_2 periods, the firm will change price in the direction previous experience (β_5) suggests.

$$PCL \leftarrow \beta_5 \, PCL$$

If there is an emergency request for price action, the department meets the recent price reduction by competition. If there is either an emergency or a standard request, or if there has been a recent price change, the firm initiates a search program. In the search routine a series of steps is taken (one each time period) until either profit goals are satisfied or the pressure for a price cut is removed. As we have already noted, the order of the steps of the search routine changes in response to success and failure. There are six possible steps:

1. Reduce slack: $SLK \leftarrow SLK + \alpha_{10}(1 - SLK)$
2. Reduce excess limit on
   inventory: $EXL \leftarrow \alpha_6 EXL$
3. Increase sales effectiveness
   pressure: $SEP \leftarrow SEP + c_1$
4. Increase sales promotion
   percentage: $SPP \leftarrow SPP + \gamma_4(1 - SPP)$
5. Decrease sales promotion
   percentage: $SPP \leftarrow \gamma_6 SPP$
6. Reduce profit goal: $PFG \leftarrow (1 - \beta_2) PFG + \beta_2 PFT$

Finally, the department checks the consistency of its proposed price, anticipated costs, profit goal, and sales goal. That is, it asks whether the mark-up indicated by comparing price and unit cost will be large enough to meet the profit goal if the sales goal is achieved. If the answer is yes, the proposed price is confirmed. If the answer is no, the firm enters a special search routine. It considers whether it should cut costs or raise price in order to try to make mark-up consistent with goals. If it has most recently cut costs and that strategy succeeded, or if it has most recently raised price and that strategy failed, the department reduces costs by cutting slack and by reducing the sales promotion percentage.

$$SLK \leftarrow SLK + \alpha_{10}(1 - SLK)$$

$$SPP \leftarrow \gamma_6 SPP$$

On the other hand, if the department has most recently raised price and that worked or if costs have been cut without success most recently, price is raised so as to be closer to that required to make the goals and mark-up consistent.

$$PCL \leftarrow (1 - \beta_3) PCL + \beta_3 (COL + PFG/SAG)$$

Detail of the sales decision. The sales decision is indicated in Figure 8.6. The decision variables are sales effectiveness pressure (SEP) and sales promotion percentage (SPP). The major goals are sales, market share, and short-run position.

The program first updates sales and market share goals and the learning parameters associated with them. If a goal is exceeded, the goal is raised, the weight attached to successful performance is increased, and the weight attached to unsuccessful performance is decreased. If a goal is not achieved,

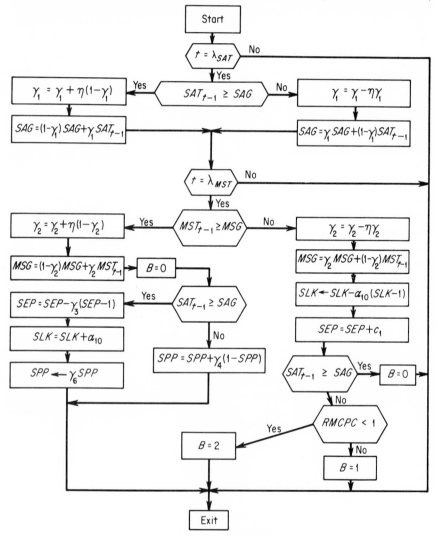

Figure 8.6 Sales strategy decision.

the goal is reduced, the weight attached to successful performance is decreased, and the weight given to unsuccessful performance is increased.

If $SAT \geq SAG$: $\gamma_1 \leftarrow \gamma_1 + \eta(1 - \gamma_1)$
$SAG \leftarrow (1 - \gamma_1)\, SAG + \gamma_1\, SAT$

If $MST \geq MSG$: $\gamma_2 \leftarrow \gamma_2 + \eta(1 - \gamma_2)$
$MSG \leftarrow (1 - \gamma_2)\, MSG + \gamma_2\, MST$

If $SAT < SAG$: $\gamma_1 \leftarrow \gamma_1 - \eta\gamma_1$
$SAG \leftarrow \gamma_1\, SAG + (1 - \gamma_1)\, SAT$

If $MST < MSG$: $\gamma_2 \leftarrow \gamma_2 - \eta\gamma_2$
$MSG \leftarrow \gamma_2\, MSG + (1 - \gamma_2)\, MST$

The firm then considers where it stands relative to its sales goals. If it is achieving either the market share goal, the sales goal, or both, no request for price action is transmitted to the pricing department. If both goals are being achieved, sales effectiveness pressure is reduced, slack is increased, and promotion expenditures are decreased.

$$SEP \leftarrow SEP - \gamma_3\,(SEP - 1)$$

$$SLK \leftarrow SLK + a_1$$

$$SPP \leftarrow \gamma_6\, SPP$$

If the market share goal is being achieved but the firm is failing in its sales goal, the proportion of sales revenue invested in sales promotion is increased.

$$SPP \leftarrow SPP + \gamma_4(1 - SPP)$$

If the sales goal is met but the market share goal is not, sales effectiveness pressure is increased.

$$SEP \leftarrow SEP + c_1$$

If neither the sales goal nor the market share goal are met, the department checks recent price competition. If competitors have recently reduced price relative to the firm, an emergency request for price reduction is made. If short-run relative price position is not worse, a standard price reduction request is made.

8.1.4 Internal parameters of the model

We can distinguish between parameters of the model that refer to internal attributes of the process by which decisions are made and parameters that are involved in the external environment (e.g., parameters of a demand function). Since we have not yet linked the internal system explicitly to the external environment, we consider here only those parameters referring to the decision process within the firm. In its present form, the model presented has 34 parameters for each firm.

1. There are three parameters constraining inventory $(INPROMAX)$, production $(PROMAX)$, and increases in sales (γ_5).

2. There are eight parameters determining certain lags and lengths of memory in the model: λ_{SAT}, λ_{MST}, and λ_{PFT}, the number of periods covered by aggregate reports on sales, market shares, and profits; π, the number of periods for which past production levels affect current limits on feasible production; Ω_1 and Ω_2, the number of periods required to elapse between certain kinds of price changes; Φ_1 and Φ_2, the number of periods for which competitors' relative price behavior is considered as long run and short run, respectively.

3. There are fourteen parameters affecting decision variables: α_1, α_2, α_4, and α_6 affect proposed inventory, and thus proposed production; γ_3 and c_1 affect sales effectiveness pressures; β_3, β_4, β_U, and β_L affect price; α_{10} and a_1 affect organizational slack; γ_4 and γ_6 affect sales promotion percentage. Each of these parameters influences the magnitude of decision reaction to a situation calling for decision change.

4. There are five parameters controlling first-level adaptation in the model: α_3 and α_5 affect inventory goals; α_8 and α_9 affect changes in production-smoothing goals; α_{11} affects changes in sales forecast.

5. There are two parameters dealing with second-level adaptation (or learning): η is the basic parameter in the learning functions for sales, market share, and profit goals; Δ is the increment of change in the price decision rule $(\beta_5 \ PCL)$ used to correct an unfavorable profit position.

6. There are two parameters affecting costs. Standard costs (STC) and the inventory cost ratio $(INCR)$ enter into the firm's cost function.

These 34 parameters remain fixed throughout a run of the model. They can be distinguished from another set of internal parameters, the initial values assigned to certain variables in the model. If we treat all of the initial values as independent (which we would not ordinarily do), the model assigns $34 + \Phi_1 + \pi$ initial values to each firm. Most of these consist in histories of various variables required to overcome the disparity between a no-history firm and the history required by many of the decision rules. Thus, we require a Φ_1-period history of price, an initial slack, an initial sales promotion percentage, an initial upper production limit, an initial lower production limit, a π-period history of production levels, an initial inventory level, an initial excess limit on inventory, an initial runout limit on inventory, an initial sales level, an initial sales forecast, a sales total, a market share total and profit total for the preceding period, an initial sales goal, an initial market share goal, an initial profit goal, an initial market share level, an initial sales effectiveness pressure, initial values for two past price change counters (W, D), initial values for the five changing values in the goal and decision rules function $(\beta_1, \beta_2, \gamma_1, \gamma_2, \gamma_5)$, the firm's initial relative (vis-à-vis the total industry) sales effectiveness pressure, relative price level, relative promotion expenditure ($RSEP$, $RPCL$, $RPEX$), and the initial search routine orders ($SR/T1$, $SR/T2$, $SR/T3$, $SR/T4$, $SR/T5$, S, A).

8.1.5 Interactions of the firms in an oligopoly marketplace

In describing our general oligopoly model of price and output, we have thus far concentrated on the model of a specific firm. The entire oligopoly model is made up of n such firms, together with some additional mechanisms that describe the interactions of these firms in the marketplace. Although an identical computer model is used to represent each of the n firms, the initial conditions and internal parameters actually used will in general differ from firm to firm.

There are two major ways in which the n oligopoly firms interact in the marketplace. In the first place, the collective actions of all the firms determine the total level of market demand. In the second place, the individual actions of each firm relative to the collective actions of all firms determine the share of demand that will be generated for each firm. In addition, as we mentioned in our discussion of pricing and sales strategy behavior of a firm, there is one minor way in which the firms interact — namely, the attention which each firm pays to relative price changes vis-à-vis its major competitors (a *major competitor* being operationally defined as any firm whose market share is at least equal to $1/n$).

In each time period the total level of market demand (in physical units), which we call DEM, is the following function of the weighted average level of prices set by all firms ($WPCL$), the weighted average level of sales effectiveness pressure for all firms ($WSEP$), the weighted average level of sales promotion expenditures by all firms ($WPEX$), and an exogenous factor (EXT):

$$DEM \leftarrow d_0 \, (EXT)^{d_1} \, (WSEP)^{d_2} \, (WPCL)^{d_3} \, (WPEX)^{d_4}$$

Each of the weighted averages in this function uses actual sales level for the previous time period (SAL) for each firm as the weighting factor.

$$WPCL \leftarrow \frac{\Sigma \, SAL_i \, PCL_i}{\Sigma \, SAL_i}$$

$$WSEP \leftarrow \frac{\Sigma \, SAL_i \, SEP_i}{\Sigma \, SAL_i}$$

$$WPEX \leftarrow \frac{\Sigma \, SAL_i \, PEX_i}{\Sigma \, SAL_i}$$

The share of market captured by the ith firm (MSL_i) is a somewhat complex function of its relative sales effectiveness pressure ($RSEP_i$), its relative price level ($RPCL_i$), its relative promotion expenditures ($RPEX_i$) and its previous share of market. (All of these relative measures are vis-à-vis the total industry levels of these variables.) The form of this function is as follows (MSL_i^* is the ith firm's un-normalized share of market, MSL_i is its normalized share of market):[2]

$$RSEP_i \leftarrow \left[w_4 \frac{SEP}{\Sigma SEP} + (1 - w_4) RSEP \right]_i$$

$$RPCL_i \leftarrow \left[w_5 \frac{PCL}{\Sigma PCL} + (1 - w_5) RPCL \right]_i$$

$$RPEX_i \leftarrow \left[w_6 \frac{PEX}{\Sigma PEX} + (1 - w_6) RPEX \right]_i$$

$$MSL_i^* \leftarrow \{ w_0 MSL + (1 - w_0) MSL [w_1 RSEP - w_2 RPCL + w_3 RPEX] \}_i$$

$$MSL_i \leftarrow \frac{MSL_i}{\Sigma MSL_j^*}$$

The level of exogenous cost factors (EXC) will change in the marketplace in response to changes in EXT in the following manner:

$$EXC \leftarrow (1 - d_5) EXC + d_5 \frac{EXT}{EXT_{i-1}} EXC$$

Thirteen market parameters whose values change over time are introduced here: $d_0, d_1, d_2, d_3, d_4, d_5, w_0, w_1, w_2, w_3, w_4, w_5$, and w_6. In addition, an initial starting value for EXC must be supplied, together with the entire time series for EXT.

A complete listing of the model in GATE for the Bendix G-20 and one set of sample input and output data are reproduced in an appendix to this chapter. In the case presented some parameter values have been generated by a special GATE random number generation subroutine. To reproduce the results without that subroutine would involve some slight modifications. The only other subroutines used are standard input-output procedures.

8.2 An Exploration of Some Properties of the Model

The general model presented in this chapter is a summary of our understanding of the key microprocesses in price and output determination by a modern firm. It is a framework for other models and a basis for exploring the reaction of such firms to characteristics of the market, variations in external (e.g., governmental) constraints, and other conventional economic questions. As a prelude to such theoretical efforts and to attempts to test the model, we have undertaken an examination of some basic properties of

[2] Subscripts outside brackets should be interpreted to apply the subscript to each variable within the brackets. Summations are over all firms in the industry.

the model. In this section we discuss the results of the first stage of that examination.

8.2.1 A multiple regression procedure for analysis

We wish to determine the extent to which behavior in the model is sensitive to variations in various internal parameters.[3] An exhaustive consideration of that question is not really feasible. The number of outputs and the number and combinations of inputs are of an intolerable order of magnitude from the point of view of complete analysis. The model generates a detailed time series of decisions, internal organizational results, goals, and so on for each firm in the industry. As we have already noted, it depends on a rather large number of initial conditions and parameters.

To make the analysis we limited attention to a few summary statistics of key output variables and to a sample of parameter inputs. The choice of output to consider and the constraints on the parameter sample were made on the basis of *a priori* judgments on importance and probable sensitivities. Within those constraints, the specific samples to be considered were determined randomly.

Industry and market simplifications. To study the impact of selected internal firm parameters on the model, we have simplified the industry by treating only the two-firm case. There are two firms in the industry, competing in the same market. There are no product differences between the two firms. In addition, we consider only one set of market parameters and a market in which the exogenous factor contributing to total demand (*EXT*) is subject only to modest random fluctuations around the mean. Values used for the market parameters and initial conditions are shown in Table 8.1. *EXT* was normally distributed with a mean 1.0 and a standard deviation 0.1. Values of *EXT* were serially independent and are listed in Table 8.2.

Output variables. For each of the two firms, we computed means of four different variables over three different time spans. Thus, we limited ourselves to 24 output variables. The four variables chosen were four common economic variables involved in the model — price, inventory, market share, and profit. The analysis considered the sensitivity of those variables to changes in internal parameter values. The time spans chosen were the last five time periods of the series, the last ten time periods of the series, and the last 25 time periods of the series. The total series consisted of 50 time periods. A complete listing of the output variables used in the analysis and their variable names in the computer program are indicated in Table 8.3.

---

[3]The multiple regression program and the analytical procedures were devised and executed by P. O. Soelberg.

Table 8.1. Market parameters and initial conditions

Variable name		Value
Flow chart	Computor program	
d_0	Z10	150
d_1	Z11	2
d_2	Z12	3
d_3	Z13	2
d_4	Z14	0.3
d_5	Z15	0.5
w_0	C140	15
w_1	C141	0.5
w_2	C142	0.5
w_3	C143	0.5
w_4	C144	0.5
w_5	C145	0.5
w_6	C146	0.5
EXC	Z16	1
EXC_{t-1}	Z17	1

Table 8.2. 50-period series of EXT

t	EXT	t	EXT
0	1.0000	26	1.0199
1	1.0464	27	1.0159
2	1.0060	28	1.2273
3	1.1486	29	1.0041
4	1.1022	30	0.8868
5	1.1394	31	1.0768
6	1.0906	32	1.0375
7	1.1179	33	0.9487
8	0.8499	34	1.0292
9	0.9310	35	1.1026
10	1.1372	36	0.8666
11	0.9518	37	0.9713
12	0.8624	38	1.0161
13	0.8990	39	0.8654
14	0.9995	40	1.1250
15	1.1393	41	1.0630
16	0.8213	42	1.0375
17	0.9895	43	0.8579
18	0.8661	44	0.9849
19	1.1041	45	0.9691
20	1.0279	46	1.0424
21	0.8195	47	1.0593
22	0.8814	48	1.0862
23	1.0658	49	1.0235
24	0.9561	50	0.9147
25	0.8601		

Table 8.3. Output variables and program names

Common variable	Fixed firm			Variable firm		
	Mean over periods 26–50	Mean over periods 41–50	Mean over periods 46–50	Mean over periods 26–50	Mean over periods 41–50	Mean over periods 46–50
Price	X47	X43	X39	X35	X31	X27
Inventory	X48	X44	X40	X36	X32	X28
Market share	X49	X45	X41	X37	X33	X29
Profit	X50	X46	X42	X38	X34	X30

Fixed internal parameter values. To simplify the analysis further, we held a substantial number of parameter values constant. In fact, we limited variation to 25 internal parameters and initial values. The number 25 was determined largely by technical requirements. The specific parameters and initial values that were kept fixed were chosen on the basis of two simple criteria. First, we fixed the parameters for one of the two firms. This "fixed" firm was the same (with respect to the values assigned to its parameters and initial conditions) throughout the analysis. The second, or "variable," firm had different values for 25 internal parameters and initial conditions. Of these 25 independent variables, five were initial conditions and 20 were parameters. We attempted to choose those variables that seemed *a priori* most likely to be important to the operation of the model. In practice, this meant that we included virtually every variable within the model that had direct effect on the decision variables, on adaptation of those decision variables, or on adaptation in goals. Table 8.4 gives the complete list of the parameters and initial conditions that were fixed for the two firms and the values assigned to each.

Variable internal parameters and sampling procedures. The 25 independent variables of the analysis defined a parameter space from which we wished to sample in order to test the effects of changes in parameter values. Our analysis is based on a sample of size 100 drawn from this parameter space in the following way:

1. For each parameter we determined a mean value, a range, and a distribution. In each case the mean value was also the value assigned to the fixed firm for the same parameter. The range was designed to restrict possible variations in parameter values to a more or less reasonable extent. The distribution could be either approximately normal or approximately rectangular.

2. From these distributions of parameter values we drew 100 random values for each of the 25 values. In effect, we created 100 different "firms" by a random combination of parameter values. The 25 variable names (in three forms — flow chart, internal computer program, and computer output), the ranges assigned, and the form of the distribution are indicated in Table 8.5. A check on the parameter values actually generated by the program indicates that the program did, in fact, choose values consistent with the specifications of range and form of distribution.

Variations in the analysis. Within the model we have not specified whether sales and market share goals are in terms of sales revenue or in terms of product units sold. By varying that aspect of the model, we have obtained three different variations of the basic model each of which has been analyzed. In Variation I sales goals are in terms of revenue, and market share goals are in terms of share of the revenue. In Variation II,

Table 8.4. Fixed parameters and initial values

Variable name		Value	Variable name		Value
Flow chart	Computer program		Flow chart	Computer program	
PCL_t	C0	1	SEP	C62	1.5
PCL_{t-1}	C1	1	MST_{t-1}	C65	0.5
PCL_{t-2}	C2	1	MSG	C68	0.5
PCL_{t-3}	C3	1	PFT_{t-1}	C75	450
PCL_{t-4}	C4	1	PFG	C78	450
PCL_{t-5}	C5	1	$RSEP$	C81	1.5
SLK	C10	1.5	$RPCL$	C82	1
SPP	C16	0.1	$RPEX$	C83	100
STC	C22	0.4	γ_5	C125	3
$INCR$	C23	0.2	β_U	C137	1.35
$PROMAX$	C24	100,000,000	β_L	C138	0.65
$UPRLIM$	C26	1,000	D	K26	1
$LPRLIM$	C28	1,000	Ω_1	K27	2
PRL_t	C30	1,000	Ω_2	K28	3
PRL_{t-1}	C31	1,000	S	K29	1
PRL_{t-2}	C32	1,000	W	K30	0
PRL_{t-3}	C33	1,000	λ_{SAT}	K33	3
PRL_{t-4}	C34	1,000	λ_{MST}	K35	3
PRL_{t-5}	C35	1,000	λ_{PFT}	K37	3
INL	C40	500	$SR/T1$	K46	1
EXL	C42	500	$SR/T2$	K47	2
RUL	C44	500	$SR/T3$	K48	3
$INPROMAX$	C48	500,000	$SR/T4$	K49	4
SAL	C50	1,000	$SR/T5$	K50	5
SFL	C52	1,000	A	K52	0
SAT_{t-1}	C55	3,000	Φ_1	structure	6
SAG	C58	3,000	Φ_2	structure	1
MSL	C60	0.5			

sales goals are in terms of product units but market share goals are in terms of share of revenue. In Variation III, sales goals are in terms of product units and market share goals are in terms of share of the product units sold.

Basic procedures of analysis. The simplification of the model permits an analysis of the following sort: we have 24 dependent variables. For each of these variables we have 25 independent variables and 100 observations of the model. This situation is repeated in each of the three variations of the model. To these data we apply a multiple regression model to determine (within the linear constraints of that model) the contribution of variations in the parameter values to variations in the output. The multiple regression procedure adds and drops variables systematically (reconsidering the entire set of variables at each stage) according to their contribution to

Table 8.5. Parameters varied randomly for the variable firm

Variable name			Range	Distribution
Computer output	Flow chart	Computer program		
X1	α_1	C101	$0.01 \leq \alpha_1 \leq 0.20$	Rectangular
X2	α_2	C102	$0.01 \leq \alpha_2 \leq 0.99$	Normal
X3	α_3	C103	$0.01 \leq \alpha_3 \leq 0.50$	Rectangular
X4	α_4	C104	$0.01 \leq \alpha_4 \leq 0.99$	Normal
X5	α_5	C105	$0.01 \leq \alpha_5 \leq 0.50$	Rectangular
X6	α_6	C106	$0.01 \leq \alpha_6 \leq 0.30$	Rectangular
X7	α_8	C108	$1.01 \leq \alpha_8 \leq 1.40$	Rectangular
X8	α_9	C109	$0.60 \leq \alpha_9 \leq 0.99$	Rectangular
X9	α_{10}	C110	$0.01 \leq \alpha_{10} \leq 0.20$	Rectangular
X10	α_{11}	C111	$0.01 \leq \alpha_{11} \leq 0.99$	Rectangular
X11	a_1	C112	$0.01 \leq a_1 \leq 0.15$	Rectangular
X12	c_1	C113	$0.01 \leq c_1 \leq 0.15$	Rectangular
X14	η	C120	$0.01 \leq \eta \leq 0.30$	Rectangular
X15	γ_1	C121	$0.10 \leq \gamma_1 \leq 0.90$	Rectangular
X16	γ_2	C122	$0.10 \leq \gamma_2 \leq 0.90$	Rectangular
X17	γ_3	C123	$0.01 \leq \gamma_3 \leq 0.20$	Rectangular
X18	γ_4	C124	$0.01 \leq \gamma_4 \leq 0.20$	Rectangular
X19	γ_6	C126	$0.80 \leq \gamma_6 \leq 0.99$	Rectangular
X20	β_1	C131	$0.10 \leq \beta_1 \leq 0.90$	Rectangular
X21	β_2	C132	$0.10 \leq \beta_2 \leq 0.90$	Rectangular
X22	β_3	C133	$0.01 \leq \beta_3 \leq 0.99$	Rectangular
X23	β_4	C134	$0.01 \leq \beta_4 \leq 0.20$	Rectangular
X24	β_5	C135	$0.81 \leq \beta_5 \leq 1.20$	Rectangular
X25	Δ	C136	$0.01 \leq \Delta \leq 0.09$	Rectangular
X26	π	K43	$1 \leq \pi \leq 11$	Rectangular

the F-values associated with the regression. It identifies all variables that meet an arbitrary criterion of contribution, the criterion being the same for all 24 regression analyses.

These procedures, although somewhat complex, are also certainly somewhat crude. They involve a host of assumptions both in the simplifications and in the use of multiple regression procedures. The multiple regression gives us only an occasional glimmer of potential interaction effects among the parameters, and we cannot be sure that the simplifications have not either concealed some important parameters or defined a specific market situation that leads to extreme results in the model. The model may behave quite differently under other reasonable initial conditions, under other market conditions, or under conditions in which there are more than two firms. Despite these obvious problems, the analysis has the virtue of feasibility. In retrospect, it also has the advantage that we have learned something from it. It has results, and the results seem to be meaningful.

8.2.2 Results of the analysis

The multiple regression analysis selects, for each output variable, those parameters to which the model is most consistently sensitive. We have identified about half of the original 25 parameters as being especially important.

Parameters affecting the output of the variable firm. We will consider only those parameters to which the model is consistently sensitive in all three variations. Differences in sensitivity from one model variation to another do not seem to be particularly consistent. Among the 25 parameters and initial values considered, there are 11 that seem to have a consistent effect in one or two classes (i.e., price, inventory, market share, or profit) of output variables. There are three that have pervasive effects in three or four classes of variables.

The parameters that have general effects are:

1. The proportional increase in the upper production limit when production is at full capacity (α_8). The larger the value of this parameter, the faster the firm can adjust its production upward.

2. The extent of adjustment in price to competitive price changes or to required mark-up to maintain profitability (β_3). The larger the value of this parameter, the greater the reaction to competition and to apparently inadequate mark-up.

3. The initial propensity to modify price in reaction to failure on profit goals (β_5). The larger the value of this parameter, the greater the initial propensity to raise price.

The generality of the effect of these parameters seems to stem, at least in part, from some key characteristics of the market postulated for the model. Relative to the initial positions of the two firms, the market was substantially underexploited. As a result, most firms tended to raise price over time, and all firms expanded production. The parameters affecting the ease with which such adjustments were made had general effects. Such general effects would probably arise under a number of market conditions, but would not necessarily appear in all.

Aside from these pervasive influences, the output was primarily sensitive to the following parameters:

Price was affected by the parameters controlling increases (a_1) and decreases (α_{10}) in slack, the amount of reduction feasible in sales promotion percentage (γ_6), and the initial responsiveness of the profit goal to profit performance (β_2). In a general way, firms that had cost change alternatives to changes in price — that is, firms that could relatively easily vary slack, reduce promotion expenditures, and reduce profit goals — were likely to be relatively low-price firms in this market.

Inventory was affected by the rate at which the forecast of sales adjusted to past sales (α_{11}). Compared with its performance elsewhere, the multiple regression model did not do an especially good job of predicting inventory levels.

Market share was affected primarily by the parameters controlling the upward adjustment of sales effectiveness pressure (c_1) and the upward (γ_4) and downward (γ_6) adjustment of sales promotion percentage.

Profit was affected primarily by the parameters controlling the initial rate of adjustment of sales goals to sales results (γ_1) and those controlling second-order learning of adjustment parameters (η, Δ).

The pattern of sensitivity to parameters is shown in Table 8.6.

Table 8.6. Major parameter effects on output variables: variable firm

Variable name	Class of output variable			
	Price	Inventory	Market share	Profit
α_8	x	x	x	x
β_3	x		x	x
β_5	x	x	x	x
a_1	x			
α_{10}	x			
γ_6	x		x	
β_2	x			
α_{11}		x		
c_1			x	
γ_4			x	
γ_1				x
η				x
Δ				x

Parameters affecting the output of the fixed firm. For obvious reasons, the analysis of the output of the fixed firm is less interesting immediately and somewhat less easy to understand. The direct parameter effects in the model are *prima facie* effects on the variable firm. The analysis of their effects on the fixed firm presupposes a detectable interaction between the firms. The parameters affecting price, inventory, and profit levels are indicated in Table 8.7. The market share analysis, of course, is identical to the previous market share analysis in a two-firm industry.

8.2.3 Implications of the analysis

On the whole, the multiple regression analysis confirms our intuitions about the model. In particular, we see five major implications:

1. The behavior of the model is partially dependent on the interaction

Table 8.7. Major parameter effects on output variables: fixed firm

Variable name	Class of output variable		
	Price	Inventory	Profit
α_8	X	X	X
η		X	X
β_3		X	X
α_{11}	X	X	
γ_6	X		
β_2		X	
α_6			X
c_1			X
γ_2			X

between one set of internal parameters and the attributes of the market within which the model operates. Both the amount and direction of price change and changes in feasible production are controlled by certain key parameters that become important as the market conditions induce pressure for the decision rule involved to be used. For example, if demand induces a pressure for an increased upper production limit or for a decreased lower production limit, the magnitude of the shift is dictated by a specific parameter in the model.

2. The output of the model is substantially independent of a number of parameters affecting adjustments within the inventory-output subroutine. Rates of adjustments in proposed inventory, runout level, and excess level (α_1, α_2, α_3, α_4, α_5, α_6) apparently do not have a major impact, nor does the number of periods of history maintained on production level (π), although this may be a special function of the fact that the market tended to expand in the cases examined.

3. Most of the parameters to which the model is sensitive have relatively localized effects on certain classes of outputs. The pairings are about what might be suspected from an inspection of the structure of the model. Price is especially sensitive to cost parameters since price is associated with profit goals and achievement of profit goals involves in part the maintenance of an appropriate cost-price spread. Market share is especially sensitive to the decision variables (sales effectiveness pressure and sales promotion percentage) in the sales area and, thus, is especially sensitive to the parameters influencing changes in those decisions.

4. Profit seems to be especially sensitive to learning parameters (η, Δ). These parameters, affecting the adaptation in other adjustment mechanisms, are logically the most "fundamental" parameters of the model. Their influence on performance (in terms of the multiple regression analysis) is most pronounced with respect to profit.

5. It is not yet obvious that a dramatic reduction in the number of

parameters in the model can be achieved by sensitivity analysis of this type. We have focused attention on about half of the original 25 parameters introduced for examination. We probably cannot reduce the number further so long as the model is in its present form. We may have to expand the number as we experiment with different market conditions and investigate some of the parameters and initial conditions rejected for *a priori* reasons in this analysis.

As we mentioned earlier, the model presented in this chapter is basically a report on the first stage of a research program. The analysis presented here was designed to facilitate two additional steps in that research program -- more detailed investigation of parameter effects and a study of the empirical implications of the model. Both of these additional steps need to be taken, and both can be accomplished more effectively on the basis of the present analysis. With respect to the empirical investigation, one of the problems with the model is the need to observe directly or to estimate a rather large number of parameters. As we reduce the number of critical parameters to a dozen or so, we can begin to see a feasible testing procedure. With respect to a more detailed study of one part of the parameter space, it is clear that an important next step is to consider more intensively the reaction of the model to the parameters identified in the present analysis.

8.3 Summary

In this chapter we have presented a detailed general model of price and output determination in a modern oligopolistic firm. The model portrays the process of decision making in terms consistent with a behavioral theory of the firm. The firm uses multiple, changing, aspiration-level goals; it solves problems in each of its decision areas more or less independently; it searches for solutions in a manner learned from experience; it adjusts its decision rules on the basis of feedback on experience. Decisions on price, output, and sales strategy are made on the basis of profit, inventory, production-smoothing, sales, market share, and competitive position goals.

The model has a rather large number of internal parameters. An examination of the sensitivity of price, inventory, market share, and profit results to variations in the values for 25 apparently key parameters identifies about half of those as having special importance. Under the market conditions used, a few have general impact on the results; the others seem to have primarily localized influence. The fact that many of the parameters that are apparently important can be seen as the product of a learning process suggests that one next step in the development of the model is the introduction of additional higher-level learning mechanisms. This conclusion is reinforced by the identification of two basic learning parameters in the model as being especially important to the profitability of the firm represented by the model.

Appendix. 20-gate Listing of Program with Sample Input and Output.

```
PERATOR-012  23 JUN 62    12:40:26  R350.004 GATE 010 060    J G MARCH GSIA
    R M CYERT - J G MARCH      GSIA                          M
                                                             M
    BEHAVIORAL THEORY OF THE FIRM                            M
    GEMPO DUOPOLY MODEL                                      M
    TREATMENT A                                              M
        FIRM I VARIABLE, FIRM II FIXED                       M
        TIME ZERO GNP = 1                                    M
        GNP NORMALLY DISTRIBUTED                             M
            MU = 1, SIGMA = .1                               M
        H1...H(K15) = GNP                                    M
                                                             M
    RUN INPUT                                                M
        J0 = RANDOM START                                    M
        K15 = TIME PERIODS PER TRIAL (K15<101)               M
        I9 = INITIAL TRIAL (-1) THIS RUN                     M
        I10 = FINAL TRIAL THIS RUN                           M
                                                             M
    MAXIMUM RUNNING TIME                                     M
        3 MIN COMPILATION AND DATA                           M
        1/2 MIN EACH 50-PERIOD TRIAL W/O DETAILED PRNT       M
        5 MIN EACH 50-PERIOD TRIAL WITH DETAILED PRNT        M
                                                             M
    MAXIMUM PRINTED OUTPUT                                   M
        10 PAGES COMPILATION AND DATA                        M
        1 PAGE EACH 50-PERIOD TRIAL W/O DETAILED PRNT        M
        43 PAGES EACH 50-PERIOD TRIAL W/DETAILED PRNT        M
                                                             M
    MODIFICATION INSERTS                                     M
        PRINT (1) PROVIDES DETAILED PRINTOUT                 M
        MSL (2) MAKES MSL UNITS = REVENUE SHARE              M
        SAL (1) MAKES SAL UNITS = REVENUE                    M
        SAL MODIFICATION CANNOT BE USED W/O MSL MOD          M
                                                             M
                                                             M
                                                             M
    FORMAT
    85 IS HIGHEST STATEMENT NUMBER
    500 ABCONS
    DIMENSION I(20) J(100) K(300) C(2175) D(85) G(50)    N
    H(100) X(58) Y(200) Z(35)
                                          M
                                                  M
1   C
    2, I0, 0, 1, 2175,                                   CLEAR MEMORY
    CI0 + 0
    YI0 + 0 IF I0 < 201
    GI0+0 IF I0<51
    KI0 + 0 IF I0 < 301
    ZI0+0  IF I0< 36
    DI0+0 IF I0<86
    JI0+0 IF I0<101
    XI0+0 IF I0<59
    HI0+0 IF I0<101
2   C
    LIST.(1)
    READ
    24,I0,0,1,40,
    C(I0+750) + KI0    IF I0 < 26                        INDU SFE DAT
    C(I0+800) + ZI0 IF I0 < 36                           INDU SFE DAT
```

183

```
        C(I0+850) ← GI0                                    INDU SFE D
024     C
        I1 ← 1
 19     C
        READ
        3, I0, 0, 1, 149,
        C(300+I0+150*I1) ← CI0                             FIRM SFE D
        K(140+I0+35*I1) ← KI0 IF I0 > 25 IF I0 < 61        FIRM SFE D
  3     C
        GO TO 19; I1 ← I1+1 IF I1 < K5
        GO TO 63
                                                    M
        START INDUSTRY CALCULATIONS                 M
                                                    M
004     C
        K0←K0+1 ; K1←K1+1 ; K3←K3+1                         TIME
        Z0←H(K0) ; K1←0 ; Z1←Z0 IF K1=K2                    INPUT GNP
        5,K19,0,1,7,
        Z(18+K19)←0
005     C
        6,K6,0,20,(K5-1)*20,
        Z18←Z18+G(4+K6)                                    S/SEP
        Z19←Z19+G(K6)                                      S/PCL
        Z20←Z20+G(1+K6)                                    S/PEX
        Z21←Z21+G(2+K6)                                    S/SAL
        Z22←Z22+G(4+K6)*G(2+K6)                            S/SEP,SAL
        Z23←Z23+GK6*G(2+K6)                                S/PCL,SAL
        Z24←Z24+G(1+K6)*G(2+K6)                            S/PEX.SAL
006     C
        7,K6,0,20,(K5-1)*20,
        G(5+K6)←G(14+K6)*(G(4+K6)/Z18)+(1-G(14+K6))*G(5+K6)   RSEP
        G(6+K6)←G(15+K6)*(GK6/Z19)+(1-G(15+K6))*G(6+K6)       RPCL
        G(7+K6)←G(16+K6)*(G(1+K6)/Z20)+(1-G(16+K6))*G(7+K6)   RPEX
007     C
        Z5←Z4 ; Z7←Z6 ; Z9←Z8 ; Z3←Z2 ; Z17←Z16
        Z4←Z22/Z21 ; Z6←Z23/Z21 ; Z8←Z24/Z21               WSEP PCL PE
        Z2←Z10*Z0+Z11*Z4+Z12*Z6+Z13*Z8+Z14                 DEM
        Z16←(1-Z15)*Z16+Z15*(Z0/Z1)*Z16                    EXC
        8,K6,0,20,(K5-1)*20,
        G(3+K6)←G(10+K6)*G(3+K6)+(1-G(10+K6))*G(3+K6)*(G(11+N
        K6)*G(5+K6)-G(12+K6)*G(6+K6)+G(13+K6)*G(7+K6))     MSL
        Z25←Z25+G(3+K6)                                    S/MSL-T
008     C
        9,K6,0,20,(K5-1)*20,
        G(3+K6)←G(3+K6)/Z25                                MSL
009     C
        Z29←G0*10+10
        10,K6,0,20,(K5-1)*20,
        GO TO 10 N
        IF G(3+K6) <Z28                                    CHECK MSL
        GO TO 10 N
        ; Z29←GK6N
        ;Z26←GK6/G(8+K6)                                   N COMPUTE MC/
        ;Z27←GK6/G(9+K6)                                   N COMPUTE MC/
        IF GK6<Z29                                         TEST PCL
 10     C
        LOCATION OF MSL MODIFICATION NUMBER 1              M
        START MSL MODIFICATION INSERT   1 OF 2             M
        Z35 ←0
        31,K6,0,20,(K5-1)*20,
```

```
        G(18+K6)  ←  Z2*G(3+K6)
        G(17+K6)  ←  GK6*G(18+K6)
        Z35  ←Z35+G(17+K6)
31      C
        32,K6,0,20,(K5-1)*20,
        G(17+K6)  ←  G(17+K6)/Z35
32      C
        END MSL MODIFICATION INSERT                          M
                                                             M
        FIRM COMPUTATIONS                                    M
                                                             M
        K7 ← 0
        59, K6, 0, 20, (K5-1)*20,
        K7 ←K7+1
        23, I0, 0, 1, 149,
        C(I0) ← C(I0+150*K7)                        FIRM OPL DAT
        K(I0) ← K(I0+35*K7) IF I0 > 25 IF I0 < 61   FIRM OPL DAT
23      C
        C84←Z26/(C0/C1)                             RMCPC
        C85←Z27/(C0/C5)                             FMCPC
        K32←K32+1 ; K34←K34+1 ; K36←K36+1           TIMING
        C51←G(2+K6)                                 UPDATE SAL
        C60←G(3+K6); C61←C60                        UPDATE MSL
        C50←C60*Z2                                  SAL
        LOCATION OF MSL MODIFICATION NUMBER 2                M
        START MSL MODIFICATION INSERT    2 OF 2             M
        C60 ←G(17+K6)
        END MSL MODIFICATION INSERT                          M
        C50←C125*C51   N                            TEST SAL
        IF C50>C125*C51
        G(2+K6)←C50
        LOCATION OF SAL MODIFICATION NUMBER 1                M
        START SAL MODIFICATION INSERT    1 OF 1             M
        C50←C0*C50
        END SAL MODIFICATION INSERT                          M
                                                     M
        INVENTORY-OUTPUT DECISIONS                   M
                                                     M
        C41←C40                                     UPDATE INL
        C40←C40+C30-G(2+K6)                         INL
        C43←C42                                     UPDATE EXL
        C42←C103*C42+(1-C103)*C51                   EXL
        C45←C44                                     UPDATE RUL
        C44←C105*C44+(1-C105)*C51                   RUL
        C44←C42 IF C44>C42                          TEST RUL
        GO TO 11  N
        ;C46←C40+C104*(C44-C40)  N                  INPRO
        IF C40<C44                                  LOW INL
        GO TO 11  N
        ;C46←C40-C102*(C40-C42)        N            INPRO
        IF C40>C42                                  HIGH INL
        C46←C101*C40+C40                            INPRO
11      C46←C48  N                                  TEST INPRO
        IF C46>C48
        C53←C52                                     UPDATE SFL
        C52←C111*C52+(1-C111)*G(2+K6)               SFL
        C25←C46-C40+C52                             PROPRO
        GO TO 12; C10←C10+C112  N                   SLK   INCR
        IF K40=0                                    IF Z= 0
        GO TO 17  N
```

```
        ;C10←C10-C110*(C10-1)   N                          SLK DECR
        ;C62←C62+C113  N                                   SEP INCR
        ; C28←C109*C28  N                                  LPRLIM
        IF K40=-1
        GO TO 16  N
        ;C10←C10-C110*(C10-1)   N                          SLK DECR
        ; C62←C62-C123*(C62-1)  N                          SEP DECR
        ;C26←C108*C26  N                                   UPRLIM
        IF K40=1
016     GO TO 17  N
        ;C26←C24 IF C26→<C24                               TEST UPRLIM
012     GO TO 14  N                                        TEST Z1
        IF K41<K43
        C26←C30
        13,K8,1,1,K12,                                     MAXPRL
        C26←C(30+K8) N
        IF C(30+K8)>C26
013     C
014     GO TO 17  N
        IF K42<K43                                         TEST Z2
        C28←C30
        15,K8,1,1,K12,
        C28←C(30+K8)  N                                    MIN PRL
        IF C(30+K8)<C28
015     C
        GO TO 17
017     18,K8,K12,-1,1,
018     C(30+K8)←C(30+K8-1)                                UPDATE PRL
        GO TO 20; C30←C25  N                               PRL←PROPRO
        ;K40←0; K41←K41+1 N
        ;K42←K42+1 IF C25→>C26   N
        IF C25→<C28
        GO TO 20; C30←C26   N                              PRL←UPRLIM
        ;K40←1; K41←0; K42←K42+1 IF C25>C26
        C30←C28  N                                         PRL←LPRLIM
        ; K40←-1 ; K41←K41+1; K42←0
020     K31←0                                              L/ CODE
                                         M
        SALES GOAL REVISION M
                                         M
        GO TO 21 N
        IF K32≠K33                                         TEST L/ SAT
        K32←0; K31←K31+1
        GO TO 21 ; C58←(1-C121)*C58+C121*C55   N           SAG INCR
        ;C121←C121+C120*(1-C121) IF C55→<C58
        C58←C121*C58+(1-C121)*C55  N                       SAG DECR
        ; C121←C121-C120*C121
                                         M
        SALES STRATEGY DECISIONS         M
                                         M
021     GO TO 25  N
        IF K34≠K35                                         TEST L/MST
        K34←0; K31←K31+2
        GO TO 22; C62←C62+C113; C68←C122*C68+(1-C122)*C65 N  MSG DECR
        ;C10←C10-C110*(C10-1)  N                           SLK DECR
        ; C122←C122-C120*C122 IF C65<C68
        K44←0
        C122←C122+C120*(1-C122)
        C68←(1-C122)*C68+C122*C65                          MSG INCR
        GO TO 25; C10←C10+C112  N                          TEST SAG
```

```
      ;C16←C16*C126; C17←C16          N
      ;C62←C62-C123*(C62-1) IF C55-<C58              DECR SFP
      GO TO 25; C16←C16+C124*(1-C16) ; C17←C16       SPP
022   GO TO 25  N
      ;K44←0 IF C55-<C58                             TEST SAG
      GO TO 25; N
      K44←2 IF C84<1                                 TEST RMCPC
      GO TO 25 ; K44←1
                                         M
      PROFIT GOAL REVISION M
                                         M
025   C5←C4
      C4←C3
      C3←C2
      C2←C1
      C1←C0
      GO TO 33 IF K36≠K37
      K31←K31+4; K36←0
      GO TO 26  N
      ;K29←K29+1 ; C78←(1-C132)*C78+C132*C75 N       PFG INCR
      ;C131←C131*(1-C120) IF C75 <C78
      C78←(1-C131)*C78+C131*C75 ; C131←C131+C120*(1-C131)   PFG DECR
                                         M
      MAIN SEARCH ROUTINE REVISION       M
                                         M
      GO TO 27 N
      IF K29=0·                                      S=0
      GO TO 27 ; K29← 0  N                           S=5
      ; C132←C132+C120*(1-C132) IF K29=5
      GO TO 27 N
      ;K29←0 ; C132←C132*(1-C120) IF K29-<1
026   C78←0  IF C78<0
      GO TO 27 ; K45←0  N                            PFG SEARCH
      IF K29=5
      GO TO 27 ; K45←K46  N                          READY SR
      IF K29=1
      GO TO 27 ; K45←K46  N                          S=6
      ; K29←1 IF K29-< 6                             S=OTHER
      K50←K46                                        REORDER SR
      K46←K47
      K47←K48
      K48←K49
      K49←K50
      K45←K46
                                         M
      PRICING DECISION                   M
                                         M
027   C0←(Z16/Z17)*C0  N                             EXC CHECK
      IF Z16 >Z17                                    PCL/FXC
      GO TO 33 N
      IF K30≠1                                       TEST W
      K30←0                                          W=0
      GO TO 29 IF C75>C76                            TEST PFT
      GO TO 30 IF C135>1                             TEST B/5
028   GO TO 33  N
      ; C135←C135+C136 IF C135+C136<C137             MIN B/5
      GO TO 33 N
      ;C135←C137 IF C135+C136-<C138
029   GO TO 28  N
      IF C135>1
```

```
030     GO TO 33 N                                          MAX B/5
        ; C135←C135-C136 IF C135-C136>C138
        GO TO 33 N
        ;C135←C138 IF C135-C136-->C138
033     K39←0
        GO TO 38 N                                          TEST 0/1
        IF K26-->K27
        GO TO 38 N
        IF C85=1
        GO TO 36 N
        IF C85>1                                            TEST FMCPC
        GO TO 37 N
        IF C65<C68                                          TEST MSG
        GO TO 38 N
        IF C55-<C58                                         TEST SAG
035     GO TO 38 N
        ; K26←0; K39←K39+10 N
        ;C0←(1-C133*(1-C85))*C0                             PCL/10
036     GO TO 37 N
        IF C65-<C68                                         TEST MSG
        GO TO 38 N
        IF C75-<C78                                         TEST PFG
        GO TO 35
037     GO TO 38; C0←C0*C85; K26←0; K39←K39+20              PCL/20
038     C
        GO TO 42; C10←C10+C112   N                          TEST PFG
        ;C62←C62-C123*(1-C62) IF C75-<C78
        GO TO 41   N                                        TEST B
        IF K44≠0
        GO TO 40   N                                        TEST EXC
        IF Z16<Z17
        GO TO 44   N                                        TEST 0/2
        IF K26-->K28
        C0←C135*C0                                          PCL/4
        K39←K39+4; K30←1
040     GO TO 54 ; K26←K26+1 ; K38←0
041     GO TO 44   N                                        B=1
        IF K44=1
        GO TO 44 N                                          B=2
        IF K26-->K27                                        TEST 0/1
        C0←C84*C0                                           PCL/3
        K26←0; K39←K39+3
        GO TO 44
042     GO TO 43 N                                          TEST 0/1
        IF K26-->K27
        GO TO 43; K26←0; K39←K39+2   N
        ;C0←C84*C0   N                                      PCL/2
        IF K44=2
        GO TO 43   N
        ;K26←0; K39←K39+1; C0←C0-C134*C0        N           PCL/1
        IF K44=1
043     GO TO 54 ; K26←K26+1 ; K38←0
                                                M
        MAIN SEARCH ROUTINE                     M
                                                M
044     C                                                   FIRE SEARC
        GO TO (45+K45) ; K38←K38+1
045     C78←(1-C132)*C78+C132*C75                           PFG SEARCH
        C78←0   IF C78<0
        GO TO 54
```

```
46      GO TO 54    N                                                    SLK SEARCH
        ;C10←C10+(1-C10)*C110
47      GO TO 54    N                                                    EXL SEARCH
        ;C42←C42*C106
48      GO TO 54    N                                                    SER SEARCH
        ;C62←C62+C113
49      GO TO 54    N                                                    SPP SEARCH
        ;C16←C16+C124*(1-C16);   C17←C16
50      GO TO 54    N                                                    SPP SEARCH
        ; C16←C16*C126 ; C17←C16
                                                    M
        COST/PRICE CHECK AND SEARCH                 M
                                                    M
54      C21←C20   IF K53=0
        C20←Z16*C10*C22+C23*(C40/G(2+K6))+C16   N                        UPDATE COL
        IF C40>0                                                         COL
        C20←Z16*C10*C22+C16   N                                          COL
        IF C40¬>0
        GO TO 53 IF K53=1
        GO TO 51  IF (C0-C20)¬<((C78/K37)/(C58/K33))                     CK COL/PCL
        GO TO (60+K52) IF K51=0                                          CK PAST EXP
        GO TO 60; K52←0 IF K52=1
        GO TO 61; K52←1
60      K51←1; K53←1
        C10←C10+(1-C10)*C110                                             CUT SLK
        C16←C16*C126 ; C17←C16                                          CUT SPP
        GO TO 54
61      K51←1; K53←1
        C0←C0*(1-C133)+C133*(C20+((C78/K37)/(C58/K33)))                  RAISE PCL
        GO TO 54
                                                    M
        BOOK-KEEPING                                M
                                                    M
51      K51←0
53      K53←0
        C71←C70 ; C72←C71; C73←C72                                       UPDATE PFL
        C70←G(2+K6)*(C0-C20)                                             PFL
        C74←C74+C70                                                      CUM PFT
        C74←0   N                                                        UPDATE PFT
        ;C75←C74; C76←C75; C77←C76; C79←C78   N                          UPDATE PFG
        IF K36=K37-1
        C54←C54+C50                                                      CUM SAT
        C54←0   N                                                        UPDATE SAT
        ;C55←C54; C56←C55; C57←C56; C59←C58   N                          UPDATE SAG
        IF K32=K33-1
        C64←C64+C60*C50; C86←C86+C50                                     CUM MST/SAT
        C64←0; C86←0 N                                                   UPDATE MST
        ; C65←C64/C86; C66←C65; C67←C66; C69←C68 N                       UPDATE MSG
        IF K34=K35-1
        C11←C10
        C63←C62
        C19←C18
        C18←C16*G(2+K6)*C0                                               COMPUTE PEX
        GK6←C0                                                           LOAD MEMORY
        G(1+K6)←C18
        G(4+K6)←C62
        G(5+K6)←C81
        G(6+K6)←C82
        G(7+K6)←C83
        G(8+K6)←C1
```

```
          G(9+K6)+C5
          K55+K55+1; K57+K57+1; K59+K59+1
055       C
          56,I6,0,1,2,
          C(87+I6)+C(87+I6)+C0                              CUM PCL
          C(90+I6)+C(90+I6)+C40                             CUM INL
          C(93+I6)+C(93+I6)+C60                             CUM MSI
          C(96+I6)+C(96+I6)+C70                             CUM PFL
056       C
          57,I7,0,3,9,
          C(87+I7) + C(87+I7)/K56              N
          IF K55=K56
          C(88+I7) + C(88+I7)/K58              N
          IF K57=K58
          C(89+I7) + C(89+I7)/K60              N
          IF K59=K60
057       C
          K6+12 IF K6=20
          K55+0; C87+0; C93+0; C96+0              N
          ;X(K18+K6+1)+C87;  X(K18+K6+2)+C90      N              LOAD K55/DE▮
          ;X(K18+K6+3)+C93;  X(K18+K6+4)+C96            N
          IF K55=K56
          K57+0; C88+0; C91+0; C94+0; C97+0            N
          ;X(K18+K6+5)+C88;  X(K18+K6+6)+C91                N
          ;X(K18+K6+7)+C94;  X(K18+K6+8)+C97      N              LOAD K57/DE▮
          IF K57=K58
          K59+0; C89+0; C92+0; C95+0; C98+0            N
          ;X(K18+K6+9)+C89;  X(K18+K6+10)+C92          N
          ;X(K18+K6+11)+C95;  X(K18+K6+12)+C98         N         LOAD K59/DE▮
          IF K59=K60
          K6+20 IF K6=12
          58, I0, 0, 1, 149,
          C(I0+150*K7) + CI0                              FIRM S-S DA▮
          K(I0+35*K7) + KI0 IF I0 >25 IF I0 < 61          FIRM S-S DA▮
58        C
          LOCATION OF PRINT MODIFICATION NUMBER 1            M
          START PRINT MODIFICATION INSERT 1 OF 1            M
          GO TO 62 IF K7 = 2
          PTK0 T70 T72
          <$PERIOD$,6S,3D,E,E,E,R6,$INDUSTRY  DATA$,E,E,R11,N
          $GNP$,6S,1D.27,10S,$DEMAND$,6S,8D,E,E,E>
                      PTC58 TC55 TC68 TC65 TC78 TC75 TC0 TC10 N
          TC30 TC62 TC40 TC20 TC16 TC42 TC44 TC28 TC26
          <R6,$FIRM  1  DATA$,E,E,R11,$FEEDBACK$,R31,  N
          $GOALS$,R51,N
          $PERFORMANCE$,E,E,R11,$SALES$,R28,8D,R54,8D,E,N
          R11,$MARKET  SHARE$,R33,.2Z,R59,.2Z,E,R11,$PROFIT$ >
          < R26,*-8D,R52,*-8D,E,E,R11,$DECISIONS$,R41,$SLACK$,N
          E,E,R11,$PRICE$,R25,*2D.2Z,R41,$ORG SLACK$,R57,N
          2D.2Z,E,N
          R11,$OUTPUT$,R23,8D,R41,$SALES  SLACK$,R56,2D.1Z,E>
          <R11,$INVENTORY$,R22,-8D,R41,$COST  LEVEL$,R55,N
          *2D.2Z,E,R11,$PROMOTION  0/0$,R28,.2Z,E,E,  N
          R11,$MISCELLANEOUS$,E,E,R11,$EXCESS  LEVEL$,R32,-8D>
          <R46,$RUNOUT LEVEL$,R64,-8D,E,R11,N
          $LOWER PROD LIMIT$,N
          R33,8D,R46,$UPPER PROD LIMIT$,R65,8D,E,E,E>
          GO TO 59
062       C
                      PTC58 TC55 TC68 TC65 TC78 TC75 TC0 TC10 N
```

```
          TC30 TC62 TC40 TC20 TC16 TC42 TC44 TC28 TC26
          <R6,$FIRM  2  DATA$,E,E,R11,$FEEDBACK$,R31, N
          $GOALS$,R51,N
          $PERFORMANCE$,E,F,R11,$SALES$,R28,8D,R54,8D,E,N
          R11,$MARKET  SHARE$,R33,.2Z,R59,.2Z,E,R11,$PROFIT$ >
          < R26,*-8D,R52,*-8D,E,F,R11,$DECISIONS$,R41,$SLACK$,N
          F,E,R11,$PRICE$,R25,*2D.2Z,R41,$ORG SLACK$,R57,N
          2D.2Z,E,N
          R11,$OUTPUT$,R23,8D,R41,$SALES  SLACK$,R56,2D.1Z,E>
          <R11,$INVENTORY$,R22,-8D,R41,$COST  LEVEL$,R55,N
          *2D.2Z,E,R11,$PROMOTION  0/0$,R28,.2Z,F,E,  N
          R11,$MISCELLANEOUS$,E,F,R11,$EXCESS  LEVEL$,R32,-8D>
          <R46,$RUNOUT LEVEL$,R64,-8D,E,R11,N
          $LOWER PROD LIMIT$,N
          R33,8D,R46,$UPPER PROD LIMIT$,R65,8D,E,E,E>
          END PRINT MODIFICATION INSERT 1 OF 1              M
59        C
          GO TO 4 IF K3<K15
          AT$$                                        FINAL OUTPUT
          AT$INDE$T$PEND$T$ENT $T$VARI$T$ABLE$T$S    $
          TX0...XK18
          AT$DEPE$T$NDEN$T$T VA$T$RIAB$T$LES $
          TX(K18+1)...X(K18+24)
          AT$$
          HALT IF I9 = TI0
                                          M
          PARAMETER SAMPLE GENERATION ROUTINE      M
                                          M
163       C
          64, I0, 0, 1, 299,
          C(I0+150) + C(I0+450)                       FIRM S-S DAT
          K(I0+61) + K(I0+201) IF I0 < 70            FIRM S-S DAT
64        C
          75,I0,1,1,K18,                              RAND DAT GEN
          GO TO 70 IF J(50+I0)=1
          D0+RAND.(LJ0,(Y(100+I0)-Y(50+I0))*1000+1)
          D0+Y(50+I0)+D0/1000
          GO TO 73
70        H0+RAND.(LJ0,100)
          H0+H0+1
          GO TO 71 IF H0>50
          GO TO 72; I1+-1
71        H0+101-H0 ; I1+1
72        D0+(Y(100+I0)+Y(50+I0))/2+((Y(100+I0)-Y(50+I0))/6)  N
          *Y(+H0)*I1
73        C
          XI0 + D0
          GO TO 75; C(JI0-1000+150) + D0 IF JI0 < 2000       FIRM GEN DAT
          GO TO 75; K(JI0-2000+35) + D0 IF JI0 < 3000       FIRM GEN DAT
          Z(JI0-3000)+D0                                    FIRM GEN DAT
75        C
          74,I0,0,1,40,
          KI0 + C(I0+750)    IF I0 < 26               INDU OPL DAT
          ZI0 + C(I0+800) IF I0 < 36                  INDU OPL DAT
          GI0 + C(I0+850)                             INDU OPL DAT
074       C
          I9+I9+1
          TI9 TJ0
          GO TO 4
          PROGRAM END
```

00:02:32

```
G0  +1,100,1000,.5,1.5,1.5,1,100,1,1,.5,.5,.5,.5,.5,.5,.5
G20+1,100,1000,.5,1.5,1.5,1,100,1,1,.5,.5,.5,.5,.5,.5,.5
H1 +1.0464,1.0060,1.1486,1.1022,1.1394,1.0906,1.1179,.8499,.9310
H10+1.1372,.9518,.8624,.8990,.9905,1.1393,.8213,.9895,.8661,1.1041
H20+1.0279,.8195,.8814,1.0658,.9561,.8601,1.0199,1.0159,1.2273
H29+1.0041,.8868,1.0768,1.0375,.9487,1.0292,1.1026,.8666,.9713
H38+1.0161,.8654,1.1250,1.0630,1.0375,.8579,.9849,.9691
H46+1.0424,1.0593,1.0862,1.0235,.9147,1.0137,.7474,.9646,.9628
H55+.9445,.9487,.8945,.9512,1.0756,1.0225,1.1678,.9850,1.0598
H64+.9101,.8837,.9739,.9643,1.1827,1.0535,.7944,.7992,1.1180,.8859
H74+1.0358,.9770,1.0208,1.027,1.0606,.9693,.7902,1.0079,.9342,.9656
H84+.9479,1.2990,1.1278,.9856,.9114,1.0193,.9801,.9463,.8059,1.0489
H94+.9757,1.0531,.9556,.9342,.9115,.9372,1.0402
J1 +1101,1102,1103,1104,1105,1106,1108,1109,1110,1111,1112,1113
J13+1114,1120,1121,1122,1123,1124,1126,1131,1132,1133,1134,1135
J25+1136,2043
J52+1          J54+1
K2 +1          K5+2
K11+35,5,5              K16+28          K18+26
K56+5     K58+10        K60+25
Y1 +2.33,2.05,1.88,1.75,1.65,1.56,1.48,1.41,1.34
Y10+1.28,1.23,1.18,1.13,1.08,1.04,.99,.95,.92,.88
Y20+.84,.81,.77,.74,.71,.67,.64,.61,.58,.55
Y30+.52,.50,.47,.44,.41,.39,.36,.33,.31,.28
Y40+.25,.23,.20,.18,.15,.13,.10,.08,.05,.02
Y50+.00,.01,.01,.01,.01,.01,.01,1.01,.60,.01
Y60++.01,.01,.01,.01,.01,.10,.10,.01,.01,.80
Y70+.10,.10,.01,.01,.81,.01,1.
Y101+.20,.99,.50,.99,.50,.30,1.40,.99,.20
Y110+.99,.15,.15,.20,.30,.90,.90,.20,.20,.99
Y120+.90,.90,.99,.20,1.20,.09,11
Z0 +1,1
Z10+150,2,3,2,.3,.5,1,1             Z28+.1
J0 +803445  I9+52  I10+53  K15+50
*
C0 +1,1,1,1,1,1,1   C10+1.5   C16+.1   C18+100   C22+.4,.2,100000000
C26+1000    C28+1000   C30+1000    ,1000,1000,1000,1000,1000
C40+500   C42+500   C44+500   C48+500000   C50+1000   C52+1000
C55+3000   C58+3000   C60+.5   C62+1.5   C65+.5   C68+.5   C75+450
C78+450   C81+1.5,1,100
C125+3   C137+1.35,.65   C140+.5,.5,.5,.5,.5,.5,.5
K26+1,2,3,1   K33+3   K35+3   K37+3   K43+6   K46+1,2,3,4,5
*
C0 +1.001
C1 +  1,1,1,1,1   C10+1.5   C16+.1   C18+100   C22+.4,.2,100000000
C26+1000    C28+1000   C30+1000    ,1000,1000,1000,1000,1000
C40+500   C42+500   C44+500   C48+500000   C50+1000   C52+1000
C55+3000   C58+3000   C60+.5   C62+1.5   C65+.5   C68+.5   C75+450
C78+450   C81+1.5,1,100
C101+.1,.5,.25,.5,.25,.15   C108+1.2,.8,.1,.5,.08,.08,.1
C120+.15,.5,.5,.1,.1,3,.9   C131+.5,.5,.5,.1,1,.05
          C137+1.35,.65   C140+.5,.5,.5,.5,.5,.5,.5
K26+1,2,3,1   K33+3   K35+3   K37+3   K43+6   K46+1,2,3,4,5
*
   I9        +.5299999999999  ₁₀+02   J0        +.1298509000000  ₁₀+07
PERIOD       1


INDUSTRY  DATA
```

```
        GNP        1.05              DEMAND              2207


FIRM   1   DATA

        FEEDBACK                GOALS                    PERFORMANCE

        SALES                   3000                            3000
        MARKET   SHARE           .50                             .50
        PROFIT                  $450                            $450

        DECISIONS                           SLACK

        PRICE           $1.00           ORG SLACK           1.60
        OUTPUT           1000           SALES   SLACK      1.6
        INVENTORY         397           COST  LEVEL        $0.83
        PROMOTION  0/0    .10

        MISCELLANEOUS

        EXCESS   LEVEL               949      RUNOUT LEVEL           779
        LOWER PROD LIMIT            1000      UPPER PROD LIMIT      1000


FIRM   2   DATA

        FEEDBACK                GOALS                    PERFORMANCE

        SALES                   3000                            3000
        MARKET   SHARE           .50                             .50
        PROFIT                  $450                            $450

        DECISIONS                           SLACK

        PRICE           $1.00           ORG SLACK           1.59
        OUTPUT           1000           SALES   SLACK      1.5
        INVENTORY         397           COST  LEVEL        $0.81
        PROMOTION  0/0    .09

        MISCELLANEOUS

        EXCESS   LEVEL               875      RUNOUT LEVEL           875
        LOWER PROD LIMIT            1000      UPPER PROD LIMIT      1000


PERIOD         2


    INDUSTRY   DATA

        GNP        1.01              DEMAND              2304


    FIRM   1   DATA

        FEEDBACK                GOALS                    PERFORMANCE

        SALES                   3000                            2256
        MARKET   SHARE           .50                             .50
        PROFIT                  $450                            $465
```

DECISIONS   SLACK

PRICE $1.00   ORG SLACK   1.54
OUTPUT   1191   SALES SLACK   1.6
INVENTORY   244   COST LEVEL $0.76
PROMOTION   O/O   .10

MISCELLANEOUS

EXCESS LEVEL   1088   RUNOUT LEVEL   961
LOWER PROD LIMIT   1000   UPPER PROD LIMIT   1191

FIRM 2 DATA

FEEDBACK   GOALS   PERFORMANCE

SALES   3000   2257
MARKET SHARE   .50   .50
PROFIT $450 $460

DECISIONS   SLACK

PRICE $1.00   ORG SLACK   1.61
OUTPUT   1200   SALES SLACK   1.5
INVENTORY   245   COST LEVEL $0.78
PROMOTION   O/O   .09

MISCELLANEOUS

EXCESS LEVEL   1046   RUNOUT LEVEL   1046
LOWER PROD LIMIT   1000   UPPER PROD LIMIT   1200

ERIOD   3

INDUSTRY DATA

GNP   1.15   DEMAND   3004

FIRM 1 DATA

FEEDBACK   GOALS   PERFORMANCE

SALES   2746   2256
MARKET SHARE   .50   .50
PROFIT $453 $465

DECISIONS   SLACK

PRICE $1.00   ORG SLACK   1.41
OUTPUT   1418   SALES SLACK   1.6
INVENTORY   -68   COST LEVEL $0.71
PROMOTION   O/O   .10

MISCELLANEOUS

```
EXCESS  LEVEL              1146     RUNOUT LEVEL           106
LOWER PROD LIMIT           1000     UPPER PROD LIMIT       141
```

FIRM 2 DATA

FEEDBACK	GOALS	PERFORMANCE
SALES	2573	2257
MARKET SHARE	.50	.50
PROFIT	$456	$460

DECISIONS   SLACK

```
PRICE          $1.07      ORG SLACK        1.63
OUTPUT          1440      SALES  SLACK     1.5
INVENTORY        -56      COST   LEVEL     $0.88
PROMOTION  0/0   .18
```

MISCELLANEOUS

```
EXCESS  LEVEL              1125     RUNOUT LEVEL          1125
LOWER PROD LIMIT           1000     UPPER PROD LIMIT      144
```

PERIOD   4

INDUSTRY DATA

     GNP   1.10   DEMAND   3780

FIRM 1 DATA

FEEDBACK	GOALS	PERFORMANCE
SALES	2746	2256
MARKET SHARE	.50	.50
PROFIT	$453	$465

DECISIONS   SLACK

```
PRICE          $1.00      ORG SLACK        1.39
OUTPUT          1689      SALES  SLACK     1.6
INVENTORY       -537      COST   LEVEL     $0.68
PROMOTION  0/0   .10
```

MISCELLANEOUS

```
EXCESS  LEVEL              1467     RUNOUT LEVEL          1311
LOWER PROD LIMIT           1000     UPPER PROD LIMIT      1689
```

FIRM 2 DATA

FEEDBACK	GOALS	PERFORMANCE
SALES	2573	2257
MARKET SHARE	.50	.50

```
PROFIT                    $456                          $460

DECISIONS                          SLACK

PRICE              $1.07          ORG SLACK        1.65
OUTPUT              1728          SALES  SLACK     1.5
INVENTORY           -508          COST  LEVEL      $0.88
PROMOTION  0/0      .18

MISCELLANEOUS

EXCESS  LEVEL                1407     RUNOUT LEVEL            1407
LOWER PROD LIMIT            1000     UPPER PROD LIMIT        1728
```

PERIOD   5

INDUSTRY   DATA

```
GNP       1.14           DEMAND          4272
```

FIRM 1 DATA

```
FEEDBACK              GOALS                  PERFORMANCE

SALES                 2746                      5511
MARKET   SHARE         .50                       .49
PROFIT                $453                      $1691

DECISIONS                          SLACK

PRICE              $1.00          ORG SLACK        1.37
OUTPUT              2012          SALES  SLACK     1.6
INVENTORY           -980          COST  LEVEL      $0.69
PROMOTION  0/0      .10

MISCELLANEOUS

EXCESS  LEVEL                1846     RUNOUT LEVEL            1634
LOWER PROD LIMIT            1000     UPPER PROD LIMIT        2012
```

FIRM 2 DATA

```
FEEDBACK              GOALS                  PERFORMANCE

SALES                 2573                      5822
MARKET   SHARE         .50                       .51
PROFIT                $456                      $1033

DECISIONS                          SLACK

PRICE              $1.07          ORG SLACK        1.66
OUTPUT              2074          SALES  SLACK     1.5
INVENTORY           -920          COST  LEVEL      $0.89
PROMOTION  0/0      .18

MISCELLANEOUS
```

```
EXCESS   LEVEL                1770    RUNOUT LEVEL              177
LOWER PROD LIMIT             1000    UPPER PROD LIMIT          207
```

PERIOD   6

INDUSTRY   DATA

    GNP   1.09   DEMAND   4010

FIRM   1   DATA

    FEEDBACK   GOALS   PERFORMANCE

    SALES   4596   5511
    MARKET   SHARE   .49   .49
    PROFIT $718 $1691

    DECISIONS   SLACK

    PRICE $1.00   ORG SLACK   1.30
    OUTPUT   2396   SALES SLACK   1.6
    INVENTORY   -966   COST   LEVEL $0.64
    PROMOTION 0/0   .10

    MISCELLANEOUS

    EXCESS   LEVEL   2103   RUNOUT LEVEL   191
    LOWER PROD LIMIT   1000   UPPER PROD LIMIT   239

FIRM   2   DATA

    FEEDBACK   GOALS   PERFORMANCE

    SALES   4234   5822
    MARKET   SHARE   .51   .51
    PROFIT $824 $1033

    DECISIONS   SLACK

    PRICE $1.07   ORG SLACK   1.68
    OUTPUT   2488   SALES SLACK   1.5
    INVENTORY   -858   COST   LEVEL $0.85
    PROMOTION 0/0   .15

    MISCELLANEOUS

    EXCESS   LEVEL   2048   RUNOUT LEVEL   204
    LOWER PROD LIMIT   1000   UPPER PROD LIMIT   248
```

PERIOD        7

INDUSTRY   DATA
```

GNP   1.12   DEMAND   3912

FIRM   1   DATA

    FEEDBACK   GOALS   PERFORMANCE

    SALES   4596   5511
    MARKET   SHARE   .49   .49
    PROFIT $718 $1691

    DECISIONS   SLACK

    PRICE $1.00   ORG SLACK   1.29
    OUTPUT   2854   SALES SLACK   1.6
    INVENTORY   -518   COST LEVEL $0.65
    PROMOTION 0/0   .10

    MISCELLANEOUS

    EXCESS LEVEL   2009   RUNOUT LEVEL   1960
    LOWER PROD LIMIT   1000   UPPER PROD LIMIT   2854

FIRM   2   DATA

    FEEDBACK   GOALS   PERFORMANCE

    SALES   4234   5822
    MARKET   SHARE   .51   .51
    PROFIT $824 $1033

    DECISIONS   SLACK

    PRICE $1.07   ORG SLACK   1.69
    OUTPUT   2986   SALES SLACK   1.5
    INVENTORY   -334   COST LEVEL $0.87
    PROMOTION 0/0   .15

    MISCELLANEOUS

    EXCESS LEVEL   2021   RUNOUT LEVEL   2021
    LOWER PROD LIMIT   1000   UPPER PROD LIMIT   2986

ERIOD   8

INDUSTRY DATA

    GNP   0.85   DEMAND   2216

FIRM   1   DATA

    FEEDBACK   GOALS   PERFORMANCE

    SALES   4596   5034
    MARKET   SHARE   .49   .48
    PROFIT $718 $1599

```
        DECISIONS                              SLACK

        PRICE            $1.00          ORG SLACK         1.29
        OUTPUT           1618           SALES  SLACK      1.6
        INVENTORY        1233           COST  LEVEL       $0.81
        PROMOTION   0/0   .10

        MISCELLANEOUS

        EXCESS  LEVEL              1954     RUNOUT LEVEL          195
        LOWER PROD LIMIT          1191     UPPER PROD LIMIT      339


   FIRM  2  DATA

        FEEDBACK          GOALS                 PERFORMANCE

        SALES             4234                      5452
        MARKET   SHARE     .51                       .52
        PROFIT           $824                       $905

        DECISIONS                              SLACK

        PRICE            $1.07          ORG SLACK         1.63
        OUTPUT           1752           SALES  SLACK      1.5
        INVENTORY        1539           COST  LEVEL       $1.02
        PROMOTION   0/0   .13

        MISCELLANEOUS

        EXCESS  LEVEL              1978     RUNOUT LEVEL         1978
        LOWER PROD LIMIT          1200     UPPER PROD LIMIT      3583


PERIOD          9

   INDUSTRY  DATA

        GNP       0.93         DEMAND            2172


   FIRM  1  DATA

        FEEDBACK          GOALS                 PERFORMANCE

        SALES             4894                      5034
        MARKET   SHARE     .48                       .48
        PROFIT           $928                      $1599

        DECISIONS                              SLACK

        PRICE            $1.04          ORG SLACK         1.27
        OUTPUT           1418           SALES  SLACK      1.7
        INVENTORY        1771           COST  LEVEL       $0.92
        PROMOTION   0/0   .10

        MISCELLANEOUS
```

```
EXCESS  LEVEL                1189      RUNOUT LEVEL               1189
LOWER PROD LIMIT            1418      UPPER PROD LIMIT           3399
```

FIRM 2 DATA

```
FEEDBACK            GOALS                 PERFORMANCE

SALES               4946                      5452
MARKET   SHARE       .52                       .52
PROFIT             $880                      $905

DECISIONS                     SLACK

PRICE           $1.28      ORG SLACK         1.87
OUTPUT           1440      SALES  SLACK      1.5
INVENTORY        2199      COST  LEVEL      $1.26
PROMOTION  0/0    .12

MISCELLANEOUS

EXCESS  LEVEL               1329      RUNOUT LEVEL               1329
LOWER PROD LIMIT           1440      UPPER PROD LIMIT           3583
```

ERIOD   10

INDUSTRY DATA

```
GNP        1.14        DEMAND          4604
```

FIRM 1 DATA

```
FEEDBACK            GOALS                 PERFORMANCE

SALES               4894                      5034
MARKET   SHARE       .48                       .48
PROFIT             $928                     $1599

DECISIONS                     SLACK

PRICE           $1.04      ORG SLACK         1.27
OUTPUT           2246      SALES  SLACK      1.9
INVENTORY         899      COST  LEVEL      $0.73
PROMOTION  0/0    .10

MISCELLANEOUS

EXCESS  LEVEL               1091      RUNOUT LEVEL               1091
LOWER PROD LIMIT           1200      UPPER PROD LIMIT           3399
```

FIRM 2 DATA

```
FEEDBACK            GOALS                 PERFORMANCE

SALES               4946                      5452
MARKET   SHARE       .52                       .52
```

```
PROFIT                    $880                        $905

DECISIONS                          SLACK

PRICE          $1.28               ORG SLACK        1.87
OUTPUT          1726               SALES  SLACK     1.6
INVENTORY       1325               COST  LEVEL     $1.04
PROMOTION  O/O    .12

MISCELLANEOUS

EXCESS  LEVEL              1151      RUNOUT LEVEL           11
LOWER PROD LIMIT          1152      UPPER PROD LIMIT       35
```

PERIOD   11

```
INDUSTRY  DATA

    GNP       0.95        DEMAND          5154


FIRM  1  DATA

    FEEDBACK          GOALS                PERFORMANCE

    SALES            4894                      6147
    MARKET   SHARE     .48                       .45
    PROFIT           $928                     $1773

    DECISIONS                      SLACK

    PRICE          $1.04           ORG SLACK        1.37
    OUTPUT          3174           SALES  SLACK     2.0
    INVENTORY        582           COST  LEVEL     $0.69
    PROMOTION  O/O    .10

    MISCELLANEOUS

    EXCESS  LEVEL              2169      RUNOUT LEVEL          17
    LOWER PROD LIMIT          1200      UPPER PROD LIMIT      33


FIRM  2  DATA

    FEEDBACK          GOALS                PERFORMANCE

    SALES            4946                      7437
    MARKET   SHARE     .52                       .55
    PROFIT           $880                     $1379

    DECISIONS                      SLACK

    PRICE          $1.28           ORG SLACK        2.03
    OUTPUT          2984           SALES  SLACK     1.6
    INVENTORY        460           COST  LEVEL     $0.96
    PROMOTION  O/O    .12

    MISCELLANEOUS
```

EXCESS LEVEL	2023	RUNOUT LEVEL	2023
LOWER PROD LIMIT	1152	UPPER PROD LIMIT	3583

ERIOD   12

INDUSTRY   DATA

   GNP   0.86   DEMAND   5012

FIRM   1   DATA

   FEEDBACK   GOALS   PERFORMANCE

   SALES   5758   6147
   MARKET   SHARE   .46   .45
   PROFIT $1151 $1773

   DECISIONS   SLACK

   PRICE $1.04   ORG SLACK   1.40
   OUTPUT   3028   SALES SLACK   2.1
   INVENTORY   1263   COST   LEVEL $0.73
   PROMOTION 0/0   .10

   MISCELLANEOUS

   EXCESS LEVEL   2523   RUNOUT LEVEL   2210
   LOWER PROD LIMIT   1200   UPPER PROD LIMIT   3399

FIRM   2   DATA

   FEEDBACK   GOALS   PERFORMANCE

   SALES   6558   7437
   MARKET   SHARE   .54   .55
   PROFIT $1249 $1379

   DECISIONS   SLACK

   PRICE $1.28   ORG SLACK   2.27
   OUTPUT   3123   SALES SLACK   1.6
   INVENTORY   924   COST   LEVEL $1.04
   PROMOTION 0/0   .11

   MISCELLANEOUS

   EXCESS LEVEL   2449   RUNOUT LEVEL   2449
   LOWER PROD LIMIT   1152   UPPER PROD LIMIT   3583

ERIOD   13

INDUSTRY   DATA

```
GNP        0.90          DEMAND              6014
```

FIRM   1   DATA

```
FEEDBACK              GOALS                    PERFORMANCE

SALES                 5758                        6147
MARKET   SHARE         .46                         .45
PROFIT               $1151                       $1773
```

DECISIONS   SLACK

```
PRICE           $1.04        ORG SLACK          1.50
OUTPUT           3399        SALES  SLACK       2.3
INVENTORY        1299        COST  LEVEL       $0.77
PROMOTION  0/0    .10
```

MISCELLANEOUS

```
EXCESS  LEVEL                2495     RUNOUT LEVEL             236
LOWER PROD LIMIT            1200     UPPER PROD LIMIT         339
```

FIRM   2   DATA

```
FEEDBACK              GOALS                    PERFORMANCE

SALES                 6558                        7437
MARKET   SHARE         .54                         .55
PROFIT               $1249                       $1379
```

DECISIONS   SLACK

```
PRICE           $1.29        ORG SLACK          2.43
OUTPUT           3430        SALES  SLACK       1.7
INVENTORY        1025        COST  LEVEL       $1.12
PROMOTION  0/0    .11
```

MISCELLANEOUS

```
EXCESS  LEVEL                2502     RUNOUT LEVEL            250
LOWER PROD LIMIT            1152     UPPER PROD LIMIT        358
```

PERIOD   14

INDUSTRY DATA

```
GNP        1.00          DEMAND              9277
```

FIRM   1   DATA

```
FEEDBACK              GOALS                    PERFORMANCE

SALES                 5758                       10550
MARKET   SHARE         .46                         .45
PROFIT               $1151                       $3224
```

DECISIONS   SLACK

PRICE $1.04   ORG SLACK   1.46
OUTPUT   4048   SALES SLACK   2.2
INVENTORY   82   COST LEVEL $0.70
PROMOTION 0/0   .10

MISCELLANEOUS

EXCESS LEVEL   2941   RUNOUT LEVEL   2715
LOWER PROD LIMIT   1200   UPPER PROD LIMIT   4048

FIRM 2 DATA

FEEDBACK   GOALS   PERFORMANCE

SALES   6558   13108
MARKET   SHARE   .54   .55
PROFIT $1249 $2057

DECISIONS   SLACK

PRICE $1.29   ORG SLACK   2.43
OUTPUT   3430   SALES SLACK   1.8
INVENTORY   -206   COST LEVEL $1.09
PROMOTION 0/0   .10

MISCELLANEOUS

EXCESS LEVEL   2892   RUNOUT LEVEL   2892
LOWER PROD LIMIT   1152   UPPER PROD LIMIT   3430

PERIOD   15

INDUSTRY DATA

GNP   1.14   DEMAND   14043

FIRM 1 DATA

FEEDBACK   GOALS   PERFORMANCE

SALES   9112   10550
MARKET   SHARE   .45   .45
PROFIT $1745 $3224

DECISIONS   SLACK

PRICE $1.12   ORG SLACK   1.36
OUTPUT   4822   SALES SLACK   2.3
INVENTORY   -2861   COST LEVEL $0.69
PROMOTION 0/0   .10

MISCELLANEOUS

```
    EXCESS   LEVEL                4447      RUNOUT LEVEL                   377
    LOWER PROD LIMIT             1200      UPPER PROD LIMIT               482
```

FIRM 2 DATA

```
    FEEDBACK              GOALS                      PERFORMANCE

    SALES                11142                          13108
    MARKET   SHARE         .55                            .55
    PROFIT              $1878                          $2057

    DECISIONS                         SLACK

    PRICE          $1.38             ORG SLACK         2.45
    OUTPUT          4116             SALES  SLACK      1.7
    INVENTORY      -3826             COST  LEVEL      $1.16
    PROMOTION  0/0   .09

    MISCELLANEOUS

    EXCESS  LEVEL                4219      RUNOUT LEVEL                   421
    LOWER PROD LIMIT            1152      UPPER PROD LIMIT               411
```

PERIOD   16

INDUSTRY DATA

```
    GNP      0.82        DEMAND            9126
```

FIRM 1 DATA

```
    FEEDBACK              GOALS                      PERFORMANCE

    SALES                 9112                          10550
    MARKET   SHARE         .45                            .45
    PROFIT              $1745                          $3224

    DECISIONS                         SLACK

    PRICE          $1.12             ORG SLACK         1.34
    OUTPUT          5743             SALES  SLACK      2.3
    INVENTORY      -2587             COST  LEVEL      $0.60
    PROMOTION  0/0   .10

    MISCELLANEOUS

    EXCESS  LEVEL                6735      RUNOUT LEVEL                   557
    LOWER PROD LIMIT            1200      UPPER PROD LIMIT               574
```

FIRM 2 DATA

```
    FEEDBACK              GOALS                      PERFORMANCE

    SALES                11142                          13108
    MARKET   SHARE         .55                            .55
```

```
PROFIT                $1878                        $2057

DECISIONS                          SLACK

PRICE            $1.38            ORG SLACK        2.38
OUTPUT            4940            SALES  SLACK     1.7
INVENTORY        -4288            COST  LEVEL     $0.99
PROMOTION  0/0    .09

MISCELLANEOUS

EXCESS  LEVEL            6343     RUNOUT LEVEL            6343
LOWER PROD LIMIT        1726     UPPER PROD LIMIT        4940
```

PERIOD   17

INDUSTRY DATA

```
GNP        0.99          DEMAND          11429
```

FIRM 1 DATA

```
FEEDBACK            GOALS                PERFORMANCE

SALES               9112                    18757
MARKET   SHARE       .45                      .45
PROFIT             $1745                    $7989

DECISIONS                          SLACK

PRICE            $1.12            ORG SLACK        1.33
OUTPUT            6840            SALES  SLACK     2.2
INVENTORY        -2545            COST  LEVEL     $0.65
PROMOTION  0/0    .10

MISCELLANEOUS

EXCESS  LEVEL           4769      RUNOUT LEVEL            4769
LOWER PROD LIMIT       3028      UPPER PROD LIMIT        6840
```

FIRM 2 DATA

```
FEEDBACK            GOALS                PERFORMANCE

SALES              11142                    23373
MARKET   SHARE       .55                      .55
PROFIT             $1878                    $5284

DECISIONS                          SLACK

PRICE            $1.38            ORG SLACK        2.32
OUTPUT            5928            SALES  SLACK     1.7
INVENTORY        -5077            COST  LEVEL     $1.05
PROMOTION  0/0    .09

MISCELLANEOUS
```

```
        EXCESS  LEVEL              5019      RUNOUT LEVEL              501
        LOWER PROD LIMIT           2984      UPPER PROD LIMIT         592
```

PERIOD   18

INDUSTRY DATA

```
      GNP       0.87         DEMAND            9199
```

FIRM 1 DATA

```
      FEEDBACK           GOALS                 PERFORMANCE

      SALES              15956                      18757
      MARKET   SHARE       .45                        .45
      PROFIT            $3679                      $7989

      DECISIONS                      SLACK

      PRICE          $1.12           ORG SLACK        1.27
      OUTPUT          7870           SALES  SLACK     2.3
      INVENTORY       -298           COST  LEVEL    $0.59
      PROMOTION  0/0   .10

      MISCELLANEOUS

      EXCESS  LEVEL              5607      RUNOUT LEVEL             529
      LOWER PROD LIMIT           3028      UPPER PROD LIMIT         814
```

FIRM 2 DATA

```
      FEEDBACK           GOALS                 PERFORMANCE

      SALES              20253                      23373
      MARKET   SHARE       .55                        .55
      PROFIT            $4642                      $5284

      DECISIONS                      SLACK

      PRICE          $1.38           ORG SLACK        2.35
      OUTPUT          7113           SALES  SLACK     1.6
      INVENTORY      -3756           COST  LEVEL    $1.00
      PROMOTION  0/0   .08

      MISCELLANEOUS

      EXCESS  LEVEL              5551      RUNOUT LEVEL             555
      LOWER PROD LIMIT           3123      UPPER PROD LIMIT         711
```

PERIOD   19

INDUSTRY DATA

GNP   1.10   DEMAND   13356

FIRM 1 DATA

FEEDBACK   GOALS   PERFORMANCE

SALES   15956   18757
MARKET   SHARE   .45   .45
PROFIT $3679 $7989

DECISIONS   SLACK

PRICE $1.12   ORG SLACK   1.37
OUTPUT   8146   SALES SLACK   2.4
INVENTORY   895   COST LEVEL $0.73
PROMOTION 0/0   .10

MISCELLANEOUS

EXCESS LEVEL   4695   RUNOUT LEVEL   4695
LOWER PROD LIMIT   3399   UPPER PROD LIMIT   8146

FIRM 2 DATA

FEEDBACK   GOALS   PERFORMANCE

SALES   20253   23373
MARKET   SHARE   .55   .55
PROFIT $4642 $5284

DECISIONS   SLACK

PRICE $1.38   ORG SLACK   2.30
OUTPUT   8536   SALES SLACK   1.6
INVENTORY   -3322   COST LEVEL $1.10
PROMOTION 0/0   .08

MISCELLANEOUS

EXCESS LEVEL   4843   RUNOUT LEVEL   4843
LOWER PROD LIMIT   3430   UPPER PROD LIMIT   8536

ERIOD   20

INDUSTRY DATA

GNP   1.03   DEMAND   14432

FIRM 1 DATA

FEEDBACK   GOALS   PERFORMANCE

SALES   15956   20670
MARKET   SHARE   .45   .45
PROFIT $3679 $7805

```
DECISIONS                              SLACK

   PRICE         $1.12                 ORG SLACK        1.35
   OUTPUT         9371                 SALES  SLACK     2.4
   INVENTORY      1815                 COST  LEVEL     $0.73
   PROMOTION  0/0   .10

   MISCELLANEOUS

   EXCESS  LEVEL              6477     RUNOUT LEVEL          58
   LOWER PROD LIMIT           4048     UPPER PROD LIMIT      97


FIRM  2  DATA

   FEEDBACK            GOALS                 PERFORMANCE

   SALES              20253                      25581
   MARKET  SHARE        .55                        .55
   PROFIT            $4642                      $6167

   DECISIONS                           SLACK

   PRICE         $1.38                 ORG SLACK        2.25
   OUTPUT        10243                 SALES  SLACK     1.6
   INVENTORY     -1993                 COST  LEVEL     $1.04
   PROMOTION  0/0   .08

   MISCELLANEOUS

   EXCESS  LEVEL              6220     RUNOUT LEVEL         622
   LOWER PROD LIMIT           3430     UPPER PROD LIMIT    1024


PERIOD       21

   INDUSTRY  DATA

      GNP       0.82        DEMAND           9217


   FIRM  1  DATA

   FEEDBACK            GOALS                 PERFORMANCE

   SALES              19345                      20670
   MARKET  SHARE        .45                        .45
   PROFIT            $5048                      $7805

   DECISIONS                           SLACK

   PRICE         $1.12                 ORG SLACK        1.41
   OUTPUT         4960                 SALES  SLACK     2.4
   INVENTORY      6565                 COST  LEVEL     $0.92
   PROMOTION  0/0   .09

   MISCELLANEOUS
```

```
        EXCESS  LEVEL              7150      RUNOUT LEVEL              6598
        LOWER PROD LIMIT           4822      UPPER PROD LIMIT          9702


 FIRM  2  DATA

        FEEDBACK            GOALS                     PERFORMANCE

        SALES               24425                        25581
        MARKET   SHARE        .55                          .55
        PROFIT             $5923                        $6167

        DECISIONS                       SLACK

        PRICE          $1.38            ORG SLACK       2.09
        OUTPUT          7210            SALES  SLACK    1.7
        INVENTORY       3654            COST  LEVEL    $1.04
        PROMOTION   0/0  .08

        MISCELLANEOUS

        EXCESS  LEVEL              6960      RUNOUT LEVEL              6960
        LOWER PROD LIMIT           4116      UPPER PROD LIMIT         12291
```

PERIOD   22

 INDUSTRY DATA

```
        GNP       0.88           DEMAND          9663
```

 FIRM 1 DATA

```
        FEEDBACK            GOALS                     PERFORMANCE

        SALES               19345                        20670
        MARKET   SHARE        .45                          .45
        PROFIT             $5048                        $7805

        DECISIONS                       SLACK

        PRICE          $1.14            ORG SLACK       1.52
        OUTPUT          4960            SALES  SLACK    2.5
        INVENTORY       6675            COST  LEVEL    $0.97
        PROMOTION   0/0  .09

        MISCELLANEOUS

        EXCESS  LEVEL              4877      RUNOUT LEVEL              4877
        LOWER PROD LIMIT           4960      UPPER PROD LIMIT          9702
```

 FIRM 2 DATA

```
        FEEDBACK            GOALS                     PERFORMANCE

        SALES               24425                        25581
        MARKET   SHARE       .55                          .55
```

```
PROFIT                    $5923                           $6167

DECISIONS                              SLACK

PRICE              $1.38             ORG SLACK         2.12
OUTPUT              4940             SALES  SLACK      1.7
INVENTORY           6051             COST   LEVEL     $1.17
PROMOTION   0/0      .07

MISCELLANEOUS

EXCESS  LEVEL                 5187    RUNOUT LEVEL               51
LOWER PROD LIMIT             4940    UPPER PROD LIMIT          122
```

PERIOD   23

INDUSTRY   DATA

```
GNP         1.07          DEMAND          17028
```

FIRM 1 DATA

```
FEEDBACK           GOALS                    PERFORMANCE

SALES              19345                      20363
MARKET   SHARE       .45                        .45
PROFIT             $5048                      $4586

DECISIONS                              SLACK

PRICE              $1.14             ORG SLACK         1.47
OUTPUT              9089             SALES  SLACK      2.8
INVENTORY           3075             COST   LEVEL     $0.81
PROMOTION   0/0      .09

MISCELLANEOUS

EXCESS  LEVEL                4853    RUNOUT LEVEL               48
LOWER PROD LIMIT            4196    UPPER PROD LIMIT           97
```

FIRM 2 DATA

```
FEEDBACK           GOALS                    PERFORMANCE

SALES              24425                      24728
MARKET   SHARE       .55                        .55
PROFIT             $5923                      $5385

DECISIONS                              SLACK

PRICE              $1.38             ORG SLACK         2.09
OUTPUT              8018             SALES  SLACK      1.9
INVENTORY           2523             COST   LEVEL     $1.05
PROMOTION   0/0      .07

MISCELLANEOUS
```

| EXCESS LEVEL | 4906 | RUNOUT LEVEL | 4906 |
| LOWER PROD LIMIT | 3952 | UPPER PROD LIMIT | 12291 |

RIOD   24

INDUSTRY DATA

GNP   0.96   DEMAND   21142

FIRM 1 DATA

FEEDBACK   GOALS   PERFORMANCE

SALES	20086		20363
MARKET SHARE	.45		.45
PROFIT	$4920		$4586

DECISIONS   SLACK

PRICE	$1.14	ORG SLACK	1.57
OUTPUT	9702	SALES SLACK	2.6
INVENTORY	1520	COST LEVEL	$0.77
PROMOTION 0/0	.09		

MISCELLANEOUS

| EXCESS LEVEL | 8185 | RUNOUT LEVEL | 6925 |
| LOWER PROD LIMIT | 4196 | UPPER PROD LIMIT | 9702 |

FIRM 2 DATA

FEEDBACK   GOALS   PERFORMANCE

SALES	24673		24728
MARKET SHARE	.55		.55
PROFIT	$5694		$5385

DECISIONS   SLACK

PRICE	$1.40	ORG SLACK	2.05
OUTPUT	12291	SALES SLACK	2.0
INVENTORY	43	COST LEVEL	$0.93
PROMOTION 0/0	.07		

MISCELLANEOUS

| EXCESS LEVEL | 7577 | RUNOUT LEVEL | 7577 |
| LOWER PROD LIMIT | 3952 | UPPER PROD LIMIT | 12291 |

RIOD   25

INDUSTRY DATA

```
        GNP        0.86            DEMAND            16930

FIRM   1   DATA

        FEEDBACK              GOALS                    PERFORMANCE

        SALES                20086                        20363
        MARKET   SHARE         .45                          .45
        PROFIT               $4920                        $4586

        DECISIONS                        SLACK

        PRICE        $1.14         ORG SLACK        1.47
        OUTPUT       11555         SALES  SLACK     2.4
        INVENTORY     2689         COST  LEVEL     $0.73
        PROMOTION  0/0  .09

        MISCELLANEOUS

        EXCESS  LEVEL            10396    RUNOUT LEVEL          90
        LOWER PROD LIMIT         4196    UPPER PROD LIMIT      115

FIRM   2   DATA

        FEEDBACK              GOALS                    PERFORMANCE

        SALES                24673                        24728
        MARKET   SHARE         .55                          .55
        PROFIT               $5694                        $5385

        DECISIONS                        SLACK

        PRICE        $1.40         ORG SLACK        1.95
        OUTPUT       11445         SALES  SLACK     1.9
        INVENTORY     3937         COST  LEVEL     $0.94
        PROMOTION  0/0  .07

        MISCELLANEOUS

        EXCESS  LEVEL             9768    RUNOUT LEVEL          976
        LOWER PROD LIMIT         3952    UPPER PROD LIMIT      147

PERIOD        26

    INDUSTRY   DATA

        GNP        1.02            DEMAND            18386

    FIRM   1   DATA

        FEEDBACK              GOALS                    PERFORMANCE

        SALES                20086                        32500
        MARKET   SHARE         .45                          .45
        PROFIT               $4920                        $10595
```

```
DECISIONS                          SLACK

    PRICE          $1.14           ORG SLACK          1.38
    OUTPUT         11326           SALES  SLACK       2.2
    INVENTORY       4968           COST   LEVEL      $0.79
    PROMOTION  0/0   .09

    MISCELLANEOUS

    EXCESS  LEVEL           8721       RUNOUT LEVEL          8721
    LOWER PROD LIMIT        4196       UPPER PROD LIMIT     13762


FIRM  2  DATA

    FEEDBACK              GOALS              PERFORMANCE

    SALES               24673                  39006
    MARKET   SHARE        .55                    .55
    PROFIT             $5694                  $11976

    DECISIONS                      SLACK

    PRICE          $1.40           ORG SLACK          1.93
    OUTPUT         10053           SALES  SLACK       1.9
    INVENTORY       6273           COST   LEVEL      $1.05
    PROMOTION  0/0   .07

    MISCELLANEOUS

    EXCESS  LEVEL           8740       RUNOUT LEVEL          8740
    LOWER PROD LIMIT       3952       UPPER PROD LIMIT     14750


RIOD       27


INDUSTRY  DATA

    GNP      1.02           DEMAND          16573


FIRM  1  DATA

    FEEDBACK              GOALS              PERFORMANCE

    SALES               29230                  32500
    MARKET   SHARE        .45                    .45
    PROFIT             $6866                  $10595

    DECISIONS                      SLACK

    PRICE          $1.15           ORG SLACK          1.54
    OUTPUT          9101           SALES  SLACK       2.2
    INVENTORY       7925           COST   LEVEL      $0.94
    PROMOTION  0/0   .08

    MISCELLANEOUS
```

```
EXCESS  LEVEL                 9220      RUNOUT LEVEL              9
LOWER PROD LIMIT             4196      UPPER PROD LIMIT         13
```

FIRM 2 DATA

```
FEEDBACK              GOALS                    PERFORMANCE

SALES                 36761                        39006
MARKET   SHARE          .55                          .55
PROFIT                $10447                       $11976

DECISIONS                          SLACK

PRICE          $1.40               ORG SLACK          1.89
OUTPUT          8959               SALES  SLACK       2.1
INVENTORY       8122               COST  LEVEL       $1.08
PROMOTION  0/0    .06

MISCELLANEOUS

EXCESS  LEVEL                 9017      RUNOUT LEVEL             90
LOWER PROD LIMIT             3952      UPPER PROD LIMIT        147
```

PERIOD   28

INDUSTRY DATA

```
GNP       1.23          DEMAND           25896
```

FIRM 1 DATA

```
FEEDBACK              GOALS                    PERFORMANCE

SALES                 29230                        32500
MARKET   SHARE          .45                          .45
PROFIT                $6866                        $10595

DECISIONS                          SLACK

PRICE          $1.15               ORG SLACK          1.52
OUTPUT         13762               SALES  SLACK       2.3
INVENTORY       3937               COST  LEVEL       $0.87
PROMOTION  0/0    .08

MISCELLANEOUS

EXCESS  LEVEL                 8455      RUNOUT LEVEL             84
LOWER PROD LIMIT             4196      UPPER PROD LIMIT        137
```

FIRM 2 DATA

```
FEEDBACK              GOALS                    PERFORMANCE

SALES                 36761                        39006
MARKET   SHARE          .55                          .55
```

PROFIT $10447 $11976

DECISIONS   SLACK

PRICE $1.39   ORG SLACK   2.05
OUTPUT   12726   SALES SLACK   2.2
INVENTORY   4273   COST LEVEL $1.11
PROMOTION 0/0   .06

MISCELLANEOUS

EXCESS LEVEL   8407   RUNOUT LEVEL   8407
LOWER PROD LIMIT   3952   UPPER PROD LIMIT   14750

ERIOD   29

INDUSTRY   DATA

GNP   1.00   DEMAND   23171

FIRM   1   DATA

FEEDBACK   GOALS   PERFORMANCE

SALES   29230   37937
MARKET   SHARE   .45   .46
PROFIT $6866 $9122

DECISIONS   SLACK

PRICE $1.15   ORG SLACK   1.48
OUTPUT   14676   SALES SLACK   2.3
INVENTORY   5979   COST LEVEL $0.82
PROMOTION 0/0   .08

MISCELLANEOUS

EXCESS LEVEL   12621   RUNOUT LEVEL   11045
LOWER PROD LIMIT   4196   UPPER PROD LIMIT   16390

FIRM   2   DATA

FEEDBACK   GOALS   PERFORMANCE

SALES   36761   45313
MARKET   SHARE   .55   .54
PROFIT $10447 $9966

DECISIONS   SLACK

PRICE $1.39   ORG SLACK   2.09
OUTPUT   14134   SALES SLACK   2.3
INVENTORY   5549   COST LEVEL $1.06
PROMOTION 0/0   .06

MISCELLANEOUS

```
        EXCESS   LEVEL              11708      RUNOUT LEVEL              1170
        LOWER PROD LIMIT            8018       UPPER PROD LIMIT          1475
```

PERIOD   30

    INDUSTRY   DATA

        GNP   0.89   DEMAND   18359

    FIRM   1   DATA

        FEEDBACK   GOALS   PERFORMANCE

        SALES   35716   37937
        MARKET   SHARE   .45   .46
        PROFIT $7687 $9122

        DECISIONS   SLACK

        PRICE $1.15   ORG SLACK   1.51
        OUTPUT   9653   SALES SLACK   2.3
        INVENTORY   11360   COST LEVEL $0.94
        PROMOTION 0/0   .07

        MISCELLANEOUS

        EXCESS   LEVEL   11811   RUNOUT LEVEL   1142
        LOWER PROD LIMIT   9101   UPPER PROD LIMIT   1639

    FIRM   2   DATA

        FEEDBACK   GOALS   PERFORMANCE

        SALES   44174   45313
        MARKET   SHARE   .55   .54
        PROFIT $10273 $9966

        DECISIONS   SLACK

        PRICE $1.39   ORG SLACK   2.05
        OUTPUT   10508   SALES SLACK   2.4
        INVENTORY   10619   COST LEVEL $1.13
        PROMOTION 0/0   .06

        MISCELLANEOUS

        EXCESS   LEVEL   11515   RUNOUT LEVEL   1151
        LOWER PROD LIMIT   8959   UPPER PROD LIMIT   1475

PERIOD   31

    INDUSTRY   DATA
```
```

GNP   1.08   DEMAND   25931

FIRM 1 DATA

FEEDBACK   GOALS   PERFORMANCE

SALES   35716   37937
MARKET SHARE   .45   .46
PROFIT $7687 $9122

DECISIONS   SLACK

PRICE $1.15   ORG SLACK   1.61
OUTPUT   13628   SALES SLACK   2.5
INVENTORY   7877   COST LEVEL $0.93
PROMOTION 0/0   .07

MISCELLANEOUS

EXCESS LEVEL   9549   RUNOUT LEVEL   9549
LOWER PROD LIMIT   9101   UPPER PROD LIMIT   16390

FIRM 2 DATA

FEEDBACK   GOALS   PERFORMANCE

SALES   44174   45313
MARKET SHARE   .55   .54
PROFIT $10273 $9966

DECISIONS   SLACK

PRICE $1.40   ORG SLACK   2.02
OUTPUT   12100   SALES SLACK   2.4
INVENTORY   8332   COST LEVEL $1.10
PROMOTION 0/0   .06

MISCELLANEOUS

EXCESS LEVEL   9677   RUNOUT LEVEL   9677
LOWER PROD LIMIT   8959   UPPER PROD LIMIT   14134

PERIOD   32

INDUSTRY DATA

GNP   1.04   DEMAND   29588

FIRM 1 DATA

FEEDBACK   GOALS   PERFORMANCE

SALES   35716   42873
MARKET SHARE   .45   .46
PROFIT $7687 $8080

```
DECISIONS                          SLACK

PRICE          $1.15              ORG SLACK        1.72
OUTPUT         16390              SALES  SLACK     2.6
INVENTORY       6505              COST  LEVEL     $0.93
PROMOTION  0/0   .07

MISCELLANEOUS

EXCESS  LEVEL            12774    RUNOUT LEVEL          115
LOWER PROD LIMIT         9101     UPPER PROD LIMIT      163
```

```
FIRM  2  DATA

    FEEDBACK            GOALS                PERFORMANCE

    SALES             44174                     50780
    MARKET  SHARE       .55                       .54
    PROFIT          $10273                    $10855

    DECISIONS                          SLACK

    PRICE          $1.40              ORG SLACK       2.10
    OUTPUT         14134              SALES  SLACK     2.4
    INVENTORY       5844              COST  LEVEL     $1.07
    PROMOTION  0/0   .06

    MISCELLANEOUS

    EXCESS  LEVEL            12016    RUNOUT LEVEL          120
    LOWER PROD LIMIT         8959     UPPER PROD LIMIT      141
```

```
PERIOD       33

    INDUSTRY  DATA

        GNP      0.95         DEMAND        28604

    FIRM  1  DATA

        FEEDBACK            GOALS                PERFORMANCE

        SALES             41106                     42873
        MARKET  SHARE       .45                       .46
        PROFIT           $7838                     $8080

        DECISIONS                          SLACK

        PRICE          $1.15              ORG SLACK       1.69
        OUTPUT         17414              SALES  SLACK     2.4
        INVENTORY       8380              COST  LEVEL     $0.91
        PROMOTION  0/0   .07

        MISCELLANEOUS
```

9+79;; ≠9]9=   1ILLJ   1>[≠^[($9]9=   HIMO
LOWER PROD LIMIT   9101   UPPER PROD LIMIT   19521

FIRM 2 DATA

FEEDBACK	GOALS	PERFORMANCE
SALES	50032	50780
MARKET SHARE	.54	.54
PROFIT	$10678	$10855

DECISIONS		SLACK	
PRICE	$1.40	ORG SLACK	1.97
OUTPUT	16961	SALES SLACK	2.4
INVENTORY	5889	COST LEVEL	$0.98
PROMOTION 0/0	.06		

MISCELLANEOUS

EXCESS LEVEL	13945	RUNOUT LEVEL	13945
LOWER PROD LIMIT	8959	UPPER PROD LIMIT	16961

PERIOD   34

INDUSTRY DATA

GNP   1.03   DEMAND   30417

FIRM 1 DATA

FEEDBACK	GOALS	PERFORMANCE
SALES	41106	42873
MARKET SHARE	.45	.46
PROFIT	$7838	$8080

DECISIONS		SLACK	
PRICE	$1.15	ORG SLACK	1.64
OUTPUT	17418	SALES SLACK	2.6
INVENTORY	10350	COST LEVEL	$0.93
PROMOTION 0/0	.07		

MISCELLANEOUS

EXCESS LEVEL	14541	RUNOUT LEVEL	14059
LOWER PROD LIMIT	9653	UPPER PROD LIMIT	19521

FIRM 2 DATA

FEEDBACK	GOALS	PERFORMANCE
SALES	50032	50780
MARKET SHARE	.54	.54

```
PROFIT              $10678                        $10855

DECISIONS                        SLACK

PRICE        $1.40              ORG SLACK        1.95
OUTPUT        17349             SALES  SLACK     2.4
INVENTORY      7877             COST  LEVEL      $1.03
PROMOTION  0/0   .06

MISCELLANEOUS

EXCESS  LEVEL            14053     RUNOUT LEVEL          1405
LOWER PROD LIMIT        10508     UPPER PROD LIMIT      2035
```

PERIOD 35

 INDUSTRY DATA

  GNP 1.10 DEMAND 38825

 FIRM 1 DATA

```
FEEDBACK             GOALS                 PERFORMANCE

SALES                41106                    56908
MARKET  SHARE          .45                      .46
PROFIT               $7838                   $10507

DECISIONS                        SLACK

PRICE        $1.15              ORG SLACK        1.75
OUTPUT        19521             SALES  SLACK     2.8
INVENTORY      8043             COST  LEVEL      $0.95
PROMOTION  0/0   .07

MISCELLANEOUS

EXCESS  LEVEL            15353     RUNOUT LEVEL          1483
LOWER PROD LIMIT         9653     UPPER PROD LIMIT      1952
```

 FIRM 2 DATA

```
FEEDBACK             GOALS                 PERFORMANCE

SALES                50032                    67268
MARKET  SHARE          .54                      .54
PROFIT               $10678                  $17038

DECISIONS                        SLACK

PRICE        $1.39              ORG SLACK        2.11
OUTPUT        20353             SALES  SLACK     2.6
INVENTORY      6126             COST  LEVEL      $1.09
PROMOTION  0/0   .06

MISCELLANEOUS
```

```
        EXCESS  LEVEL              14743      RUNOUT LEVEL              14743
        LOWER PROD LIMIT           10508      UPPER PROD LIMIT          20353
```

PERIOD   36

INDUSTRY DATA

```
     GNP        0.87          DEMAND          31063
```

FIRM 1 DATA

```
     FEEDBACK               GOALS                    PERFORMANCE

     SALES                  53132                        56908
     MARKET   SHARE           .45                          .46
     PROFIT                 $8916                       $10507

     DECISIONS                        SLACK

     PRICE         $1.15             ORG SLACK        1.71
     OUTPUT        19492             SALES  SLACK     2.5
     INVENTORY     11771             COST   LEVEL    $0.92
     PROMOTION  0/0   .07

     MISCELLANEOUS

     EXCESS  LEVEL            19284      RUNOUT LEVEL            17568
     LOWER PROD LIMIT          9653      UPPER PROD LIMIT        23249
```

FIRM 2 DATA

```
     FEEDBACK               GOALS                    PERFORMANCE

     SALES                  65609                        67268
     MARKET   SHARE           .54                          .54
     PROFIT                $15398                       $17038

     DECISIONS                        SLACK

     PRICE         $1.39             ORG SLACK        1.98
     OUTPUT        19376             SALES  SLACK     2.6
     INVENTORY     11210             COST   LEVEL    $1.02
     PROMOTION  0/0   .06

     MISCELLANEOUS

     EXCESS  LEVEL            18011      RUNOUT LEVEL            18011
     LOWER PROD LIMIT         10508      UPPER PROD LIMIT        24424
```

PERIOD   37

INDUSTRY DATA

```
        GNP      0.97          DEMAND          33097


FIRM  1  DATA

        FEEDBACK            GOALS                   PERFORMANCE

        SALES              53132                         56908
        MARKET  SHARE        .45                           .46
        PROFIT            $8916                        $10507

        DECISIONS                       SLACK

        PRICE          $1.15    ORG SLACK         1.66
        OUTPUT         17722    SALES  SLACK      2.7
        INVENTORY      14430    COST  LEVEL      $0.96
        PROMOTION  0/0   .06

        MISCELLANEOUS

        EXCESS  LEVEL            16146      RUNOUT LEVEL          1614
        LOWER PROD LIMIT        13628      UPPER PROD LIMIT      2326


FIRM  2  DATA

        FEEDBACK            GOALS                   PERFORMANCE

        SALES              65609                         67268
        MARKET  SHARE        .54                           .54
        PROFIT           $15398                        $17038

        DECISIONS                       SLACK

        PRICE          $1.39    ORG SLACK         2.03
        OUTPUT         16937    SALES  SLACK      2.8
        INVENTORY      14321    COST  LEVEL      $1.11
        PROMOTION  0/0   .05

        MISCELLANEOUS

        EXCESS  LEVEL            15955      RUNOUT LEVEL          1595
        LOWER PROD LIMIT        12100      UPPER PROD LIMIT      2442


PERIOD      38


INDUSTRY  DATA

        GNP      1.02          DEMAND          43846


FIRM  1  DATA

        FEEDBACK            GOALS                   PERFORMANCE

        SALES              53132                         62925
        MARKET  SHARE        .45                           .46
        PROFIT            $8916                        $11288
```

DECISIONS   SLACK

PRICE $1.15   ORG SLACK   1.77
OUTPUT   23249   SALES SLACK   2.9
INVENTORY   9841   COST LEVEL $0.94
PROMOTION 0/0   .06

MISCELLANEOUS

EXCESS LEVEL   16764   RUNOUT LEVEL   16530
LOWER PROD LIMIT   16390   UPPER PROD LIMIT   23249

FIRM 2 DATA

FEEDBACK   GOALS   PERFORMANCE

SALES   65609   73817
MARKET   SHARE   .54   .54
PROFIT $15398 $16143

DECISIONS   SLACK

PRICE $1.39   ORG SLACK   2.19
OUTPUT   22059   SALES SLACK   3.0
INVENTORY   9723   COST LEVEL $1.12
PROMOTION 0/0   .05

MISCELLANEOUS

EXCESS LEVEL   16187   RUNOUT LEVEL   16187
LOWER PROD LIMIT   14134   UPPER PROD LIMIT   24424

ERIOD   39

INDUSTRY DATA

GNP   0.87   DEMAND   42292

FIRM 1 DATA

FEEDBACK   GOALS   PERFORMANCE

SALES   60659   62925
MARKET   SHARE   .46   .46
PROFIT $9920 $11288

DECISIONS   SLACK

PRICE $1.15   ORG SLACK   1.73
OUTPUT   26166   SALES SLACK   2.7
INVENTORY   11558   COST LEVEL $0.88
PROMOTION 0/0   .06

MISCELLANEOUS

EXCESS   LEVEL   21751   RUNOUT LEVEL   1976
LOWER PROD LIMIT   17414   UPPER PROD LIMIT   2769

FIRM   2   DATA

    FEEDBACK   GOALS   PERFORMANCE

    SALES   73146   73817
    MARKET   SHARE   .54   .54
    PROFIT $15980 $16143

    DECISIONS   SLACK

    PRICE $1.39   ORG SLACK   2.22
    OUTPUT   24381   SALES SLACK   3.3
    INVENTORY   11022   COST   LEVEL $1.07
    PROMOTION 0/0   .05

    MISCELLANEOUS

    EXCESS   LEVEL   20198   RUNOUT LEVEL   2019
    LOWER PROD LIMIT   16937   UPPER PROD LIMIT   2442

PERIOD   40

INDUSTRY   DATA

    GNP   1.12   DEMAND   71304

FIRM   1   DATA

    FEEDBACK   GOALS   PERFORMANCE

    SALES   60659   62925
    MARKET   SHARE   .46   .46
    PROFIT $9920 $11288

    DECISIONS   SLACK

    PRICE $1.15   ORG SLACK   1.83
    OUTPUT   27690   SALES SLACK   2.9
    INVENTORY   1419   COST   LEVEL $0.94
    PROMOTION 0/0   .06

    MISCELLANEOUS

    EXCESS   LEVEL   21554   RUNOUT LEVEL   2075
    LOWER PROD LIMIT   17418   UPPER PROD LIMIT   2769

FIRM   2   DATA

    FEEDBACK   GOALS   PERFORMANCE

    SALES   73146   73817
    MARKET   SHARE   .54   .54

```
PROFIT                 $15980                              $16143

DECISIONS                              SLACK

PRICE              $1.39              ORG SLACK          2.24
OUTPUT             24424              SALES  SLACK       3.5
INVENTORY            404              COST  LEVEL        $1.11
PROMOTION  0/0     .05

MISCELLANEOUS

EXCESS  LEVEL              20619      RUNOUT LEVEL              20619
LOWER PROD LIMIT          16937      UPPER PROD LIMIT          24424
```

PERIOD   41

INDUSTRY DATA

```
     GNP       1.06          DEMAND          90169
```

FIRM 1 DATA

```
FEEDBACK              GOALS                  PERFORMANCE

SALES                 60659                      118845
MARKET  SHARE          .46                        .46
PROFIT                $9920                      $26363

DECISIONS                              SLACK

PRICE              $1.15              ORG SLACK          1.73
OUTPUT             32979              SALES  SLACK       2.8
INVENTORY         -16814              COST  LEVEL        $0.86
PROMOTION  0/0     .06

MISCELLANEOUS

EXCESS  LEVEL              34815      RUNOUT LEVEL              29446
LOWER PROD LIMIT          17722      UPPER PROD LIMIT          32979
```

FIRM 2 DATA

```
FEEDBACK              GOALS                  PERFORMANCE

SALES                 73146                      139104
MARKET  SHARE          .54                        .54
PROFIT                $15980                     $30872

DECISIONS                              SLACK

PRICE              $1.39              ORG SLACK          2.20
OUTPUT             29309              SALES  SLACK       3.5
INVENTORY         -19418              COST  LEVEL        $1.06
PROMOTION  0/0     .05

MISCELLANEOUS
```

```
EXCESS  LEVEL              31405     RUNOUT LEVEL              31405
LOWER PROD LIMIT          16937     UPPER PROD LIMIT          29309
```

PERIOD   42

INDUSTRY DATA

GNP   1.04   DEMAND   89966

FIRM 1 DATA

FEEDBACK   GOALS   PERFORMANCE

```
SALES                 105816                    118845
MARKET   SHARE          .46                       .46
PROFIT                $17180                    $26363
```

DECISIONS   SLACK

```
PRICE          $1.15      ORG SLACK         1.70
OUTPUT         39278      SALES  SLACK      2.6
INVENTORY     -29668      COST   LEVEL     $0.83
PROMOTION  0/0   .06
```

MISCELLANEOUS

```
EXCESS  LEVEL             44801     RUNOUT LEVEL             38656
LOWER PROD LIMIT         17722     UPPER PROD LIMIT         39278
```

FIRM 2 DATA

FEEDBACK   GOALS   PERFORMANCE

```
SALES                 134518                    139104
MARKET   SHARE          .54                       .54
PROFIT                $28099                    $30872
```

DECISIONS   SLACK

```
PRICE          $1.39      ORG SLACK         2.05
OUTPUT         35171      SALES  SLACK      3.5
INVENTORY     -34242      COST   LEVEL     $0.98
PROMOTION  0/0   .05
```

MISCELLANEOUS

```
EXCESS  LEVEL             41036     RUNOUT LEVEL             41036
LOWER PROD LIMIT         16937     UPPER PROD LIMIT         35171
```

PERIOD   43

INDUSTRY DATA

I   PWR   0 6 ✓ /   8NVAWR   * * ≠ ≠ 2

FIRM 1 DATA

    FEEDBACK   GOALS   PERFORMANCE

    SALES   105816   118845
    MARKET   SHARE   .46   .46
    PROFIT $17180 $26363

    DECISIONS   SLACK

    PRICE $1.15   ORG SLACK   1.62
    OUTPUT   46780   SALES SLACK   2.6
    INVENTORY   -18913   COST LEVEL $0.73
    PROMOTION 0/0 .06

    MISCELLANEOUS

    EXCESS LEVEL   45728   RUNOUT LEVEL   42668
    LOWER PROD LIMIT   17722   UPPER PROD LIMIT   46780

FIRM 2 DATA

    FEEDBACK   GOALS   PERFORMANCE

    SALES   134518   139104
    MARKET   SHARE   .54   .54
    PROFIT $28099 $30872

    DECISIONS   SLACK

    PRICE $1.39   ORG SLACK   2.03
    OUTPUT   42205   SALES SLACK   3.5
    INVENTORY   -26540   COST LEVEL $0.89
    PROMOTION 0/0 .05

    MISCELLANEOUS

    EXCESS LEVEL   43359   RUNOUT LEVEL   43359
    LOWER PROD LIMIT   16937   UPPER PROD LIMIT   42205

PERIOD   44

INDUSTRY DATA

    GNP   0.98   DEMAND   62541

FIRM 1 DATA

    FEEDBACK   GOALS   PERFORMANCE

    SALES   105816   121657
    MARKET   SHARE   .46   .46
    PROFIT $17180 $38489

```
DECISIONS                          SLACK

PRICE          $1.15               ORG SLACK        1.56
OUTPUT         51021               SALES SLACK      2.6
INVENTORY      -3992               COST LEVEL      $0.76
PROMOTION  0/0   .06

MISCELLANEOUS

EXCESS LEVEL          30261        RUNOUT LEVEL          30261
LOWER PROD LIMIT      23249        UPPER PROD LIMIT      55715
```

```
FIRM  2  DATA

FEEDBACK            GOALS                    PERFORMANCE

SALES              134518                      142273
MARKET  SHARE         .54                         .54
PROFIT            $28099                      $45558

DECISIONS                          SLACK

PRICE          $1.39               ORG SLACK        2.00
OUTPUT         50646               SALES SLACK      3.5
INVENTORY      -15017              COST LEVEL      $0.94
PROMOTION  0/0   .05

MISCELLANEOUS

EXCESS LEVEL          31441        RUNOUT LEVEL          31441
LOWER PROD LIMIT      22059        UPPER PROD LIMIT      50646
```

```
PERIOD       45

INDUSTRY  DATA

GNP       0.97         DEMAND          61162

FIRM  1  DATA

FEEDBACK            GOALS                    PERFORMANCE

SALES              118224                      121657
MARKET  SHARE         .46                         .46
PROFIT            $26970                      $38489

DECISIONS                          SLACK

PRICE          $1.15               ORG SLACK        1.58
OUTPUT         39839               SALES SLACK      2.5
INVENTORY      15874               COST LEVEL      $0.86
PROMOTION  0/0   .05

MISCELLANEOUS
```

```
            EXCESS  LEVEL              31697      RUNOUT LEVEL             31154
            LOWER PROD LIMIT           26166      UPPER PROD LIMIT         55715
```

FIRM 2 DATA

```
    FEEDBACK               GOALS                  PERFORMANCE

    SALES                 141814                     142273
    MARKET   SHARE           .54                        .54
    PROFIT               $42794                     $45558

    DECISIONS                          SLACK

    PRICE        $1.39                 ORG SLACK        1.89
    OUTPUT       43730                 SALES   SLACK    3.6
    INVENTORY     5621                 COST   LEVEL    $0.92
    PROMOTION  0/0    .05

    MISCELLANEOUS

    EXCESS  LEVEL              30872      RUNOUT LEVEL             30872
    LOWER PROD LIMIT           24381      UPPER PROD LIMIT         60775
```

PERIOD   46

INDUSTRY   DATA

```
    GNP       1.04            DEMAND           70863
```

FIRM 1 DATA

```
    FEEDBACK               GOALS                  PERFORMANCE

    SALES                 118224                     121657
    MARKET   SHARE           .46                        .46
    PROFIT               $26970                     $38489

    DECISIONS                          SLACK

    PRICE        $1.15                 ORG SLACK        1.68
    OUTPUT       41962                 SALES   SLACK    2.7
    INVENTORY    19628                 COST   LEVEL    $0.94
    PROMOTION  0/0    .05

    MISCELLANEOUS

    EXCESS  LEVEL              31209      RUNOUT LEVEL             31154
    LOWER PROD LIMIT           27690      UPPER PROD LIMIT         55715
```

FIRM 2 DATA

```
    FEEDBACK               GOALS                  PERFORMANCE

    SALES                 141814                     142273
    MARKET   SHARE           .54                        .54
```

```
PROFIT                  $42794                              $45558

DECISIONS                               SLACK

PRICE               $1.39              ORG SLACK          2.05
OUTPUT              40766              SALES  SLACK       3.8
INVENTORY           14574              COST  LEVEL       $1.08
PROMOTION   O/O      .05

MISCELLANEOUS

EXCESS  LEVEL               30224       RUNOUT LEVEL             3022
LOWER PROD LIMIT           24424       UPPER PROD LIMIT         6077
```

PERIOD   47

INDUSTRY DATA

```
GNP      1.06            DEMAND            94500
```

FIRM 1 DATA

```
FEEDBACK            GOALS                 PERFORMANCE

SALES               118224                     132337
MARKET   SHARE         .46                        .46
PROFIT              $26970                    $30066

DECISIONS                               SLACK

PRICE               $1.15              ORG SLACK          1.64
OUTPUT              55715              SALES  SLACK       2.9
INVENTORY           13480              COST  LEVEL      $0.87
PROMOTION   O/O      .05

MISCELLANEOUS

EXCESS  LEVEL               35593       RUNOUT LEVEL             3391
LOWER PROD LIMIT           32979       UPPER PROD LIMIT         5571
```

FIRM 2 DATA

```
FEEDBACK            GOALS                 PERFORMANCE

SALES               141814                     154641
MARKET   SHARE         .54                        .54
PROFIT              $42794                    $40705

DECISIONS                               SLACK

PRICE               $1.39              ORG SLACK          2.09
OUTPUT              52011              SALES  SLACK       4.1
INVENTORY            8949              COST  LEVEL      $1.05
PROMOTION   O/O      .04

MISCELLANEOUS
```

EXCESS LEVEL	33639	RUNOUT LEVEL	33639
LOWER PROD LIMIT	29309	UPPER PROD LIMIT	60775

PERIOD   48

INDUSTRY DATA

GNP   1.09   DEMAND   131376

FIRM 1 DATA

FEEDBACK   GOALS   PERFORMANCE

SALES	129375	132337
MARKET SHARE	.46	.46
PROFIT	$28446	$30066

DECISIONS   SLACK

PRICE	$1.16	ORG SLACK	1.62
OUTPUT	66356	SALES SLACK	2.7
INVENTORY	2322	COST LEVEL	$0.82
PROMOTION 0/0	.05		

MISCELLANEOUS

EXCESS LEVEL	46845	RUNOUT LEVEL	41848
LOWER PROD LIMIT	39278	UPPER PROD LIMIT	66356

FIRM 2 DATA

FEEDBACK   GOALS   PERFORMANCE

SALES	153997	154641
MARKET SHARE	.54	.54
PROFIT	$42153	$40705

DECISIONS   SLACK

PRICE	$1.41	ORG SLACK	1.95
OUTPUT	60775	SALES SLACK	4.2
INVENTORY	-3542	COST LEVEL	$0.96
PROMOTION 0/0	.04		

MISCELLANEOUS

EXCESS LEVEL	43203	RUNOUT LEVEL	43203
LOWER PROD LIMIT	35171	UPPER PROD LIMIT	60775

PERIOD   49

INDUSTRY DATA

```
GNP        1.02           DEMAND          122460
```

FIRM 1 DATA

FEEDBACK	GOALS	PERFORMANCE
SALES	129375	132337
MARKET SHARE	.46	.46
PROFIT	$28446	$30066

DECISIONS   SLACK

PRICE	$1.16	ORG SLACK	1.56
OUTPUT	79030	SALES SLACK	2.7
INVENTORY	6372	COST LEVEL	$0.78
PROMOTION 0/0	.05		

MISCELLANEOUS

EXCESS LEVEL	64850	RUNOUT LEVEL	5583?
LOWER PROD LIMIT	39839	UPPER PROD LIMIT	7903?

FIRM 2 DATA

FEEDBACK	GOALS	PERFORMANCE
SALES	153997	154641
MARKET SHARE	.54	.54
PROFIT	$42153	$40705

DECISIONS   SLACK

PRICE	$1.41	ORG SLACK	1.85
OUTPUT	72930	SALES SLACK	3.9
INVENTORY	-2921	COST LEVEL	$0.89
PROMOTION 0/0	.04		

MISCELLANEOUS

EXCESS LEVEL	59178	RUNOUT LEVEL	59178
LOWER PROD LIMIT	40766	UPPER PROD LIMIT	72930

PERIOD   50

INDUSTRY DATA

```
GNP        0.91           DEMAND          82383
```

FIRM 1 DATA

FEEDBACK	GOALS	PERFORMANCE
SALES	129375	198247
MARKET SHARE	.46	.46
PROFIT	$28446	$57286

DECISIONS   SLACK

PRICE $1.16   ORG SLACK   1.51
OUTPUT   53539   SALES SLACK   2.6
INVENTORY   43500   COST LEVEL $0.91
PROMOTION 0/0   .05

MISCELLANEOUS

EXCESS LEVEL   62563   RUNOUT LEVEL   59453
LOWER PROD LIMIT   39839   UPPER PROD LIMIT   94125

FIRM 2 DATA

FEEDBACK   GOALS   PERFORMANCE

SALES   153997   231754
MARKET SHARE   .54   .54
PROFIT $42153 $79232

DECISIONS   SLACK

PRICE $1.41   ORG SLACK   1.77
OUTPUT   63491   SALES SLACK   3.6
INVENTORY   29528   COST LEVEL $0.95
PROMOTION 0/0   .04

MISCELLANEOUS

EXCESS LEVEL   59910   RUNOUT LEVEL   59910
LOWER PROD LIMIT   40766   UPPER PROD LIMIT   87516

INDEPENDENT VARIABLES
X0   +.0000000000000   10+00   X1   +.9800000000002   10-01
X2   +.7090666666663   10+00   X3   +.1010000000000   10+00
X4   +.5636999999996   10+00   X5   +.4409999999998   10+00
X6   +.8600000000005   10-01   X7   +.1191000000000   10+01
X8   +.8459999999991   10+00   X9   +.1840000000000   10+00
X10   +.1279999999999   10+00   X11   +.5100000000000   10-01
X12   +.4499999999998   10-01   X13   +.1869999999999   10+00
X14   +.3199999999998   10-01   X15   +.6799999999997   10+00
X16   +.2159999999998   10+00   X17   +.1170000000000   10+00
X18   +.3599999999996   10-01   X19   +.9629999999990   10+00
X20   +.1610000000000   10+00   X21   +.2859999999999   10+00
X22   +.2159999999999   10+00   X23   +.6899999999998   10-01
X24   +.9959999999991   10+00   X25   +.6199999999998   10-01
X26   +.7191999999997   10+01
DEPENDENT VARIABLES
X27   +.1158649103839   10+01   X28   +.1539007837642   10+05
X29   +.4610590225742   10+00   X30   +.1567770597854   10+05
X31   +.1152020769148   10+01   X32   +.3178928561830   10+04
X33   +.4609840634257   10+00   X34   +.1389881767510   10+05
X35   +.1147735087191   10+01   X36   +.6245212036128   10+04
X37   +.4592123291558   10+00   X38   +.7775481283872   10+04
X39   +.1403211661077   10+01   X40   +.6173713311121   10+04
X41   +.5389409774252   10+00   X42   +.2118489137787   10+05

X43	+.1397083858755	$_{10}$ +01	X44	-.4300701451060	$_{10}$ +04
X45	+.5390159365737	$_{10}$ +00	X46	+.1800802128265	$_{10}$ +05
X47	+.1394931275803	$_{10}$ +01	X48	+.2903130647462	$_{10}$ +04
X49	+.5407876708439	$_{10}$ +00	X50	+.1014346715395	$_{10}$ +05

00:07:22

9

A MODEL OF RATIONAL

MANAGERIAL BEHAVIOR[1]

by O. E. Williamson

In his 1952 essay indicating the need for revisions to the theory of the firm, Papandreou suggested that profit maximization was an unnecessarily special assumption and that a more fruitful theory of the firm would employ a general preference function.[2] More recently, Alchian and Kessel have also proposed that firms may maximize a utility function that includes components other than profits[3] and Becker has joined them in this suggestion.[4]

[1]A series of discussions that I had with Professors R. M. Cyert and J. G. March contributed importantly to my decision to formalize the "organizational slack" propositions that underlie this model. Their comments, as well as those of Professors A. H. Meltzer and J. F. Muth, have been appreciated. The study resulting in this paper was made in part under a fellowship granted by the Ford Foundation. However, the conclusions, opinions, and other statements in this paper are my own.

[2]A. G. Papandreou, "Some Basic Problems in the Theory of the Firm," in *A Survey of Contemporary Economics*, ed. B. F. Haley (Homewood, Ill.: Richard D. Irwin, 1952), vol. 2, 211.

[3]A. A. Alchian and R. A. Kessel, "Competition, Monopoly, and the Pursuit of Pecuniary Gains," paper given at the University-National Bureau Conference on Labor Economics, April 22–23, 1960.

[4]G. S. Becker, "Irrational Behavior in Economic Theory," *Journal of Political Economy*, **70** (1962), 12.

Although Baumol has developed a model that substitutes revenues for profits in the objective function of the firm,[5] "general preference functions" of the sort imagined by Papandreou have not been forthcoming.

It is the purpose of this chapter to propose what appears to be a particularly fruitful general preference function. This is accomplished by employing the assumption that managers conduct the affairs of the firm so as to attend to their own best interests and by introducing into the utility function of the firm certain of the organizational slack propositions that have been given in Chapter 3. After reformulating the firm's objectives in this way, maximization techniques are employed to derive testable theorems about the firm's behavior. Contrary to Papandreou's conjecture, we show that it is *not* necessarily "harder to derive operationally meaningful theorems concerning firm behavior from a construction . . . directly based on preference-function maximization than . . . from the profit-maximization construction."[6]

In order to develop this position, a brief review of the profit maximization assumption will be given in Section 9.1. The view is expressed there that if the goals of the firm are to be consistent with the self-interest seeking hypothesis that underlies so much of economic analysis, greater attention must be paid to the interests of the management. Section 9.2 gives specific content to this proposal for reformulation. A mathematical model is constructed in Section 9.3 and the equilibrium and comparative statics properties of this behavioral model are obtained by employing the techniques of maximization. When the model is applied to public utilities, conditions said to be characteristic of their operations are obtained as direct implications.

9.1 Managerial Rationality and Profit Maximization

As indicated in Chapter 2, the profit maximization hypothesis has been subject to repeated criticism. Some of this criticism has been directed at the notion of marginal analysis itself. We shall not be concerned with this class of criticism. More fundamental, perhaps, have been the criticisms that challenge the propriety of treating profit maximization as being the entire objective of the firm without regard for the conditions of competition in which the firm operates. Thus, whereas the assumption of profit maximization may lead to accurate predictions of behavior where competition is vigorous, it is not clear that this assumption should be carried over uncritically to firms for which the conditions of competition are weak.

However, as long as it was plausible to assume that the ownership interests in the firm played the dominant role in determining the firm's activi-

---

[5]W. J. Baumol, *Business Behavior, Value, and Growth* (New York: Macmillan, 1959).
[6]Papandreou, *op. cit.*, 211.

ties, the profit maximization hypothesis could be supported on grounds other than competitive necessity — namely, on grounds of self-interest seeking. But, given the conditions of absentee ownership characteristic of many of our major corporations, this basis also becomes suspect.[7] Indeed, as Shackle has pointed out, a broader framework than profit maximization is needed to understand the performance of firms sheltered from the rigors of competition: "Security surely ranks in importance, amongst the ideas which should concern the economist [and presumably *do* concern the manager], with scarcity itself; but how different is its place in the theoretical literature."[8] Although offering stock options to management and tying bonuses to profit performance can enhance the profit incentive,[9] there is little reason to believe that, for a management operating on a general preference function, this will lead to the single-minded pursuit of profits.[10] Moreover, the relation between managerial rewards and profits is often much less than explicit. Yet, despite the fact that *both* the incentive *and* the necessity for profit maximization may well be weak, the profit maximization hypothesis has continued to play a dominant role in economics both for the class of firms for which its *a priori* claims are clear and for the firms where its claims are less certain. That this is true may speak highly for the power of the hypothesis, but this may also be due to " . . . the failure of any coherent, self-consistent alternative to be developed and be widely accepted."[11]

It is the purpose of this chapter to examine an alternative to profit maximization by isolating for special consideration the objectives of the group that effectively controls the activities of the firm — the management. Thus, whereas the logic of self-interest requires that managers operate the firm in their self-interest, their effective control insures that this objective will be pursued. Although a state of vigorous competition will prevent a management from manipulating the activities of the firm to conform to personal objectives, the absence of such competitive conditions will permit

[7]*Ibid.*, 197–200; also, R. A. Gordon, *Business Leadership in the Large Corporation* (Berkeley: U. of Cal., 1961), chaps. 2, 8; A. A. Berle, Jr., and G. C. Means, *The Modern Corporation and Private Property* (New York: Macmillan, 1932).

[8]G. L. S. Shackle, "Professor Keirstead's Theory of Profit," *Economic Journal*, **64** (1954), 120.

[9]W. H. White, "The Changing Criteria in Investment Planning," in *Variability of Private Investment in Plant and Equipment*, Part II, Joint Economic Committee, Washington, D. C., 1962, 21.

[10]Although it is difficult to document the proposition that the firm is pursuing goals other than profit maximization without encountering a claim that the firm's activities are somehow consistent with "long-run profit maximization," a case study of management goals that is particularly difficult to reconcile with the "long-run" dodge is provided by C. West Churchman, Russell T. Ackoff, and E. Leonard Arnoff, *Introduction to Operations Research* (New York: Wiley, 1957), 150–152.

[11]M. Friedman, *Essays in Positive Economics* (Chicago: University of Chicago Press, 1953), 23.

managers to pursue their own goals. In these circumstances, therefore, the rules of profit maximization will not necessarily allocate the residual funds in firms which, after satisfying their minimal profit demands, possess additional uncommitted resources. Although our preference function allows the single-minded pursuit of profit maximizing-objectives, this occurs not as a general, but as a *special case*.

Whether, as in the usual treatment of the theory of the firm, this special case is the only interesting one is an empirical question. Although the evidence from the studies of the firm's decision-making processes (see Chapters 3-7) indicates that our model is based on more "reasonable" assumptions than is the profit-maximizing hypothesis, there may well be less than unanimity on this matter. Moreover, the differences will not be settled by conjecture. Thus, it is less the assumptions of the behavioral model (as discussed in Section 9.2) than the implications that flow from them (as developed in Sections 9.3 and 9.4) that put our model to the hard test.

9.2 Motivating the Model

Considerations of space permit only a cursory treatment of the question of managerial motivation. The emphasis, therefore, will be on those aspects of motivation that are neglected by the profit maximization hypothesis, but which are essential to the present model. However, this shift of emphasis should not be construed to mean that such goals as self-fulfillment and organizational achievement are unimportant. Rather, since these occupy the center of attention in the usual treatments of motivation, their omission here is merely a device for drawing particular attention to those aspects of managerial behavior that properly should be added to achievement goals in studying the behavior of the business firm. These latter goals, although neglected in the discussion, nevertheless are included in the model. They occur as profits in the "discretionary spending for investment" term.

Modern organization theory treats the firm as a coalition (managers, workers, stockholders, suppliers, customers) whose members have conflicting demands that must be reconciled if the firm is to survive.[12] In the sense that each group in the coalition is essential to the firm's continuing existence, the members of the coalition can be regarded as "equals." This view, however, is more useful when observing the firm in a period of crisis than when survival is not a pressing problem.[13] Where survival is not a current concern, restoring a hierarchy among the members based on the attention they give to the firm's operations may lead to more productive insights. From this viewpoint, management emerges as the chief member of the coalition; its role as the coordinating and initiating agent as well as its preferred access

---

[12]J. G. March and Herbert A. Simon, *Organizations* (New York: Wiley, 1958).

[13]For example, in a period of financial troubles, withdrawal of the firm's suppliers (refusal to extend trade credit) may force the coalition to be dissolved.

to information permit it quite naturally to assume this primacy position. Thus, although in certain circumstances it may be necessary to give special attention to shifts in demands made by members of the coalition other than managers, under "normal" conditions it may be entirely appropriate to take the demands of the other members (for wages, profits, product, and so forth) as *given* and leave to the discretion of the management the operation of the firm in some best sense.[14]

Our departure from the conventional view of the firm is in the assumption of what is "best." Traditionally, this requires that managers choose to operate the firm in a stewardship sense of attending to the stockholders' best interest by maximizing profits. The behavioral model proposes that managers operate the firm in the only fashion consistent with the assumption of self-interest seeking — in their *own* best interests. By adapting the notion of "organizational slack" in Chapter 3, specific content is provided to this hypothesis.[15]

In the present model, managers are held to operate the firm so as to maximize a utility function that has as principal components (1) salaries, (2) staff, (3) discretionary spending for investments, and (4) management slack absorbed as cost.[16] This utility function is maximized subject to the condition that reported profits be greater than or equal to minimum profits demanded.

The objective function can be simplified by eliminating the salary component — not because this does not represent an essential element in management's reward schedule, but because it can be subsumed in the "staff" term. Thus, Simon has shown that executive compensation can be explained by the interaction of the (competitive) salary demands of new employees at the lowest executive levels with a process of social determination within the organization that basically amounts to "staffing."[17] A perceptive management, therefore, can obtain its salary objectives indirectly

[14]Such a proposal appears to be generally in accord with Gordon's findings (*op. cit.*) in his classic study of business leadership where he indicates that: (1) profits are perhaps properly considered as a constraint (pp. xii and 337); (2) in the absence of adversity the nonmanagement members of the coalition tend to be passive (pp. 163 and 195); (3) management effectively controls the operations of the enterprise (chap. 14).

[15]The notion of "organizational slack" was also present, if not quite explicit, in the early work of Reder. See M. W. Reder, "A Reconsideration of the Marginal Productivity Theory," *Journal of Political Economy*, **55** (1947), 450–458.

[16]It might be noted that the argument runs in terms of "managers" rather than "top management." Thus, even in those situations where the goals of top management might be approximately those of the stockholders, the subgoals of middle managers may be sufficiently different to prevent the intended objectives from being realized (March and Simon, *op. cit.*, 121–129). Ordinarily, however, it will require an attitude of permissiveness if not outright cooperation on the part of top management for these nonprofit objectives to absorb any sizable amount of the firm's resources.

[17]H. A. Simon, "The Compensation of Executives," *Sociometry*, **20** (1957), 32–55.

(and less ostentatiously) by building pressure from below through staffing rather than by operating on the salary goal directly. Moreover, managers may find staff attractive for reasons other than the relation it bears to salaries; staff is a source of job *security*, prestige, and flexibility as well.

That staffs have a tendency, sometimes legitimate and certainly natural, to grow has been widely observed. What may appear originally as a legitimate expansion, however, can, in the absence of binding constraints, easily lead to a general condition of excessive staff throughout the firm. Indeed, the steady accumulation of excess staff may be difficult to resist as long as the firm is not confronted with adversity. When economic pressures appear, however, the excess will tend to be removed. Thus it will often be after adversity has set in rather than contemporaneously that the evidence of excess staff will appear.[18]

Quantitatively, the expenditures on extra emoluments will ordinarily represent a smaller diversion of resources than will the excess staff activity. Nonetheless, it is clear that managers do indulge in superfluities which themselves appear to be a function of the condition of the environment (the amount spent for expense accounts, office improvements, and so forth tends to be correlated with economic conditions), and in some circumstances these amounts may not be insignificant.[19] Although it may be claimed that these superfluities are salary substitutes to the management, it is not clear that the amounts of resources involved could in fact be taken as salary without creating counterpressures from the labor and stockholder members of the coalition. Indeed, it seems entirely plausible that a significant amount of these superfluities arise from the political position that a manager enjoys and that they are economic rents which, if removed, would not cause him to seek other employments.

Discretionary spending for investment represents the difference between reported profits and minimum profits demanded. It reflects investment decisions of the firm that are made less on the basis of their economic necessity than on the successful influence of managers in diverting resources to their area. This does not mean that the apparent justification for investment

---

[18]As an example of management slack absorbed as "staff," A. M. Hartogensis reports the case of a firm under pressure being able to reduce its production control staff from 500 to 350 over a weekend without serious difficulty. "Cost Reduction by Brute Force," *N.A.C.A. Bulletin* (November 1953), 344–356. In the same vein, but more recently, a large paper manufacturer has cut its office force by 32 per cent and reduced total overhead by $14 million (on sales of about $180 million) as part of a vigorous cost reduction program. *Forbes* (December 1, 1961), 18. Very likely, neither of these situations would have been easily identified *ex ante* as ones where excess staff abounded.

[19]An example of what, presumably, was a noninsignificant diversion of resources for these purposes is afforded by the report of a firm whose management realized that the profits which it was going to show in its forthcoming annual report would be unusually large. Hastily, an office modernization program was launched with the objective of "bringing the year's earnings into line and avoid spoiling the stockholders." Baumol, *op. cit.*, 90.

proposals will not remain economic; it merely means that the real basis contains important elements that have ordinarily been neglected.

Investments that are made necessary out of economic considerations are included in the minimum profits demanded constraint for this static model.[20] That the firm's investments both affect and are affected by the strategies of rivals can be made explicit in a dynamic model. For the present, however, necessitous investments are taken as given. Introducing necessitous investments not as a component of the objective function but rather as a constraint gives preferred status to this class of resource demands. That is, necessitous investments together with dividend demands have a first claim on the firm's "surplus"; after these have been satisfied, the residual is distributed according to management's utility function.[21]

To define these notions more precisely requires us to introduce some profit taxonomy. "Maximum" profits (π^*) are profits that the strictly profit-maximizing firm would obtain by equating marginal revenue to marginal cost. "Actual" profits (π_A) are profits actually earned by the firm that has its objective function augmented to include a "staff" component. That is, the firm that has as its objective function a combination of staff and profit terms will employ staff in the region where the marginal value product is less than the marginal cost of the factor. Hence, actual profits are less than maximum profits — a condition that should be clear when we examine the model in Section 9.3. "Reported" profits (π_R) are the profits the firm admits to and are actual profits reduced by the amount of management slack absorbed as cost. It is out of reported profits that taxes, dividends, and internal growth funds are obtained. "Minimum" (after tax) profits (π_0) are profits negotiated by the other members of the coalition that are just sufficient to satisfy their demands. Reported profits must be greater than or equal to minimum profits as corrected for taxes. If we let $MS_1 =$ management slack absorbed as staff, $MS_2 =$ management slack absorbed as cost, and $t =$ tax rate, we can summarize the above notions as follows:

$$\pi_A \equiv \pi^* - MS_1 \qquad \text{or} \qquad MS_1 \equiv \pi^* - \pi_A$$

$$\pi_R \equiv \pi_A - MS_2 \qquad \text{or} \qquad MS_2 \equiv \pi_A - \pi_R$$

$$\pi_R \geq \pi_0 + T$$

$$\pi_R \geq \frac{\pi_0}{1 - t} \qquad \text{when} \qquad T \equiv t\pi_R$$

[20]The notion of necessitous investments has been borrowed from my colleague, Louis R. Pondy, who has found this a meaningful category in his empirical studies of the capital budgeting decision.

[21]Although within the context of the present paper I am deliberately avoiding the question of how the demands among coalition members interact over time, it might be pointed out that if management wanted to neutralize stockholders' demands it would probably adopt the policy of (1) paying nearly fixed dividends and (2) moderating the normal fluctuation of earnings by alternately easing and tightening its own performance demands in response to rises and declines in business conditions.

Discretionary spending for investments is defined as the difference between reported profits and minimum profits and taxes. That is, if I_D = discretionary spending for investment:

$$I_D \equiv \pi_R - (\pi_0 + T)$$

The above discussion has emphasized a condition of discretion in the firm's operations that economic theory has tended to ignore, presumably because these conditions represent a variety of friction that can be safely neglected. For a large class of firms this is probably true. However, it is not *a priori* evident that all firms belong to this class. Indeed, many firms possess considerable latitude in selecting their strategies for dealing with their environments. This latitude may be due to industry arrangements, local advantages, or simply a buoyant, growing market. Whatever the case, for firms that find themselves sheltered from the rigors of competition, a model drawn more closely along the lines of the one proposed in this chapter than along the lines of the profit maximization hypothesis may be appropriate. On the other hand, since the special advantages that insulate a firm from the pressures of competition are often eroded with time (and may fail to be replaced by others), the behavioral model may best be restricted to predicting short and intermediate run phenomena and other constructions used for the long run.

9.3 The Model

The task now becomes one of selecting a set of variables that permits us to translate management's objective function into mathematical terms. This requires that two new variables be defined: (1) the fraction of actual profits that is reported and (2) staff. The first of these is necessary in order to identify the management slack absorbed as cost component. The second is essential because the staff and production decisions, contrary to the standard theory of the firm, are no longer made symmetrically.[22] With these two exceptions, all the variables entering the model are conventional ones. Thus, the variables we consider are:

$$R \equiv \text{revenue} = P \cdot X$$

$$P \equiv \text{price} = P(X, S; \epsilon); \frac{\partial P}{\partial X} < 0; \frac{\partial P}{\partial S} \geq 0; \frac{\partial P}{\partial \epsilon} > 0$$

$$X \equiv \text{output}$$

---

[22]The argument for neglecting the staff term in the standard treatment of the theory of the firm is that the manufacturing and staff decisions are symmetrical. And indeed they are — for the standard theory. See G. J. Stigler, *The Theory of Price* (New York: Macmillan, 1949), 251.

$S \equiv$ "staff" (in money terms)

$C \equiv$ production cost $= C(X)$

$\rho \equiv$ the fraction of actual profits reported (and $(1 - \rho)$ is the fraction of the actual profits absorbed as cost)

$\epsilon \equiv$ the condition of the environment, a demand shift parameter

$T \equiv$ taxes where $t =$ tax rate and $\bar{T} =$ lump sum tax

Second order (stability) conditions are satisfied by assuming both well-behaved cost and revenue functions and diminishing marginal utility characteristics in the utility function.

As proposed above, the components of the objective function can be reduced to three: (1) staff (S), (2) management slack absorbed as cost $(\pi_A - \pi_R)$, and (3) discretionary spending on investments (I_D). If we let U be the utility function, management's objective becomes:[23]

$$\text{maximize} \quad U = U(S, \pi_A - \pi_R, I_D)$$

$$\text{subject to} \quad \text{(i)} \ \pi_R \geq \pi_0 + T$$

$$\text{(ii)} \ 0 \leq \rho \leq 1$$

where $\pi_A \equiv R - C - S$

$\pi_R \equiv \rho \pi_A$

$I_D \equiv \pi_R - (\pi_0 + T)$

$T \equiv t \pi_R$

It turns out that both constraints are redundant so that both can be ignored in the subsequent analysis and the problem becomes one of finding an unconstrained maximum.[24] Thus, the problem is to

$$\text{maximize} \quad U = U[S, (1 - \rho)(R - C - S), \rho(1 - t)(R - C - S) - \pi_0]$$

[23]A less general formulation of the preference function would be to consider it as additive in each of the terms. Thus the objective would be to

$$\text{maximize} \quad U = \alpha_1 S^{\beta_1} + \alpha_2 (\pi_A - \pi_R)^{\beta_2} + \alpha_3 I_D^{\beta_3}$$

$$\text{subject to} \quad \text{(i)} \ \pi_R \geq \pi_0 + T$$

$$\text{(ii)} \ 0 \leq \rho \leq 1$$

where $\alpha_1, \alpha_2, \alpha_3 > 0$; $\alpha_1 + \alpha_2 + \alpha_3 = 1$; $0 < \beta_1, \beta_2, \beta_3 < 1$.

Since it is unnecessary to restrict the form of the utility function in order to obtain our results, the more general formulation is to be preferred.

[24]That the first constraint is redundant is due to the fact that it takes exactly the same form as the last term in the utility function. Thus, whenever the constraint becomes binding (i.e., satisfied as an equality), the third term in the utility function itself goes to zero and with diminishing marginal utility characteristics (and assuming no corner solutions), the marginal utility becomes infinite. Given this property, the firm

The following first-order results are obtained by taking partial derivatives of U with respect to X, S, and ρ.[25]

$$\frac{\partial R}{\partial X} = \frac{\partial C}{\partial X} \tag{1}$$

$$\frac{\partial R}{\partial S} = \frac{-U_1 + U_2(1 - \rho) + U_3\rho(1 - t)}{U_2(1 - \rho) + U_3\rho(1 - t)} \tag{2}$$

$$U_2 = U_3(1 - t) \tag{3}$$

From Eq. (3) it follows that ρ will be chosen so as to preserve a positive proportional relationship between the amounts of management slack absorbed as cost and discretionary spending on investments. Thus, only in the limiting case when the environment is so severe as to drive both these slack type activities to zero will ρ be chosen equal to one. Otherwise, values of ρ less than unity will be selected. Substituting Eq. (3) into Eq. (2) yields

$$\frac{\partial R}{\partial S} = \frac{-U_1 + U_2}{U_2} \tag{2'}$$

The corresponding profit-maximizing relationships are

$$\frac{\partial R}{\partial X} = \frac{\partial C}{\partial X}, \qquad \frac{\partial R}{\partial S} = 1$$

and ρ chosen identically equal to unity. Hence, only for the production decision do we obtain results for the behavioral model that are consistent with profit-maximizing behavior. That is, whereas the profit-maximizing firm employs staff at the level where the marginal value product equals the marginal cost of the factor (i.e., $\partial R/\partial S = 1$), the behavioral firm ordinarily employs staff in the region where the marginal value product is less than the marginal cost (i.e., $\partial R/\partial S < 1$). Moreover, only under conditions where $U_1 = 0$ or when the firm is confronted with severe adversity (so that U_2 takes on very large positive values) will the profit-maximizing choice of

---

will, so long as it is possible, choose values for its decision variables that maintain positive values for I_D (i.e., satisfy the constraint as an inequality). Thus, as the condition of the environment becomes increasingly more severe, the firm will converge to profit-maximizing behavior independent of the constraint. That the second constraint is redundant obtains from first-order conditions that require that the second and third terms in the utility function bear positive proportional relationships to one another. The analysis, however, is not dependent on the fact that both constraints are redundant. Had this not been true, the resulting inequality-constrained maximization problem could have been handled by making use of the Kuhn-Tucker theorem. All of our results would be preserved as long as the constraints were not binding.

[25]In these expressions, U_1 is the first partial of the utility function with respect to S, U_2 is the first partial with respect to $\pi_A - \pi_R$, and U_3 is the first partial with respect to I_D.

staff obtain under the behavioral model. Since a value of $U_1 = 0$ requires an elimination of the staff term from the utility function entirely, this possibility can be ignored. Also, since by hypothesis we are dealing with firms for which economic pressures are not continuously severe, the second condition under which profit-maximizing rules would determine the staff employment decision can be treated as the unusual rather than the normal situation.

Only when the behavioral firm is confronted by conditions of economic adversity that would cause it to employ staff profit-optimally will ρ be chosen equal to one. In all other circumstances it will choose values of ρ less than unity; i.e., it will absorb some fraction of actual profits as nonproductive cost.

The fact that the behavioral model shows the production decision being made along lines consistent with profit maximization while the staff decision is not warrants further examination.[26] This result flows directly from our assumption that staff is valued by the managers for reasons apart from productivity whereas (by implication) the only satisfaction that management derives from employing labor is that associated with the productive value of this resource. Indeed, by introducing a staff term into the utility function as we have, this result follows deductively. However, the result also accommodates itself to our observations of the business enterprise. Thus, given favorable economic conditions, staff expenditures (for selling expense, research and development, community relations, and so forth) are typically permitted to absorb large amounts of the uncommitted resources that the firm is generating. In the behavioral model, this derives from the managerial rewards associated with such expenditures — namely, from the relation these expenditures bear to salary, prestige, flexibility, and job security.

Given these equilibrium conditions, how do the decision variables adjust to a change in the parameters — to a displacement of equilibrium?[27] In particular, how does the system adjust to a change in the condition of the environment (the demand shift parameter ϵ), a change in the profit tax rate (t), and a lump sum tax ($\bar{T}$)?

It will facilitate the argument to compact the notation and designate each decision variable by X_i and each parameter by θ_j. Then the function $U(X, S, \rho; \epsilon, t, \bar{T})$ can be represented as $U(X_1, X_2, X_3; \theta_1, \theta_2, \theta_3)$. The

[26]Although the argument may be raised that the difference between hiring additional labor and hiring additional staff is that the costs and benefits are much more precisely known for the former, this does not provide a basis for the persistent *bias* in favor of hiring additional staff. Rather, the reason must lie elsewhere.

[27]The treatment here follows P. A. Samuelson, *Foundations of Economic Analysis* (Cambridge: Harvard University Press, 1958), 12–14.

general form for determining the response of the pth decision variable to a change in the mth parameter becomes

$$\left(\frac{\partial X_p}{\partial \theta_m}\right)^o = \frac{-\sum_{i=1}^{3} \frac{\partial^2 U}{\partial X_i \, \partial \theta_m} \cdot C_{ip}}{|D|}, \qquad \begin{cases} p = 1, \ldots, 3 \\ m = 1, \ldots, 3 \end{cases}$$

where C_{ip} is the cofactor of the ith row and pth column of D and $|D|$ is the determinant of the second partials $|\partial^2 U/(\partial X_i \, \partial X_j)|$.

The results for a displacement by each of the parameters are summarized in Table 9.1. The direction of adjustment of any particular decision variable to a displacement from its equilibrium value by an increase in a particular parameter is found by referring to the row and column entry corresponding to this pair.

Table 9.1. Responses to displacements from equilibrium for the behavioral model

Variable	Parameter		
	ϵ	t	$\overline{T}$
X^o	+	+	−
S^o	+	+	−
ρ^o	−	−	+

The significance of these responses can best be discussed by comparing them to the corresponding results obtained for the profit-maximizing model. These are shown in Table 9.2.

Table 9.2. Responses to displacements from equilibrium for the profit-maximizing model

Variable	Parameter		
	ϵ	t	$\overline{T}$
X^o	+	0	0
S^o	+	0	0

The qualitative differences between the two models are substantial.[28] Thus, whereas the profit-maximizing firm chooses values for ρ^o identically equal to one, the behavioral firm chooses values for ρ^o less than unity and adjusts the value of ρ in response to a parameter change. More important are the tax effects. Whereas the profit-maximizing firm responds to neither a profit tax rate nor a lump sum tax, the behavioral firm adjusts both its output and staff decisions (as well as its choice of ρ) when taxes are changed.

[28]There are also quantitative differences in the output and staff response to the change in the demand shift parameter between the two models, but these are not differences which will concern us here.

Both models predict that the output and staff will be increased in response to an increase in the demand shift parameter (ϵ). However, the behavioral model also indicates that the fraction of profits reported will be reduced (i.e., the fraction of profits absorbed as cost will increase). Thus the management slack absorbed as cost will increase not only absolutely but also relatively as the demand for the firm's products increases (and a deterioration of the environment will lead to a reversal of these profit absorption activities). The behavioral model therefore predicts that expenditures for travel, expense accounts, office improvements, and so forth will be very much a function of business conditions.[29] Implicitly, the profit-maximizing model denies that such a relationship should exist.

With respect to an increase in the profit tax rate, our model predicts that the firm will shift out of profits and into staff and output as well as managerial superfluities as the penalty associated with reporting profits is increased. In the presence of an excess profits tax, for example, the behavioral firm will increase expenditures on advertising, customer services, public relations, and so forth and at the same time increase the proportion of management slack absorbed as cost. Under the profit-maximizing hypothesis, however, the optimum choice of factors is unaffected by a rate increase; it therefore predicts that there will be no response to any change in the profits tax rate. Although it is possible to interpret our experience with excess profits taxes in a manner somehow consistent with a "long-run" version of profit maximization, at the level of the models we are considering here the gross evidence clearly conforms to that predicted by the behavioral model and contradicts that predicted by the profit-maximizing model.

When a lump sum tax is levied, the behavioral firm is no more able to avoid it than is the traditional firm. Since the traditional firm is already maximizing profits, it continues its operations unchanged. However, the behavioral firms, which are operating in a region that is suboptimal from the profit-maximizing standpoint, revise their strategies so as to maintain a balance between their rewards and move their decision variables in a direction that increases profits. Thus, staff, output, and the amount of management slack absorbed as cost are all reduced as the lump sum tax is increased. It might be noted that the lump sum tax is really doing triple duty inasmuch as its effect is identical to that of increasing the minimum profit constraint or imposing any sort of fixed charge on the firm. That is, the behavioral model predicts that, contrary to the traditional theory (but

---

[29]It is sufficient that ρ^0 be less than unity and $(\partial \rho / \partial \epsilon)^0 = 0$ for this correlation to obtain. Indeed, even with $(\partial \rho / \partial \epsilon)^0$ slightly positive, the relationship would hold. As it turns out, the sign of $(\partial \rho / \partial \epsilon)^0$ cannot be deduced from the model unambiguously. However, on reasonable assumptions its sign is negative. This same qualification holds for the signs of $(\partial \rho / \partial t)^0$ and $(\partial \rho / \partial T)^0$; i.e., on reasonable assumptions these signs are minus and plus, respectively.

perhaps more in accord with standard business practice), fixed costs do influence the firm's choice of an optimum configuration of variable factors.[30] Although the property does not derive from the comparative statics of our model, the fact that a newly installed executive with the assigned objective of reducing costs can remove staff with ease is an event that is entirely consistent with the behavioral model. The explanation requires only that we recognize that the objective of cost reduction implies a low preference for staff. Hence, the manager with a lower preference for staff than his predecessor will typically be able to achieve significant reductions in staff without impairing performance. Moreover, when these changes in personnel and objectives occur at the top executive levels (especially at the level of the president), shrinkage of the entire staff structure may be both attempted and achieved.

9.4 A Particular Application of the Analysis

Although a number of possible applications of the model suggest themselves (e.g., in the area of tax policy), most of these are best deferred until the model has been subjected to empirical test. However, departures from profit-maximizing behavior that are said to exist in the operations of public utilities are captured so nicely by our model that it may be worthwhile to develop them.

The rates a public utility is permitted to charge are set at levels intended to allow the utility to cover its costs and earn a fair rate of return. Ordinarily rates are not adjusted continuously as conditions change but are revised only periodically. In the short run, therefore, a utility may earn above or below normal profits but this is not a situation that will continue for very long; profits will eventually be restored to a fair level by rate adjustments.

Since above-normal profits can not long continue and since supernormal profits may invite the early attention of the regulatory commissions, the management of a public utility that has other than profit-maximizing objectives has an incentive to hold profits at or below some "safe" level. This tendency to absorb profits is further reinforced by the fact that the penalty for inefficient operations is particularly weak among the regulated monopolies. Not only is there a virtual guarantee that rates will be set to cover costs and permit the utility to show earnings sufficient to attract new capital; in addition, the regulatory commissions have not attempted to control costs. Hence, there is a positive reward for absorbing profits without an offsetting penalty. This situation is said to be responsible for the conditions of excessive staff and excessive managerial accommodations among the public utilities.

[30]This point has also been made by Baumol, *op. cit.*, 78.

By inserting a maximum (or safe-level) profit constraint into the behavioral model, this sort of behavior can be shown to follow as a direct implication. Thus the objective is to

$$\text{maximize} \quad U[S, \pi_A - \pi_R, \pi_R - (\pi_0 + T)]$$

$$\text{subject to} \quad \text{(i)} \ \pi_R \geq \pi_0 + T$$

$$\text{(ii)} \ \pi_R \leq \pi_M$$

where π_M = maximum safe level of profits to report.

By hypothesis, the minimum profit constraint is ineffective but the maximum profit constraint may be encountered. When this occurs, $\pi_R = \pi_M$ and this can be handled by substituting π_M for π_R in the objective function. The problem then is reduced to

$$\text{maximize} \quad U[S, R - C - S - \pi_M, \pi_M - (\pi_0 + T)]$$

but the last term in this expression is a constant. Hence, the only terms that are relevant for maximization purposes are the staff and management slack absorbed as cost terms. Thus, the effect of encountering a safe-level profit constraint shifts the firm all the more into excessive staff expenditures and excessive managerial accommodations, which are indeed the implications we were looking for.[31]

This sort of behavior need not be limited to public utilities, of course. Any firm which, for whatever reason (e.g., to discourage entry), finds itself encountering a maximum safe-level profit constraint could be expected to exhibit this behavior.

9.5 Conclusion

By taking advantage of the notion of "organizational slack," the firm's objective function has been reformulated along lines that reflect not the traditional "best interests of the stockholders," but rather the (entirely natural) self-interest seeking of managers. The techniques of maximization analysis have been employed to discover the equilibrium and comparative

[31]Averch and Johnson, in a paper titled, "Behavior of the Firm Subject to External Regulatory Constraint" [*RAND* (March 1962), P-2488-1], have also examined the effect of introducing a safe-level profit constraint. Their behavioral assumption, however, is different from ours. They assume that the utility seeks to maximize *profit* subject to regulatory constraint. As a result they do not obtain any of the slack responses that we show but find instead that the firm will attempt to inflate its rate base by investing in plant beyond the level called for in traditional theory. By expressing output as a function of labor and capital and making the regulatory constraint a maximum rate of return rather than a maximum profit level, we can also obtain this investment response (in addition to the slack responses) with our model.

statics properties of the resulting model. These properties appear to be both intuitively sensible (indeed, at the level of casual empiricism the conformity to experience of the behavioral model is striking) and capable of being tested. What is needed, however, is a systematic study of the data to discover under what circumstances the model holds.

Among the virtues of the model are:

1. The basic behavioral assumption of the model is the same as the basic rationality assumption in all of economics: people seek their own self-interest.

2. Under conditions where forces of competition are weak, the model returns implications different from those of the traditional profit-maximizing model — implications that it would appear are capable of being tested. These implications include (a) staff expenditures (for advertising, customer services research and development, and so forth) will be permitted to absorb excessive amounts of resources when the firm's environment is favorable, but these excesses will tend to disappear in the face of adversity; (b) expenditures for managerial superfluities (entertainment, travel, office improvements, etc.) will vary directly with the business cycle; (c) staff expenditures will increase if an excess profits tax is imposed; (d) this will also be true of management slack absorbed as cost; (e) fixed costs will affect the firm's optimum configuration of variable factors; (f) newly installed executives with a lower preference for staff than their predecessors will be able to achieve significant reductions in staff with ease.

3. The model preserves the results of the profit-maximizing hypothesis under conditions of pure competition.

4. Conditions said to be characteristic of public utilities are obtained by a straightforward application of the model.

5. The welfare implications of the model are easily obtained and readily translated into policy proposals.

In addition, the model subsumes a rather general set of arguments that have been raised, but seldom tested, against the profit maximization hypothesis. Thus, if the behavioral model should be disconfirmed in all but an unimportant subset of circumstances, a large number of arguments contradictory to the traditional model can be disregarded.

10

A MODEL OF TRUST

INVESTMENT BEHAVIOR[1]

by G. P. E. Clarkson

In the preceding chapters we have seen how specific models of price and output behavior have reflected in detail the general theory summarized in Chapter 6. In the theory, an organizational decision is conceived as a choice in terms of objectives among a set of alternatives on the basis of available information. This approach has led to an examination of how organizational objectives are formed, how decision strategies are evolved, and how decisions are made using those strategies. It has also led to the problem of identifying some concepts of organizational goals, expectations, and methods of choice. The models in Chapters 5, 7, 8, and 9 illustrate and elaborate various parts of the general theory. In particular, they show that models of organizational decision making can be built that predict not only actual price, output, and other decisions but also patterns of decision-making behavior that are generally consistent with observable organizational behavior.

In this chapter we reverse this approach — that is,

[1]This chapter is based on G. P. E. Clarkson, *Portfolio Selection: A Simulation of Trust Investment* (Englewood Cliffs, N.J.: Prentice-Hall, 1962).

we first present a detailed model of individual decision-making behavior within the context of a larger organization. After presenting the model, we shall examine how closely the behavior of our model of an individual conforms to the general behavior of individuals implicit in the theory outlined above.

10.1 General Considerations

This study concerns the investment of trust funds held by banks in the United States — funds that currently amount to nearly $60 billion. Our model focuses on the investment of trust funds in common stocks. When making a decision, a trust officer in a bank is confronted with a mass of information. Information abounds on the operation of firms and the market valuation of their stocks, and published reports make predictions about the future state of the general economy and the stock market. When an investor acts in an agency or fiduciary capacity, legal restrictions and the desires of his client must also be considered. These factors, when evaluated and combined into an investment program, ultimately result in a decision to buy specific quantities of particular stocks and bonds. Thus, an investor choosing a portfolio is processing information: he sorts the useful from the irrelevant and applies the parts of the total information flow that are most important.

This process involves decision making under uncertainty. Our model, written as a computer program, simulates the procedures used in choosing investment policies for particular accounts, in evaluating the alternatives presented by the market, and in selecting the required portfolios. The analysis is based on the operations at a medium-sized national bank[2] and the decision maker of our model is the trust investment officer.[3] We require our simulation model to select portfolios using the same information that is available to the trust officer at the time his decisions are made.

10.2 Postulates and Data for the Model

Since our model is a theory of individual decision-making behavior, the method of analysis is based on the theory of human problem solving.[4] In keeping with the postulates of this theory, the main postulates for the analysis of the investment decision process are that there exist:

[2]The trust assets of this bank are approximately equal to the average for all national banks.

[3]It should be noted that our model reflects the behavior of one investor and hence may not describe the general case. The implications of this study for more general theories of investment are discussed in Clarkson, *op. cit.*, chap. 8.

[4]A. Newell, J. C. Shaw, and H. A. Simon, "Elements of a Theory of Human Problem Solving," *Psychological Review*, **65** (1958), 151–166.

1. A *memory* that contains lists of industries each of which has a list of companies associated with it. The memory also contains information associated with the general economy, industries, and individual companies.[5]

2. *Search* and *selection* procedures that perform the task of searching the lists of information stored in memory, selecting those items that have the required attributes, regrouping the selected items of information into new lists, and performing algebraic operations when necessary. These procedures function like a clerk who prepares lists of stocks suitable for current investment by scanning a master list.

3. A *set of rules* or criteria that guide the decision making by stipulating when and how each decision process is to be used. The set of rules constitutes the structure of the decision processes for an individual investor. It might be compared to the "rules of thumb" of the traditional "expert," but there is an important difference — namely, the set of rules must be defined unambiguously.

In common with other problem-solving programs, the processes are used iteratively and recursively. Lists of industries and companies are searched for particular attributes; sublists are created, searched, and divided again. For example, to obtain a high growth portfolio, the list of companies stored in memory is searched to obtain securities with the desired characteristics. Additional criteria are employed to narrow (or expand) this list. Further search and testing against desired criteria yields the specific selection of stocks to buy.

Like the investor it simulates, the program stores the final result (list) for future use. If the same problem recurs, the entire process need not be repeated. The list may be judged by present criteria, accepted, adapted to meet new conditions, or completely rejected. In the latter event the program would renew search and selection activity until a new list had been formed.

To define a model of trust investment behavior within this general framework, we require the basic rules (operations) used in making a decision to purchase particular securities. To obtain these data, trust departments of several local banks were studied by interviewing departmental officers and by observing behavior at committee meetings called to review past and future decisions. Attention was then focused on an investment officer who was chiefly responsible for all decisions on the choice of portfolios within a particular bank. The histories of several accounts were examined and

---

[5]Investors categorize companies by industry. Not all investors may associate identical companies with a given industry, but the process of classification by industry remains invariant as the primary basis for listing companies in the memory. The information associated with each company also varies among investors, but each may be represented as having a list of attributes with their values stored in memory, e.g., growth rate, dividend rate, price earnings ratio, expected earnings, expected yield, etc.

naive behavioral models were constructed to help uncover those decision processes that appeared to be invariant among accounts.

In an attempt to confirm or refute these hypotheses, the trust officer was asked to permit "protocols" to be made of his decision processes.[6] The protocols recorded the trust officer's decision processes for accounts that arose in the course of his work. The decisions made during those problem sessions determined the particular securities that were purchased for these accounts.

Close inspection of the protocols revealed that many of the decisions pertaining to the formulation of expectations and the evaluation of industries, companies, and stocks were made before the selection of a particular portfolio began. In an attempt to discover how these prior decisions were made, a new approach was taken. The trust officer was asked to read articles from financial journals and analysts' reports to which he subscribed and to comment on the ideas, forecasts, facts, and so forth presented in these articles. Protocols of these thought processes were more successful, for the reason that they revealed many of the decision processes subsumed in the earlier transcripts.

On the basis of these data and analytic techniques, a model was constructed. The model considers the problem of investing the funds of new accounts in common stocks. It does not directly consider the problem of allocating the funds among bonds, preferreds, and common stocks. The trust investment model is stated in terms of a computer model, which is presented in the next section.

10.3 The Decision Model

The investment decision process can be divided into three parts: (1) the analysis and selection of a list of stocks suitable for current investment, (2) the formulation of an investment policy, and (3) the selection of a portfolio (see Fig. 10.1). Although the selection process contains rules on diversification and on how to determine the number of shares to buy, the essence of the investment process lies in carrying out the prior analysis — Steps 1 and 2. Thus, a major part of the model's function is to convert the information on the economy, industry, and companies as found in financial journals and reports into a list of stocks suitable for current investment. The next part (Step 2) consists of formulating an investment policy from

---

[6]A "protocol" is a transcript of the verbalized thought and actions of a subject when the subject has been instructed to think or problem-solve aloud. Thus, the transcript is a record of the subject's thought processes while engaged in making a decision. Since a protocol is a detailed description of what a person does, it avoids some of the problems inherent in interview and questionnaire techniques that ask the subject to state his reasons for behaving as he does. For further discussion, see Newell, Shaw, and Simon, *op. cit.*

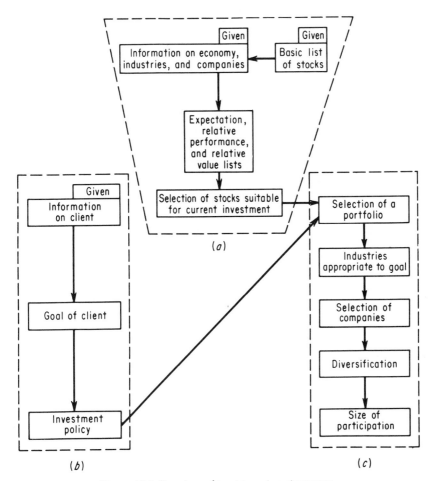

Figure 10.1 Structure of trust investment process.

the information about the beneficiary or client involved. The final section of the model performs the task of actually selecting the required portfolio.[7]

Now that we have outlined the investment process and the method of analysis used in constructing the model, the only remaining question before we proceed to describe the model is the effect of the organization and the fiduciary relation on the trust investment process.[8]

Since banks are responsible for all investments made in their name,

[7]To keep this paper to a reasonable length, the description of the model's processes must perforce be somewhat brief. A complete discussion can be found in Clarkson, *op. cit.*, chap. 4.

[8]As we are principally concerned with the investment of trust funds for individual accounts, the important constraints are those that are imposed on the investor by the banking institution and the fiduciary relation with the client.

elaborate procedures are set up to review and approve all investment decisions. Also, the necessity of being able to justify their investment decisions in a court of law has led trust investors to create a set of criteria for judging the quality of any given portfolio or investment. For all practical purposes these criteria can be reduced to one maxim: A security is of investment quality *if and only if* it is being held or is being bought by other leading trust funds.[9] Clearly, this maxim is circular in nature and if strictly true would preclude change. However, the smaller the bank the truer the maxim, so that innovations come from the larger banks acting by themselves or in small groups. If innovations do not occur frequently, this maxim then asserts that the general list of stocks that are considered suitable for trust investment will remain fairly stable over time. The addition of a further observation — namely, that trust investors eschew taking losses, i.e., selling stocks whose prices have fallen below the purchase price — allows an even stronger prediction to be made: The basic list of stocks that are considered to be suitable for trust investment by a particular bank will remain fairly stable over time, any changes being in the form of additions. Thus, for any given trust investor, the basic list of stocks from which he can choose is given to him by the historical record. At a particular point in time, however, an investor selects stocks from a subset of his basic list. This subset is defined by a concept of relative valuation. As expectations, prices, yields, and so forth change with time, so does the content of this subset.

10.3.1 Selection of stocks suitable for current investment

The information used to derive the current list of stocks is classified into three main categories: general economy, industry, and company. The content of the information processed and the manner in which interrelations are formed differ among these categories, but the basic mechanisms that sort and process the information are the same.

For each category there is a set of attributes that corresponds to the important variables in that category.[10] For example, the set of attributes for individual companies contains such attributes as sales, earnings per share, cash flow per share, profit margin, dividends per share, and so forth. The specific values are determined by the information given to the model.

Processing the data. All information except that dealing with economy and industry forecasts is fed into the model in numerical form. These data consist of the historical values of each attribute in the system for the last

---

[9] By a simple substitution of words this maxim can roughly be applied to the composition of portfolios, i.e., the ratio of common stock to bonds and preferred stock.

[10] The attributes themselves are taken as given. They were derived by an analysis of investors' decision processes and by observing which variables are considered important by investment services.

ten years. The data are entered in the form of lists, and from these basic lists the model creates, for each attribute, three additional lists. The first list contains the mean value of the ten historical values; the second contains a set of nine values that record the rate of increase (or decrease) of each value in the historical record over the value immediately preceding it; the third list contains the average rate of change of the values for the entire ten-year period. Thus, the basic information given to the model is processed so that it is expressed in terms of rates of change, ratios, or both. The rates and ratios are directly comparable throughout the system.

Information on forecasts is entered into the model in two different forms. Forecasts for economy and industry variables are converted for input into a three-valued scale — "above," "below," or "equal to." The values are based on published predictions in financial reports and journals that a given variable is going to rise, fall, or stay the same over the next interval of time.[11] For the analysis of company performance, however, numerical forecasts are needed, and in a further attempt to avoid conflicting opinions, forecasts are taken from the *Value Line Investment Survey.*

Only current forecasts are used. Previous forecasts are not kept and the model makes no attempt to evaluate them. This procedure may not be too realistic, for it ignores the effects of personal preferences on perception. However, since the model is not equipped to handle second guessing and other judgmental modifications, the forecasts are assumed to be reliable.

Before we discuss the role of expectations in the model, it is worth emphasizing that this is a model of trust investment behavior. By and large, trust investment is long-term investment. Trust investors do not engage in trading stocks for their clients and they do not look to the long-term growth of the economy and the market to justify their investments. This is not to say that they remain aloof from daily, monthly, or yearly fluctuations, but rather that their emphasis is on the analysis of industries and their respective companies. Their basic belief is that the market will eventually recognize a company's "true value." Thus, in general, trust investors analyze companies and not the market.

Evaluating the data. The model uses two main processes to evaluate company performance: the first determines the relative performance of each company with respect to the other companies in its industry; the second determines the relative value of each company's stock with respect to current market valuation.

The *relative performance* of a company is determined by deriving the relative performance of each attribute of a company with respect to the same attributes of all other companies within the same industry. This

---

[11]Numerical data are not used in an attempt to avoid the chaos of averaging the array of forecasts found in financial literature.

measure is computed as the difference between the mean value for the attribute and the mean of the distribution of the attribute means. This difference is taken as a per cent of the distribution mean and is then converted into the three-valued scale of "above," "below," or "equal to." Thus, the Relative Performance List for a company contains measures of the performance of each of its attributes with respect to the attributes of the other companies within its industry.

The *relative value* of each company's stock is determined by a pair of measures. The objective of these measures is to determine whether the current market price can be justified in the light of expected earnings and the price investors have been willing to pay for the stock in the past. The two metrics consist of (1) the difference between the mean (ten-year) price-earnings ratio and a price-earnings multiple obtained by dividing the current market price by the expected earnings per share three to five years from now, and (2) the difference between the mean and the current price-earnings ratios. These differences are taken as a per cent of the historical mean price-earnings ratio and are recorded as "above," "below," or "equal to" the historical mean. Thus, for each company the *Relative Value List* is a pair of "aboves," "belows," or "equals to" that under two possible conditions will form a pattern of only "aboves" or "belows."

The many interrelations. Up to now we have described the mechanisms that process the data as though they were independent of each other. Although this is true to a certain extent, these mechanisms are related by the process that selects the stocks suitable for current investment.[12] This selection process is composed of two parts: a scanner and a selector.

The *scanner* examines the expectation lists of the industries and economy, notices the patterns of "aboves" and "belows" generated by these lists, and reports these findings to the selector. The *selector* takes these results and, depending upon what the pattern is, applies a set of tests to all the companies in the system. These tests are applied to the two values on the Relative Value List and consist essentially of a relaxing of constraints during prosperous times and a tightening up of constraints during recessions. Those companies that pass the tests are placed on the special list known as the A-list. It is from this list that the portfolio selections are made.

10.3.2 Formulation of an investment policy

In order to determine a client's goals, the investment officer has two main sources of information — an administrative officer's interview with

---

[12]It is worth noting that information can be fed into the various categories (e.g., economy, industry, and company) at different intervals of time. Although published reports do not appear simultaneously, these intervals can be chosen to suit any particular set of requirements.

the client and the written record. The former provides the investor with some subjective impressions of the client, the latter with a copy of the legal instrument (often a will) setting up the trust. In most cases this instrument contains information about the beneficiary, the investment powers of the bank, the disposition of the principal, the desired amount of income, and so forth. The instrument also contains information on the beneficiary's age, marital status, number and age of dependents, place of legal residence, and income tax bracket. Armed with this information, the investment officer must now decide on an account investment policy lying somewhere along the continuum between the extremes of growth and income.

The model simulates this process by another "pattern-recognition" process.[13] The information on the client is entered into the model as a set of attributes — e.g., client's profession, income tax bracket, age, etc. — whose values are recorded on the three-valued scale: "high," "med," or "low." As in the previous case, the function of the scanner is to examine the list of attributes, to notice the pattern that they form, and to report the result to the selector. The function of the selector is to take the pattern of values given to it by the scanner and to convert it into an investment policy. Although there are a large number of possible combinations of growth and income, in practice only four categories are used:[14]

1. *Growth account.* Assets are expected to appreciate at an average rate of 10 per cent per year, income is not stressed, and fluctuations in principal are tolerated.

2. *Growth and income account.* Assets are expected to appreciate at 5–6 per cent per year; dividend yield should approach 2–3 per cent per year.

3. *Income and growth account.* Dividends are expected to yield 3–4 per cent per year; assets are only expected to appreciate at 3–4 per cent per year.

4. *Income account.* Size and stability of income are important, growth is not stressed, and expected dividend yield is 4–6 per cent per year.

To each investment policy there corresponds a pattern of "highs," "meds," and "lows" (see Fig. 10.2). Thus, the selector takes the pattern of values generated by the scanner and by a series of tests selects the appropriate investment policy.

---

[13]Although this is neither a new idea nor the first time it has been used, the model states explicitly how these patterns are formed and recognized. For further discussion of this concept, see J. S. Bruner, J. J. Goodnow, and G. A. Austin, *A Study of Thinking* (New York: Wiley, 1956); J. Feldman, "An Analysis of Predictive Behavior in a Two-Choice Situation" (Ph.D. thesis, Carnegie Institute of Technology, 1959).

[14]These figures are in no way fixed and will vary with changing market conditions. For a flow chart of the investment policy selector, see Fig. 10.2.

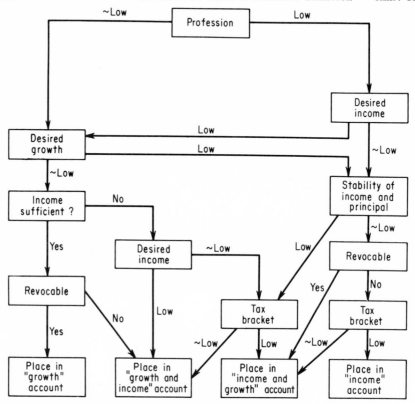

Figure 10.2 Selector for investment policy.

10.3.3 Selection of a portfolio

As mentioned earlier, the selection of a specific portfolio is essentially a process of mapping the set of industries and companies found on the A-list onto the desired investment policy. The mapping yields a subset of industries and companies that is further reduced to a specific set of stocks for a portfolio by the addition of some extra constraints. This process is divided into the following four sections:

Selection of industries appropriate to investment policy. Despite the large overlap among the characteristics of various industries, the trust investment officer associates a set of industries with each goal. Since this association depends on the characteristics of the goal as well as the general characteristics of the companies within each industry, the particular set of industries associated with a given goal may include some of the industries that are associated with other goals. Some industries on the list contain companies that vary only slightly in their individual characteristics, e.g., banks or utilities; others, such as oils, are more heterogeneous and appear on several lists. Since the investment officer's classification of an industry's characteristics changes slowly, the model takes these lists as given. Thus, for each investment policy there is now a list of industries whose companies are both currently acceptable and appropriate to the investment performance desired from the portfolio.

Selection of companies. Once the list of industries has been generated, the companies are selected for participation by the application of still another scanner-selector mechanism.

The scanner performs the task of ordering the companies in each industry on the basis of the dominant attribute of the investment policy. For example, if an income portfolio is being selected, the scanner ranks the companies in each industry on the basis of yield. The selector takes the first company from the industry that heads the list and applies a set of tests to it.

These tests consist of a series of binary decisions on the performance and expectations of important attributes. Since the importance of specific

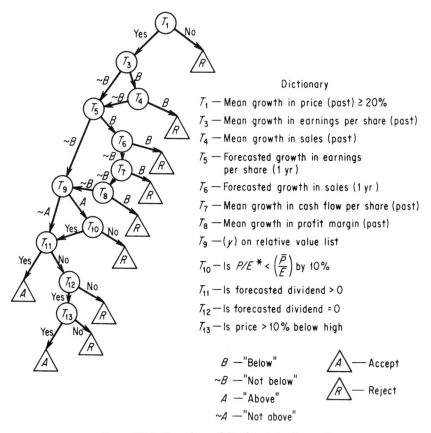

Dictionary

T_1 — Mean growth in price (past) $\geq 20\%$

T_3 — Mean growth in earnings per share (past)

T_4 — Mean growth in sales (past)

T_5 — Forecasted growth in earnings per share (1 yr)

T_6 — Forecasted growth in sales (1 yr)

T_7 — Mean growth in cash flow per share (past)

T_8 — Mean growth in profit margin (past)

T_9 — (y) on relative value list

T_{10} — Is $P/E * < \left(\dfrac{\bar{P}}{E}\right)$ by 10%

T_{11} — Is forecasted dividend > 0

T_{12} — Is forecasted dividend $= 0$

T_{13} — Is price $> 10\%$ below high

B — "Below" A — Accept

$\sim B$ — "Not below"

A — "Above" R — Reject

$\sim A$ — "Not above"

Figure 10.3 Growth portfolio discrimination net.

attributes depends upon the investment policy that is being applied, the series of tests will vary with each investment goal.[15]

The tests, which are qualitative in nature, are applied in turn to the companies within each industry. Unless the actual value of some attribute deviates considerably from the test value, the selector will accept the first company that is processed. If, for some reason, the first company does not pass the tests, the selector moves on to the second company and repeats the process. If no company from that industry is able to pass through the set of tests, the selector moves on to the next industry. If after processing all the industries, funds still remain to be invested, the selector returns to the first industry from which no selection was made and recommences processing. This time, processing begins at that test which immediately precedes the spot where the selector stopped on the first run. As soon as a company is selected, the selector moves on to the next industry.

Diversification. Diversification is achieved by insisting that all accounts participate in at least *five* industries and that participation in stocks be limited, in general, to *one* per industry. When the portfolio includes bonds and preferred stocks, each $10,000 invested in bonds or preferreds is taken to be equivalent to a participation in one industry. Hence, for an account of $50,000 with $20,000 invested in government bonds, the model would require that the remaining funds be invested in at least three industries.[16]

Size of participation. The number of shares to be purchased of each company that is selected is determined by a process that computes the average number of dollars to be invested in each company and then divides this figure by the price of the particular company's stock. In small accounts — that is, accounts with less than $50,000 to invest in common stocks — this figure is rounded to the nearest multiple of five; in large accounts round lots (100 shares) are purchased whenever possible.

The selection process continues as long as there are funds remaining for investment. When the funds have been used up, the selection process stops and the stocks that have been chosen become the required portfolio.

10.4 Testing the Model

In order to test the model's ability to reproduce the actual behavior of the trust investor — i.e., to simulate the trust investment process — the model

---

[15]The series of tests for a growth portfolio is shown in Fig. 10.3.

[16]As can be seen from the above, the investment officer's "rule of thumb" seeks to spread risk by diversification. However, as Markowitz has shown [H. Markowitz, *Portfolio Selection* (New York: Wiley, 1959), 109], when the returns on securities are correlated, this may not be accomplished if the amount invested for the client is relatively small.

was required to select portfolios for a specific set of actual trust accounts. In particular, the model was required to generate portfolios for four accounts with which the trust officer had dealt but which were not used in developing the model. These portfolios are presented below along with the selections made by the trust officer for the same accounts. The generated

SIMULATION OF ACCOUNT 1 (1/8/60)

Growth Account

Funds available for investment: $22,000

The **program** *selected the following portfolio*	*The portfolio selected by the* **trust officer** *was*
60 General American Transportation	30 Corning Glass
50 Dow Chemical	50 Dow Chemical
10 I.B.M.	10 I.B.M.
60 Merck and Company	50 Merck and Company
45 Owens Corning Fiberglas	50 Owens Corning Fiberglas

SIMULATION OF ACCOUNT 2 (6/10/60)

Income and Growth Account

Funds available for investment: $37,500

The **program** *selected*	*The* **trust officer** *selected*
100 American Can	100 American Can
100 Continental Insurance	100 Continental Insurance
100 Equitable Gas	100 Equitable Gas
100 Duquesne Light	100 General Public Utilities
100 Libbey Owens Ford	100 Libbey Owens Ford
100 International Harvester	50 National Lead
100 Philadelphia Electric	100 Philadelphia Electric
100 Phillips Petroleum	100 Phillips Petroleum
100 Socony Mobil	100 Socony Mobil

SIMULATION OF ACCOUNT 3 (7/8/60)

Income and Growth Account

Funds available for investment: $31,000

The **program** *selected*	*The* **trust officer** *selected*
100 American Can	100 American Can
100 Continental Insurance	100 Continental Insurance
100 Duquesne Light	100 Duquesne Light
100 Equitable Gas	100 Equitable Gas
100 Pennsylvania Power and Light	100 General Public Utilities
100 International Harvester	100 International Harvester
100 Libbey Owens Ford	100 Libbey Owens Ford
100 Socony Mobil Oil	100 Socony Mobil Oil

SIMULATION OF ACCOUNT 4 (8/26/60)

Income Account

Funds available for investment: $28,000

The **program** *selected*	*The* **trust officer** *selected*
100 American Can	100 American Can
100 Continental Insurance	100 Continental Insurance
100 Duquesne Light	100 Duquesne Light
100 Equitable Gas	100 Equitable Gas
100 Pennsylvania Power and Light	100 General Public Utilities
100 International Harvester	100 International Harvester
100 Phillips Petroleum	100 Phillips Petroleum

portfolios were then compared with portfolios generated by various random and naive models. The results of these tests indicate that the trust investment program selected a greater proportion of correct securities than did any one of the alternative models.

To obtain additional confirmation, the testing process was carried one step further — that is, the processes by which the portfolios are generated were submitted to empirical test. The test consisted of comparing the stream of output of the trust investment model to the recorded decision behavior of the trust investor. This test was applied to several of the mechanisms incorporated in the model. Although it is not possible to state that all the decision processes were unequivocally confirmed, the evidence strongly supports the hypothesis that the model's mechanisms have captured a considerable portion of the trust investment process.[17]

10.5 The Model and the Behavioral Theory of the Firm

A description of an organizational choice process was presented at the end of Chapter 5. In brief, it assumed multiple, acceptable-level goals, sequential consideration of alternatives with acceptance of the first satisfactory one, and the dominance of the choice process by standard operating procedures and rules of thumb. Patently, a similar choice process is involved in the trust investment model. Although it deviates in detail from the price and output models and devotes more attention to information processing, the model presented in this chapter (like the earlier models) depicts a decision-making process that assumes a relatively simple-minded, computationally constrained, adaptively rational system.

Similarly, a comparison of the model with the key concepts summarized in Chapter 6 shows a close — though not complete — agreement between the basic attributes of the theory and the major features of the model.

---

[17]For a complete presentation of the evidence and a discussion of the tests, see Clarkson, *op. cit.*, chaps. 5, 6, and 7.

With respect to the quasi resolution of conflict, two features of the model are conspicuous. First, the remarkable independence of the trust department from the rest of the organization suggests a considerable degree of local rationality within the organization as a whole. Second, the form and function of goals in the model is almost indistinguishable from the form and function specified in the theory. With respect to uncertainty avoidance, the trust investment model clearly exhibits behavior directed toward establishing a standardized, legitimized environment. The trust officer has negotiated a substitution of "good investment practice" for the less certain "good investment." With respect to problemistic search and organizational learning, the model is less strikingly consistent with the behavioral theory of the firm (although not inconsistent). Both long-run organizational learning and short-run reactions to failure are outside the domain of the investment model.

In general, it seems reasonable to conclude that the basic theory used to develop models of price and output determination may be useful as a basis for models of other decisions made by (or in) complex organizations. This possibility is explored briefly in Chapter 11.

11

SOME IMPLICATIONS

The theory of the firm serves four major purposes within the framework of economic theory:

1. It describes how individual business firms make decisions in a market system. It specifies a set of rules or motivational assumptions that describe a firm's decisions on output, price, and resource allocation. With respect to this purpose, the adequacy of the theory is determined by comparing the predictions of the theory with observations on individual firms.

2. The theory prescribes how individual business firms should make decisions in a market system. On the basis of assumptions about the goals of the firm, it specifies a set of decision rules for decisions on output, price, and resource allocation. The rules have some properties of optimality vis-à-vis the goals. With respect to this purpose, the adequacy of the theory is tested by using it as a basis for decisions and comparing the result with the result obtained from decisions derived from alternative rules.

3. The theory is a basis for describing the behavior of certain aggregates of firms — specifically for an industry, a particular sector of the economy, or the economy as a whole. Simple propositions, from the theory, about the behavior of individual firms are used to derive predictions of aggregate behavior. With respect to this purpose, the

adequacy of the theory is assessed by comparing the predictions of aggregate behavior with the actual behavior of the specified aggregates.

4. The theory is a tool for deciding among some alternative economic policies. Since many policy recommendations are designed to influence the decisions made by business firms, the theory is used to deduce the probable consequences of alternative policies. With respect to this purpose, the adequacy of the theory is evaluated by comparing the results of public policy with the desired results.

We suggested in Chapter 2 that the same theory of the firm would not necessarily be appropriate for each of these purposes. For instance, the conventional theory of the firm is more appropriate for the second and third functions than it is for the first and the fourth. In this chapter we consider the behavioral theory of the firm in the same way and inquire about its relevance to the four classic functions. At the same time, we examine the possible relevance of the general concepts for theories of organizational decision making in organizations other than the business firm. In general, we will conclude that the theory is most obviously relevant to a description of how individual firms behave, but also that it has some implications, not yet fully explored, for prescriptive theories of the firm, for aggregate economic theories, for economic policy, and for theories of organizational decision making by organizations other than firms.

11.1 Descriptive Analysis: The Firm

The arguments in this volume can be summarized by three statements: (1) The business firm is a relevant unit for investigation. (2) It is possible to construct a theory of decision-making behavior within such a unit. (3) Such a theory must focus explicitly on actual organizational decision process. We have tried both to show how to construct behavioral models of firm decision making and to indicate the basic theoretical framework within which such models lie. We have tried to specify reasons for preferring a behavioral theory of the firm to more conventional theories for purposes of descriptive microanalysis. In this section we elaborate briefly the implications of the theory for descriptive analysis of the firm.

11.1.1 Price and output determination

We will not attempt to discuss in any detail the implications of the theory for price and output models. Most of the work reported in previous chapters has dealt specifically with that problem. A microeconomic theory of price and output has to explain the quasi resolution of conflict within business organizations, problemistic search behavior, uncertainty avoidance as a basic decision commitment, and organizational learning.

The models presented in this book represent price and output determination as an adaptively rational, multiple-objective process rather than an omnisciently rational, single-objective process. Prices and outputs change primarily in response to short-run feedback on performance, and the extent to which solutions to organizational problems are sought in price and output changes depends on past learning about the consequences of such changes. Firms do not resolve potential conflict between share-of-market, profit, and production stability goals primarily by a procedure of explicit mediation. Rather, they ameliorate conflict by accumulating excess resources (organizational slack), by decentralizing information, and by attending sequentially to crises. Firms attempt to avoid the uncertainties of competition by using standard industry practice and negotiated risk-avoiding agreements.

11.1.2 Internal resource allocation

The procedures (e.g., budgeting, transfer pricing) by which a firm allocates resources to the various units within the organization are procedures for solving a classic economic problem — the efficient utilization of resources. By assuming the effective operation of an external price system, the theory of the firm has largely by-passed internal allocation as a focus of attention.[1] If the theory of organizational decision making that we have suggested has validity, the classical assumptions are incomplete. In fact, we should be able to identify some general implications of our theory for a model of internal allocation.

Consider the quasi resolution of organizational conflict. In budgeting (as in pricing), we expect to find that goals tend to enter as more or less independent constraints (each of which must normally be satisfied). Where an allocation plan apparently meets the constraints, we expect rather loose evaluation of the accuracy of the estimates and other assumptions on which it is based. Where resource rationing is necessary, we expect two general kinds of reactions: first, a tendency to use arbitrary allocative rules that maintain the relative positions of the members of the coalition; second, a tendency to re-evaluate those estimates that are relatively difficult to defend in terms of traditional organizational practice, standard accounting procedure, or immediacy of tangible return.

[1]Not completely, however. See T. Koopmans, *Three Essays on the State of Economic Science* (New York: McGraw-Hill, 1957); R. H. Coase, "The Nature of the Firm," *Economica*, **4** (1937), 386–405; J. Hirshleifer, "Economics of the Divisionalized Firm," *Journal of Business*, **30** (1957), 96–108; K. J. Arrow and L. Hurwicz, "Decentralization and Computation in Resource Allocation," in *Essays in Economics and Econometrics; A Volume in Honor of Harold Hotelling*, ed. R. W. Pfouts (Chapel Hill: University of North Carolina Press, 1960).

Consider search behavior. We expect to find the same general form of problem-oriented search as in the case of price and output. That is, search occurs in response to a problem facing the firm and is directed by learned rules for associating search behavior with particular problems. The search for alternative internal allocations is stimulated by failure on some criterion of relevance to a subunit of the organization. Thus, one type of search is stimulated by a need to reduce immediate expenditures, a second type by a need to improve profitability, a third type by a need to increase sales, and a fourth type by a need to maintain the position of a subgroup within the organization. Each type of search has a different organizational locus and a different set of organizational consequences. In general, for an alternative investment opportunity to have a significant chance of being introduced in the system, two conditions have to be met. A problem must be perceived by the organization, and the investment must be visible to that part of the organization in which search is stimulated by the problem.

Consider uncertainty avoidance. We expect to find extensive dependence of budgeting on standard industry and firm rules. Widely shared operative criteria (e.g., share of sales dollar invested in advertising) both standardize dimensions within the environment and, in effect, standardize decisions by permitting cross-firm comparisons. They also induce various kinds of rule-directed behavior. A case in point occurs when there is interdependence among activities. Under such conditions, evaluation depends on partially arbitrary rules for allocating common inputs and outputs. The rules tend to be biased in the direction of producing data leading to organizational acceptance of projects favored by particular subunits. For example, we expect to find a tendency to combine projects that do not meet explicit criteria with projects that more than meet them in order to obtain funds for projects desired on other grounds.

Consider organizational learning. We expect the same general kind of behavior as for price and output. We expect changes in the goals over time, changes in the search and decision rules, and changes in the learning rules. For example, in the case of a budget allocation, we expect adjustments over time in the aspirations of the various subunits, in the criteria applied to proposals, and in the search reactions to failure. In general, we expect a behavioral model of resource allocation to be heavily history-dependent in the same way, and for the same reasons, as our suggested models of pricing.

On the whole, we think models of resource allocation that build upon these concepts of a market price system are likely to be useful first attempts at a theory of resource allocation within a firm. We think the concepts are generally consistent with descriptions of actual budget behavior. However, we are far from confident that we can identify *a priori* all of the major relevant factors in allocation decisions. Our only intention here is to outline some possible first approximations.

Project allocation. At least at the outset we will distinguish between allocation decisions involving projects (e.g., capital budgeting, some kinds of operating budgets) and allocation decisions involving organizational subunits without immediate reference to projects. We may wish to abandon the distinction ultimately, but it corresponds roughly to a distinction made by many organizations and thus has face validity for a process theory. It is convenient to think of project allocation decisions as resulting from three relatively independent activities: (1) the determination of a target total project budget, (2) the allocation of that budget to specific projects and subunits, and (3) the implementation of that allocation through expenditure.

The target total budget is a calculation of what the organization in some sense "can afford to spend" during the next budget period. In classic investment theory such a total is not independent of the investment opportunities, but we expect a relatively independent calculation. Presumably it is subject to some modest revision subsequently on the basis of opportunities (if the opportunities are not suppressed by the system), but the target probably depends heavily on distinctions between internal and external capital, on total revenue expectations, and on past actual total budgets. We expect the target to have two major consequences. On the one hand, it should be strongly self-confirming upward; that is, if the target exceeds the probable total normal demands of subunits for projects, the search for new projects on the part of subunits and the optimistic inflation of estimates of returns from pet projects will assure the authorization of the full budget. On the other hand, it should also be self-confirming downward — subject to some possible revision in the target if project demand exceeds target funds by a large amount. Given these self-confirming attributes of the target, the determination of total funds available becomes a critical determination in the allocation decision. It is, however, a determination that has not been studied intensively from the point of view of a positive theory.

In contrast, some preliminary work has been done on the allocation of a project budget to specific projects and subunits in the organization. On the basis of a study of actual capital-budgeting procedures and practices in a few large firms, L. R. Pondy has suggested that projects are selected by a sequence of allocations to project classes.[2] That is, the organization first allocates an approximate share of the budget to major types of projects (e.g., "normal," "major," etc.). The shares allocated depend on such considerations as historical legitimacy, current organizational emphasis, and presumed performance. This major allocation is taken substantially as given at the next step, and another approximate allocation is made to a

---

[2]L. R. Pondy, "A Theory of the Capital Budgeting Process," unpublished manuscript, Graduate School of Industrial Administration, Carnegie Institute of Technology.

more refined project class. This continues until the number of projects within a class is small enough and goals are ·shared enough to allow an explicit, complete ranking of individual projects. In general, different criteria are applied at the different stages; the segmentation of the decision makes final allocation decisions substantially dependent on the classification, the differences among criteria, and the nonuniqueness provided by multigoal, acceptable-level ranking procedures. Thus, a theory of project allocation would focus on the processes by which project classes are defined, class criteria for evaluation of projects are developed, and specific individual projects are assigned to classes.

Frequently a theory of organizational decision making must distinguish between the choices made by the organization and the specific action implemented. Such a distinction is especially important here because the execution of a project allocation ordinarily involves a relatively long time and the organizational separation of the "decision" from the "implementation."

Two simple case reports will illustrate this phenomenon. In a study of capital budget decisions in a large manufacturing firm, Pondy discovered that the procedures for making "technical" revisions in project plans after approval yielded somewhat different projects from the projects as approved.[3] In some cases this involved the modification or elaboration of approved projects with partial substitution of projects that either were not approved or would probably not have been approved originally. We made a similar observation in a study of capital budgeting in another large firm during a period of marked inflationary pressure on project costs. Differences between organizational rules for changing budget authorizations and organizational rules for changing project specifications predictably affected both the project characteristics and the relation between budgeted and actual project expenditures. In this situation, cost estimates were consistently low because of inflationary pressure and organizational rules required reauthorization if expenditures exceeded authorization by more than a fixed percentage. When project costs threatened to exceed authorization by more than the fixed percentage, the usual response was to redesign the project and search for alternative sources of components rather than seek a new authorization. As a result, the frequency distribution of the ratio of actual project expenditures to estimated project expenditures shows a sharp drop at the point where the reauthorization rule became operative, and the projects actually constructed were somewhat different from the projects authorized.[4]

As in the case of price and output models, it seems probable that the

---

[3] L. R. Pondy, private communication.
[4] At the request of the company involved, we have not presented the specific data.

first successes in models of project allocation will deal with the setting of target budgets and with the allocation of a target budget to specific projects or subunits. The implementation problem will have to await a convenient way of representing the kinds of modifications characteristically introduced at that stage.

Subunit allocation. There are two important ways in which subunit allocation tends to differ from project allocation. First, because the subunit persists whereas only classes of projects persist, historical precedents for allocating resources among alternatives are likely to be of greater importance in allotments to departments than in allotments to projects. Second, because it is a more complicated mixture of activities, the subunit is likely to be harder to evaluate in widely accepted terms than is the project. Thus, it is harder to obtain agreement on procedures for ranking subunits than on procedures for ranking projects. Because of these differences, we would expect that decisions on allocations to regular subunits would be quite sensitive to past experience, to the experience of comparable subunits, and to the *prima facie* relevance of the subunit to other parts of the organization. We would expect learning with respect to these decisions to be rather crude and subject to substantial short-run error.

Consider, for example, the allocation of resources to research and development within a business firm. Partly because it appears to represent an extreme case of the characteristics we have attributed to organizational subunits and partly because of contemporary interest in research, a number of students have considered predictive models of research and development allocation. If our general conception of an organization is correct, expenditures for research and development will be based on simple rules that change slowly over time on the basis of experience and are voided in the short run by the pressure of failure. The recent work of Seeber seems to be consistent with such a conception.[5]

Seeber's studies of the process of budget decisions for research and development seem to indicate four important features of the process from the present point of view:

1. Most organizations are aware of and probably use such simple rules as per cent of revenue as a guide to research and development allocation.

2. The pressure of subunits for maintaining absolute dollar allocations, the logic of research appropriations, and the difficulties of forecasting revenues lead to considerable attempts to smooth allocations so that they vary less from year to year than do revenues.

[5]N. E. Seeber, "Research and Development Decision Making in the Business Firm," unpublished manuscript, Graduate School of Industrial Administration, Carnegie Institute of Technology.

3. Target allocations are substantially influenced by estimates of allocations (per cent of sales) in other "comparable" organizations.

4. Organizational failure on profit or sales goals leads to pressure to revise the allocation rules.

These gross features of the process can be considerably refined on the basis of Seeber's research. The refinement is obviously necessary to provide specific understanding of the ways in which the demands of the various organizational subunits are mediated in the face of scarcity, the ways in which the allocation rules change over time, and the ways in which causes are attributed to failures of various kinds. For the present, however, we will simply note that (1) the results of this research on subunit allocation seem to be generally consistent with the organizational models we have outlined and (2) studies of research and development expenditures (because of the conspicuous difficulties in evaluating research and development performance) should be especially useful in providing clues to the ways in which organizations avoid uncertainty and learn in ambiguous situations.

Transfer payments. With diversification, vertical integration, and growth in firm size have come various methods for determining the payments among organizational subunits. The effect is to allocate resources; the major motivation is to allocate responsibility for aggregate organizational performance. Thus, although the term "transfer pricing" has come to have a rather specific meaning both in the literature of economics and the parlance of management, we can focus more generally on the class of allocative procedures by which the organization disaggregates performance and transfers accounting credit for performance from one divisional ledger to another. These procedures include the allocation of overhead, various preferential-treatment market systems for the purchase of goods and services by one subunit from another, organizational conventions for determining subunit responsibility for receipts or disbursements (in money or other criteria of performance), and an assortment of informal devices for exchanging budgetary allotments.

In recent years these procedures have been elaborated by the development of transfer pricing schemes and by the demonstration of various theorems about the efficiency of such schemes.[6] Some form of modified market system has been used by a number of firms to allocate charges for key goods and services. More ancient procedures for cost and revenue allocation have an apparent purpose that is quite similar — if somewhat cruder. They attempt to make a "fair" division among the subunits.

[6] J. Hirshleifer, "On the Economics of Transfer Pricing," *Journal of Business*, **29** (1956), 172–184; K. J. Arrow, "Optimization, Decentralization, and Internal Pricing in Business Firms," in *Contributions to Scientific Research in Management* (Los Angeles: University of California, 1959).

If, however, we are primarily interested in a positive theory of allocation and if we view the organization as a coalition of participants in which conflict is only partially resolved, the concepts of "efficiency" and "fairness" have limited utility. In fact, we expect to find that organizational participants view the rules for making transfer payments as largely arbitrary (at least within wide limits). From the point of view of the subunits, performance is determined partly by the return from the external environment and partly by the transfer payment rules they can arrange by bargaining with the other parts of the organization. Subunit success involves dealing effectively with the environment and negotiating effectively with the organization on accounting conventions.

If our model of an organization is correct, we should find that transfer payment rules result primarily from a long-run bargaining process rather than a problem-solving solution. We should find that renegotiation of transfer payments will be viewed as a primary activity for solving subunit problems, especially where the subunit does not perceive the external environment as being susceptible to further exploitation. We should find that the same factors that produce organizational slack with respect to the external environment will produce slack with respect to transfer payments. Subunits that have been successful will be less active in seeking new transfer rules than will units that have been unsuccessful. In general, we should find that transfer payments are made on the basis of a few simple rules that (1) have some crude face validity and (2) have shown some historic viability. We should find that they are the focus of conflict among subunits in the same way as other allocative devices.[7]

Wage payments. One way of approaching the allocation to wage payments would be to focus explicitly on the wage decision and build a model roughly comparable to the pricing models outlined in this book. That is, we would view the firm as "solving" the wage decision problem the same way it "solves" the pricing problem — by comparing wage payments with aspiration levels, searching when the aspiration levels are not being met, applying simple decision rules on the basis of short-run feedback, and adapting gradually to experience. Perhaps the major way in which the theory would have to be structurally different would be in the relative independence of the labor union, as compared with the functional subunits considered in the price and output models, from the other subunits in the organization. The independence has two consequences. First, it would probably be necessary to pay greater attention to the internal processes of conflict resolution within the subunit (labor union) than we have previously done. In general, we have been able to ignore the fact that our subunits

---

[7]For a brief look at transfer payments as they operate in a major industry, see A. Whinston, *Price Coordination in Decentralized Systems* (Ph.D. thesis, Carnegie Institute of Technology, 1962).

are also rather complex organizations; we probably could not do so here. The union also "solves" the wage decision, presumably following the same general kind of decision process. Second, we would have to attend to the difference between *ritual* bargaining (i.e., bargaining between two groups in which conflict of interest is explicitly conceded although agreement is required by both) and *informal* bargaining (i.e., bargaining between groups in which conflict of interest is implicit). Because of the traditions of the relations between unions and management, most wage bargaining is ritual bargaining. Some of the procedures for the quasi resolution of conflict we suggested earlier are more relevant for informal bargaining than they are for ritual negotiations.

Where union negotiation is not involved, we would expect most wage decisions to be based on the same types of rules of thumb we have observed in other contexts. The organization faces a series of constraints on its decisions. For example, there might be constraints on the total salary budget, on the salary differentials among positions, on the minimum or maximum amounts payable to some specific individuals or positions, and on consistency within positions. The organization considers whether the existing allocation (or a proposed alternative) satisfies the constraints. If it does, fine; if not, the organization searches for an alternative. The constraints and the search procedures are subject to adjustment in the face of experience, but in the short run they dominate the decision. Thus, Simon has argued that much of the observed variance in executive compensation is consistent with an extremely simple organizational constraint model.[8] Basically, the model assumes a market determination of lowest-level executive salaries and an organizational constraint on salary differentials within the system. Although Simon does not claim much for the model as an actual representation of salary determination within a firm, it is not hard to see why simple internal consistency rules might easily control both salary aspirations and salary levels.

Stockholder payments. Periodically, a firm allocates resources to stockholders. These resources generally are in the form of money, stock, stock options, or other closely related variants. We can outline roughly a process for determining stockholder payments. Suppose we imagine an organization with a set of financial goals of an aspiration-level type. The firm wishes to maintain at least a certain liquidity position; it wishes to maintain a particular stock value relative to the value of other stocks in the industry, to avoid governmental intervention in stockholder allocation, to avoid a stockholder revolt, and so on. The firm obtains information on how well it is doing vis-à-vis its goals. If there is a problem, search is undertaken to determine a new strategy. So long as no problems arise, some simple

---

[8]H. A. Simon, "The Compensation of Executives," *Sociometry*, **20** (1957), 32–35.

computational rules are used to determine the appropriate payments. These rules emphasize historical legitimacy and conformity to simple partial-ordering constraints (e.g., if profits are up, dividends should not go down). Studies by Lintner, Walter, and others indicate that some such process seems reasonable as a first approximation.[9]

11.1.3 Innovations

One persistent problem in the development of a theory of the firm is the problem of dealing with innovations. Technology changes, and, for purposes of analysis over time, the production function must be viewed as adaptive rather than simply given. Products and product preferences change, and therefore the product mix and business of a firm change. We would like to predict who will introduce what kind of innovation when. We would like to know how to stimulate or discourage particular classes of innovations.

At one level, it appears that our general theory — especially the concept of problemistic search — is of considerable relevance to the prediction of innovations. We have argued that failure induces search and search ordinarily results in solutions. Consequently, we would predict that, everything else being equal, relatively unsuccessful firms would be more likely to innovate than relatively successful firms. Such a prediction is a legitimate derivation from the theory we have outlined where "innovation" means a new solution to a problem that currently faces the organization. Unfortunately, the evidence does not support the prediction for major technological changes. Data collected by E. Mansfield do not support the innovation-in-the-face-of-adversity hypothesis with respect to the introduction of twelve different innovations in four industries.[10]

It is possible that this means our theory cannot be used to predict innovations. We prefer initially, however, to modify the theory to accommodate both what we think is an accurate portrayal of the mechanisms involved and the data on acceptance of new technological innovations. To do this we need to reconsider our discussion of organizational slack. As we pointed out in Chapter 3, slack is the difference between the payments required to maintain the organization and the resources obtained from the environment by the coalition. In general, success tends to breed slack. One of the main consequences of slack is a muting of problems of scarcity. Subunit demands are less closely reviewed (since they are less likely to conflict with other demands). Resources are more likely to be

---

[9]J. Lintner, "Distribution of Incomes of Corporations among Dividends, Retained Earnings, and Taxes," *American Economic Review*, **46** (1956), 97–113; J. E. Walter, "Dividend Policy and the Process of Choice," unpublished manuscript, Wharton School of Finance and Commerce, University of Pennsylvania.

[10]E. Mansfield, "Technical Change and the Rate of Imitation," *Econometrica*, **29** (1961), 741–766.

allocated if they are sought strongly by a single subunit. Thus, distributed slack is available for projects that would not necessarily be approved in a tight budget. We have also argued that the criteria of acceptance for organizational courses of action are heavily influenced by traditional procedures and historical rules of thumb. In general, therefore, the tighter the budget, the more expenditures will be controlled by essentially conservative rules. Slack provides a source of funds for innovations that would not be approved in the face of scarcity but that have strong subunit support. As we observed in our study of the magnetic controllers in Chapter 4, such innovations typically include improvements in the technology (better engineering, newer forms of products). These are not problem-oriented innovations. In the short run they contribute mostly to subunit goals (professional status, subunit prestige, and so forth), but some portion of them turn out to be major technological improvements. As a result, when we study the firms that have made specific significant technological improvements, we find that they were made by firms with substantial slack (and thus mostly successful firms).

Since we now have a prediction that firms will innovate both when successful and when unsuccessful, we need some operational criteria for distinguishing between the kinds of innovations in the two cases. The distinction is not hard to make in principle. Problem-oriented innovation will tend to be justifiable in the short run and directly linked to the problem. Slack innovation will tend to be difficult to justify in the short run and remotely related to any major organizational problem. The classification of innovations is, however, difficult. Consider, for example, the introduction of a computer to process a payroll. We might suspect that in most cases this represents a case of slack innovation, but we can imagine circumstances under which specific problems with labor costs or labor inaccuracies would make it a problem-oriented innovation.

We think that this view of innovations is a reasonable approach, if the problem of distinguishing between the two types of innovations is not insuperable. It will become an even more plausible approach if we can devise a measure for slack that will distinguish between distributed and undistributed slack. In the theory the two types of slack are clearly distinct, but they are difficult to distinguish empirically.

11.2 Descriptive Analysis: Aggregates of Firms

It is a common practice in economic theory to make a series of behavioral assumptions for micro-units and to generate from these assumptions a parallel series of implications for aggregations of such units. Assumptions about the firm, consumer, and investor lead to a series of predictions of the behavior of markets, segments of the economy, and the economy as a whole.

Since these aggregate predictions can be compared with aggregate data gathered from the real world, implicit confirmation of the whole model (including the underlying behavioral assumptions) is obtained by testing aggregate predictions. Although the traditional justification of this methodology is questionable (see Appendix A), the methodology itself is, in principle, unexceptionable.

We have reviewed some of the classic assumptions of firm behavior used in aggregate models. Although most of them seem to us implausible as descriptions of the actual behavioral processes used by firms, they have been useful for certain kinds of aggregate models. In fact, much of macro-economic theory is built upon such assumptions even if the assumptions are not always necessary to the theory.

The approach pursued in this book and the models outlined here make it possible to develop alternative aggregate models built upon alternative assumptions about business firms. Provided we can solve the computation problems of aggregation, we should be able to elaborate behavioral theories of markets or economies. To a limited extent, we have already shown some of the implications of our models for the simplest forms of oligopoly — the duopoly models of Chapters 5 and 8. Although those efforts are not conclusive, they do indicate both some kinds of aggregate implications and some procedures for evaluating the implications. In this section, we will suggest briefly some general implications for aggregate systems and some approaches to the problem of constructing useful aggregate models.

11.2.1 Oligopoly theory and the behavioral theory of the firm

Although we have presented some models that involve interacting firms within an oligopolistic market, we have not attempted to consider oligopoly theory in any detail. Such a consideration must await further empirical work on oligopoly market behavior and its relation to the predictions generated by behavioral models. However, we can suggest a few implications of the theory for work on oligopoly markets. The suggestions include proposals for modification of both the substantive content of theories of firm behavior and the theoretical objectives of oligopoly theory. The substantive modifications were discussed at some length earlier. For the most part, a behavioral model of oligopoly behavior should emphasize adaptation, problem solving, uncertainty avoidance, and incomplete rationalization of decisions. It should tend to de-emphasize explicit omniscience and goal clarity.

These substantive modifications stem from the modifications we have proposed in the theoretical objectives of oligopoly theory. Conventionally, oligopoly theory considers the ways in which the theory of competition must be modified to deal with a market dominated by a few major firms. The shift in "competition" from a large number of essentially anonymous small firms to a small number of readily identifiable large firms leads to an explicit treatment of expectations about the behavior of specific competitors. The objective is to develop a model containing a few variables capable of yielding a determinate result of considerable generality. In order to reduce the decision process to manageable proportions, the classical theory ignores some phenomena and aggregates others into a handful of constructs. As we have observed above, such a strategy assumes that at some meaningful level of generality it is possible to construct a relatively simple model of an oligopolistic market. We are constrained to consider only those phenomena that are susceptible to prediction by such models.

The behavioral theory of the firm relaxes considerably the requirements of simplicity in the models, expands considerably the phenomena that can be considered explicitly, and reduces considerably the need for aggregation of phenomena into summary variables. As a result, the theory gives up some attributes of generality. The distinctions made among firms and industries are finer and the predictions, therefore, tend to be more specific. Since the predictions depend on a larger number of variables, the model's require more knowledge in order to generate firm predictions. The reaction of one variable to movement in another variable depends on a number of other contingencies within the model.

To illustrate the differences between the two approaches, consider the treatment of competition within oligopoly theory. If we acknowledge the relevance of specific competitors for decisions, we are constrained to introduce some form of the conjectural variation term — an expectation about behavior by key competitors. For such models we assume that firms have (or form) some expectations about the reaction of other firms to their own behavior. In most forms of the theory, the conjectural variation term is quite simple. It is a crude aggregate construct to summarize the way in which the firm anticipates competitor's behavior.

No one would seriously argue either that, in fact, a conjectural variation term is explicitly formulated by many business firms or that we can represent all of the processes by which firms attempt to deal with competition in an oligopoly by introducing such a simple concept. However, the conjectural variation term is consistent with the general theoretical strategy of oligopoly theory and allows some kinds of solutions to some problems.

An alternative strategy is to examine the actual processes by which firms deal with the problem of oligopolistic competition. Such an approach — as reflected in the behavioral theory of the firm — identifies two conspicuous techniques used by the business organization. The firm attempts to learn from its experience. That is, rather than "calculate" a conjectural variation term, it "learns" one on the basis of market feedback. Even more important, the firm attempts to avoid the uncertainties of competition by developing information systems that substitute direct knowledge for forecasts. The possibility that business firms might in a general way be adaptive and that they might develop procedures for sharing information is a feature of imperfect competition that few students of oligopoly would deny. What distinguishes the behavioral theory of the firm from most other theories of the firm is the attempt to consider relatively slow adaptation and partial information systems rather than limiting attention to immediately adaptive or complete information systems.

The significance of the difference hinges on the extent to which the firms with which we deal can, in fact, be adequately described in the terms encompassed by more conventional theories. For example, one possible information system for firms in an oligopoly is complete collusion. Normally, it provides the maximum amount of information sharing within the industry. It can also be encompassed rather easily within the theory. Such collusion has, however, two major drawbacks for the typical firm. First, social regulation of market systems ordinarily inhibits the development of collusive information sharing. Various prohibitions of conspiracy and collaboration among competitors (in combination with erratic enforcement) make the costs of manifest collusion highly uncertain. Second, the full effectiveness of collusion depends on assured cooperation among the several firms in the industry, and for at least some firms in the industry the uncertainties of polyarchy within a cartel are at least as forbidding as the uncertainties of oligopolistic markets. Because of the costs involved, the difficulties in enforcing cooperation, and the substantial commitment in the culture to the immorality of complete collusion, such a strategy is generally not considered except when the organization — or some part of it — feels under considerable pressure from actual or impending failure to achieve critical goals. Attempts at some form of collusion are certainly common. The conditions necessary often exist somewhere in a complex organization, and the conventional delegation of authority and decentralization in an organizational coalition lend themselves to decentralized collusion. However, the collusion ordinarily associated with legal action by the government is apparently not a standard operating procedure for most large business firms in the United States.

There are, however, a number of alternative information systems much more commonly in use, some of which were mentioned in earlier chapters. Salesmen exchange information with each other directly. Customers serve as brokers of information gathered from their various alternative suppliers. Information on plans, styles, product mix, and expectations are both systematically leaked and diligently pirated. Trade and professional associations provide for the systematic exchange of information. Widely shared standard operating procedures make explicit information redundant in many cases. Various kinds of external consultants serve as indirect means of pooling information. Some of these information systems are customarily viewed as unilateral intelligence activities, but, in fact, most of them thrive as accepted devices not simply for acquiring information but also for sharing it. The firm or subunit that refuses to offer information is at a disadvantage in gathering it from the information broker involved.

If this description is accurate, the difficulty of oligopoly theory is clear. It deals relatively effectively with complete exchange of information and relatively effectively with no exchange of information but it deals poorly with the intermediate information systems that are apparently typical of most firms in oligopolistic industries. At the same time, it should be clear that the behavioral theory of the firm can — at least thus far — treat intermediate systems precisely only in special situations (e.g., the department store model, the general price and output model). Beyond such special situations the theory provides only a general framework for understanding the operation of oligopolies.

In a similar way, if we examine the possibilities for dealing with organizational learning in an oligopolistic market, we must admit that aside from a few special applications we are not yet in a position to make effective use of the observation that firms adapt to their environments. Some efforts (Chapter 5) to examine adaptive conjectural variation terms have been useful, and some more general adaptive models (Chapter 8) seem to portend more general applicability of detailed learning constructs.[11] However, at this level of theory the main contribution the behavioral theory of the firm can offer is a different set of general considerations for the development of a theory of oligopoly.

11.2.2 Computer models of aggregates of firms

The research strategy of expanding the range of phenomena explicitly treated in a theoretical model makes little sense for oligopoly theory unless it is feasible to develop computer models of aggregates of firms. There does not appear to be any alternative method of dealing with the kinds of models described here. Conversely, the step from a predictive computer model of a specific firm to a predictive computer model of a specific industry does not seem in principle overwhelming. In fact, we have moved rather easily back and forth from one to the other (e.g., in the can industry model, the department store model, and the general model).

For comparative statics these models do not seem to have any particular advantage over other models except in special cases. For describing changes over time in a complex system of interrelated decisions and reactions, however they open to study a large class of economic phenomena that have not yielded to previous theoretical efforts. The general model of price and output, for example, predicts time series of prices, profits, market shares, inventory levels, output, general sales strategies, costs, and organizational

[11]C. E. Ferguson and R. W. Pfouts, "Learning and Expectations in Dynamic Oligopoly Behavior," *Behavioral Science*, **7** (1962), 223–237.

slack. In order to generate such output, of course, the models require not only the parameters describing attributes of the firms involved but also an adequate characterization of the external environment — as represented particularly by the demand function. The individual firms represented may consist of all of the firms in the market (or segment of the economy) being simulated, or the model may be restricted to a sample of firms from which some prediction can be made. The latter procedure seems more feasible from the point of view of model construction, but it does pose some difficult technical problems in extrapolation. Aggregation to still larger units (e.g., the economy) is also possible through sampling. Although such aggregation may not involve major conceptual difficulties, the problems in obtaining relevant microdata are large enough to make detailed economy-wide aggregation seem somewhat farther in the future.[12]

11.3 Descriptive Analysis: Nonbusiness Organizations

The business firm is a major decision-making organization. It is not the only type of large, complex organization that makes decisions, however. Even in a society using a market economy, many important decisions are made outside the framework of the firm. Most conspicuous among such institutions are the political institutions of the modern nation state. Governmental bureaucracies are complex, decision-making organizations. So also are military organizations and schools, the Presidency, and many local political systems. Outside of the government, we might add such organizations as labor unions, hospitals, eleemosynary institutions, and private and professional associations.

Viewed as a theory of organizations, the behavioral theory of the firm belongs to the third, "decision-making," branch of organization theory described in Chapter 2. It postulates the same basic structure of the decision-making process and the same fundamental psychological mechanisms as does the other literature belonging to that branch, applying them to the specific context of the business firm. Hence, the behavioral theory of the firm is one of the important potential sources of evidence about the validity of this structure and these mechanisms. It is also a source of new evidence and new insights for further modifying and developing the theory. We have not, as yet, explored in detail the relation of the models that have emerged from our studies to possible models of other types of organizations. As a result, we will limit ourselves in this section to a general discussion of the next steps that are required to exploit developments in the behavioral theory of the firm for organization theory as a whole.

[12]G. H. Orcutt, M. Greenberger, J. Korbel, and A. M. Rivlin, *Microanalysis of Socioeconomic Systems — A Simulation Study* (New York: Harper, 1961).

11.3.1 Firms and nonfirms

The verbal theory of a firm presented in Chapters 3–6 is idiosyncratic to business firms in many specific ways. The kinds of information it considers, the kinds of goals it assumes, and the kinds of choices it predicts are, if not unquie to firms, at least more characteristic of firms than of other organizations. Profit, sales, inventory, and production goals are the basic goals we consider. Feedback on these goals, on costs, and on competitors' behavior is the information we emphasize. Decisions on price and output are the choices we predict. Other organizations may have analogs of such specific dimensions, but the possible utility of the theory does not depend upon straining for specific analogs; it depends upon the relevance of more general theoretical concepts.

If we view the concepts alone, it is clear that they are not intrinsically unique to the firm. The processes they stipulate are general decision processes. On the whole, the concepts of the theory seem to be consistent with much recent work on organizations outside the business world; but most recent work on organizations, as in the case with the business firm, has not had as distinct a decision-making orientation as would be required to test the model. For example, there are a number of points of tangency between the behavioral theory of the firm and studies of hospitals by Perrow and studies of foundations by Sills.[13] None of these studies, however, attempts to specify a model of decision making within the organization. The closest thing to an explicit model of which we are aware is found in a discussion of planning in the British National Health Service by Eckstein.[14] In a brief epilogue to a more comprehensive study of the operation of the Health Service, Eckstein summarized the planning and decision making process he observed.[15] Paraphrased only slightly, Eckstein found that:

> 1. Health Service objectives consist in a large number of relatively independent, not necessarily internally consistent, imperatives.

[13]C. Perrow, "The Analysis of Goals in Complex Organizations," *American Sociological Review*, **26** (1961), 854–865; D. L. Sills, *The Volunteers* (Glencoe, Ill.: Free Press, 1957).

[14]H. Eckstein, *The English Health Service* (Cambridge: Harvard University Press, 1958).

[15]There are a number of other studies in which some of the same processes are described. A few of these studies are: R. L. Chapman, J. L. Kennedy, A. Newell, and W. C. Bril, "The Systems Research Laboratory's Air Defense Experiments," *Management Science*, **5** (1959), 250–269; H. Kaufman, *The Forest Ranger* (Baltimore: Johns Hopkins University Press, 1960); C. E. Ridley and H. A. Simon, *Measuring Municipal Activities* (Chicago: International City Managers' Association, 1938); H. A. Simon, "Birth of an Organization: The Economic Cooperation Administration," *Public Administration Review*, **13** (1953), 227–236; V. A. Thompson, *The Regulatory Process in OPA Rationing* (New York: Kings Crown, 1950).

2. The extent to which the potential conflict among goals becomes an actual conflict depends on the level of abundance provided by the environment of the Service.

3. In order to reduce the difficulty of dealing with a complicated, uncertain, and threatening world, the organization uses routine and stereotyped rules and arbitrary accounting procedures.

4. Rules are revised primarily when a problem exists and is made conspicuous by a complaint.

5. Problems are solved by searching for a solution that "works" (i.e., eliminates the complaints) rather than an explicitly optimal solution.

6. Rules tend to be learned as appropriate responses to particular situations independent of their original justification.

7. Goals change over time as a result of experience with the consequences of decisions.

The British Health Service may conceivably be representative of only a small class of public organizations, but it is hard to read Eckstein's study without feeling that the Health Service and the firms we have described in this book belong to the same decision-making species.

Our reading of the literature on political institutions suggests that the concepts needed for a theory of decision making by political organizations are not strikingly different from those needed in dealing with the firm. However, political organizations (and other nonbusiness decision-making organizations) differ from firms in several important ways. They differ in the mythology surrounding them, in the character of their relations with external control groups, and in the traditions surrounding their standard operating procedures. Such differences probably lead to important differences in the detailed process by which the organizations make decisions. For example, the extended social isolation of firms from other organizations should lead to differences in behavior simply through learning in a world where acceptable solutions are not unique.

11.3.2 Prerequisites for a theory

Quite aside from the considerations advanced in Chapter 1 for the study of the firm, it is no accident that models of organizational decision making can be developed in a detailed, quantitative form in the area of business behavior. Specifically, in the case of the theory of the firm we have a rather large number of more or less comparable organizations making repeated decisions on a quantifiable dimension. These characteristics permit the development of the theory. Without them, a theory is possible but handicapped both with respect to being developed and with respect to being general.

Comparable organizations. Students of public organizations are especially plagued by the apparent uniqueness of their subject organizations. Whereas there are many large oligopolistic firms in the world, there are few British National Health Services. One solution to the problem has been to shift to comparative studies of administration, to consider national health services in all countries in which they are found. Nevertheless, such a study, useful as it is, is not the only solution. The statement that there are many large oligopolistic firms in the world is less a statement of fact than a classificatory fiat. Nature did not decree that two such dissimilar systems as General Motors and U.S. Steel should both belong to the class of large oligopolistic firms. Economic theory and economists made the classification with no more (and no less) justification than that the classification permits a useful distinction between generic and specific statements and that there are a reasonable number of generic statements.

When we leave the area of the firm, we are likely to hear with impressive frequency that the structure, position, task, or history of a certain organization is unique. What we tend to forget is that uniqueness in this sense is not an attribute of the organization alone; it is an attribute of the organization and our theory of organizations. An organization is unique when we have failed to develop a theory that will make it nonunique. Thus, uniqueness is less a bar to future theoretical success than a confession of past theoretical failure. Whether our study of "comparative administration" is a study of how the same (in some sense) task is performed under different cultural traditions, how different tasks are performed under the same cultural tradition, or how the same task is performed at different levels in a social system, the basis for the classificatory system is the presumption that generic statements can be generated. On the whole it must be conceded that organization theory has not been conspicuously fortunate in its *a priori* guesses on a useful classificatory system for studying politics. Our own faith that this misfortune is not a necessary feature of political systems stems in large part from an observation that the classifications ordinarily used are justified primarily by recourse to Montesquieu or to the U. S. Government Manual.

Repeated quantifiable decisions. There is nothing intrinsically more repetitious or quantifiable about economic decisions than there is about decisions by organizations other than firms. The differences between the two lie almost entirely in our habitual ways of thinking about them. Economists have conditioned us to focus attention on a small set of decisions made by firms repeatedly and in quantifiable form — prices, outputs, resource allocations. These represent only a small portion of the decisions made within firms. Even these decisions are frequently not seen by the firm as the simple numerical choices that the theory represents. For example, "pricing" decisions often include a variety of considerations such as discounts, preferential treatment, credit arrangements, and so forth. Thanks to the widespread acceptance of economic concepts in firms, it is relatively easy to impose those concepts on the decision-making data. The organization collects data and makes decisions in terms of such concepts as "profit," "cost," "price," and "production." A theorist need merely relax and reap the benefit of his predecessors' genius in educating generations of subjects in the efficacy of such measurable dimensions.

Such a happy condition does not exist to any significant extent in other organizations. Consider foreign policy making in the U.S. State Department, for example. A student who wishes to study policy making in the State Department faces a double handicap that is not faced by the student of the firm. First, he has no ready-made decision concepts. If he accepts the ideology that each decision is unique, he is obviously lost. If he does not accept such a doctrine, then he must create some reasonable decision variables. Second, he has no general acceptance within his subject organizations of a set of concepts. Even if he generates some reasonable dimensions of his own, he has no assurance that the organization will contribute to his data-gathering problems. Even though the student of the firm may have some scepticism about the relation between accounting profits and economic profits, he can at least be sure that the firm will have some records of profit. The student of the State Department has no comparable confidence that the department will record relevant information on his theoretical decision variables.

The major exception to this distinction is in the area of internal resource allocation. It is budgeting that has been studied in most detail in nonbusiness organizations.[16] Earlier in this chapter, we suggested an approach to the study of budgeting in the firm. With only slight modification such an approach can be transferred to other kinds of organizations. In fact, the ideas for a model of budgeting in the firm are quite similar to the ideas on governmental budgeting expressed by Wildavsky.[17] Governmental organizations are accustomed to dealing in the language of appropriations and budgets, and such allocations provide a ready decision that is both repetitive and immediately quantifiable. Similar knowledge of and attention to a budgetary allocation are characteristic of most other noneconomic organizations. Because of this fact, it seems likely that the first major work on decision-making models (in the sense that we have used the term in this book) of nonfirms will be in the area of internal resource allocation. Ultimately, however, we must go beyond such a limit. We will have to create decision variables with which to analyze the decision behavior of organizations that do not now use theoretically useful decision variables.

[16]Ridley and Simon, *op. cit.*

[17]A. Wildavsky, "Political Implications of Budgetary Reform," *Public Administration Review,* **21** (1961), 183–190.

11.4 Normative Analysis: The Firm

The problems of how business firms ought to make decisions — as contrasted with how they do — form the basis for an extended, growing, and sophisticated literature. Substantial parts of such analytical tools as modern statistical decision theory, linear, quadratic, dynamic, heuristic, and integer programing, various kinds of direct search methods, game theory, and theory of teams have been developed in the context of generating normative solutions to problems of the firm. Few of the major economic decisions of the firm have escaped assault by some new technique of operations research or management science. It is natural, therefore, to ask whether positive models of organizational decision making based on a behavioral theory of the firm have any implications for a normative theory.

On the whole, we think an honest answer must emphasize both the severe limitations on the theory as a normative model and the modest amount of effort that has been directed at considering normative implications. The main positive thing that can be said is that the theory offers some glimmers of possible approaches to a few problems with which current normative theory has difficulty. Specifically, we will consider four kinds of problems: (1) finding an analytically useful way of describing one's own organization, (2) building an operations research model that considers explicitly both the organizational structure and the implementation of "optimal" decision rules, (3) predicting the behavior of other organizations within the environment, and (4) managing an organization rationally from the point of view of the manager.

Organization description. Traditionally, organizations are described by organization charts. An organization chart specifies the authority or reportorial structure of the system. Although it is subject to frequent private jokes, considerable scorn on the part of sophisticated observers, and dubious championing by archaic organizational architects, the organization chart communicates some of the most important attributes of the system. It usually errs by not reflecting the nuances of relationships within the organization; it usually deals poorly with informal control and informal authority, usually underestimates the significance of personality variables in molding the actual system, and usually exaggerates the isomorphism between the authority system and the communication system. Nevertheless, the organization chart still provides a lot of information conveniently — partly because the organization usually has come to consider relationships in terms of the dimensions of the chart.

Alternative ways of describing organizations have been suggested from time to time. The most common alternatives focus on dimensions of the organization that are poorly reflected by the usual organization chart, but they retain the basic representation in terms of a set of relations between pairs of individuals. Thus, we conceive the organization as a communication system and describe it in terms of some dimension of communication (channels actually used, channels available, and so forth). Or, we view the system in terms of sociometric choices and describe it as a sociometric network. In either case, we use a simple linear graph or a matrix representation of the system.

The kinds of models presented in this book provide another possible alternative descriptive view of an organization. We can describe the organization as a decision-making process. Such a description tends to be quite different — in terms of the organizational features it highlights — from an organization chart or the more common alternatives to it. By opening for examination a different set of attributes, it is likely to stimulate the consideration of a different set of alternative changes in the system. Beyond this, a description in terms of the decision process has something to recommend it for a primary position in a system having decisions as a primary output. In either case, however, a description does not necessarily solve problems. It abstracts from a complicated organization some attributes of the organization. In order to be useful, the persons using the description must be able to do something with it.

Supplement to operations research models. Much of modern effort in operations research and management science is directed toward developing decision rules and strategies for making the classic decisions within business firms. These decisions — pricing, production, inventory, advertising, investing — overlap considerably with the decisions considered in the previous chapters from a positive point of view. Quite literally, therefore, widespread shifts in the decision rules used by firms would require us to reconsider the details — if not the basic framework — of our theory.

The converse is also true. Two of the persistent difficulties in generating and implementing management science recommendations seem to stem from implicit acceptance of the classical model of an omnisciently rational firm. First, despite considerable sophistication gained by hard experience, few operation research workers are fully satisfied with the criterion functions provided them by the organizations with which they work. It is one thing to start a textbook discussion with the qualifier, "Given a well-defined preference order . . . ." It is quite another thing to find an organization that will give you one. Second, management science models frequently experience difficulty in moving from "acceptance" by the organization to full implementation. Both of these difficulties are typical manifestations of an adaptive, multiple-goal system.

Our models do not suggest an obvious solution to the problem of dealing normatively with such a system. However, they may help in understanding the nature of the problem. If our description of the objectives of an organization is accurate, it is not surprising that operations research efforts occasionally stumble on inconsistent or ambiguous criterion functions. It is even less surprising that they frequently encounter problems in implementation. The "goals" of an organization are subject to the decentralization and attention factors with which we have been concerned. As a result, it is virtually impossible to specify them *a priori*. It is also virtually impossible for a "responsible executive" to specify them accurately. Recent efforts to determine criterion functions are a response to one form of this difficulty. They attempt to avoid the intrapersonal problems of defining a utility function. To be more successful in an organization, however, the management scientist must expose a wider part of the organizational system to the implications of the decisions. The "responsible executive" can at best predict the situations in which his organization (or a part of it) will protest. Even the best executive makes errors in prediction — especially if he is accustomed to keeping the organization viable by responding to feedback rather than relying exclusively on predictions of trouble.

If our analysis is correct, a behavioral theory of the firm has implications for operations research models at two different levels of generality. First, a model of a specific decision-making process could form a basis for identifying organizational constraints on a decision rule. Thus, it would be one basic device for defining the precise problem facing the organization. Second, the theory seems to indicate that efforts to improve an organization as an adaptive system might be more relevant than efforts to generate some kind of optimizing decision rule. In the final accounting, it will probably be the first of these implications that will prove the more significant. Effective normative treatment of organizational decision making is particularly dependent on a precise specification of the institutional and behavioral limits on organizational design. In the short run, however, the theory may also be useful as a guide to developing adaptive procedures using the organization's limited capacities more effectively.

Predicting the behavior of other organizations. Business organizations exist in an environment consisting largely of other organizations. Effective management requires knowledge of the probable behavior of suppliers, customers, competitors, governmental regulatory bodies, labor unions, and a host of other complex organizational decision-making systems. As in every case in this section, we have no direct evidence that the models are useful for such a purpose. It should be obvious, however, that if we can predict the ordering behavior of a retail department store, we should be able to provide some useful information to a manufacturer selling to such a store. If we can understand the search behavior of the department store, we can adopt a sales strategy that will increase the likelihood that our products will be visible to the store when it is searching. Similarly, if we can predict the price, output, and sales strategy reactions of a class of firms to certain kinds of situations, we should be able to provide some help to a firm operating in an industry composed of firms of that class.

Use of such models will scarcely eliminate the use of other more classic devices of tactical intelligence — spying, trial balloons, analysis of public information, and direct observation. Classical intelligence devices are (as we have noted) means for avoiding uncertainty by using short-run feedback. An organization will continue to need such feedback even if the models are much more successful than we as yet have any reason to hope they will be. An organization will continue to use such feedback even if it does not need it. For special purposes and in special situations, however, it should be possible to provide some additional aids to decision making involving other organizations by developing models of those other organizations and testing alternative strategies against the models.

In order for behavioral models of organizations to be useful for predicting organizations within the environment, we require a knowledge of the internal operation of those organizations. Such knowledge may be difficult to obtain; few competitors will knowingly provide detailed information for such a purpose. Effective normative use, therefore, will depend on the extent to which the development of the theory will limit the number of organization-specific characteristics that have to be determined and on the extent to which the standard devices for gathering information about other organizations can be used to estimate the key parameters. At present, the theory is not well enough developed to offer much immediate hope except in a few areas.

The rational manager. We have argued that the business firm is basically a coalition without a generally shared, consistent set of goals. Consequently, we cannot assume that a rational manager can treat the organization as a simple instrument in his dealings with the external world. Just as he needs to predict and attempt to manipulate the "external" environment, he must predict and attempt to manipulate his own firm. Indeed, our impression is that most actual managers devote much more time and energy to the problems of managing their coalition than they do to the problems of dealing with the outside world. "Optimal" allocation to a particular subunit cannot be determined independent of the effect of an allocation on the goals (and thus the demands) of subunits in the organization and on the development of organizational slack. These more or less elementary lessons in the administrative facts of life have not as yet been adequately considered by management science. Since O. E. Williamson has pursued (in Chapter 9) some of the possible implications of using the present theory as a guide to a rational manager, we will not attempt to suggest any further detail.[18]

[18]We are quite aware of the ideological ambivalence in the contemporary American business creed with respect to managerial responsibility and managerial rationality.

11.5 Normative Analysis: Economic Policy

Finally, we can consider the implications of the theory for economic policy. Insofar as economic policy is directed toward influencing the behavior of business firms, it seems reasonable that a behavioral theory of the firm might cast some light on policy alternatives. With the appropriate cautions, we think it does. As in the case of other problems considered in this chapter, the main cautions stem from the incomplete nature of our present knowledge.

Control of firms through policy action. Short-run economic policy can impinge on an adaptive, problem-solving business organization in three main ways: (1) Policy decisions can change the routine inputs to standard decision rules. Decisions can be modified more or less automatically by modifying the data fed into the rules. (2) Public policy can create a problem for the firm. Failure of the firm to achieve some goal can be induced by public action. (3) Economic policy can modify the attributes of potential solutions to potential problems. New alternatives can be added to the search list or the attributes of existing alternatives can be modified.

Manipulating firms by changing the inputs to routine decision rules is so common we scarcely are aware of it as a tool for policy making. Changes in accounting or tax rules, product specifications, work regulations, and some kinds of minor taxes are examples of inputs that are almost automatically coded in the organization's language and fed into its decision rules. So long as the resulting modifications in the behavior of the firm (in interaction with the behavior of the external environment) do not result in goal failure, changes are induced almost without awareness on the part of the organization. Such changes can be made easily because the organization typically has a set of goals that can be met by more than one "solution." Any shift from one feasible solution to another — especially when it can be presented as a technical adjustment in low-level classificatory rules — is likely to pass virtually unnoticed.

Manipulating firms by forcing failure on some goal is typical of some major policy efforts. An external, explicit constraint on costs, prices, profits, sales, production policy, or inventory policy, for example, would — if severe enough — clearly induce failure for an organization having the general characteristics we have imputed to business firms. The failure would, in turn, clearly stimulate search for a new solution to the problem. The policy problem is to induce failure in such a way as to direct search toward a socially desirable solution.

Manipulating firms by modifying attributes of potential solutions to

---

By suggesting that predictive models of organizational decision-making may permit a manager to act rationally, we do not mean to preclude "unselfish" acts of trusteeship by the manager. If the models are applicable, they can be applied to further the interests of the manager, the stockholders, the public, or virtue.

problems is really an intermediate-run rather than short-run economic policy. To be effective in modifying actual behavior, changes in the available alternatives must be accompanied by some stimulus for the firm to seek new alternatives or new information about old ones. The strategy tends to be a relatively subtle one, but where the problems to be faced by a class of firms can be anticipated and the objective is to produce a gradual shift in behavior, modifications in alternatives can be achieved — sometimes without the heavy emotional content of efforts to force organizational search immediately.

If we consider the major short-run repertoire of the economic policy maker (e.g., changes in reserve requirements, interest rate adjustments, selective and aggregate shifts in taxes and public expenditures, wage and price restrictions, anti-trust regulation),[19] it is clear that the behavioral theory of the firm is far from providing precise answers to policy problems. If the theory is substantially correct, however, the difficulty is not that knowledge about the internal decision process of the firm is irrelevant to policy formation, but rather that our knowledge is incomplete.

To illustrate the problem, consider the following question. Suppose that we wish to stimulate the substitution of capital for labor in manufacturing a particular basic product. In general, we have a number of potential policy actions. For example, we can reduce the cost of capital by changing the interest rate, granting tax rebates, or subsidizing the development of labor-saving machinery. We can increase the cost of labor by wage legislation, support of unions in collective bargaining, or a reduction in the labor supply (e.g., through lowering retirement age). For purposes of this illustration only, let us ignore the political feasibility of the various alternatives. Then it becomes obvious that the appropriateness of a given policy strategy hinges on the way in which the policy action enters the decision process of the firms involved. A change in the interest rate, for example, might influence the shift from capital to labor in two possible ways. If the firm routinely scanned interest rates for investment implications, the change would enter routinely. Otherwise, the interest rate change would consist in a change in a set of alternatives that would be examined if the firm were forced to search by failure to achieve a particular goal. The shift would influence firm behavior in the desired direction only if there were

---

[19]We have called all of these policy procedures "short-run" procedures not to deny their importance. They are, and will continue to be, our main tools for influencing firm behavior. There are, however, some possibilities for long-run modifications in the decision processes used by firms. We have ordinarily viewed policy as operating on the information available to the firm and on the constraints within which the firm functions. Although there are serious technical problems in the way, there is no theoretically compelling reason for not modifying basic decision procedures. The major problem is that we do not have an adequate theory of firm rearing from which to derive appropriate techniques of socialization.

some problem that led the firm to consider capital alternatives to the use of labor. A direct change in the cost of labor, on the other hand, would be more likely to produce a goal failure and search for an alternative solution. If no other solution (e.g., a price increase, decrease in slack) were discovered first, the firm might turn to substitution of capital.

In this specific case, and in the case of virtually any policy we can think of, the impact of the policy depends on such factors as:

1. The type of manipulation it attempts to accomplish.

2. The extent to which the organization to be manipulated deals routinely with the variables being modified externally.

3. The extent to which organizational problems can be solved by reducing internal slack.

4. The standard problem-solving and search rules used by the organization.

These factors represent a set of intervening mechanisms between economic policy and the results of such policy.

Anti-trust policy. In a similar way, it seems clear that we cannot really deal effectively with the problems of anti-trust policy without more explicit attention to the procedures, motivations, and conflicts of the modern business firm. We have argued that the business firm will attempt to avoid uncertainty in its environment by developing information systems that permit the exchange of information on price, product changes, and so forth. Current concepts of anti-trust policy, on the other hand, are directed toward enforcing competition by enforcing uncertainty, by restricting the exchange of information. The resulting strains are described by Hazard:

> To those who labor in the system, a philosophy which makes the good society depend upon blind competition carried on in ignorance of market facts and in disregard of the profit which, and which alone, can give the business institution permanence — such a philosophy seems irresponsible. Such men find themselves pressed on the one hand by the dogma: Compete yourself out of profits. On the other hand, they are pressed to conserve the business, to make it grow, from peace to war, from old styles to new styles, from obsolete technology to advanced technology. The businessman does not understand why his quest for certainty is wrong, why the dogma of competition should be pressed so far as to make a guessing game of the system.[20]

In principle, anti-trust policy can deal with the pressures toward uncertainty avoidance in four different ways: (1) Make it impossible to avoid uncertainty by creating an environment in which the best imagination and most compelling motivations will not suffice to eliminate a significant

[20]L. Hazard, "Are Big Businessmen Crooks?," *Atlantic Monthly* (November 1961).

part of the uncertainty. (2) Restrict by legal fiat the use of any device for avoiding uncertainty. (3) Encourage the development of devices for avoiding uncertainty that do not involve the exchange of information or collusion. (4) Change the internal structure and motivations in the firm that lead toward avoiding uncertainty.

The first two procedures are typical of current techniques. Either we attempt to make information exchange hopelessly complicated by populating the industry with many firms or we attempt to outlaw various forms of information systems. Quite aside from other consequences (e.g., on productive efficiency), both procedures have some treadmill features to them. The law seems to stay at most a half-step behind the ingenuity of its objects. Consider, for example, what would be involved if we really wanted to restrict interfirm information flow as it now exists. We would be required to force the modification of financial statements so that only limited information on costs and performance of firms is available. We would have to prohibit trade association activity designed to standardize accounting methods, operating procedures, and record keeping. We would have to outlaw the information brokerage functions of customers, and so on. As the quotation from Hazard suggests, the legal constraints stimulate search for alternative procedures for avoiding uncertainty. That search is usually successful and the procedures discovered tend to be at most only slightly less objectionable than the procedures prohibited by the law.

Perhaps this is the best we can do. The legal system has been pursuing the perversities and ingenuity of man for many years in many different areas with only moderate success. However, we think it may be possible to explore new alternatives as we improve our understanding of the decision process of the firm. Suppose, for example, that the pressure toward collusion among firms is really (as we have suggested) a pressure toward avoiding uncertainty. Can we develop procedures that will permit the firm substantially to avoid uncertainty without avoiding competition? Two possibilities suggest themselves. First, we might improve predictive devices. We have suggested that many of the procedures adopted by firms stem from the unreliability associated with current forecasting techniques. A firm that had a good predictive model of pricing behavior by its competitors would hardly need to obtain additional direct information about that firm's pricing intentions. Second, we might stimulate the development of uncertainty buffers of organizational slack. As B. Naslund and A. Whinston have pointed out to us, organizational slack can play an important role in permitting the organization to deal with uncertainty. A firm that can absorb the consequences of uncertainty in slack does not need other devices for controlling its environment. Procedures of this sort may well have side consequences that are unfortunate. For example, it is not clear that we would be any better off if firms could accurately predict behavior than we are if they freely exchange information. At least they have the merit of attempting to channel a pressure from the firm into socially acceptable activities rather than simply trying to constrain the pressure by legislation. All of these policy efforts accept as given the uncertainty avoidance motivation of the firm. As we indicated earlier, a final procedure that in principle would work is the modification of the motivation. Because we see only dimly what lies behind the characteristic behavior of the firm and understand only partly the learning processes within the firm, we cannot articulate a serious policy proposal for changing the behavior pattern.[21] In the long run, however, improvements in anti-trust policy probably depend more on such an approach than on the others we have discussed.

11.6 Summary

We have tried to suggest some possible implications of recent work on a behavioral theory of the firm. The implications for descriptive economics, for studies of noneconomic organizations, and for normative analysis are not always easy to see at this stage. They are even harder to validate. In the area of the descriptive analysis of the firm, we can claim some modest validation. We think a behavioral theory of the firm has a major contribution to make to the understanding and prediction of decision making within economic organizations and we have tried to present the theoretical constructs, models, and empirical observations upon which that belief is based. Beyond the area of positive theories of business decision making, we believe the concepts of a behavioral theory of the firm may have some potential relevance. The rough ideas in this volume are offered to indicate possible directions for further empirical and analytical work.

---

[21] It seems reasonable to expect, for example, that some more general changes in social training may be necessary.

A

ASSUMPTION,

PREDICTION,

AND EXPLANATION

IN ECONOMICS

by R. M. Cyert and E. Grunberg

Within recent decades economists have made great strides towards the elimination of nonoperational terms from their lowest-level propositions and the construction of theories in rigorous form. Thereby attention has been increasingly centered on prediction, no longer just as a basis for economic policy — that is, as the social justification of economics — but as a crucial step in theorizing: the verification of hypotheses.

The problems of prediction become entangled with issues involving the nature of assumptions and the role of prediction and explanation in economic models. The positions taken on these issues have implications for the research methodology that should be followed in economics. We hope to clarify the basic issues and discuss in a general way the broader implications for research.[1]

[1]See M. Friedman, *Essays in Positive Economics* (Chicago: University of Chicago Press, 1953), 3–43, for another discussion of many of the same points.

A.1 Nature of Prediction and Explanation

Since we will be using the terms *prediction* and *explanation* throughout this paper, it is important to examine in more detail the meaning of these terms in methodology.[2] In closed systems, where the *ceteris paribus* condition is fulfilled or can be made to hold effectively, explanation and prediction are symmetrical: the model is explanatory if the implied set of observation-statements (initial conditions) refers to an event that has already occurred; it is predictive if the implied set of observation-statements refers to a future event.[3] The time element enters into both concepts because real world processes have measurable duration and duration extends backwards and forwards. If knowledge of a specific event at a future date is desired, it is necessary to know the process by which — in due time — this event will be brought about. In the same way, if an event that has already occurred is to be explained by relating it to other prior events, a process in time is involved. In either case reference is made to specific space-time regions.

In nonclosed systems the symmetry of explanation and prediction does not hold. Before the event has happened it is not known what exogenous variables may influence the course of events. After the event has actually occurred, it is (in principle) always possible to identify all the variables that had a measurable effect on it. Thus, in nonclosed systems, hindsight is better than foresight.

In a *complete* explanatory model (which, being complete, is also a predictive model) the set of general laws must, in addition to empirical laws, also contain laws of the highest available order: laws which explain all other laws of lower order used in the explanation and prediction. The empirical laws (laws of lowest order) must contain terms that refer directly to observables and thus must be directly verifiable. Laws of higher order, used to explain lower-order laws, need not contain terms referring directly to observables although they may, of course, contain such terms. The same law may, in fact, appear in one predictive model as a lowest-level empirical law and in another model as a higher-order law. However, in the hierarchy of a theoretical structure, the higher the order of a general law (that is, the more steps it is removed from the lowest-order laws and the

---

[2]Because some confusion on this point still lingers, it is perhaps worthwhile to restate explicitly that the function of methodology is not to provide rules of discovery. There are no such rules, and, in fact, we know little about the process by which new ideas and hypotheses come to be formulated and discoveries are made. Rather, the function of the methodology of science is to evaluate the content, significance, and status of propositions dealing directly or indirectly with observables. It provides the procedural rules for the verification of such propositions *after they have been formulated.* The methodology itself is in the metalanguage, which would not be the case if it provided rules for discovery.

[3]C. G. Hempel and P. Oppenheim, "Studies in the Logic of Explanation," *Philosophy of Science*, **15** (1948), 135–178.

broader the scope of the explanation that it provides), the less are the chances that it will contain terms referring directly to observables. To the extent that it does contain such terms, the law remains, of course, rigorously subject to direct empirical verification. If, however, it does not contain any terms referring directly to observables, it *can* be only indirectly verified: empirical laws must be validly deducible from it in a finite number of steps. These lowest-order laws must be empirically verifiable.

In predictive models the higher-order general laws appear as premises from which the lower-order laws are validly deducible. This should not obscure the fact that in the actual enterprise of discovery they may yield priority to the empirical hypothesis. This is well expressed by saying that the higher-order laws *explain* the lower-order laws that are implied by them. By explaining the lower-level laws, the higher-level law makes possible the building of a consistent theoretical structure out of originally isolated and unrelated empirical hypotheses. Once such a theoretical structure (even the simplest one) exists, it becomes possible to derive from it new empirical hypotheses that are not obtained from observations but which, instead, predict observations. It is important to remember that the deduction of a new empirical hypothesis from an existing (and thus accepted) theoretical structure does not establish the truth of the hypothesis nor make the ultimate empirical test unnecessary. The derivation of empirical laws from more general laws is a source of tentative hypotheses, not a procedure of verification.

The fact that an empirical hypothesis, or a higher-order law explaining it, is inconsistent with an accepted theoretical structure does not strictly disconfirm the hypothesis. In fact, it is possible that the entire previously accepted theoretical structure may be disconfirmed by such an inconsistency. Actually, inconsistent hypotheses may be held simultaneously. The point is that such a situation will be considered to be unsatisfactory and, hopefully, will not be permanent. Efforts will be made to reconcile the inconsistent hypotheses or to replace them by others that are consistent with each other. Such inconsistencies are viewed as flaws in the theoretical structure — excused by reference to the fact that science cannot be omniscient.

Thus, because we cannot be certain that any of our laws is really true, the valid derivation of an empirical hypothesis from higher-order laws cannot establish its truth.[4] On the other hand, hypotheses obtained in this way do normally command a high degree of confidence because we obviously must have confidence in the body of accepted laws. The history of science abounds with examples where hypotheses first deduced from existing theoretical structures have later been empirically verified and have survived

---

[4]Thus Hempel and Oppenheim, *op. cit.*, point out that all general laws are considered to be "lawlike sentences" since it can never be known whether they are empirically valid. At the same time the general laws are viewed as logically true propositions.

confrontation with actual observations. In turn, the theoretical structure that has served as premise commands increasing confidence as more empirical hypotheses — later verified and accepted — are deduced from it. The possibility of thus indirectly verifying hypotheses that for some reason cannot be directly verified is of great importance for the social sciences.

With this background we will examine the prediction problem in economics.

A.2 Prediction in Economics

At the heart of the current methodological discussion in the social sciences in general and in economics in particular is (we believe) the predictive weakness of existing theory.[5] The cause of this weakness is the indefinitely large number of variables that can affect the course of economic events. Since predictive models can take into consideration only a limited and, in fact, quite small number of variables, the failure of a prediction made with such a model is not decisive for the fate of the hypothesis. The prediction is made subject to the *ceteris paribus* condition and it is usually difficult, if not impossible, to ascertain whether this condition has been fulfilled in a specific case. Economics is often compared with meteorology, which for similar reasons also suffers from a notable predictive weakness. However, the economist cannot derive much solace from this comparison. Closer scrutiny reveals a fundamental difference between the two situations. Like economics, meteorology deals with an indefinitely large number of variables, i.e., with "unique events." This leads, at times, to spectacularly wrong predictions. After the event, a satisfactory explanation is usually given in terms of the interference of unforeseen factors — that is, the nonfulfillment of the *ceteris paribus* condition.

The essential difference between meteorological and economic models lies in the fact that meteorology uses chiefly physical laws. These laws are verified independently from their use in meteorological predictions and explanations; they are used in (physical) models referring to situations for which the set of relevant variables is considered to be exhaustive — that is, for which it is successfully assumed that no exogenous variable can measurably affect the outcome.

On the other hand, as has been pointed out elsewhere in greater detail, the majority of the laws used in economic prediction and explanation are economic laws containing only economic terms.[6] Therefore, they cannot be verified independently from their use in economic predictions and they

[5]This seems to be true of most if not all methodological discussion in the domain of social events. Thus, the most famous of these discussions, the *methodenstrait* between Gustav Schmoller and Karl Menger, would hardly have been possible if economic hypotheses could be rigorously tested by using them in predictive models.

[6]E. Grunberg, "Notes on the Verifiability of Economic Laws," *Philosophy of Science*, **24** (1957), 337–348.

cannot be strictly verified through their use in economic predictions because of the difficulty of disconfirming them. This difficulty prevails because economic models are usually incomplete, which means that exogenous variables can measurably affect the outcome. Thus the economist finds himself in a worse position than the meteorologist.

If the difficulty of validation by prediction of contemporary economic models is accepted, it is necessary to turn to an appraisal of the status of economic hypotheses.[7] Specifically, we are interested in the class of hypotheses called "assumptions." Formally these assumptions are presented as major premises in valid arguments leading to the formulation of predictions of specific economic observations. Beyond that, considerable doubt and little agreement prevail with regard to the status and content of these propositions. In the next section an attempt is made to determine the nature and the function of assumptions in economic prediction and explanation.

A.3 Nature and Use of Assumptions

The inability strictly to disconfirm economic laws has raised the issue of the status and the function of assumptions in economic reasoning. Although a history of such propositions as the so-called "rational principle," or the principle of profit maximization, transcends the scope of this work, it should be noted that these and similar propositions were originally thought to have immediate empirical content and thus to be "realistic." Certainly, Bentham did not think of his felicific calculus as a mere formal postulate but rather as a set of propositions about some aspect of the real world. Adam Smith viewed the basic behavioral propositions used in *The Wealth of Nations* similarly — although he certainly considered the propositions as relevant only to certain aspects of human behavior. The same attitudes would seem to apply to the first formulations of the model of perfect competition.

In the course of the development of economics, the basic behavioral propositions met with increasing dissatisfaction. In recent years they have come under heavy attack because of the lack of empirical content. Now, it is a familiar occurrence in science that concepts that at first are thought

---

[7]K. Klappholz and J. Agassi, "Methodological Prescriptions in Economics," *Economica*, **26** (1959), 60–74, affirm that economic laws have been definitely rejected, if not by confrontation with observations, then at least by other means, presumably by inconsistency with the bulk of accepted theory. They cite as example the theories held by the mercantilists. However, this statement invites grave doubts. First, there is really no identifiable "theory of mercantilism" in the sense in which there is a theory of phlogiston. The writers classified as *mercantilists* held a variety of views that hardly form a consistent body of theory. Moreover, whatever views they held, they can still be found in contemporary arguments. Only 25 years ago economists spoke about "neomercantilism" in reference to the protectionist tendencies of the late twenties and the thirties.

to have immediate empirical content (to refer to observables) are later found to have no such content. Normally such concepts are simply eliminated when they are no longer useful. If they appear in higher-level laws, they are replaced by other concepts more satisfactory in the explanation of lower-level laws. This procedure, of course, requires the constant control of empirical verification. Economics, however, is still essentially based on "intended empirical laws."[8]

The role of assumptions in the physical sciences is nothing like their role in economics. Almost any law may be treated as an assumption if this is convenient for the purpose at hand, but there are no laws that occupy the position of "basic assumptions." There are, of course, laws that explain other laws, but these remain subject to constant control through the process of verification of their empirical implications.

In physics, too, the issue of the "realism" of propositions has been debated. What was involved, however, was the operational nature of theoretical concepts. On the other hand, in economics, what is meant by "lack of realism" is inconsistency of propositions with observables. This problem, of course, is one of substantive economics, which must be solved by empirical research. The fact that it could become a basic methodological problem is surprising.

A brief review of Friedman's argument may help to clarify the main issues. Friedman argues that "assumptions" need not be "realistic." They are judged exclusively by the predictive success of their implications. Thus, he concludes that criticism of assumptions as unrealistic is ill-founded and, indeed, that the search for more realistic assumptions is illicit.

Friedman himself is well aware of the ambiguity of the term "assumption." He offers three interpretations: "(a) they are often an economical mode of describing or presenting a theory; (b) they sometimes facilitate an indirect test of the hypothesis by its implications; and (c) . . . they are sometimes a convenient means of specifying the conditions under which the theory is expected to be valid."[9]

As an example of the first interpretation he offers the case of the leaves of trees, which behave as if they were maximizing the amount of sunshine to which they are exposed. He defends this form of expression essentially by asserting that the alternative to it would be to enumerate each tree. Rotwein has pointed out that this is false since Friedman's formulation simply amounts to saying that the density of leaves on trees is a positive function of the amount of sunshine (a consequence of heliotropism).[10] Even

---

[8]By "intended empirical laws" we mean propositions that have the form of empirical laws but that cannot be verified because they are formulated subject to the *ceteris paribus* condition.

[9]Friedman, *op. cit.*, 23.

[10]E. Rotwein, "On 'The Methodology of Positive Economics,' " *Quarterly Journal of Economics*, **73** (1959), 554–575.

if, within the narrow limitation of a reference to the density of leaves on tree trunks, the two statements may be accepted as equivalent, the question remains as to why the unrealistic statement, couched in anthropomorphic terms, should be used in preference to the other. Although it seems to have no advantage, it does have a serious disadvantage. Since the statement does not fit into the existing theoretical structure of plant biology and chemistry, it would seriously impede explanation. Friedman himself realizes this and gives up his formulation in preference to those more realistic. Thus, in the end it would seem that in some cases crude generalizations are better than exhaustive enumeration, and no one would dispute this.

Friedman's second interpretation is not concerned with the nature of assumptions at all but with experimental design. The specific example offered by Friedman is a good design and is used routinely.[11] Again, what is involved is no special type of proposition that is an "assumption" but simply general hypotheses to be verified by routine procedures.

What is meant by an "assumption" as a convenient way to state the conditions under which a theory is expected to be valid is not quite clear. Obviously these conditions must always be stated. They are, in fact, normally incorporated into the general hypothesis: a general law, after all, must state to what it applies. More likely, what Friedman has in mind is the state description rather than lawlike statements. In the terms of Hempel-Oppenheim, this means that Friedman refers to C-statements and not at all to L-statements.[12]

For example, consider "perfect competition." This is a state description; from it alone nothing follows. In order to obtain an explanatory model L-statements must be supplied. Here these L-statements may be, for example, the hypothesis of profit-maximizing behavior, the law of variable proportions, and the Marshallian demand curve. The usual "results of perfect competition" now follow from this model.

[11]The example is a proposition taken from G. J. Stigler, "A Theory of Delivered Price Systems," *American Economic Review*, **39** (1949), 1143–1157.

[12]Hempel and Oppenheim use the following diagram to summarize their analysis of explanation and prediction:

$$\left.\begin{array}{l} \left\{\begin{array}{l} C_1\, C_2 \ldots C_k \quad \text{Statements of antecedent conditions} \\ L_1\, L_2 \ldots L_r \quad \text{General laws} \end{array}\right\} \quad \text{Explanation} \\ \hline \rightarrow E \quad \left.\begin{array}{l} \text{Description of the empirical} \\ \text{phenomenon to be explained} \end{array}\right\} \quad \text{Explanation} \end{array}\right.$$

Logical deduction

If E is given (that is, has been observed) and the C's and L's are provided afterwards, then we have explanation. If E is deduced from the C's and L's before it occurs, then we have prediction. Thus the requirements for explanation are also appropriate for prediction.

Whether such a state description is realistic is a question of substantive economics or, in general, an empirical question. As a matter of fact, the particular state description of perfect competition is believed to be unrealistic. It is normally introduced by such words as: "Let it be assumed . . . ." Here we seem at last to have come across the generally accepted usage of the term "assumption": a state description (a set of C-statements). Normally, such a state description is called an "assumption" when the C-statements of which it consists are known to be all or in part untrue — and, in fact, are chosen because they are untrue. In this sense assumptions are part of an experimental design. They are used primarily when it is not feasible to produce actually desired conditions (as can be done where laboratory experiments are possible). The desired state is then imagined (assumed) and the consequences of a hypothesis under these conditions are explored. Whether a particular set of assumptions is adequate for the purpose at hand is not a question of general methodology.

In the end, it becomes clear that Friedman uses the term "assumption" in reference to quite different things: (crude) generalizations — especially those actually known to be unrealistic, the uses of hypotheses in certain experimental designs, and the counterfactual state description used again for purposes of experimental design.

It is submitted that the last-mentioned usage is the most legitimate and seems to correspond with general usage. In this sense "assumptions" refer to what is usually called a "mental experiment."[13] It would be helpful for methodological discussion if the term "assumption" were used only in the context of mental experiment.

Friedman's interpretation of the term "assumption" as a hypothesis known to be unrealistic raises the question as to whether there ever is any justification for the use of such propositions. This question leads to the heart of the matter. Consider his example of the expert billiard player whose shots are predicted on the basis of the assumption that, before each shot, he solves the mathematical problems involved. What has occurred here is the following: after having observed the successful play of an expert billiard player, we ask how he goes about making the billiard balls go where he wants them to go. The hypothesis is offered that he may with lightning rapidity solve the mathematical problem of the path of the balls required for success. This hypothesis may be borne out by the correct prediction of further shots.

Now the first difficulty arises from the fact that the hypothesis will not yield consistently correct predictions; we do know that even the most expert billiard player makes bad shots, loses games, and may even have days on which he plays poorly. Thus, the hypothesis may not yield

---

[13] N. Goodman, "The Problem of Counterfactual Conditionals," *Philosophy of Science*, **44** (1947).

completely correct predictions. However, it may be argued that perhaps the illustration is poorly chosen and that some other illustration might serve us better. Therefore, let us simply assume that the hypothesis actually does yield consistently correct predictions.

Another, more significant, difficulty now arises: it is actually known that billiard players, expert or otherwise, do not solve the relevant mathematical problems before making their shots. This is easily proved by testing expert billiard players for their mathematical knowledge. The mathematics required for the purpose is complex and quite beyond the grasp of all but well-trained mathematicians. In other words, the hypothesis that expert billiard players solve their problems by the use of higher mathematics can easily and unambiguously be disconfirmed. We may, indeed, safely consider it to be actually disconfirmed.

Friedman's whole argument rests on the assertion that an assumption — which now we know to be a lawlike statement — is verified exclusively by its predictive power. In fact, he defines the "truth" of such a statement as its power to yield correct predictions. This is the generally accepted definition of the "truth" of a law. It follows from Friedman's argument that the hypothesis that billiard players solve the problems encountered in the game by the use of higher mathematics must be considered to be true. It is not even permissible to speak of it as unrealistic — even though we positively know most billiard players to be ignorant of the required mathematical techniques. The point is that, although the hypothesis may yield consistently correct predictions of the shots made by expert billiard players, it yields consistently wrong predictions of the solutions obtained by the same players when confronted with the mathematical formulation of the problem of making a good shot. Three possibilities emerge:

1. The hypothesis that expert billiard players make their shots by solving mathematical problems is considered to be disconfirmed and is, therefore, discarded.

2. The hypothesis is known to be strictly disconfirmed. Since, however, it yields correct predictions in a given class of events (for unknown reasons), it is retained in the theoretical structure *until a better hypothesis can be formulated.* The situation is considered to call for a search for a more satisfactory hypothesis. In this context the fact that the disconfirmed hypothesis yields correct predictions for a given class of events must also be considered as a problem that requires solution. This is, of course, the situation that prevails in all areas of the scientific enterprise, as long as we are not omniscient, and, therefore, the solution of each problem raises new problems. Mutually inconsistent hypotheses and hypotheses yielding correct predictions in one area, whereas failing in another, are routinely retained in a theory.

3. Finally, the hypothesis may, as it were, be split in two: a hypothesis b_1 (expert billiard players solve the relevant mathematical problems before making a shot) and b_2 (expert billiard players have mathematical training to solve the mathematical problems presented by the game). Whereas b_2 is now considered to be strictly disconfirmed, b_1 is considered to be true.

Friedman chooses the third alternative. Such a choice means that in the process of verification only those implications of a hypothesis that yield correct predictions are considered. Now, although the retention of a hypothesis in spite of its failure in one or more classes is heuristically defensible, it may not be established as a methodological principle or rule. It would, indeed, lead to a complete fragmentation of science and make impossible the subsumption of apparently quite different events or attributes under one general theoretical structure. That is, it would prevent explanation beyond the lowest-level laws. Since its inception, however, science has considered as its major task the explanation of observable regularities by ever more general laws.

The fundamental difference between laws containing references to observables and laws that no longer contain references to immediately observable entities or attributes must be recognized. Although not all higher-level laws are free from references to observables, only higher-level laws can be of this kind.

Laws that thus do not contain references to observables can, in the way Friedman indicates, be verified *only* by deriving from them L-statements that do contain such references. These L-statements, in combination with C-statements, are then used in predictive models. Hypothetical constructs of this high level are obtained finally by successively asking why things are behaving in the observably regular way in which they actually do behave. Such hypotheses can be neither "realistic" nor "unrealistic" — the terms do not apply here.

On the other hand, if lawlike statements do contain terms purporting to refer directly to observables, there must be actual observations corresponding to these terms. Otherwise, the lawlike statement is obviously falsified. This proposition follows from the fact that any reference to direct observables implies predictions. To say, for instance, that billiard players solve mathematical problems implies the prediction that if a billiard player is confronted with a mathematical problem, he will in due time be observed either to state or write down an arrangement of symbols that constitutes the correct solution to the problem. If it is now said that the L-statement about the mathematical abilities of billiard players is "unrealistic," this means that the players in the situation described above will either say or write nothing at all or will produce symbols that do not constitute the solution of the problem.[14] According to Friedman's own argument, the hypothesis that billiard players solve complex mathematical problems is thereby disconfirmed and should be discarded. If no more satisfactory hypothesis can be found at the time, the disconfirmed hypothesis will remain in use for those classes of events for which it has been found to lead to correct predictions. In fact, additional applications of the hypothesis may be found. All of this, however, means only that the hypothesis will be used *until* a more satisfactory hypothesis can be formulated. If some hypothesis yields correct predictions for one class of events and fails to do so for another class of events to which it is claimed to apply, then it follows that there must exist at least one more satisfactory hypothesis. This may turn out to be a single hypothesis yielding correct predictions in all cases to which the old hypothesis has been applied; it may also be found that the cases in which the old hypothesis held are really special cases. That is, an explanation will be found as to why the old hypothesis has failed in some cases to which it had erroneously been believed to apply. The fact that a hypothesis is found to be "unrealistic" indicates the need to search for better hypotheses. Our disagreement with Friedman is not over his refusal to discard unrealistic hypotheses. This procedure, as we have seen, is legitimate as long as nothing better is at hand. Our disagreement is over the fact that his position seems to imply that an unrealistic hypothesis, because it seems to yield correct predictions in some cases, is beyond the principle of permanent control (any accepted proposition can be dropped at some later stage of investigation) and must be accepted. His argument, if followed literally by economists, would prohibit further research in a number of areas.

A.4 A Positive Approach

Summing up the argument of the preceding sections, we find that the difficulties encountered in economics flow from the fact that hypotheses cannot be strictly disconfirmed. As long as it is logically impossible to disconfirm a hypothesis, the hypothesis remains in doubt no matter how much confirmatory evidence is accumulated in its support.[15] This does not mean that such a hypothesis may not be used nor that it may not command

---

[14]Friedman's reference to abstract propositions as also "unrealistic" in the sense of the statement about the billiard players confuses two quite different things: neglecting certain attributes of reality and making observably false statements about reality. *Abstraction* means including an event or entity into a class defined by one or at best a few attributes (dark red, heavy things, etc.). Consequently an abstract proposition cannot refer to *all* attributes of the elements of the particular class, but it may not contain empirically untrue references.

[15]In his entire argument Friedman mentions only confirmatory evidence which he describes as "dramatic" and as "conclusive," but confirmatory evidence is never conclusive. It merely indicates that a hypothesis has so far not been disconfirmed. Thus, no

some degree of confidence. The point is not that *intended* empirical laws may not be used nor command confidence; it is rather that *no* evidence need be recognized as disconfirming them.

Our purpose in this section is to recommend certain approaches through which we may develop hypotheses that can be disconfirmed. While we would not argue that there is a unique methodology, we do maintain that our recommendation can lead to the discovery of general laws and hence to models with predictive and explanatory power. Essentially, we argue that economics should be viewed as part of the study of human behavior and that the empirical laws of economics should be based on propositions of behavior that can be disconfirmed independently from the economic situations. In a basic sense our position is consistent with J. M. Keynes' assertion that economics presupposes psychology. However, we will elaborate our position and show the operational significance for research.

Perhaps the issue can best be joined by referring again to the Friedman-Savage billiard player. Friedman proposes a theory based on the assumption that the billiard player makes his shots "as if he knew the complicated mathematical formulas that would give the optimum directions of travel, could estimate accurately by eye the angles, etc., describing the location of the balls, could make lightning calculations from the formulas, and could then make the balls travel in the direction indicated by the formulas." He then goes on to argue that quite obviously the confidence in such a hypothesis is not based on any actual belief that a billiard player would have such abilities, but rather from the belief that "unless in some way or other they were capable of reaching essentially the same results they would not in act be expert billiard players." Further, Friedman, at least by implication, excludes the possibility of utilizing empirical methods to develop a more detailed theory of behavior in this case. He argues that if one asked the billiard player how he decides where to hit the ball, the billiard player might say that he "just figures it out" but then might also rub a rabbit foot to make sure. Friedman is here taking the position that it is impossible to find out from the decision maker himself the process by which the decision is made. This means that it is impossible to gain any insight into the actual processes of decision making in the two primary micro-units of economics, the firm and the household. If such an inference were correct, economists would be forever condemned to making counterfactual hypotheses of the billiard-player type.

---

matter how much confirmatory evidence for a hypothesis has been accumulated, it can never lead to the definitive acceptance of this hypothesis nor can it make methodologically illicit further attempts to disconfirm it. Indeed, verification of a hypothesis does not mean collecting confirmatory evidence but means trying as hard as possible to disconfirm the hypothesis.

In fact, however, such a limited view of our potential knowledge of decision-making behavior is not justified. A variety of decision-making behavior has been studied by a number of methods — including interviewing, observation, and analysis of the records of past decisions (see Chapters 7 and 10). Models that predict and explain decisions have been developed in a number of areas.[16] The trend of the evidence leads to the view that any decision can be successfully subjected to scientific analysis.

If we look at the billiard player as an example, the approach we suggest would be to study his decision-making process, build a model of the process, and test the model by making predictions and comparing the predictions with the actual result. In this way we can not only join our knowledge with that of other disciplines studying similar behavior, but we will gain explanatory value for our models as well as predictive ability.

One of the methodological breakthroughs that makes complicated models of a decision-making behavior feasible is the digital computer (see Appendix B). The computer model written in computer language makes it possible to build "positive" models of processes that were previously too complicated to be viewed as legitimate units of study.

Thus, one program of research that would lead out of the difficulties described in earlier sections involves the following suggestions:

1. There should be a concentration of empirical study of the micro-decision-making units — firms and households.

2. The empirical study should be directed toward determining the actual decision-making processes involved, which requires the use of such techniques as interviews, observations, and analyses of records.

3. The models formed as a result of such study should be decision-process models. They should show the complete map of alternatives under the variety of conditions of the real world. Thus we will be able to eliminate the usual *ceteris paribus* condition.

4. The language of the computer should probably be used because of the complex and dynamic character of such models.

In short, we are striving for a science of economics that is based on behavioral propositions relating to the micro-units. These propositions

[16]There are a number of papers, many unpublished as yet, that have been written in this area. See, for example, J. Feldman, "An Analysis of Predictive Behavior in a Two-Choice Situation," (Ph.D. thesis, Carnegie Institute of Technology, 1959); A. Newell, J. C. Shaw, and H. A. Simon, "Elements of a Theory of Human Problem Solving," *Psychological Review*, 67 (1958); W. R. Reitman, "Programming Intelligent Problem Solvers," *I.R.E. Transactions* HFE-2 (1961); G. P. E. Clarkson and H. A. Simon, "Simulation of Individual and Group Behavior, "*American Economic Review*, 50 (1960). For a general discussion of the approach suggested in this section, see H. A. Simon, "Theories of Decision-Making in Economics and Behavioral Science," *American Economic Review*, 49 (1959).

would relate to the decision-making behavior of the micro-units and would be disconfirmable either by direct behavioral tests or by inference from economic tests. The propositions would no longer refer to phenomena observable only as unique events but would refer to repetitive situations.

B

COMPUTER MODELS IN
DYNAMIC ECONOMICS[1]

by K. J. Cohen and R. M. Cyert

The development of the electronic digital computer has
been an extremely significant technological innovation for
science, probably ranking on a par with the inventions of
the telescope and the microscope. As the first such
computer, the ENIAC, was completed less than 15 years
ago, our experience with electronic computers is still too
limited for anyone to predict the ultimate significance of
these machines in both the natural and the social sciences.
However, our knowledge has increased so rapidly from the
years immediately after World War II, when computers
were viewed only as larger and faster desk calculators,
that it seems worthwhile to examine some of the implications that electronic digital computers have for research
methodology in the social sciences.

It is undeniable that electronic computers, when used
as routine calculating devices for performing statistical
analyses and clerical data-processing operations, can be
extremely useful in social science research. The purpose

[1]This appendix is substantially the same as K. J. Cohen and
R. M. Cyert, "Computer Models in Dynamic Economics," *Quarterly
Journal of Economics,* **75** (1961), 112–127.

of this appendix is not to consider the importance of such "routine" uses of computers in the social sciences, but, rather, to explore the possibilities of using computers to simulate the behavior of complex social systems. The specific illustrations used are all drawn from the field of economics, but the concepts seem equally relevant to other fields of social science. We shall use the term *computer model* to refer to a formal model designed for digital computer simulation. In this appendix we propose to examine the characteristics of computer models and to survey some of the economic computer models that have been formulated. In addition, we shall attempt to evaluate the future achievements that might reasonably be expected from further work with computer models.

B.1 Theory Construction (Model Building)

The professional in any science works within a framework of definitions and concepts that becomes second nature to him. As a result, basic methodological points are frequently taken for granted. In appraising a methodological innovation, however, it is useful to re-examine such points. The explanation and evaluation of computer models can be simplified by examining the nature of theory construction (model building) itself.

A theory consists of three elements — *definitions*, *assumptions*, and *conclusions*. The following is a simple and familiar example of a theory:[2]

Assumptions

1. Firms attempt to maximize profits.
2. The marginal revenue curves intersect the marginal cost curves from above.
3. The marginal curves are continuous.

Conclusion

A firm will produce that output corresponding to the point of intersection of its marginal revenue and marginal cost curves.

It is obvious that this theory also depends on a set of subject matter (extralogical) definitions — profits, marginal cost, and marginal revenue. There are a number of relevant points that can be noted from this example. The conclusion is a logical implication of the assumptions. The language in which the conclusion is derived from the assumptions is a matter of the theoretician's choice. In general, there are three languages that have been commonly used by economists for drawing a conclusion from a set of assumptions — ordinary prose, pictorial geometry, and formal mathematics. In the specific theory under discussion, it is obvious that the conclusion can be derived using any of the three languages. It would also,

[2]G. J. Stigler, *The Theory of Price* (New York: Macmillan, 1946), 4–6.

of course, be possible to state the assumptions and the conclusions in any of the three languages. Generally it is most convenient to state assumptions and conclusions in prose alone or in a combination of prose and mathematics. The question of which language to use is answered quite nicely in the following quotation:

> If mathematics is no more than a form of logical reasoning, the question may be asked: why use mathematics, which few understand, instead of logic, which is intelligible to all? It is only a matter of efficiency, as when a contractor decides to use mechanical earth-moving equipment rather than picks and shovels. It is often simpler to use pick and shovel, and always conceivable that they will do any job; but equally the steam shovel is often the economic proposition. Mathematics is the steam shovel of logical argument; it may or may not be profitable to use it.[3]

Another point to note is that the conclusion is true only in the sense of logically following from the assumptions. The theory must be tested empirically before it can be said that the theory "proves" anything about the world. As has been said a number of times, it is not possible to "prove" by an *a priori* argument that a particular proposition is true of the real world. With most economic theories, unfortunately, testing is difficult, as it is with any nonlaboratory science.[4] One important reason for this difficulty in economics is that for the most part we are dealing with static theories, whereas the world in which we must test the theory is dynamic. As a result, it is usually difficult to find satisfactory data for testing purposes. As we shall argue below, we feel that computer models can reduce the difficulties of developing models that can be directly tested, although some new statistical problems may arise.

An additional point that is relevant to the problem of testing should be recognized about the nature of most economic theories. The point has been effectively made by Professor Samuelson:

> The general method (of economic theory) involved may be very simply stated. *In cases where the equilibrium values of our variables can be regarded as the solutions of an extremum (maximum or minimum) problem, it is often possible, regardless of the number of variables involved, to determine unambiguously the qualitative behavior of our solution values in respect to changes of parameters.*[5]

This means that the testing procedure consists in making numerical measurements to determine whether the direction of change of certain parameters is in the predicted direction. In general, economic theory

---

[3]R. G. D. Allen, *Mathematical Economics* (London: Macmillan, 1957), xvi.

[4]See Appendix A.

[5]P. A. Samuelson, *Foundations of Economic Analysis* (Cambridge: Harvard University Press, 1947), 21.

seems more successful in yielding propositions about directions of change than propositions about numerical magnitudes of particular variables.

B.2 General Characteristics of Computer Models

A computer model is a model in which the implications of the assumptions — that is, the conclusions — are derived by allowing an electronic digital computer to simulate the processes embodied in the assumptions. Computer programs can thus be considered to be a fourth language in which the assumptions of a theory can be expressed and its conclusions derived. Actually, computer models might be viewed as special cases of mathematical models. We shall not pause to debate taxonomic subtleties, however, for it is more important to examine some of the features which characterize computer models.

We have stated above that there are a number of languages that *could* be used in model building. There are also a number of criteria that might be used to determine which language *should* be used. It seems obvious, however, that one important criterion is efficiency, as R. G. D. Allen argued. Computer models may be the most efficient approach when the model portrays a dynamic process and numerical answers in the form of time series are desired.

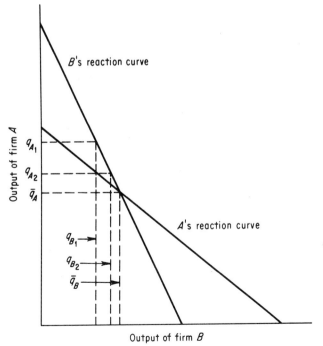

Figure B.1 Reaction curves of **A** and **B**.

The notion of a dynamic process can perhaps be made clear by reference to the simple Cournot duopoly model.[6] In Fig. B.1, the reaction curves for rivals A and B are given. Each reaction curve shows the optimum output for one firm as a function of the output of its rival. In accordance with the model, the curves are drawn on the assumption that the conjectural variation terms ($\partial q_A/\partial q_B$ and $\partial q_B/\partial q_A$) are equal to zero. The dynamic process of the model can be started at any point. Assume that A is producing q_{A_1}, then B will produce q_{B_1}. In answer to this, A will produce q_{A_2}; B will then produce q_{B_2}, and so forth. If this simple model were analyzed as a computer model, the computer would generate the time series of outputs for each firm. After the model had been run for a large number of periods, it would be clear that the outputs were tending toward equilibrium values where A is producing q_A and B is producing q_B.

In a model as simple as the Cournot model, we are generally not interested in tracing through the process by which equilibrium is reached but only in deriving the equilibrium values. These values are easy to find by simple mathematical analysis. However, the addition of a few assumptions about the behavior of the two firms can complicate the model sufficiently so that a computer simulation will be the most efficient method for determining the implications of the model. The volume of conclusions derived from a model is within the control of the model builder. However, in complicated computer models there are, generally, a large number of potential implications generated, many of these being time series of particular numerical values.

The fact that conclusions drawn from computer models may consist of a series of numerical values has in itself a number of interesting consequences. Numerical solutions should be contrasted with the analytic solutions usually derived from mathematical models. In terms of our earlier discussion on theory construction, we could say that the conclusions sought from a mathematical model are usually in the form of relations among the variables and parameters (including, frequently, derivatives or differences of the variables or parameters), whereas in computer models the conclusions obtained typically are in the form of time series of specific numerical values. This suggests that computer models are less general than mathematical models, for the reason that the amounts of input for computer models are greater than for the usual mathematical models. The increased input places greater restrictions on the relationships among the variables and parameters and, therefore, produces a less general but more specific model. To economists, one advantage of computer models is that their conclusions are presented in immediately testable form.

It should be emphasized that the above characterization does not imply

---

[6]A. Cournot, *Researches into the Mathematical Principles of the Theory of Wealth,* trans. Nathaniel T. Bacon (New York: Macmillan, 1897), chap. 7.

that computer models are necessarily less general nor mathematical models necessarily less specific. Our considerations are related primarily to questions of convenience and efficiency. It is possible to use a computer model, for example, to gain insight into the effects of rates of change of particular parameters on the results of the model. This end is accomplished by varying the parameters of the model from one simulation run to another and comparing the output time paths that are generated. If the model can be solved analytically, however, such a result could be more easily achieved by mathematical analysis.

B.2.1 Comparison of computer models with operations research simulations and econometric models

In order better to understand the nature of computer models and the problems of using them, it is desirable to examine the use of simulation in the burgeoning field of operations research.[7] Additional clarification can be gained by comparing computer and econometric models.

There are two basically different approaches that can be followed in using computer simulation to study a complex system. The actual approach taken, of course, depends on the questions to be answered and the kind of information known at the time of the investigation. The approach generally taken in operations research or management science might be entitled "synthesis." This approach aims at understanding the operating characteristics of a total system when the behavior of the component units is known with a high degree of accuracy. The basic questions answered by this approach relate to the behavior of the over-all system. In principle, the entire system response is known once the characteristics of the structural relations are specified. If the system is complex, however, it may be difficult or impossible to determine the system behavior by current mathematical techniques. In this situation, simulation by an electronic computer can be utilized to determine the time paths traced by the system.

In social science, generally, the situation is quite the reverse. The behavior of the total system can be observed. The problem is to derive a set of component relations that will lead to a total system exhibiting the observed characteristics of behavior. The usual procedure is to construct a model that specifies the behavior of the components, and then to analyze the model to determine whether or not the behavior of the model corresponds with the observed behavior of the total system. When this model

[7]A broad survey of the scope of operations research simulations can be found in D. G. Malcolm, ed., *Report of the Systems Simulation Symposium* (American Institute of Industrial Engineers, 1958). The number of operations research simulation studies that have been discussed in professional meetings or journals is too numerous to permit us to undertake here any further discussion of them (e.g., at the Sixteenth National Meeting of the Operations Research Society of America in Pasadena, California, November, 1959, there were approximately twenty papers presented dealing with computer simulation).

is sufficiently complex, either because of the nature of the underlying functions, the number of variables contained in it, or both, computer simulation may be the most convenient technique for manipulating the model. It is logical to call this approach to simulation "analysis." The actual output of the model is a set of time paths for the endogenous variables being studied by the model.

Traditional econometric models are essentially one-period-change models. Any lagged values of the endogenous variables are, in effect, treated as exogenous variables. They are assumed to be predetermined by outside forces rather than by earlier applications of the mechanisms specified in the model. Hence the output of econometric models is the determination of the values of the endogenous variables for a given time period. To determine these values for the next period, new values would have to be assigned to the lagged endogenous variables. For this reason, most econometric models should be regarded as determining the changes that take place in the world from one period to another. They should be contrasted with process or evolutionary models, which attempt to exhibit the unfolding of dynamic processes over time.

The mechanisms of a computer process model, together with the observed time paths of the exogenous variables, are treated as a closed, dynamic system. In such a model, the values of the lagged endogenous variables are the values previously generated by the system. Computer models may thus be forced to operate with errors in the values of the endogenous variables made in previous periods, there being no correction at the end of each period to assure correct initial conditions for the next period as in econometric models.

The contrasts between econometric and computer models have not been offered as invidious comparisons. It is clear that economics has benefited and will continue to benefit in the future from work in econometrics. Rather, our analysis is aimed at showing the nature and peculiar attributes of an important new research technique for social science.

B.3 Methodological Problems of Computer Models

As with any new research technique, there are methodological difficulties connected with the efficient utilization of computer simulation. There are three basic classes of problems that arise in using computer models — the specification of functional forms, the estimation of parameters, and the validation of the models.

The problem of specifying functional forms is literally an example of the "embarrassment of riches." Most mathematical models have been formulated in terms of linear equations in order to facilitate the attainment of analytic solutions. Since this restriction is unnecessary for computer models, the way is opened for nonlinear functions having a wide variety of forms. The solution to this problem will probably come from two sources. First, as our empirical information (the collection of which will be stimulated and guided by attempts to formulate computer models) increases, some clues as to the proper forms to use to explain and predict behavior will be available. Second, technical statistical criteria will be developed to select efficiently the proper forms of the equations, presumably on the basis of predictive power.

The problems of parameter estimation have, of course, been much discussed in statistical and econometric literature. A major advance has been the proof that unbiased and efficient estimates can be obtained only by acknowledging the simultaneity of the equations of a model.[8] If this result carries over to computer process models, obtaining maximum likelihood estimates of all the parameters in such models will be a forbidding task.

A more feasible approach to the parameter estimation problem may be to restrict attention to the joint determination of only the current endogenous variables within a single period and to consider that the values of the lagged endogenous variables are subject to errors. The parameter estimation problem must then be considered within the framework of an "errors in the variables" model rather than an "errors in the equations" model. A few econometricians have investigated this kind of estimation problem, and their results may prove applicable to computer models.[9]

The likelihood that a process model will incorrectly describe the world is high, because it makes some strong assertions about the nature of the world. There are various degrees by which any model can fail to describe the world, however, so it is meaningful to say that some models are more adequate descriptions of reality than others. Some criteria must be devised to indicate when the time paths generated by a process model agree sufficiently with the observed time paths so that the agreement cannot be attributed to mere coincidence. Tests must be devised for the "goodness of fit" of process models with the real world. The problem of model validation becomes even more difficult if available data about the "actual" behavior of the world are themselves subject to error.

Although the formal details have not yet been adequately developed, there appear to be at least three possible ways in which the validation problem for process models can be approached:[10]

[8]See, e.g., L. R. Klein, *A Textbook of Econometrics* (Evanston, Ill.: Row, 1953), chap. 3.

[9]Recent surveys of the state of econometric methodology regarding errors in the variables models can be found in J. D. Sargan, "The Estimation of Economic Relationships Using Instrumental Variables," *Econometrica*, **26** (1958), 393–415, and in Madansky, "The Fitting of Straight Lines Where Both Variables Are Subject to Error," *Journal of American Statistical Association*, **54** (1959), 173–205.

[10]These have all been suggested by Professor Jack Johnston of the University of Manchester in private conversations with the authors.

1. Distribution-free statistical methods can be used to test whether the actual and the generated time series display similar timing and amplitude characteristics.

2. Simple regressions of the generated series as functions of the actual series can be computed, and then we can test whether the resulting regression equations have intercepts that are not significantly different from zero and slopes that are not significantly different from unity.

3. We can perform a factor analysis on the set of generated time paths and a second factor analysis on the set of observed time paths, and we can test whether the two groups of factor loadings are significantly different from each other.

B.4 Review of the Literature

Although the notion of utilizing the computer as a tool in model building is still relatively new, there are several research projects in process and several completed segments of research in economics that have followed this approach. A review of some of this work will give some specific indications of the versatility of computer models; our review is intended to be illustrative, rather than exhaustive, of the applications of computer models in economics that have been reported in the literature. It also deliberately excludes the work reported in this volume.

Simulation of households. A large-scale simulation that has as its ultimate goal the simulation of the total economy of the United States has been underway for several years under the direction of Professor Orcutt.[11] Currently the project is concentrating on the analysis of households. The ultimate goal is to develop a general model consisting of the 10 flow-of-funds sectors used in national income accounting.

The first step in Orcutt's approach is to develop a stratified sample of households classified along the dimensions of some 23 variables. These variables — such as race, age, sex, education, income, debt, stocks of assets — are the inputs to the decision units in the model. The outputs of the household model include relevant data for forecasting population — purchases of durables, nondurables, services, and housing, net change in debt, and net change in assets for the household sector.

The individual decision units of the model must be endowed with values of the various input variables in accordance with the actual system being simulated. The unit is viewed as having alternative types of behavior available. With each alternative there is associated a probability, empirically determined. Random numbers are generated to select specific actions

---

[11]G. H. Orcutt, M. Greenberger, J. Korbel and A. M. Rivlin, *Micro-analysis of Socioeconomic Systems — A Simulation Study* (New York: Harper, 1961).

for each unit in a manner consistent with the assigned probabilities. In this way outputs are determined for each unit: The outputs are then used to modify the inputs for the next series of decisions.

The above description, of course, is only the skeleton of the model. Orcutt discusses many other problems connected with the model, such as parameter estimation, discrepancies between generated and actual series, and so forth. Orcutt sees his model as providing an instrument for "consolidating past, present, and future research efforts of many individuals in varied areas of economics and sociology into one effective and meaningful model; an instrument for combining survey and theoretical results obtained on the microlevel into an all-embracing system useful for prediction, control, experimentation, and analysis on the aggregate level."[12]

Firm models. In another early work, Hoggatt has developed a simulation of a perfectly competitive industry.[13] His objective was to study the stability of a model in which entry and exit conditions, as well as the formation of price expectations, are specified. The model consists of the following:

1. A market demand function dependent on two parameters.

2. A long-run average cost curve dependent on two parameters.

3. A total cost curve for each firm dependent on the same parameters as Condition 2.

The assumption is made that entering firms will expect the then-current price to prevail in the future, and they therefore select that plant size that will maximize profits given the current price. The usual neoclassical decision rules for determining output of the firms prevail. The model is ready to operate when the four parameters in Conditions 1 and 2, the initial number of firms, and the size of plant for each firm are specified.

Hoggatt begins by choosing values that give an equilibrium position for the industry. He assumes all firms to be of equal size. The output of the model is the price in the market and the production and profits for each firm. (There are also a number of other outputs that are used for analyzing the system.) The demand curve is then shifted to the right by changing one of the parameters, and the results are studied. One interesting conclusion the model brings forth is the "possibility that the market variables (price and industry supply) may be nearly stationary even though there is considerable entry and exit activity on the part of firms in the industry."[14] The model is especially interesting as an example of the type of complex questions that can be asked of an old model with the technique of simulation.

---

[12]*Ibid.*, 40–41.

[13]A. C. Hoggatt, "Simulation of the Firm" (I.B.M. research paper, RC-16, August 15, 1957).

[14]*Ibid.*, 62.

Industrial dynamics. Another use of computer models has been made by J. W. Forrester.[15] He utilizes time lags within a system to demonstrate the types of fluctuations that can develop within a company as a result of a shock to the system — for example, an increase in demand. The model utilized consists of five component parts: factory, factory warehouse, distributors, retailers, and customers. The customers' order rate is as an exogenous variable. There are given time lags through the whole system in terms of the delivery of goods from retailer to customer, distributor to retailer, and so forth back to the factory lead time for production. There are also a series of time lags in the information system. The lags are in the timing of orders for goods, transmitted from component to component. The last aspect of the model is a description of the policy followed in placing orders at each level and the rules for maintaining inventory.

Once the parameters (time lags and policies) are fixed, the system is set in motion and can be analyzed for any given customer order rate. The model is nonlinear and would be difficult to analyze by any method other than computer simulation.

Forrester also analyzes a further model in which advertising is introduced with a similar set of time lags. It is clear that a number of additional variables can be introduced, and their effects on fluctuations in production, employment, and investment analyzed for the firm. Forrester's main aim is to utilize such analysis for the improvement of business management.

Industry analysis. Perhaps the most detailed published attempt at using computer models in economics is the study of the shoe, leather, and hide industries by K. J. Cohen.[16] This work was designed to explore the usefulness of computers in economic analysis. The models in the study are based on the empirical research of Mrs. Ruth P. Mack.[17] Several different models are constructed in Cohen's study, but only the outline of the general approach will be discussed here.

The industry can be divided vertically into five segments — consumers, shoe retailers, shoe manufacturers, cattlehide leather tanners, and hide dealers. The major variables on which attention is focused are the selling prices of each sector (other than consumers), the purchases of each sector (other than hide dealers), and the production of retailers, manufacturers, and tanners. The models are an attempt to explain the monthly values of each of these variables from 1930 to 1940. The major exogenous variables

[15]J. W. Forrester, "Industrial Dynamics — A Major Breakthrough for Decision Makers," *Harvard Business Review*, **36** (1958), 37–66, and also *Industrial Dynamics* (New York: Wiley, 1961).

[16]K. J. Cohen, *Computer Models of the Shoe, Leather, Hide Sequence* (Englewood Cliffs, N.J.: Prentice-Hall, 1960).

[17]R. P. Mack, *Consumption and Business Fluctuation: A Case Study of the Shoe, Leather, Hide Sequence* (New York: National Bureau of Economic Research, 1956).

used are disposable personal income, the Bureau of Labor Statistics' consumers' price index, and hide stocks in the hands of hide dealers. As can
be seen from the above descriptions, the models are formulated in terms of
two major classes of variables — prices and physical flows.

The dollar expenditure on shoes by consumers is determined by disposable personal income and a seasonal factor, both exogenous variables.
The physical volume of retailers' sales is simply the consumers' expenditures
divided by the retail price of shoes. The retailers' receipts of shoes are
determined basically by demand considerations accompanied by some price
speculation on inventories: retailers always try to have available for sale
at least enough shoes to meet their anticipated demand; the extent to which
they try to push their inventory levels beyond this point depends upon
their changing evaluations of future market prospects. The manufacturers
plan their shoe production in response to retailers' orders for shoes, spread-
ing these orders evenly over the available lead time to obtain some smoothing of production. The leather purchases by manufacturers are designed
at least to provide for their current production requirements, but the
manufacturers frequently build up their leather inventories beyond current
needs in response to price speculation motives. The production of finished
leather by tanners depends upon the relation between their leather ship-
ments and their leather stocks, but, because tanners attempt to smooth
production rates, finished leather production is also tied to the previous
month's production and hide wettings. Tanners' hide wettings depend
upon the turnover rate of tanners' finished leather stocks, but again efforts
are made to prevent rapid changes from occurring in the rate of production.
Tanners' purchases of hides are determined by a reduced form relation that
reflects both their current needs (the higher the rate of wettings, the more
hides the tanners will order) and their view of the supply situation (the
lower the price of hides last month, the more hides tanners will buy).

The retail price of shoes is determined in the models by a rigid mark-up
on factory shoe prices. In setting the factory shoe price, manufacturers
consider both the strength of consumer demand and the costs of production,
as reflected in recent leather prices. Current leather price depends upon
lagged leather price and current and lagged hide prices. Current hide price
is determined in the models by a reduced form relation that reflects
interactions between supply and demand considerations. The supply
aspects are summarized in the final reduced form equation in terms of the
ratio of leather and hide stocks in the hands of buyers to the leather and
hide stocks in the hands of sellers; the higher this ratio, the lower the
relative size of sellers' inventories and the higher the price the sellers
require to induce them to sell hides. The demand side is reflected in the
reduced form equation by actual uses of hides by tanners — i.e., by hide
wettings and finished leather production — and by factory shoe price,

which serves as a proxy for underlying forces causing shifts in the demand schedule for hides.

There are several important interactions between prices and physical flows in the models. The physical volume of retail shoe sales is directly affected by retail shoe price. Retailers' purchases of shoes, manufacturers' purchases of leather, and tanners' purchases of hides are affected, largely through price speculation on inventories, by prices that are endogenously determined. The most important converse effect in the models is the dependence of hide price upon the purchases of leather by manufacturers and the finished leather production, hide wettings, and hide purchases by tanners.

Both one-period-change and process models were formulated. Mathematically, the forms of the models are nonlinear systems of lagged simultaneous difference equations. Simulation techniques were used to trace the time paths generated by the models for all endogenous variables. These generated series were then compared with the observed values of these variables between 1930 and 1940. Although these comparisons do not result in complete agreement between the hypothetical and the actual time series for the endogenous variables, they do indicate that the models may incorporate some of the mechanisms that in fact determined behavior in the shoe, leather, and hide industries.

B.5 Future of Computer Models

We have examined the nature of computer models, the associated methodological problems, and some of the current literature utilizing computer models. It is now appropriate to evaluate the role of computer models in social science research. We clearly maintain that computer models are an important new tool for the social sciences. Computer models should be viewed as a supplement to available procedures rather than as a replacement for all existing techniques.

The basic advantage of computer models is that they provide a language within which complex dynamic models can be constructed. In addition, and because of the richness of the language, such models can incorporate the relevant empirical variables. This does not imply that economists should no longer be interested in general models, but it does mean that economists are no longer forced to deal *only* with general models.

Computer models provide a bridge between empirical and theoretical work. The requirements of a computer model can provide a theoretical framework for an empirical investigation, and, in return, the empirical information is utilized in developing a flow diagram for the model. Through this process of working back and forth, it is possible to know when enough empirical information has been gathered and whether it is of the proper quality. Once the model is simulated, a more rigorous test of the validity of the model can be made, as indicated earlier, by comparing the time series generated by the model against the actual observed behavior of the system.

Because computer models have such a large capacity for utilizing empirical data, a burden may be placed on the actual collection of empirical information. We know of no obviously optimal procedure for gathering information that exists inside firms or inside consumers' heads. Nevertheless, this is the kind of information that economists desire and that computer models can readily handle.

INDEX